CONTENTS

4
PROTECTOR OF THE FREE WORLD   85

5
THE LIBERAL PROMISE: JFK AND LBJ   103

6
THE PERILS OF POWER: FOREIGN POLICY IN THE 1960s   133

7
THE "YOUTH REVOLT" AND THE "NEW POLITICS," 1960-1968   153

8
PROTEST AND THE SEARCH FOR POWER,
1968-1976   177

9
THE POLITICS OF THE 1970s   199

10
THE OVERSIZED SOCIETY:
LIFE DURING THE 1960s and 1970s   245

INDEX   289

PREFACE
AND ACKNOWLEDGMENTS

In preparing this revised edition of *In Our Times* we have followed the same guideline we used in the initial edition—our insistence that history is not simply "one damn thing after another." We have continued, therefore, to depart from a strictly chronological narrative in favor of a more interpretive view of the post-World War II era. We have been heartened at the number of positive responses to this approach from both fellow historians and from students. We have also been humbled by some justifiable criticism, and this revision is intended to respond to the limitations of the first edition as well as to carry the history of "our times" through the 1970s. Obviously, even with this heavily-revised edition, not everyone will agree with our choice of emphasis or accept all of our judgments. We believe, however, that readers will find that we have provided a useful framework within which to study the history of postwar America.

As in the first edition, we have gone beyond a conventional narrative of politics and diplomacy to explore social, economic, and cultural affairs. We have tried to be thorough without being encyclopedic; we have sought to be colorful and illustrative without being simply anecdotal; and, above all, we have tried to encourage students of recent American history to reflect seriously upon the complex relationship between the past, the present, and the future.

In the process of revising this book, we have found our intellectual debts continuing to soar. The views expressed in this work continue to be informed by our own experience teaching courses in recent American history and by the responses of our students at Macalester College. The heavily-revised reading lists at the end of each chapter only begin to suggest how this new edition has benefited from the insights we have gained from other interpreters of America's recent history. Special thanks go to three anonymous critics who carefully reviewed this revision and to our editors at Prentice-Hall, especially Anne Armeny. Finally, we gratefully acknowledge the assistance of Professor James R. Moore of Southampton College. He contributed three chapters to the first edition and remains our collaborator on Chapters 4 and 6 of this edition.

Although they have not been a direct part of this book, our colleagues at Macalester—especially Ernest R. Sandeen and James B. Stewart—have encouraged our work and cheerfully overlooked the problems that two people can encounter while they share both one teaching position and the care of four small children. This book, like our teaching career, is in every way a joint effort. For any errors that have slipped through, there is the same disclaimer sometimes given to students and colleagues: "you must be looking for the other Professor Rosenberg."

THE WORLD'S SUPERPOWER

Collapse of the Old Order, Rise of the New

The war was over! Japan had surrendered! At seven in the evening on September 6, 1945, President Harry S Truman made the official announcement. Across the country people began to celebrate the end of World War II. Outside the White House, a crowd that had been waiting all day struck up the chant, "We want Harry, we want Harry." The president appeared, said a few words, and left, only to be called back twice more by repeated shouts. Finally, he sank into a chair and expressed the universal sentiment: "I'm glad that it's over."

Pressing problems and hard decisions did not end with the war. Postwar reconstruction and the development of a cold war between the United States and the Soviet Union kept international affairs in a state of perpetual crisis.

A War-Shattered World

Before World War II Europeans believed that they occupied the center of progress, civilization, and world power. London and Paris set the trends in world culture, held the reins of government for colonial peoples throughout the globe, and provided financial institutions for the business of far-flung empires. But World War II, coming only two decades after the tremendous financial strain of World War I, dramatically altered Europe's position. The costs of the long struggle left the nations of Europe—both victor and vanquished—exhausted and bankrupt. As Europeans spent their military and economic strength in what some historians have called a European civil war, their grasp over colonial areas weakened. Worldwide fighting strengthened local nationalist movements and whetted tastes for independence and self-determination. Revolution threatened to dismember the great European empires and to create a host of new, potentially unstable nations in Asia and Africa.

As the old order of European dominance and colonialism disintegrated after the war, few dared to predict what would happen. Cordell Hull, Franklin D. Roosevelt's secretary of state, warned that "the people of many countries will be starving. . . homeless. . . their factories and mines destroyed; their roads and transport wrecked. . . .Disease will lurk everywhere. In some countries confusion and chaos will follow the cessation of hostilities." Hull advised that "victory must be followed by swift and effective action to meet these pressing human needs."

It fell to America, Hull and other internationalists believed, to supply the blueprint for a postwar order. Untouched by battle, enriched by wartime profits, and free from scarcity, instability, and serious left-wing challenges, the United States emerged as victor of the victors. With much of the world in its debt, America became the undisputed superpower. American leaders tried to devise ways of using this power in postwar diplomacy. The supposed folly of isolationism and the "lessons" of appeasement during the 1920s and 1930s had turned many American policymakers into internationalists. Throughout the war they planned for postwar reconstruction.

One of the architects of American policy, Undersecretary of State Dean Acheson (later Truman's secretary of state), entitled his memoirs of this period *Present at the Creation*. The title was revealing. It reflected the belief that America would have to construct a new world order. It also displayed confidence—even arrogance—in America's ability to shape events. To policy makers like Acheson, forming a postwar settlement would involve little give-and-take diplomacy; it would be primarily an act of creation, a monumental American-directed effort affecting the well-being of future generations.

The American Vision

How did American policymakers envision the postwar world? Drawing upon tradition, they focused on two articles of faith deeply rooted in the American past: open access for trade and investment, and federalism.

A trading nation with a dynamic, expanding economy, America had always opposed restrictions to the free flow of its overseas trade and investment. During the depression decade of the 1930s, Americans watched uneasily as economic restrictions threatened to close large parts of the world to their businessmen: Great Britain moved toward an "imperial preference" system that placed nations outside of the British Empire at a commercial disadvantage; Japan's expansionist leaders threatened to create a closed economic sphere in Asia; fascist Germany reached out to encompass new sources of raw materials. Americans hoped to eliminate restrictionist trends in the postwar world. They believed that unhampered commerce brought peace, while economic restrictions—such as unequal tariffs, preferential commercial arrangements, and currency inconvertibility—bred jealousy and war. "If we could get a freer flow of trade," Cordell Hull wrote, "the living standards of all countries might rise, thereby eliminating the economic dissatisfaction that breeds war." While ushering in prosperity and peace, freer trade would, not incidentally, also enhance

United States influence worldwide because of America's dominant financial position. In planning a postwar world, as in most other endeavors, ideology and self-interest dovetailed.

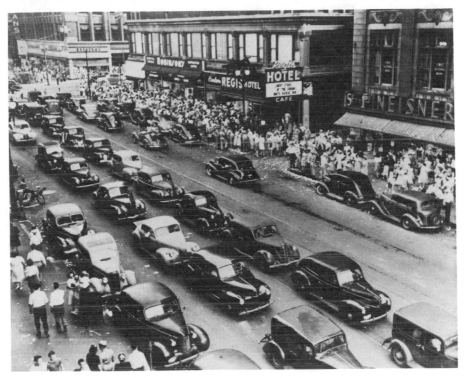

Nebraska State Historical Society

V-J Day in Omaha. All across the country, people were celebrating victory over Japan.

Since the time of Woodrow Wilson, Americans had also periodically sought to apply principles of representative federalism to international relations. Many Americans felt that their country's refusal to join the League of Nations after World War I had contributed to the breakdown of peace in 1939, and during World War II Roosevelt revived the Wilsonian dream of an international federation. This time the idea commanded more domestic support. The creation of a world body, the United Nations, became one cornerstone of America's plan for lasting peace.

Why did Americans place so much hope in a multinational body? The notion that a free exchange of ideas promoted understanding, compromise, and consensus had been a persistent American belief. Americans believed that under their constitution representative bodies forged the diverse interests of individual states into a unified national policy, and that except for the Civil War this federal system had functioned fairly successfully. Americans understandably felt that a similar federal arrangement, with modification, might also work on a grander scale. Influential Americans became convinced that internationalism would serve, not undermine, national interests. Behind this conviction lay certain assumptions: that international conflicts often stemmed from breakdowns in communication, that free debate would produce a consensus in support of the most convincing argument, and that the American point of view would invariably triumph in an open forum. A representative world assembly, policy makers believed, would provide a means of moderating tensions and building a world community under the aegis of the United States, Britain, France, and the Soviet Union. Working through an international body, these powers would become the collective guarantors of postwar peace.

American postwar plans sounded selfless and impartial. Free trade and an open forum for debate appeared to give everyone an equal chance and to set aside narrow nationalism. But critics of American policy claimed that free trade and international assemblies would inevitably advance the interests of that nation that was economically and politically the strongest—the United States. Americans used internationalist rhetoric, critics charged, only to camouflage self-interest and their desire to dominate the world.

Did American policy serve the world or itself? Could it do both? These questions have formed the basis for many of the debates on postwar American foreign policy. They have also been central to interpreting the cold war that developed between America and the Soviet Union. In the period immediately following the war few American observers doubted that their country's policy was righteous and benign. But a newer generation of analysts, writing mostly after the debacle of Vietnam, severely criticized an America that tended to identify the world's well-being with its own. America's role in the postwar world—benevolent giant or avaricious colossus—promises to remain a great problem of historical interpretation.

Reconstructing an International Economic System

Secretary of State Hull made America's position on economic issues clear: it expected equal access to trade and raw materials in the postwar world. As a condition for receiving lend-lease assistance from the United States during the war, Allied nations had to promise to work toward the "elimination of all forms of discriminatory treatment in international commerce." And in July 1944 representatives from forty-four countries gathered at Bretton Woods, New Hampshire, to work out a postwar economic structure. The Soviet Union did not attend. Although they did not adopt every American proposal, the Bretton Woods delegates formulated a system that generally reflected American goals.

Stable monetary exchange rates and full convertibility among the world's currencies seemed essential to free-flowing trade and investment. The delegates consequently created the International Monetary Fund (IMF) and charged it with maintaining a stable international system of exchange in which each national currency was convertible into any other at a fixed rate. A country could alter its exchange rate (that is, adjust the value of its money in relation to other currencies) only by agreement with the IMF. The architects of the IMF hoped that the system would combat the economic nationalism of the 1930s and believed that it would forge an interdependent world economy that would contribute to peace. The system of exchange rates did provide the foundation for unparalleled growth and prosperity in the developed nations of the Western world.

The delegates to Bretton Woods also created the International Bank for Reconstruction and Development, now called the World Bank. This institution was to encourage loans for postwar economic recovery. Loans would help restore war-ruined economies and bring resumption of normal trading patterns; financial stabilization, it was believed, would also help curb radical political movements that fed on economic discontent. Since its creation, the World Bank has been dominated by American capital and headed by an American director. It gained its most prestigious head when Robert McNamara, former secretary of defense under presidents Kennedy and Johnson, assumed command in 1967. (McNamara remained at the bank until 1981.)

United States support for the World Bank stemmed not only from a desire to stabilize and assist needy nations, but also from the pragmatic realization that America's trade would suffer unless other countries possessed the money to buy its products. In addition, the World Bank advanced American interests by promising to foster private investment. The bank would participate in or guarantee private American loans made in foreign nations. America was by far the richest nation in the postwar world, and the bank helped many Americans invest their excess capital around the globe, particularly in the development of raw materials needed by American industry. The outflow of American investment reduced the pressures toward inflation at home and greatly increased America's financial holdings abroad. Americans believed that the World Bank served world reconstruction and America's domestic prosperity equally well.

The Bretton Woods agreements stabilized the international economy and helped revive trade and investment. They helped sustain America's postwar economic predominance, and the American dollar became the kingpin of international finance. Until 1971, when a system of floating exchange rates replaced the fixed system set forth at Bretton Woods, the economic agreements of 1944 remained the foundation for the world economy outside of the Soviet bloc. For the developed nations, Bretton Woods provided a structure for nearly three decades of dynamic growth. But some less-developed nations, in whose interest the system was also supposed to work, have consistently charged that the IMF and the World Bank have worked largely to advance the interests of the already wealthy nations and have rendered the less wealthy increasingly dependent.

The Creation of the United Nations

During World War II, American officials revived Woodrow Wilson's idea of a League of Nations. They proposed an international body that would mediate disputes and create a multinational force to deter potential aggressors. They hoped to substitute collective security for old-style balance-of-power diplomacy.

At Dumbarton Oaks in Washington, D.C. in August 1944 and at San Francisco in April 1945, the wartime Allies hammered out the structural details of the United Nations. They established a General Assembly, in which all member nations had one vote; a Security Council composed of five permanent members (the United States, Great Britain, France, the Soviet Union, and Nationalist China) and six rotating temporary members; a Secretariat to handle day-to-day business; and an Economic and Social Council comprising committees for worldwide social rehabilitation and economic development.

The Security Council, which according to the UN charter had the "primary responsibility for the maintenance of international peace and security," consisted of the major victors in World War II. The inclusion of China, at American insistence, always seemed incongruous. At the time of the UN charter, China possessed an unpopular and corrupt government led by Chiang Kai-shek. Many observers doubted that Chiang could maintain control at home, much less play an active role in international affairs. But the inclusion of Chiang's China represented the Roosevelt administration's desire to turn China into a friendly Pacific power that would fill the vacuum left by Japan's defeat. In 1949, however, Chiang's Nationalist government fled to the small island of Formosa and a communist regime headed by Mao Tse-tung came to power. Under Mao, China did become a major power, but the Nationalist regime continued to sit on the Security Council until 1971. This discrepancy between the realities of world power and Security Council membership proved to be a weakness of the United Nations.

The provision for veto power within the Security Council also undermined the U.N.'s effectiveness. The charter provided that each permanent member of the Security Council could exercise an absolute veto over U.N. decisions. None of the great powers would have joined the U.N. without this means of safeguarding their national interests. But the veto provision meant that the United Nations could act only when all five permanent members agreed, and unanimity was rare in the postwar world. The U.N.'s strongest action, sponsoring a military force to assist South Korea in 1950, was approved during the absence of the Soviet Union's delegate.

If the Security Council did not always fulfill the peace-keeping role that its founders envisioned, other U.N. bodies did serve useful functions. The General Assembly provided a forum in which nations could articulate their positions; it was a barometer of international tensions and a gauge of shifting views on various issues. It also provided a platform for smaller nations whose viewpoints might not otherwise be heard. In some respects the most successful parts of the U.N. structure were the social and economic agencies, such as the World Health Organization (WHO) and the United Nations Educational, Scientific, and Cultural Organization (UNESCO). Their humanitarian programs boosted U.N. prestige. The U.N. did not fulfill the hopes of American internationalists during the 1940s, but neither was it a failure.

The Onset of the Cold War

The Allies Fall Out

The political and economic order American leaders had planned depended upon cooperation among the great powers. But divisions within the wartime Grand Alliance eventually undermined the kind of stable world that American policymakers had hoped to create.

Throughout the war, tensions had existed between the Soviet Union and the other allies. The greatest disputes centered on the issue of wartime strategy. British planners, eventually supported by the United States, favored peripheral campaigns against Germany, first into French North Africa and then up through Sicily and Italy. Soviet Premier Joseph Stalin denounced these Anglo-American offensives because they delayed the opening of a second front to the west of Germany and forced the Soviet Union to bear the main thrust of German power. Stalin came to believe that his allies were carving out spheres of influence in Northern Africa, Italy, and the Middle East while allowing Germany and the Soviet Union to exhaust each other. The long delay in opening a second front, Stalin reasoned, indicated that the wartime alliance against Nazism had not softened capitalist hostility toward Soviet communism.

The fierce fighting on the eastern front and the Soviet army's tremendous casualties helped shape Stalin's postwar policies. The Soviet leader wanted to eliminate the German menace that had repeatedly threatened his country. Thus, he viewed the creation of a pro-Soviet zone in neighboring Eastern Europe as vital to his country's national security.

During 1944 and 1945 Stalin believed he had some Allied support for his goal of creating a Soviet sphere of influence. At a meeting in 1944, Winston Churchill and Stalin reached an informal agreement: Churchill would grant Soviet predominance in Rumania and Bulgaria in return for British preeminence in Greece. Roosevelt refused to endorse this agreement, but he did not protest it. Publicly, Americans talked of eliminating spheres of influence; privately, American policymakers seemed to understand their inevitability. At the Yalta Conference in February 1945, Allied harmony reached its high tide with the implicit recognition of spheres of influence: Germany was divided into four zones of occupation; Russia agreed to sign a treaty of friendship with America's client in China, Chiang Kai-shek; the Allies agreed to a vague promise to hold "free elections" in liberated Europe, but Anglo-American negotiators implied their understanding of Stalin's need to have Poland as a friendly neighbor.

In the end, the course of battle largely determined the postwar power situation. Soviet troops marched into Berlin from the east as American forces advanced through Germany from the west, and the separate zones of occupation eventually hardened into a divided Germany. The nationality of occupation forces likewise helped determine the destiny of the countries surrounding Germany. Anglo-American influence was strong in France, Italy, Greece, and the Middle East; Soviet power predominated in Eastern Europe. The United States assumed exclusive control of the Japanese-dominated Pacific islands and of defeated Japan itself.

Stalin largely ignored the Yalta declaration supporting free elections in Eastern Europe. Pro-Soviet governments came to power in Rumania, Hungary, Bulgaria, Albania, and Poland; Latvia, Lithuania, and Estonia were absorbed completely by the Soviet Union. Stalin refused to include an Anglo-American-sponsored group in the new government of Poland, and some Americans cried that that country had been betrayed. Polish communists, however, who had remained in their country and organized underground resistance to the Nazi occupiers, may well have had more popular support than the Anglo-American-backed group that sat out the war in London as a government-in-exile.

To Stalin, a Soviet-dominated zone in Eastern Europe represented a minimal guarantee of future security. It seemed a just reward for having borne the brunt of Germany's force and for having suffered staggering casualties. (The Soviet Union lost more than ten times as many soldiers as the United States.) Stalin also recalled that Anglo-American commanders had not allowed Soviet participation in governments under their military influence. In Italy after Benito Mussolini's overthrow, for example, England and the United States had installed a rightist regime committed to purging any leftist or pro-Soviet sentiment.

Stalin regarded his Eastern European policy as defensive, but to many people in the United States it appeared aggressive. Republicans blamed President Roosevelt especially for failing to obtain stronger guarantees for Eastern Europe at the Yalta Conference. They felt he had betrayed the cause of democracy. Americans of Eastern European descent and others who had expected the war to open all of Europe to American trade and ideas began to view the Soviet Union as a new threat to peace similar to Nazi Germany. Both Roosevelt and Truman had acknowledged the importance of the six million Polish-Americans to the Democratic party's strength. And Stalin's brutal, iron-handed supression of domestic dissent made him a convincing villain. Accustomed to thinking in terms of an evil and aggressive enemy, a growing number of Americans substituted the Soviets for the Germans as the new arch enemies. A former State Department official, William C. Bullitt, expressed this attitude: "The Soviet Union's assault upon the West is at about the stage of Hitler's maneuvering into Czechoslovakia." This analysis could have only one conclusion—that there could be no appeasement, no compromise with Soviet power.

Mounting Distrust

American–Soviet relations degenerated from an atmosphere of cooperation at Yalta in early 1945 to one of deep distrust by the end of the same year. Stalin's Eastern European policies provided the backdrop to this cooling of relations, but events in the United States also contributed.

Harry S Truman, who had become president in April 1945, lacked

Roosevelt's cool self-confidence, easy affability, and cosmopolitan world view. He had not been close to Roosevelt and knew little of his policies or intentions. In attempting to form guidelines for his new administration, Truman quickly sided with those advisers who advocated a harder line against the Soviet Union, and he rejected the notion of a Soviet sphere of influence in Eastern Europe. Setting a style for his successors, he began to talk tough to the Russians, especially at the Potsdam Conference of July 1945.

Truman and his advisers had two potent weapons in bargaining with Stalin. The first was atomic power. Even before Roosevelt's death, some advisers had suggested that the bomb might be an effective diplomatic lever. After demonstrating the horrible power of this weapon at Hiroshima and Nagasaki to bring about Japan's rapid surrender, some officials believed that Stalin could no longer ignore American demands to open Eastern Europe. Truman also hoped that the Soviet's need for postwar economic assistance would bring Stalin into line. After the termination of lend-lease, Stalin requested additional aid to help rebuild Russia's war-damaged economy. But Truman's tough tone indicated that assistance would be contingent upon a change in the Soviet Union's Eastern European policy. Possessing overwhelming nuclear and economic power, American leaders were in no mood to compromise.

National Archives.

The A-Bomb, 1946. The tremendous power of the atom bomb created a terrible new military weapon; it also stimulated false hopes of a bountiful and cheap energy source in peacetime.

Rather than forcing Stalin into accommodation, Truman's hard-line policy reinforced Stalin's apprehensions about Soviet security and Western hostility. Fearful of the strings America might attach to any economic-aid package, he eased his country's difficulties in other ways: a new Five-Year Plan to rebuild Soviet industry and an expropriation of materials from occupied territories, particularly East Germany. Just as the United States had removed thousands of tons of military materials and scientific documents from West Germany, so the Soviet Union carried away whatever it could use—in some cases whole factories. More and more, Stalin closed the Soviet zone to Anglo-American influence.

Some Americans believed that Truman's hard line was at least partially responsible for Stalin's growing hostility. Secretary of Commerce Henry A. Wallace, for example, advocated a more cooperative attitude toward the Soviet Union, warning that the United States had everything to lose by "beating the tom-toms against Russia." In a speech in 1946 he pleaded "[We] should recognize that we have no more business in the political affairs of Eastern Europe than Russia has in the political affairs of Latin America." Wallace argued that a secure and prosperous Russia would be more accommodating than a frightened and hungry one. But this view ran counter to Truman's foreign policy. Embarrassed by the public display of disunity within his administration, the president asked for Wallace's resignation.

From allies in a hot war the United States and the Soviet Union became enemies in a "cold war." In 1946 Stalin publicly expressed distrust of his old capitalist allies. Their objections to Soviet policy in Eastern Europe, he believed, indicated their intention to crush socialism and isolate the Soviet regime. On the other side, Winston Churchill denounced Soviet actions, charging that Stalin had dropped an "iron curtain" across Europe. With the collapse of the wartime alliance, the world plunged into a period of bipolar politics in which America and the Soviet Union vied for worldwide influence.

Cold-War Aid Programs

By 1947 the American government faced a dilemma. It had almost completed a period of rapid military demobilization, and the public longed for the "normalcy" of peace. At the same time, government policymakers perceived Russia as a new aggressor and decided to adopt a hard line. In 1946 Secretary of State James Byrnes wrote, "We must help our friends in every way and refrain from assisting those who either through helplessness or for other reasons are opposing the principles for which we stand." But would the American Congress and public approve the appropriations that such "help" required?

By early 1947 the issue could no longer be postponed. A leftist revolution threatened the conservative regime in Greece, and Great Britain, which had previously considered Greece within its sphere of responsibility, announced that it could no longer provide economic and military assistance. The State Department wanted to grant extensive military aid to Greece, a move that would have established a precedent for America's entry into other areas as a replacement for European power. But the chances for such a commitment seemed slim. Senator Arthur Vandenberg correctly assessed the situation: "If Truman wants it, he will have to go and scare hell out of the country."

Truman was equal to the task, and he set out to sell Congress and the public on both the aid program and his cold-war viewpoint. A leftist victory in Greece, he explained, would lead to communist takeovers in other parts of Europe. Before a joint session of Congress in March 1947, the president advanced the Truman Doctrine. He explained that the struggle in Greece represented a conflict between two ways of life, one "distinguished by free institutions, representative government, free elections, guaranties of individual liberty, freedom of speech and religion, and freedom from political oppression." The other system relied upon "terror and oppression, a controlled press and radio, fixed elections, and the suppression of personal freedoms." By failing to act, Truman concluded, "we may endanger the peace of the world—and we shall surely endanger the welfare of our own nation." These arguments helped cast anticommunism in global terms, and brought a $400-million authorization to extend assistance, primarily military aid, to Greece and neighboring Turkey.

The rationale for the Truman Doctrine set the terms of Americans' analysis of foreign affairs for years to come and formed the core of a policy later called *containment*. The classic and most sophisticated statement of containment came in a 1947 article in *Foreign Affairs* written by George Kennan, a respected foreign-service officer. Writing under the pseudonym "Mr. X," Kennan analyzed the Soviet Union's "expansive tendencies" and advocated a "firm and vigilant" application of counterforce to meet Soviet maneuvers until internal change in Russia moderated the threat to the West.

In December 1947 the president again requested a strong commitment of economic aid—this time to European nations, including Germany. Initially Congress balked, but a procommunist coup in neutralist Czechoslovakia convinced many people that Soviet aggression threatened Europe and that containment had to be implemented. The new aid program—the Marshall Plan—passed by an overwhelming margin.

The Marshall Plan sprang not only from a genuine desire to alleviate human suffering but also from a very practical assessment of America's national interests. The entire economic and political system that American policymakers had arduously constructed in postwar conferences depended upon the economic revival of European nations. But European economies were faltering, and West Germany remained a weak and defeated nation. American leaders recognized that their own country's prosperity ultimately required a prosperous and stable Europe. In addition, as hostility toward the Soviet Union mounted, it seemed increasingly necessary to counter Soviet power with a strong, industrialized West Germany. Germany, the Nazi enemy that had once united capitalists and communists, now became the focal point of the cold war, ominously divided between the two competing camps. As Russia changed from ally to enemy, West

Germany changed from enemy to ally. Germany would later provide the first real showdown in the cold war.

From the enunciation of the Truman Doctrine through the most troubled years of the cold war, the United States would continue to employ economic and military aid as major weapons against instability. Money often brought needed assistance to poverty-ridden areas and helped boost America's trade and investment abroad. American aid helped revitalize Europe. But if the policy was sometimes successful, it also frequently led to expensive or impossible commitments. While the Soviet Union sometimes took advantage of global postwar disruption by backing revolutionary and anticolonial movements, the United States tried to "contain" instability. Threats to the status quo became suspect, and nationalist movements in the third world, even when they had little connection with Moscow, were too often viewed solely as part of a cohesive international communist conspiracy. At a time when Europe's empires were breaking down, the United States moved into these power vacuums and often continued to back unpopular regimes. Once the champion of social justice and the right of revolution, the United States increasingly pitted its might against any change that it did not control.

Cold-War Crises

The cold war grew more menacing during Truman's second term, and Dean Acheson, who became secretary of state in 1949, tried to bring order to a disorderly world. He reorganized and enlarged the State Department, hoping to make it more efficient and productive. He called for a new approach to foreign affairs: broader perspectives, bolder actions, more centralization in planning and direction. Acheson, who liked to quote his predecessor General George C. Marshall's advice, "Don't fight the problem. Decide it!" never doubted the accuracy of his assessments or the morality of his decisions. He hoped that later generations would recognize the "truly heroic mold" of the Truman administration's reactions to cold-war crises; that Americans would realize, as the less polished chief of state put it, that Harry Truman "done his damnedest."

The Berlin Crisis

By 1947 American policymakers had accepted the need to contain Soviet aggression by stabilizing Europe through economic assistance. The reestablishment of Germany as an industrial power and its reintegration into Europe's economy seemed essential for the continent's full recovery. Consequently the United States, Great Britain, and France decided to merge their zones of occupation into one federal republic and to institute a program of economic rehabilitation. On June 18, 1948, the three powers announced a currency reform for what would become, in 1949, the Federal Republic of Germany.

The Soviet Union saw the strengthening of West Germany as a provocation. Stalin wanted Germany to remain weak and divided; he desired German reparations for war damage; and he sought to dismantle the country's industrial capacity, not to rebuild it. In retaliation for the West's actions, he formed the German Democratic Republic in East Germany and closed off West Berlin, an Anglo-American-controlled sector of the capital city that was wholly within the Soviet zone.

Only one way remained into the blockaded city—by airplane. American planes began flying around the clock to deliver food, fuel, and medicine to the 2.5 million people in West Berlin. In Montana pilots practiced landings at a flight-training center with an air corridor, runways, and navigational aids exactly duplicating those in Berlin. Assisted by the latest radar techniques, Operation Vittles, as the pilots dubbed the airlift, landed almost 13,000 tons of provisions during its peak day. By the spring of 1949 the airlift was bringing as much into Berlin as water and rail had provided before the blockade. To underscore how seriously he viewed the crisis, Truman also reinstated the draft and sent two squadrons of B-29s to Great Britain. In the face of this commitment the Soviet Union backed off. In May 1949 Stalin reopened certain corridors of surface travel into West Berlin, and the city returned to its uneasy equilibrium. The divided city would remain a symbol and point of tension throughout the cold war.

During the year-long Berlin crisis, which had closely followed the communist coup in Czechoslovakia, the nations of Western Europe grew increasingly anxious about cold-war tensions. With United States encouragement, Britain, France, Belgium, the Netherlands, and Luxembourg signed the Brussels Pact, pledging cooperation in economic and military matters. They also appealed for a stronger United States commitment to their security. Finally, in the spring of 1949 twelve nations, including the United States and the Brussels Pact countries, established the North Atlantic Treaty Organization (NATO). This collective-security pact provided that an attack against one of the signatories would be considered an attack against all. Furthermore, the contracting nations promised to encourage economic ties among one another. NATO laid the groundwork for America's long-lasting military presence in Western Europe and formed a pattern for later collective-security pacts, CENTO and SEATO, in other parts of the world. NATO, together with the Marshall Plan, brought Western Europe under America's economic and military umbrella.

The Chinese Revolution

Throughout World War II, civil war plagued China. The United States consistently supported the Nationalist government of Chiang Kai-shek, providing it with arms, money, advisers, a prestigious position on the United Nations Security Council, and an assurance of Soviet support. Yet most American diplomats in Asia believed that Chiang's government could not last. Joseph Stilwell, who went to China in 1942 to organize its military effort against the Japanese, reported that Chiang was too corrupt and incompetent to gain wide support among the Chinese people. The communist forces under Mao Tse-tung were both more effective in fighting the Japanese and more popular with the peasants.

Statistical comparisons made Chiang's victory over the communists seem a sure thing: by 1947 he had twice the number of men under arms and three or four times the number of rifles. From 1945 through 1948 the United States extended him a billion dollars in military aid and another billion in economic assistance. Yet these figures only measured his incompetence and lack of support. Despite American help, Chiang's armies rapidly lost ground; Chinese peasants flocked to the communist side, which promised land reform and popular government.

Realizing Chiang's limitations, American officials attempted to mediate between the opposing sides after World War II. But the effort failed. The United States government was left uncomfortably supporting Chiang at the very time that most officials came to believe his downfall inevitable. At the end of 1948 the director of the American military advisory group in China, Major-General David Barr, reported that "the military situation [had] deteriorated to the point where only the active participation of United States troops could effect a remedy." And this adviser "certainly [did] not recommend" allying with what he termed "the world's worst leadership" to attempt the impossible: regaining the enormous expanse of Chinese territory that Chiang had lost to the communists.

Early in 1949 the Nationalist government withdrew to the island of Formosa (Taiwan), leaving Mao Tse-tung in complete control of the mainland. To Secretary Acheson the turn of events was disturbing, but in a white paper presented to the president he wrote that the situation in China was "beyond the control of the government of the United States." America's containment policy as yet applied principally to Europe, and policymakers recognized some realistic limits to their ability to shape world events. But the United States government was now trapped by its previous attempt to strengthen Chiang. Not wishing to harm the Nationalist cause, American officials had concealed the full extent of Chiang's unpopularity and ineptness. What seemed inevitable to officials knowledgeable about China looked like a sell-out to communism by Americans who viewed Chiang as the strong and respected leader of "free" China. By the time Chiang retreated, it was too late to revise the public's view of him. The news of China's "fall" hit America like a bombshell, and following swiftly upon this news came word that the Soviet Union had exploded a nuclear device. America had "lost" China and no longer had sole possession of the ultimate weapon.

The Anticommunist Crusade

The constant crises of 1949—Berlin, China, and Russia's new bomb—unsettled many Americans. The communist threat appeared to be everywhere; American power seemed in retreat. Many Republicans and some Democrats sought the source of America's problems not in the world at large but in traitors in their midst. The charge gained credibility when a former State Department officer, Alger Hiss, was accused of passing government papers to the Soviet Union. The search for Soviet spy rings became the order of the day; Republican Senator William E. Jenner of Indiana charged that the Truman administration consisted of a "crazy assortment of collectivist cutthroat crackpots and Communist fellow-traveling appeasers." Acheson's assessment regarding China—that America could not control all world events—sounded to some like a new doctrine of appeasement, and many Republicans demanded Acheson's resignation. The cry for an all-out crusade against communism, including suppression of dissent at home and of revolution abroad, would affect American life and policy for years to come.

The international shocks of 1949 and the fire from Republican leaders prompted senior officials in the State and Defense departments to draw up a paper outlining foreign-policy assumptions and future strategy. The paper, called N.S.C. 68, was approved by the National Security Council and the president. In 1950 Acheson traveled throughout the country trying to regain his credibility as a tough anticommunist by preaching the assumptions upon which N.S.C. 68 was based. The report's logic eventually became the conventional wisdom of the cold war. According to N.S.C. 68, The Soviet Union was determined to stamp out freedom and dominate the world. Negotiation with the communists was futile, for they did not bargain in good faith. And there could be no valid distinction between national and world security. The United States could not, as Acheson put it, "pull down the blinds and sit in the parlor with a loaded shotgun, waiting." The country had to embark upon a massive military buildup at home and create "situations of strength" abroad, regardless of cost. N.S.C. 68 provided the blueprint for what one historian has called a "national security state": a leviathan with overwhelming military power, a wide variety of economic weapons, and an extensive capacity for covert operations.

In his cold-war speeches Acheson argued that freedom meant simply anticommunism. Those people who wanted to go from ally to ally "with political litmus paper testing them for true-blue democracy" were "escapists." Furthermore, domestic consensus served freedom while differences of opinion aided the enemy. The "fomenters of disunity" who advocated negotiation with the Soviets, Acheson explained, contributed to American weakness. Other observers, noting how often "freedom" was invoked to support dictators abroad and to suppress dissent at home, suggested that language, and therefore communication, was one of the first serious casualties of the cold war.

Korea

In June 1950 the assumptions and fears articulated in N.S.C. 68 seemed to come alive: communist North Korea attacked South Korea. There was no evidence that Stalin had ordered the attack across the thirty-eighth parallel or that he knew of it in advance, yet Americans still viewed the Korean conflict as a showdown with the Soviets and their "satellites." Using the same logic he had outlined in his Truman Doctrine for Greece and Turkey, the president announced that "if aggression is successful in Korea, we can expect it to spread through Asia and Europe to this hemisphere." One weak spot in the "free world" defense would start the "dominoes" falling.

In line with this new worldwide containment policy, Truman responded immediately. He gained United Nations support for an American-controlled defense of Syngman Rhee's South Korean regime (the Soviet delegation was boycotting the United Nations and could not exercise its veto); he also announced protection for Chiang Kai-shek's exiled regime in Formosa and ordered support for the French in their efforts to hold off communist-led nationalists in Vietnam. Assistance was also extended to the Philippine attempts to suppress leftist Huk rebels. In Europe, more troops were added to the NATO military force and a program for rearming West Germany was announced. The front line against communism lay everywhere, and America committed its power, prestige, and treasure as though they had no limits.

Americans were torn between two goals during the Korean War: simple containment (which would leave Korea divided) and rollback (which would unite it, totally under American influence). As long as South Korean and American troops were retreating southward early in the war, restoration of a boundary at the thirty-eighth parallel seemed victory enough. But when a regrouped force under General Douglas MacArthur landed at Inchon behind enemy lines and drove the North Koreans back from the thirty-eight parallel, decisions became more complicated. Could MacArthur "liberate" North Korea, and would Russia and China intervene if he did? The president gave MacArthur authority to pursue the war in the north as long as it did not bring a wider war with China, but the general underestimated Chinese reaction. After crossing the thirty-eighth parallel American soliders began to encounter Chinese "volunteers." Then, as American forces penetrated farther into North Korea and approached the border of China, the dam broke. Chinese troops streamed into Korea and sent MacArthur's armies reeling backward across the thirty-eighth parallel once again. When MacArthur again regrouped and began pushing northward, Truman ordered him to seek a negotiated settlement.

Truman's order provoked a dramatic clash between civilian and military authority. The general publicly opposed Truman's "limited war" and balked at his instructions. He pressed for a full-scale commitment to victory over North Korea, even over China, and claimed that this was America's chance to roll back communism in Asia. Truman, however, held to his position that a lengthy conflict in Korea would weaken America's defense posture in other, more vital areas. He viewed the Soviet Union as the real enemy and believed a costly Asian land war would only play into Stalin's hands. In the face of MacArthur's challenge to presidential authority, Truman had only one choice: he removed the general from his command.

Those "Asia-firsters" who had excoriated Truman following Chiang Kai-shek's fall in China now had new ammunition and a popular martyr. They condemned the "no-win policy" against communism, and MacArthur returned home a hero. Telegrams demanding Truman's impeachment flooded the White House. Huge crowds greeted the general in San Francisco, Washington, and

New York. A parade in New York on the general's behalf attracted seven and a half million people (compared with four million for Eisenhower at the end of World War II) and produced over three thousand tons of litter. George Gallup reported that only 29 percent of those polled supported President Truman's action against MacArthur.

The outpouring in favor of MacArthur, including a MacArthur-for-president boomlet, subsided quickly. Senate hearings on the general's dismissal convinced the public that most military strategists opposed a wider conflict in Asia, and few Americans wanted full-scale war. Admiration for MacArthur's military achievements remained, but most Americans welcomed negotiation. When the 1952 Republican nominee for president, General Dwight D. Eisenhower, promised to go to Korea and end the struggle, he received applause and votes. By the end of Truman's presidency the war in Korea had grown less intense and both sides had gathered around a conference table. Hammering out the details of a negotiated settlement (which eventually reestablished the thirty-eighth parallel as a dividing line) would fall to the new Republican administration.

Long-Term Trends in Foreign Policy: A Look Toward the Future

World War II vastly changed the United States government bureaucracy. Before the war the federal government employed about 800,000 civilians, 10 percent of whom were involved with national security; by the end of the war the figure had risen to nearly four million, with 75 percent working for national-security agencies. Although the new government bureaus were designed to increase the efficiency of wartime operations, their sheer size and complexity often complicated decisionmaking. New photocopying techniques brought additional problems. The "paper revolution," designed to assist interdepartmental communication, often beleaguered policymakers, burying both the important and the trivial under a mountain of duplicate copies.

The State Department, the agency traditionally responsible for creating and executing foreign policy, was transformed during the war. The department and its related agencies outgrew old quarters and, during the 1950s, expanded into twenty-nine buildings throughout Washington, D.C. When all of these offices were finally brought together in 1961, it took eight stories covering a four-block area to house them. Before the war a few men would meet in the secretary of state's office, discuss world problems, and set policy. By the end of the war cozy familiarity and easy communication had given way to faceless bureaucratic routine. Truman's secretary of state, Dean Acheson, once asked Cordell Hull, Franklin Roosevelt's secretary of state, to come by the department and meet the assistant secretaries. Hull declined, wryly commenting that he had never done well in crowds.

The cold war also helped swell the State Department's staff. In its new role as global superpower, the United States seemed to need a resident expert on every conceivable topic so that it could react quickly to a wide variety of situations. In this era of confrontation, the most casual decision could suddenly mushroom into a matter of major importance.

After 1949 the crisis atmosphere of the cold war delivered even stronger blows to the State Department's effectiveness. Mao's victory in China in 1949 outraged those Americans who believed that communism could never triumph on its own merits. A number of influential people were convinced that State Department officials must have sold out China, and pressure mounted to purge the "old China hands" who had advised against an open-ended commitment to Chiang Kai-shek. Throughout the 1950s many seasoned diplomats lost influence to newer men who took a harder anticommunist line. The immediate suspicion of anyone who questioned cold-war verities submerged healthy differences of opinion. The State Department became less involved in forming policies according to world realities and more caught up in interpreting the world according to a preestablished cold-war viewpoint. The cold-war consensus of the early and mid-1950s, combined with the attacks upon experienced diplomats, damaged the effectiveness, and ultimately the prestige and power, of the State Department.

Other agencies challenged the State Department's preeminence in international concerns. Before the war, nearly all foreign-policy functions were centralized at State; after the war, other departments—especially Agriculture, Treasury, and Commerce, as well as independent agencies such as the Central Intelligence Agency—assumed responsibilities in foreign nations. Policymaking became a complex process involving many different bureaucracies, each with its experts and points of view.

Overlapping jurisdictions sometimes even produced conflicting policies, particularly between the Central Intelligence Agency (CIA) and the State Department. The CIA grew out of the Office of Strategic Services (OSS), a wartime intelligence-gathering agency. After the war the State Department, the armed services, and the FBI all sought to assume the functions of the OSS. As a compromise, the CIA was created as an independent agency under the new National Security Council. Under the influence of its activist director, Walter Bedell Smith, the CIA began to lose the cosmopolitan character of the OSS and to narrow into a preoccupation with anticommunism. (Smith reportedly once confided that he even believed Eisenhower was a communist.) Although the CIA's finances and operations were kept secret, scholars have estimated that the agency rapidly surpassed the State Department both in number of employees and in budget. Personnel of the two departments frequently worked at cross-purposes. In Indonesia, Burma, and Costa Rica, to name just a few examples, CIA agents helped movements attempting to overthrow governments with which the State Department was dealing. American ambassadors in foreign lands often complained that their ignorance of the CIA's clandestine activities undermined their prestige.

The Pentagon also became a powerful rival in handling foreign affairs. During the war Roosevelt increasingly turned to the military for advice, and the Joint Chiefs of Staff, created in 1941, eroded the secretary of state's position as preeminent foreign-policy expert. In the 1960s this trend accelerated when Secretary of Defense Robert McNamara, mastermind of Ford Motor Company's postwar reorganization, easily out-maneuvered Secretary of State Dean Rusk in bureaucratic power plays. Armed with ironclad self-confidence, detailed statistics, and convincing analyses, McNamara solidified the Pentagon's position, and the views of generals, rather than of civilians, tended to shape decisions regarding Vietnam.

Some elements of foreign policy were altogether external to the government. Although private businessmen in foreign lands had always influenced international affairs, the giant United States-based multinational corporations that mushroomed in the postwar era exerted an unparalleled impact upon foreign relations. For example, the great oil giants—the so-called seven sisters—profoundly affected the world's economy through their agreements that set the world price of oil and divided up spheres of production and distribution. Many companies with far-flung investments began to view themselves as wholly new forces in international relations, developing company interests that could surpass national loyalties.

SUGGESTIONS FOR FURTHER READING

There are numerous studies of the onset and conduct of the early cold war. A good place to begin is Thomas G. Patterson's *On Every Front* (1979); the book offers a good blend of primary research and synthesis of recent "revisionist" scholarship and contains a thorough bibliography. Other general accounts include John Lewis Gaddis, *The United States and the Origins of the Cold War, 1941–1947* (1972); Stephen G. Ambrose, *Rise to Globalism* (2nd rev. ed., 1980); and Walter LaFeber, *America, Russia and the Cold War, 1945–75* (rev. ed., 1980). Thomas H. Etzold and John Lewis Gaddis, eds., *Containment: Documents on American Policy and Strategy, 1945–1950* (1978), is a very useful collection of documents.

In addition to these general studies, there is a growing body of more specialized work on the cold war. *The Politics of War* (1968) by Gabriel Kolko and *The Limits of Power* (1972) by Gabriel and Joyce Kolko are two important studies. See also Daniel Yergin, *Shattered Peace* (1977); Diane Shaver Clemons, *Yalta* (1973); Lisle Rose, *After Yalta* (1973); Lloyd C. Gardner, *Architects of Illusion* (1970); Lynn Etheridge Davis, *The Cold War Begins* (1974); Bruce Kuklick, *American Policy and the Division of Germany* (1972); John Gimbel, *The Origins of the Marshall Plan* (1976); and Akira Iriye, *The Cold War in Asia* (1974). On economic issues, see David P. Calleo and Benjamin M. Rowland, *America and the World Political Economy* (1973); Alfred E. Eckes, Jr., *A Search for Solvency: Bretton Woods and the International Monetary System, 1941–1971* (1975); and Fred Block, *The Origins of International Economic Disorder* (1977).

There has been considerable controversy among scholars over the meaning of cold-war events. All of the books cited above reflect the historiographical give-and-take, but students can sample conflicting interpretations for themselves in Thomas G. Patterson, ed., *The Origins of the Cold War* (2nd ed., 1974). The memoirs of some of the leading architects of cold-war policy also reflect the clash of opinions. See, for example, Dean Acheson's *Present at the Creation* (1969) and George F. Kennan's *Memoirs, 1925–50* (1967).

The complex interrelationship between foreign and domestic affairs is examined in Robert A. Divine, *Foreign Policy and United States Presidential Elections, Vol. I* (1974); Richard Freeland, *The Truman Doctrine and the Origins of McCarthyism* (1972); and Richard J. Barnet, *Roots of War* (1972). See also Stanley Hoffman, "Thirty Years Overview," in his *Primacy or World Order* (1979).

POSTWAR READJUSTMENTS, 1946–1953

The Nation Wages Peace

Reconversion

President Truman and his close advisers had awaited the end of the war with both hope and fear. The return of peace, they hoped, would allow the Democratic party to retrieve the fallen standard of domestic reform, to revive the New Deal spirit. But the end of war also brought the possibility of economic stagnation. Economists recognized that it was not New Deal programs but World War II, with its huge government outlays for weaponry, that had finally ended the Great Depression of the 1930s. Remembering the sharp economic downturn that had followed the first Great War—and the bitter social conflicts that the depression of 1919 had brought—many people dreaded the transition from war to peace. What would happen when wartime production slowed? Only a few weeks after the final victory in 1945, almost 100,000 defense workers in Detroit alone lost their jobs. Could production for civilian consumption take up the slack and put people back to work?

Liberal economists and many Democratic politicans argued that the national government should continue the social and economic programs—and also solidify the political gains—of the Roosevelt era. Government welfare measures should not be limited to times of acute depression, liberal economists contended, but must become a permanent part of the postwar economic system. Increased spending for social-welfare programs would pump money into the economy, easing the problem of reconversion and providing a cushion against social conflict. Unless the national administration took decisive action, some forecasters claimed, postwar unemployment might reach 11 million workers.

Only three weeks after the Japanese surrender President Truman sent Congress a message proposing twenty-one domestic spending programs. These included an increased minimum wage, money for hospital construction, funds for small businesses, permanent government price supports for farmers, and legislation to ensure full employment. The Truman administration faced congressional opposition from a coalition of anti-New Deal Republicans and southern Democrats, but the Seventy-ninth Congress did pass a number of Truman's proposals, including the Hospital Construction Act, the Veterans Emergency Housing Act, funds for power and soil-conservation projects, and a modified version of the highly controversial Full Employment Bill of 1945.

The Full Employment Bill of 1945 and the Employment Act of 1946

The Full Employment Bill produced bitter political and economic debates. The bill's drafters announced that it would "establish a national policy and program for assuring continuing full employment," largely through continual planning, direction, and spending by the national government. Washington would take responsibility for ensuring that the "free enterprise" system would produce full employment. But the specter of government planning and massive spending in peacetime alarmed many conservatives; to them the Full Employment Bill seemed another giant leap toward a centrally planned economy, or even toward socialism.

The employment bill and similar economic proposals drew their inspiration not from socialism but from the theories of British economist John Maynard Keynes. A complex capitalist economy, Keynesians argued, required active governmental intervention. Whenever consumer spending declined, for example, increased spending by government could take up the slack, maintain full employment, and prevent recession. Funds for public housing, hospitals, schools, and social welfare would provide assistance for the poor while maintaining a high level of economic growth. In addition, government officials could use controls over taxation as an economic tool: in times of slow growth they could lower personal and business taxes to stimulate buying power and output; when inflationary pressures developed they could raise taxes as one means of reducing the amount of spending. Keynes's American disciples did not follow all of his ideas—political pressures, for example, made it difficult to raise taxes or reduce government expenditures—but the "new economics" became orthodoxy to most Democratic liberals after World War II.

By the late 1940s most Americans saw the need for some type of continuing economic role for the federal government, and a modified version of the Full Employment Bill did become law in 1946. Economic oversight and heavy government spending became prominent features of the postwar welfare state. The modern "free enterprise" system was too fragile to be left entirely to the mechanisms of the marketplace.

Although it did not entirely satisfy advocates of centralized planning, the Employment Act of 1946 established an important precedent and provided the institutional framework for more extensive government action. Congress created a new executive body, the Council of Economic Advisers, and charged it with advising the president and establishing policies to "promote free competitive enterprise, to avoid economic fluctuations. . . and to maintain employment, production, and purchasing power." Since 1946 the council has gained more and more influence over economic policy. Citizens have come to expect that the national government, especially the presidency, will deal firmly with economic problems. Any administration that fails to develop effective programs, to maintain high levels of employment, or to curb inflation invites political disaster. In retrospect, the Employment Act of 1946 was more than a legislative pronouncement. With its authorization of positive action by the national government, the measure assumed almost the status of a constitutional amendment. It mandated a new political-constitutional order that one analyst has called "the positive state."

Inflation, Black Markets, and Strikes

Despite all the analyses and governmental involvement, a variety of economic problems beset the nation in the period immediately following the war. Most liberal economists had feared that peacetime consumer spending would not maintain wartime levels of production and employment, but the gloomy forecasters were proved wrong. Consumers took the money in their savings accounts—funds that they had been unable to spend because of wartime rationing and production controls—and went on a buying spree. They wanted all the items that had been scarce or out of production during the war: refrigerators, new-model cars, nylon stockings, cameras and film, rubber-centered golf balls, and even wire coat-hangers. Toy manufacturers promised to fill the demand for electric trains. Taking advantage of greater supplies of gasoline, Americans began to travel again, and hotel and cabin owners (plastic-coated, chain motels were still in the future) complained that they could not handle the crowds of tourists.

In all areas of the economy supply could not equal demand, and a steep inflationary spiral began. As prices continued upward, supplies dwindled. Producers could not provide enough meat, cars, and new homes. In June 1946 a deliveryman in Denver lost his entire truckload of bread to a crowd of women who overpowered him outside a grocery store; rumors of a shipment of meat produced an angry, shoving crowd of over two thousand in front of a Brooklyn store; and outside a Detroit supermarket employees served coffee and doughnuts to placate angry shoppers who were waiting in line. A thriving black market soon developed. If people wanted a new car or a juicy steak, they often had to tip the automobile salesman or the butcher. When one woman walked into a Detroit meat market the butcher asked his boss if she was a regular customer. "No," the boss replied; "starve the bitch." Some butchers tried a barter system: a meat cutter in Atlanta offered steaks and roasts in exchange for nails, flooring, and plumbing fixtures for his new home.

Harry Truman received much of the blame for postwar economic problems. While Republicans berated him for rising prices and black-market conditions, he also faced opposition from labor unions, which had been firm supporters of the Democratic party and Roosevelt's New Deal. A series of labor strikes in 1946, including walkouts in the coal and auto industries, tried the president's patience. When a nationwide rail shutdown threatened to disrupt the transportation sytem, Truman proposed drafting striking workers into the army. This threat won him the enmity of many labor leaders and the title of the nation's foremost strikebreaker. A number of pro-Democratic labor leaders questioned Truman's capacity for leadership; many liberal Democrats also became disenchanted, dismissing Truman as an inept politician with a weak social conscience.

Throughout his first year in office Truman did appear scarcely able to handle his responsibilities. Seeking political popularity by promising rapid discharges for service personnel, he mishandled demobilization of the armed forces. At one point the navy found it lacked the ships to transport the large number of soldiers scheduled to return to the States. By Truman's admission the process soon "was no longer demobilization . . . it was disintegration." Although he did face extremely difficult economic decisions, Truman made things even worse by failing to develop clear and consistent policies. He hesitated to support the Office of Price Administration (OPA), an executive agency that regulated wages and prices, and listened instead to people who favored a quick end to economic controls after the war. In June 1945 Truman vetoed a bill that would have renewed the OPA's authority while limiting its powers. But after a short period with no controls at all, he signed a second bill that differed very little from the first. (Finally, in November 1946, Truman proclaimed an end to virtually all controls.) In all of these matters Truman projected the image of an indecisive leader, a person who leaned too heavily upon old political cronies and representatives of special-interest groups. Even Truman's supporters could find few examples of effective leadership during his first year in the White House.

A Republican Victory: 1946

Republicans hardly lacked campaign issues in 1946: soaring prices, black-market conditions, labor strikes, an unpopular president. By October the Gallup polling organization reported that only 32 percent of their sample approved of Truman's performance, compared with a figure of 87 percent a little over a year earlier. One pro-Republican columnist suggested that the Democrats nominate W. C. Fields for president: "If we're going to have a comedian in the White House, let's have a good one." Other Democrats were the targets of similar jibes, and after nearly fifteen years as the minority party, Republicans found themselves almost back in control. Summing up all the Democratic sins, Republicans posters asked, "Had enough?" In the November 1946 elections Republicans gained control of the new Eightieth Congress and captured twenty-five governorships. Jersey City's political boss, Frank Hague, was philosophical about the defeats. "The Republicans would have won even had they put up a German, " an aide quoted Hague. And 1948 promised to be an even better year for Republicans.

Truman made little effort to work with the new Republican-controlled Eightieth Congress (1947-49) on domestic issues. He challenged Republicans to pass legislation he knew they opposed and refused to seek any common ground on measures such as a higher minimum wage and labor legislation. At the same time, the president consulted congressional Democrats infrequently, failing to give them any clear indication of the White House's domestic priorities. At one point Democratic Senator Alben Barkley grumbled that working with Truman was like playing a night baseball game in the dark: "I'm supposed to be the catcher and I should get the signals. I not only am not getting the signals, but someone actually turns out the light when the ball is thrown." Thus, while Truman proposed expensive social-welfare programs, he also urged reductions in federal expenditures. Such double-talk showed little executive leadership, but it helped Truman build a record upon which to run in 1948.

In reality, Truman could point to few domestic innovations of his own and could not cite many instances of Republicans trying to tear down popular programs begun during Roosevelt's New Deal. By the late 1940s many Republican politicians were coming to recognize that outright opposition to liberal Democratic measures such as Social Security offered little hope for increasing the GOP's vote totals. This pragmatic attitude gained most of its support from younger Republicans, particularly those who came from larger northern cities or held state offices. Increasingly, they battled older, more tradition-bound Republicans in Congress for influence within the party.

Ridiculed by Democrats as a do-nothing body, the Eightieth Congress actually passed several significant pieces of legislation. The National Security Act of 1947 reorganized the armed forces and the entire military establishment. In recognition of the new importance of air power, the air force became a separate branch of the military; a new Department of Defense, under a civilian head, replaced the old departments of War and Navy; top-ranking uniformed officers from the air force, navy, army, and marines sat on a new coordinating body called the Joint Chiefs of Staff; and the new National Security Council and Central Intelligence Agency assumed important tasks in planning and executing foreign policy. In a highly popular move, the Eightieth Congress also approved and sent to the states the Twenty-second Amendment, which prohibited presidents from serving more than two terms. In addition, Congress accepted Truman's suggestion that it create a special commission to study reorganization of the federal bureaucracy. Under the chairmanship of former President Herbert Hoover, the commission submitted a plan that became the basis of the Reorganization Act of 1949. By clarifying lines of authority and reducing the number of executive agencies, the Hoover Commission hoped to make government administration more efficient.

Robert Taft, Republican majority leader in the Senate, emerged as the dominant figure in the Eightieth Congress. Son of President William Howard Taft, the middle-aged Ohioan was a shy, thoughtful man who often seemed uncomfortable in the glare of national politics. Certainly he lacked the charm of Roosevelt or the fire of Truman. But Taft's close attention to detail won him respect from Senate colleagues, and his reputation for honesty and integrity gained him the admiration of older, more conservative Republicans. "Mr. Republican" argued that liberal Democrats were abandoning the New Deal measures of Roosevelt and moving toward socialism. Their programs, he charged, threatened to bankrupt the country and to place individual liberties at the mercy of an overbearing federal bureaucracy. By 1946 Taft was also moderating some of his more extreme anti-New Deal views: to the consternation of more reactionary Republicans, he even supported some federal aid to education, a limited program of public housing, and some social-welfare measures. In view of Truman's increasing problems, Taft hoped that his vision of "modern Republicanism" would make him the GOP's nominee in 1948.

Passage of the Taft-Hartley Labor Act of 1947 demonstrated the Ohio senator's economic ideas and legislative skills. The law, aimed at reducing the political and economic power of organized labor, outlawed the closed shop (the practice of hiring only union workers), prohibited use of union dues for political activities, and authorized presidential back-to-work orders whenever labor strikes threatened national security. The law, Taft claimed, would not destroy labor unions; it would actually help workers by curbing the abuses of corrupt labor bosses. Taft skillfully managed the bill through the Senate and worked out a compromise with House Republicans who wanted a stronger antiunion statute. Truman vetoed the measure, but Taft collected the votes to override the president's action. Labor leaders denounced the bill as "a slave-labor act" and the "Tuff-Heartless Act"; pickets appeared at the wedding of Taft's son carrying

National Archives

President Truman throws out the first ball, 1948. In the late 1940s baseball ruled, unchallenged by football, as the national pastime.

placards that read "CONGRATULATIONS TO YOU. _____ TO YOUR OLD MAN."

The Election of 1948

Despite his impressive leadership in Congress, Robert Taft lost the 1948 presidential nomination to Governor Thomas E. Dewey of New York, the GOP's standard-bearer in 1944. Taft's reputation as a poor vote-getter and a conservative worked against his nomination. Republicans, who had not nominated a winning candidate in twenty years, desperately wanted a winner, and Dewey and his running mate, Governor Earl Warren of California, appeared to be shoo-ins. Dewey had run well against FDR in the last presidential contest, had won a smashing victory in the 1946 New York gubernatorial race, and belonged to the more progressive, Eastern wing of the GOP.

But the victor in 1948 was not Tom Dewey: Harry Truman surprised almost all the political "experts," his Democratic critics, and the entire Republican party. "You've got to give the little man credit," admitted

National Archives.

The man from Independence. Harry Truman liked to portray himself as an ordinary citizen, one who never lost the common touch after he gained office.

Republican Senator Arthur Vandenburg. "Everyone had counted him out, but he came up fighting and won the battle. That's the kind of courage the American people admire." To the extent that the presidential sweepstakes was a "beauty contest" between competing images, Truman emerged the clear winner. Dewey displayed little of Truman's warmth and personality. "I don't know which is the chillier experience—to have Tom ignore you or shake your hand," claimed one of his detractors. "You have to get to know Dewey to dislike him," another complained. Overconfident and overly cautious, "Thomas Elusive Dewey" made far fewer personal appearances than Truman. When Dewey did speak, he fell back upon platitudes and bland appeals to national unity.

In contrast, Harry Truman sounded more like a country politician—which he had been—than the president of the United States. Speaking from notes rather than prepared texts, Truman slashed away at the Republicans' Eightieth Congress. With his arms in perpetual motion, Truman denounced Republican representatives as "errand boys of big business" and bragged that he had vetoed more legislation than any other president since Grover Cleveland. During the interval between the Democratic convention and the November election Truman called the Eightieth Congress into special session and presented it with a list of "must" legislation. When the Republican-controlled legislature predictably adjourned after passing only a few minor bills, Truman escalated his attacks upon Dewey and the Eightieth Congress. The president's seventeen-car, armor-plated campaign train whistle-stopped across the country to shouts of "Give 'em hell, Harry."

When he was not roasting the "no-account, do-nothing" Republican Congress, Truman emphasized his own welfare proposals. His chief strategists, especially Washington lawyer Clark Clifford, advised him that an aggressively liberal stance would keep urban Democrats from supporting Henry Wallace—FDR's former vice-president, who was running on the Progressive-party ticket—and not seriously hurt Truman's campaign in the South. Truman called for a higher minimum wage, repeal of Taft-Hartley, more public housing, and higher farm prices. During the final week of the campaign he became the first president to appear in Harlem. There he told a crowd of 35,000 blacks that he supported the "goal of equal rights and equal opportunitites" for all Americans.

The civil-rights question, which would become a more pressing political issue after 1948, did cost Truman some southern votes. His advisers had hoped that the party convention would adopt a mild statement in support of civil rights, but liberals and big-city bosses, who relied upon black voters, pushed through a stronger proposal. Following the heated floor fight, delegates from Alabama and Mississippi stalked out of the convention, and segregationists eventually formed the States Rights, or "Dixiecrat," party. The Dixiecrat platform denounced "totalitarian government" and advocated "segregation of the races." With Strom Thurmond of South Carolina as their presidential nominee, the Dixiecrats hoped to gain one hundred electoral votes in the South—enough ballots, they thought, to throw the presidential election into the House of Representatives. Thurmond, however, lacked sufficient financial support to

Democrats stayed with Truman, and Thurmond gained only 39 electoral votes.

Truman survived another revolt within his party: the Progressive-party candidacy of Henry Wallace. Truman had fired Wallace as secretary of commerce because Wallace had publicly criticized the administration's hard-line anti-Soviet foreign policy. With the support of a wide range of left-wing groups, including the Communist party, Wallace launched a new party that advocated greater cooperation with the Soviet Union, an end to the military draft, more federal money for social and economic programs at home, and American support for a United Nations Reconstruction Fund to promote world-wide economic recovery. If the United States could avoid conflict with the USSR, Wallace believed, American liberals could not only revive the New Deal at home but extend its spirit of social reform overseas. Wallace's early appearances drew large and enthusiastic crowds. His rallies resembled old-time revival meetings, as folk singers such as Pete Seeger and Woody Guthrie campaigned for Wallace and his running mate (another guitar player) Senator Glen Taylor of Idaho. One of Guthrie's songs, sung to the tune of "The Wabash Cannonball," reflected the hope of Wallace's left-wing supporters that they could create a party based on class consciousness.

> *There's lumberjacks and teamsters and sailors from the sea,*
> *And there's farming boys from Texas and the hills of Tennessee,*
> *There's miners from Kentucky and there's fishermen from Maine,*
> *Every worker in the country rides that Wallace-Taylor train.**

But the Wallace-Taylor special never reached the White House. Following Clark Clifford's advice, Truman highlighted his own role as the nation's commander-in-chief while allowing subordinates to tie Wallace to the enemy in Moscow. "A vote for Wallace," the Democratic National Committee claimed, "is a vote for the things for which Stalin, Molotov, and Vishinsky stand." Wallace's acceptance of support from the Communist party of the United States, bitter opposition from large labor unions, the defection of anticommunist liberals, his forthright stand on civil rights, and the insurmountable problems of any newly formed party all caught up with Wallace. In December 1947 a poll showed that 13 percent of the electorate favored Wallace's candidacy; by election day his campaign had collapsed, and he received less than 3 percent of the popular ballots and not a single electoral vote.

In the end, Truman's victory demonstrated the staying power of the old Roosevelt coalition. Middle western farmers, urban ethnic voters, organized labor, blacks, and most southerners continued to support the Democratic party. Many voted Democratic because of family tradition and because of the social and economic programs begun during the New Deal. Truman's energetic campaign, like most political efforts, did not suddenly convince great numbers of voters to support the Democratic party; it revived many Democrats' party loyalty and raised fears that GOP reactionaries would mount a general assault on New Deal measures. The four-way contest apparently confused some voters. The 1948 election was what political scientists call a "decline election," and only 54 percent of the electorate turned out. The election maintained the basic political configuration of the late 1930s and provided a mandate for following the basic outlines of the New Deal's welfare state.

The Fair Deal

Truman's Domestic Program

After the uphill Democratic victory of 1948, Truman and his advisers planned a new set of domestic proposals that they hoped would move beyond Franklin Roosevelt's New Deal. FDR's programs had been designed to stop the Great Depression and to restore the prosperity of the 1920s; Truman's Fair Deal offered measures aimed at sustaining an ever expanding economy.

Truman's liberal economists believed that they had solved the mysteries of economic management. One aide, Charles F. Brannan, championed an ambitious proposal that he claimed would give farmers higher prices while providing consumers with cheaper food. Under Brannan's program the government would lift New Deal restrictions on the number of acres planted and would maintain farm income through direct price supports.

Another of Truman's economic advisers, Leon Keyserling, predicted that the national government could guarantee full employment, higher wages, and greater profits through well-planned and well-executed spending programs. Americans had no need to take from the rich to care for the poor. Properly managed, America's capitalist economy could outproduce any socialist system in the world. In 1948 nearly two-thirds of all American families lived on incomes of less than $4,000 a year; by 1958 it would be possible, Keyserling predicted, to generate enough economic growth to make $4,000 the minimum income for *every* family. "The people of America need to be electrified by our limitless possibilities," he proclaimed.

In addition to government measures designed to stimulate economic growth, the Fair Deal promised a variety of programs that would ensure social and economic justice. Truman proposed expansion of Social Security, generous federal funding for public-housing projects, a national plan for medical insurance, federal aid to education, and civil-rights legislation for black Americans. Truman and his liberal advisers believed that the Fair Deal represented the middle way between socialism and fascism. "Between the reactionaries of the extreme left with their talk about revolution and class warfare, and the reactionaries of the extreme right with their hysterical cries of bankruptcy and despair, lies the way of progress," Truman declared. The Democratic historian Arthur Schlesinger, Jr., provided an appropriate title for this postwar liberalism—"the vital center."

Following World War II, the Truman administration achieved some of its social programs, and government and business leaders built upon the economic gains of the war years. Congress passed measures that extended Social Security benefits; raised the minimum wage (to seventy-five cents an hour); and appropriated federal funds for soil conservation, flood control, and public power. Despite some fluctuations, the economy performed fairly well during the late 1940s and early 1950s. The United States came nowhere near Leon Keyserling's optimistic predictions, but real income did rise. People who had survived the Great Depression of the 1930s with help from the New Deal continued to do well in the era of the Fair Deal.

The Fair Deal: An Assessment

Sandwiched between FDR's New Deal and LBJ's Great Society, the Fair Deal of Harry Truman has too often been ignored. Many historians have viewed it as an addendum to the New Deal, as a grab bag of social-economic programs left over from the 1930s; others have seen it primarily as a prelude to the burst of legislation enacted during Lyndon Johnson's second term. But the Fair Deal deserves to be assessed on its own terms: the Fair Dealers' optimistic assumptions about economic and social policies helped to shape a broad consensus about the nation's future and about the role of government.

The Fair Deal rested upon an abiding faith that the United States economic system, so severely criticized by intellectuals during the 1930s, had ultimately proved itself far superior to any type of planned economic order. Capitalism, not socialism or Soviet communism, seemed to be the wave of the future. Classical defenders of the "free enterprise" system, of course, had always argued that a marketplace economy maximized individual freedoms and efficiently allocated resources and finished products. But during the cold-war era, capitalism's liberal defenders also claimed that it could advance the cause of social justice, the banner under which the political left marched. One of the main virtues of America's economic system, postwar liberals argued, was its apparently unlimited ability to generate economic growth, a fact of American life that economists proudly measured by a relatively new statistical gauge, the gross national product (GNP). A steadily rising GNP attested to the fact that the economic collapse of the 1930s would not reoccur. Indeed, given the new economic wisdom now available, it could not!

The vision of economic growth bedazzled postwar social planners. An ever-expanding economy, Truman's economic advisers promised, ensured continued economic security for those people, and for those organized interests that had already benefited from the reforms of the New Deal era. More important, the promise of an ever-expanding economic pie offered some hope to those Americans, estimated in 1939 by Roosevelt himself to be one-third of the population, who had been largely untouched by New Deal programs. In seeking to aid the poor and to achieve greater social justice, the United States could deftly sidestep difficult issues involving redistribution of wealth, income, and political power. As long as there were a growing GNP, the new economic growth could provide the material basis for aiding those who had somehow fallen behind in the race for success. As Walter Heller, an economist who began his distinguished career during the Truman era, later explained, economic growth was both "the pot of gold and the rainbow."

But, as the dwindling band who still embraced classical laissez faire complained, proponents of the new economic wisdom did not place their faith in capitalism alone. The economic collapse of the 1930s, liberal economists warned, showed that a complex market economy was not always self-regulating. One of the lessons of the Great Depression was the necessity for governmental policies that would assist, and guarantee, economic growth. As passage of the Employment Act of 1946 suggested, even a majority of Congress, hardly a body known for its radical economic ideas, agreed that government officials had some responsibility to intervene in the "free enterprise" economy. Liberal economists welcomed this responsibility. Possessing new tools for monitoring the economy and for diagnosing its health, America's economic doctors were generally confident that they could administer the kind of remedies—including measures to adjust interest rates, levels of taxation, and amounts of government spending—that could cure an ailing economy or merely pep up a sluggish one.

Confidence in the essential soundness of American capitalism and in their own expertise allowed the Fair Dealers to think beyond the old goals of the New Deal—economic recovery and reform. Instead, they could frame programs and establish bureaucratic institutions that could ensure economic growth; they could then use the results of this growth to attack ancient social problems, such as the grossly unequal access to medical care. Truman's proposals for domestic reform, more than anything envisioned by FDR, remained the basic aims of the Democratic party for almost two decades. A whole generation of Democratic liberals—individuals like Hubert Humphrey and John Kennedy—began their careers during the Fair Deal. Most never moved beyond it or questioned its basic assumptions.

The Fair Deal, like the whole postwar liberal program, contained significant limitations. Despite its general affluence, especially in contrast with the economic situation in other parts of the post-war world, the American welfare state expanded its boundaries relatively little in the two decades after 1945. In 1962 Michael Harrington's *The Other America* reminded affluent liberals that nearly one-fourth of the population of their country still lived in deep poverty, largely unaided by federal programs. Defenders of the Fair Deal's approach could, of course, argue that the more ambitious portions of Truman's program never got through Congress. Determined lobbying by the American Medical Association, which raised the cry of "socialized medicine," helped kill the plan for national health insurance. Opposition from other powerful pressure groups encouraged a coalition of Republicans and conservative southern Democrats to block repeal of the Taft-Hartley law, a program for general federal aid to state school systems, and the Brannan plan for agricultural subsidies. In addition, many of the Fair Deal's programs lacked broad popular support. Most middle-class Americans, the people who made up the bulk of the electorate, wanted to enjoy the benefits of expanding economic production themselves—in the form of a new home, a second car, new consumer goods, and greater recreational opportunities.

But the failure of the Fair Deal cannot be blamed solely on the conservative coalition in Congress, on special-interest groups, or on public apathy. The Truman administration itself placed greater weight on foreign than on domestic issues. America's national security and its economic well-being, Truman and his internationalist advisers believed, depended primarily upon the successful conduct of a global foreign policy. Preoccupied with foreign affairs and often inept in his dealings with Congress, Truman failed to provide vigorous domestic leadership. America's liberal crusaders focused most of their attention, and most of their energies, on problems overseas.

Civil Rights

The lack of enthusiasm for new domestic crusades was most evident in the fate of civil-rights legislation. Revulsion against Nazi racism helped encourage greater rhetorical denunciations of discrimination at home; wartime economic gains produced a desire among blacks for broader attacks on discrimination; and the outbreak of racial violence immediately after the war intensified liberal efforts to calm racial hatreds. Even the climate of the cold war seemed to call for measures to improve race relations at home. As the United States proclaimed that it, not the Soviet Union, offered the proper model for other nations to follow, continued legal discrimination against nonwhites in the United States itself proved difficult to explain. Despite these forces for change, however, the Fair Deal meant only small gains for most black Americans.

As part of his broad domestic program President Truman pushed for a variety of civil-rights measures, including a ban on poll taxes, an antilynching law, and legislation to guarantee equal employment opportunities. During the 1948 presidential campaign he issued executive orders that ended (at least on paper) discrimination in federal employment. Truman took great pride in his civil-rights record; he once went so far as to claim that desegregation of the armed forces, which began during his second term, was "the greatest thing that ever happened to America."

The Truman administration also played a role in several important Supreme Court decisions that affirmed the legal rights of black Americans and other minority groups. In *Shelly* v. *Kraemer* (1946) the justices unanimously held that no court could enforce restrictive covenants, agreements that prevented minority groups from acquiring real estate in certain areas. In two other cases—*Sweatt* v. *Painter* (1950) and *McLaurin* v. *Oklahoma Board of Regents* (1950)—the Court ruled that a separate law school established for blacks violated the Fourteenth Amendment's requirement for equality in education and that graduate schools could not segregate students according to race. Although these cases did not declare all segregated educational facilities inherently unequal, they did point the way toward the broader school-desegregation decision in *Brown* v. *Board of Education* (1954). And in *Henderson* v. *United States* (1950) the Supreme Court outlawed racial segregation in railroad dining cars. In all these cases Truman's Justice Department supported the claims of the black plaintiffs.

Despite these positive marks on Truman's record, civil rights provided another example of the gap between liberal promise and performance. Some civil-rights activists blamed Truman himself for the lack of new legislative initiatives: they claimed that the president gave their cause a low priority and too often deferred to the feelings of southern Democrats. Truman did try to avoid a direct stand on civil rights; the threat of black voters defecting to Henry Wallace in 1948, for example, prompted his executive orders barring racial discrimination in federal hiring. But Truman was not entirely to blame for his administration's failure to achieve more. The conservative coalition in Congress effectively bottled up legislation that would have aided black Americans, and some military officials did their best to delay desegregation of the armed forces. Similarly, the president's initiatives in ending job discrimination ultimately depended upon the attitude of other officials in the federal bureaucracy. No executive order could be self-enforcing.

There was also a good deal of popular opposition to even limited moves

National Archives.

A shack for "colored only." The rural South in 1945.

toward racial equality. In the southern states the Confederate flag became the symbol of resistance: one flag company estimated that Virginians owned more Confederate banners in 1951 than during the Civil War, and a New York City firm reported that the demand for rebel flags exceeded orders for the Stars and Stripes. Throughout the nation, racists violently opposed the drive for integration. When a black couple attempted to move into an apartment in Cicero, Illinois, a mob of about 5,000 angry whites broke through National Guard lines and set the building ablaze. In the same year, 1951, a black school principal and civil-rights leader died when explosives destroyed his Miami home on Christmas Day. Decrying the increased use of explosives in racial attacks, Walter White of the National Association for the Advancement of Colored People observed that "the bomb has replaced the lynchers' rope" as the main weapon of racist resistance.

The upsurge in white violence was one more brake on the pace of national action against racial discrimination. White America's long-delayed commitment to legal equality for blacks barely began during the Truman years. Still, Truman's record looked better than that of any previous twentieth-century president. He was the first chief executive to make civil rights a national political issue, and his administration at least proposed a comprehensive legislative program.

Anticommunism at Home

The Communist Issue

Although the Truman administration moved cautiously on civil rights, it acted decisively against the alleged threat of communist subversion in the United States. In 1947 Truman established a comprehensive "internal security" program designed to uncover "subversives" in the federal bureaucracy. Employing flimsy procedural safeguards and broad definitions of disloyalty, agencies purged a number of supposed security risks. The president did oppose suggestions for more Draconian measures—such as abolition of the Fifth Amendment in national-security cases—but the White House often failed to restrain the Department of Justice. J. Edgar Hoover's FBI, with the administration's consent, pried into the private lives and political beliefs of alleged subversives. Extending a practice begun during the Roosevelt years, the FBI also used wiretaps in violation of the Federal Communications Act of 1934. In 1949 Truman rejected the American Civil Liberties Union's suggestion that a special commission investigate the FBI. "Hoover has done a good job," the president told a press conference. The Attorney General's List of Subversive Organizations, first issued in 1947, demonstrated the Justice Department's propensity for establishing guilt by association. Noncommunists who happened to belong to one of these groups sometimes found themselves branded as reds, "pinkos," or fellow travelers. Libertarians charged that the government too often equated legitimate political dissent with communist subversion.

How real was the domestic threat of communism? Did the White House and the Justice Department exaggerate the dangers? Although no researcher has uncovered any evidence that procommunists shaped United States policies, the government did possess reliable intelligence about the activities of communist agents and the passing of military information to the Soviet Union. The FBI captured several authentic spies, and J. Edgar Hoover firmly believed that "the ignorant and the apologists and the appeasers of Communism in our country" consistently minimized the "danger of these subversives in our midst." Still, the amount of subversive activity and its danger to national security remain open questions. Historians, for example, continue to debate whether or not the Justice Department possessed sufficient evidence against Ethel and Julius Rosenberg, who were executed in 1953 for passing atomic secrets to the Soviets, and whether or not the couple fell victim to anticommunist hysteria. Greater access by scholars to previously classified materials, released through new government regulations or through suits under the Freedom of Information Act of 1974, has only provided new ammunition with which to refight the old cold-war battles. Thus, new books and articles have helped to intensify, not to settle, disputes over the reality of the communist threat during the 1940s and the 1950s.

Whatever the real domestic danger from communism, the Truman administration had reasons to mount a vigorous anti-red crusade. Since the late 1930s, anti-New Deal Democrats and conservative Republicans—particularly members of the House Un-American Activities Committee—had claimed that communists and fellow travelers infested the Roosevelt administration. Charges of communist influence in the federal government often accompanied general attacks upon the "socialistic" New Deal welfare programs. Responding to Republican taunts of being "soft on communism," the Truman administration tried to improve its anticommunist credentials. Truman hoped that a tough policy of his own would prevent Republicans from seizing the anticommunist issue for themselves.

Fears of an active communist conspiracy within the United States also dovetailed with the administration's strong anti-Soviet foreign policy. During the period immediately following the war, public-opinion polls revealed that few Americans considered communism a major problem. Truman's advisers feared that such attitudes—along with the strong popular sentiment in favor of avoiding expensive overseas commitments—might hamstring the president's foreign policy. A tough stand against a supposedly growing red menace at home and a constant barrage of anticommunist rhetoric, administration strategists hoped, would counteract domestic resistance to Truman's sweeping foreign-policy proposals.

Consequently, the Truman administration dramatically publicized its plans for dealing with internal subversion; officials continually stressed the need for greater vigilance; and the government orchestrated a vigorous pro-American campaign. In 1947, for example, Attorney General Tom Clark developed the "Freedom Train" program. This historical society on rails carried important documents, including a copy of the Truman Doctrine, to more than two hundred major cities. When the train returned to Washington in the fall of 1947, the government staged a "week of rededication." At a series of patriotic demonstrations, government employees took a "freedom pledge" and everyone sang "God Bless America." In a similar vein, the Office of Education promoted its "Zeal for Democracy" program: Washington encouraged local schools "to vitalize and improve education in the ideals and benefits of democracy and to reveal the character and tactics of totalitarianism."

Government leaders, of course, did not simply manufacture a spirit of 100-percent Americanism. But their efforts did strengthen the inevitable postwar nationalism and gave it an increasingly anticommunist tone. The actions and rhetoric of the Truman administration helped shift attention from the specific problem of Soviet espionage to the highly emotional issue of a general communist "invasion" of American institutions. Many people became less concerned about Russian spies in Washington than about communist sympathizers spreading heretical ideas throughout a too tolerant society.

More extreme anticommunists claimed that government leaders, even President Truman, failed to perceive the nation's grave peril. To these modern Paul Reveres, Soviet spies were only part of the problem. Anticommunists could find sinister forces almost everywhere. Self-appointed vigilantes, for example, moved against "communist" movie stars, left-wing writers, and "subversives" in the radio industry. Several hundred people whose political ideas seemed suspect found themselves unofficially blacklisted. Some on the blacklist could find no work at all. Others were luckier. Writing under the pseudonym of "Robert Rich," blacklisted screenwriter Dalton Trumbo even won an Academy Award. Protectors of 100-percent Americanism also invoked official sanctions. The Post Office obtained authority to ban communist materials from the mails; many states adopted laws barring subversives from state-government jobs; bar associations and school boards required prospective attorneys and teachers to take loyalty oaths. The House Un-American Activities Committee (HUAC) examined "communist penetration" into the entertainment industry and the federal bureaucracy. Members of HUAC—including young Richard Nixon—claimed that their committee had discovered extensive procommunist activity in the United States. Critics of the committee charged that members had only smeared the reputations of innocent people in order to advance their own political careers. More important, the opponents of militant anticommunism charged, the impact of such witch-hunts even fell upon those not directly touched by investigations: many people may have decided to censor themselves lest some official or self-appointed body step in and embroil them in controversy. The extreme cold-war atmosphere, civil libertarians argued, helped to chill the type of free expression that was supposed to characterize an open society.

A series of disturbing events appeared to give credence to the tales of communist machinations. The fall of China in 1949 and Russia's first atomic test frightened Americans who wrongly believed that the United States had "lost" China to the communists and that the "backward" Russians had stolen vital atomic secrets from the United States. Stories about communists in the State Department and atomic spies offered attractive explanations. The year 1950 brought new shocks: the government uncovered a Soviet spy ring in the United States, and American troops entered the Korean conflict. If these developments were not troubling enough, there were a series of scandals within the Truman administration, corruption in the Internal Revenue Service, a televised investigation of organized crime, and even an assassination plot against the president by Puerto Rican nationalists. Although only a few people blamed all these problems on one giant communist conspiracy, the events did generate the kind of anxieties and fears that encouraged a paranoid style in American politics.

McCarthyism

Militant anticommunism reached its apogee in—and eventually took its name from—Senator Joseph McCarthy. McCarthyism existed before McCarthy ever discovered the anticommunist issue, and other McCarthyites made even wilder charges than the Wisconsin senator. But McCarthy captured most of the headlines. His tactics were disarmingly simple: he flung accusations as fast as newspapers could print them but avoided specific proposals for fighting the communist "menace." When an acquaintance asked McCarthy how he would change the Voice of America's allegedly ineffective programs, "the Senator looked blank; obviously he had never thought about it." Nor did McCarthy spend much time documenting his sensational charges. His famous Wheeling, West Virginia, speech of 1950—in which he charged that the State Department employed more than two hundred communist sympathizers—rested upon a hodgepodge of questionable evidence from old congressional files. Even though the Senate later gave him broad investigatory powers, McCarthy never bothered to pursue his allegations against the State Department. Instead, he went after new demons whom he claimed were hiding in other government bureaus. According to the social critic Dwight McDonald, McCarthy dealt in "dead souls": his targets were not "actual, living breathing Communists but rather people who once were or may have been" communists.

Because of the widespread publicity he received, McCarthy soon gained an undeserved reputation as a powerful new political force. The Wisconsin senator, his opponents feared, led a massive right-wing movement that seemed to appeal to the great numbers of lower-middle-class people with little formal education. McCarthy, who looked more like a heavy in a B movie than a tribune of the people, exaggerated his image as a tough guy and a rebel. He railed against "establishment Democrats" such as Alger Hiss, a former New Dealer who was charged with espionage for the Soviet Union, and Dean Acheson, Truman's Yale-bred secretary of state. All these "bright young men who were born with silver spoons in their mouths" and all those "striped-pants diplomats," McCarthy charged, were "selling the nation out." As McCarthy escalated his attacks, many liberals and moderates worried about this new threat from the radical right.

In fact, however, McCarthy's power did not come from the support of great numbers of populist fanatics. Instead, he gained attention because important people, such as members of the United States Senate, either supported his attacks or failed to oppose him. Influential middle western Republicans, who formed the traditional base for anti-New Deal conservatism, gave McCarthy vital political assistance. His charges of communist influence in government, which linked Democratic liberalism with socialistic ideas, reechoed the familiar theme of GOP conservatives. Republicans who would not personally stoop to McCarthy's smear tactics—Robert Taft of Ohio, for example—tacitly encouraged the Wisconsin senator. Anything that hurt the Democrats, Taft reasoned, would help the Republican party regain power. In addition to aid from conservative Republicans, McCarthy received help from other important sources. Most newspapers, regardless of their political allegiances, splashed McCarthy's unproven charges over their pages. Sensational scoops about communist influence provided good copy—and greater sales. And many prominent liberal politicians avoided direct confrontation with McCarthy and his supporters for fear of being labeled "soft" on communism.

The passage of the McCarran Internal Security Act of 1950 demonstrated most politicians' fear of opposing anticommunist measures. Rather than openly fighting Senator Pat McCarran's harsh proposals, the White House and Democratic congressmen offered their own internal-security bills. In so doing, they accepted the McCarthyites' basic position: communists should not expect the same civil liberties as other Americans. In its final form, the McCarran Act required communist and "communist-front" organizations to register with the attorney general, barred foreign communists from entering the United States, and authorized secret prison camps for detention of domestic subversives during wartime. Only seven senators and a handful of representatives voted against the McCarran Act. In one of his most courageous political acts, Truman vetoed the bill, but Congress quickly overrode the president's action. McCarthyism and McCarthy continued to influence national policy.

Eventually, however, McCarthy ran out of obvious targets and overstepped even his fertile imagination. By 1953 he was charging that Voice of America, the new Republican administration of Dwight Eisenhower, and the United States Army had played into the hands of the communists. In one celebrated incident, two of McCarthy's aides traveled around Europe to search for procommunist literature in libraries run by the United States Information Service. His agents and other witnesses charged that these libraries contained many communist books and few pro-American works; one investigator even suggested that librarians manipulated card catalogs so that readers would not find books critical of communism. Finally, McCarthy's charges of communist influence in the army resulted in a special Senate investigation. The Army-McCarthy hearings—a daytime television spectacular as popular as the later Watergate hearings of 1974—contributed to McCarthy's demise. Some people resented his brash manner and bullying tactics. Many others simply became bored with the whole communist issue. Emboldened by McCarthy's problems, his critics escalated their attacks. Some of his Republican allies began to temper their support, and a few anticommunists claimed that McCarthy's extremist position discredited the fight against Moscow and unwittingly aided the

Kremlin. Finally, the United States Senate, the source of his prestige, turned against him. In 1954 a majority of senators voted to "condemn" McCarthy for conduct unbecoming a member of the Senate. Stripped of his prestige and influence, McCarthy disappeared from the headlines, began drinking heavily, and died in 1957 at the age of forty-eight.

The Cold-War Consensus

McCarthyism represented only the most visible, extreme segment of a general anti-communist consensus. Influential American leaders, people who dismissed Senator Joe as a simplistic vulgarian, espoused a more sophisticated brand of anti-communism. Most prominent American leaders agreed that a vicious totalitarian conspiracy threatened "the American way of life" and that Marxism was a pernicious doctrine without any intellectual respectability. The United States, virtually every writer and commentator argued, was engaged in a kind of holy war against world communism. In the words of the liberal journalist Tom Braden, this was a war "fought with ideas instead of bombs." During the 1950s a number of prominent American intellectuals joined the Congress for Cultural Freedom, an international organization devoted to promoting the doctrines of liberty and opposing "state-sponsored ideologies" such as Soviet communism. In reality, the CCF and its influential journal, *Encounter,* received secret funding from the United States Central Intelligence Agency. Although the CIA certainly did not tell members of the CCF what to say or write, the leaders of the organization rarely sponsored writers who seriously criticized United States policy.

The American press remained free from government censorship, and many papers vigorously criticized official execution of specific programs. But except for ultraconservatives who decried communist influence and Democratic welfare schemes, few journalists questioned basic domestic- and foreign-policy assumptions of the "vital center." Making the round of fashionable cocktail parties and listening to officials' off-the-record explanations, influential Washington journalists almost became members of the government themselves. Members of the Washington press corps sometimes provided outlets for carefully contrived "pseudo-events"—trial balloons, distortions, and outright lies that government officials and prominent politicians wanted to place before the public. Truly independent journalists such as I. F. Stone, who assumed that every government statement was suspect until proven otherwise, were rare in cold-war Washington. Serving as reporter, editor, and publisher, he made *I. F. Stone's Weekly* an impressive example of democratic journalism. Some other writers and publications also probed beneath the surface of events, but too many journalists remained content to rely upon prepackaged stories supplied by the growing corps of government "information" specialists.

The same cold-war consensus pervaded the American academic community. No government or academic censors prevented scholars from writing studies that stressed social conflict or expressed an anticapitalist viewpoint. In some cases professors with "radical" connections did lose their jobs or suffer overt discrimination, but in general the pressures to conform were more subtle. In history, economics, and the social sciences radical analysis simply became old-fashioned and was dismissed as too simplistic. The undeniable terrors of Stalinist Russia and the Soviet-American cold war caused many former Marxists to renounce communism and to reject the Marxist and class-conflict theories that had been so influential during the 1920s and 1930s. After World War II writers invariably emphasized the positive side of American society—the general social harmony, the political democracy, the material abundance, and the economic opportunity. Most political scientists, for example, praised American politicians for their pragmatism and for creating a pluralistic system in which all legitimate groups could compromise their differences. At the same time, most historians contended that consensus rather than conflict had always character- ized the American experience. Louis Hartz, a professor of government at Har- vard, spoke for most academicians and journalists when he concluded that the United States had always been—and would undoubtedly remain—a nation of moderate capitalists.

Although scholars and social commentators still criticized specific short- comings—the inefficiency of government bureaucrats was a popular theme—most generally praised the kind of pragmatic liberalism represented by Harry Truman's Fair Deal. Rejecting both romantic conservatism and radical social theories, the vast majority of American intellectuals believed that tough- minded problem solvers could unravel even the most complex social puzzles. Moderate liberal reformers in the tradition of Franklin Roosevelt, they con- cluded, would advance social and economic justice without any fundamental restructuring of capitalist institutions or change in basic social values. During the late 1940s and 1950s, most influential Americans occupied the broad middle ground between the political right and socialism—Arthur Schlesinger's "vital center." Prominent left-wing dissenters C. Wright Mills and I. F. Stone were not officially silenced, as they would have been in totalitarian regimes; their kind of passionate radicalism was simply dismissed by the intellectual establishment as methodologically or politically naive.

Society During the Truman Years

Science and Technology

Most Americans praised the new developments in science and technology. The atomic explosions that ravaged Hiroshima and Nagasaki reflected the United States' growing scientific and technological prowess. "The bomb" raised terrify- ing images of worldwide destruction, but it also seemed to offer more optimistic possibilities. Correctly developed and properly harnessed, atomic energy could power America's growing cities, run naval vessels, even carry people into outer space. And radioactive material promised exciting new advances in scientific research and in the treatment of diseases such as cancer. But first the United States needed a way to regulate atomic activities.

In response to a request from President Truman, Congress passed the Atomic Energy Act of 1946. The military implications of nuclear power, of course, made some system of national control imperative, and the act gave the president sole authority to order the use of atomic weapons. In addition, the law vested day-to-day control over nuclear energy and materials with the Atomic Energy Commission. Run by civilians, the AEC possessed authority to conduct nuclear research and make policy decisions affecting the use of nuclear energy. Under the 1946 law the government controlled all fissionable material, but with the new Atomic Energy Act of 1954 the federal nuclear monopoly ended. Establishing the goal of encouraging rapid growth of privately owned nuclear-power plants, the new act instituted a program for federal licensing and regulation of the nuclear industry. By the mid 1950s the granting of licenses and the providing of overall regulation by administrative agencies had become common practices. Few people questioned the wisdom or propriety of these important steps in the development of a private nuclear-power industry.

The national government became more involved in a wide range of other scientific activities after World War II. The wartime experience demonstrated the need for continued support of military research, and advocates of federal aid also urged the government to appropriate more money for nonmilitary experimentation. In a report to the president entitled *Science—The Endless Frontier* (1945), Vannevar Bush called for the creation of a single national agency to administer grants for scientific research. Scientists, he argued, were about to make important breakthroughs, new discoveries that could protect Americans from foreign enemies and dramatically improve the quality of their daily lives. In 1950 Congress established the National Science Foundation, and NSF grants soon allowed scientists to explore subjects unknown a generation earlier. Within two decades federal funds underwrote most scientific research.

Encouraged by government funds (and by grants from tax-exempt private foundations), scientific activity accelerated in postwar America. Ever since the late nineteenth century the number of scientists and technicians had been growing faster than the general population, and this trend continued after 1945. The United States had always been a nation of basement tinkerers: individuals such as Thomas Edison simply applied their common sense and mechanical aptitude to existing knowledge and came up with new inventions. But the corps of highly trained specialists who dominated science and technology after World War II could not proceed by trial and error or build their own laboratories, as Edison did at Menlo Park. The new discoveries—in fields such as chemistry, biology, electronics, and nuclear energy—rested upon highly sophisticated equipment and complex scientific theories about the physical universe.

New developments in science and technology seemed to promise almost unbelievable changes for American society. Instead of merely adapting human institutions to the natural environment, scientists could now go beyond the natural to create an artificial world. Knowledge of scientific theories permitted them to rearrange molecular structures and to produce synthetic fibers, high-strength adhesives, man-made construction materials, and many other new products. In 1944 scientists at Rockefeller Institute isolated a compound called DNA, which opened the secrets of genetic reproduction. Throughout the 1940s biochemists tried to unravel the molecular structure of DNA, and finally in 1953 an American and a Briton constructed a model of a DNA molecule. Science, it seemed, was on the threshold of creating life itself. Abstract theoretical knowledge and sophisticated technology were becoming important national resources, like iron and coal. In the coming years, people predicted, scientific know-how and up-to-date technology would be the most vital resources of all.

The computer revolution perhaps best symbolized the possibilities of the new science and technology. World War II had provided the impetus for development of machines capable of storing and retrieving great amounts of data and of systems capable of organizing and analyzing all this information. Not until 1946, however, did scientists and engineers construct the first really usable computer—ENIAC. Later, technicians improved design and efficiency, and Remington Rand marketed the first commercial computer in 1951. But IBM soon came to dominate the industry, providing systems for government, private business, and academic institutions. Computers enabled doctors to check their research more closely, social scientists to analyze human behavior more effectively, and business institutions to control accounts and other records more efficiently. Everyone, it seemed, had a use for computers. During the 1960s one enterprising promoter even used them to simulate radio versions of imaginary prize fights between all the heavyweight champions of the twentieth century. Fortunately, the computer decided that the relatively young Rocky Marciano should meet Muhammad Ali in the filmed finale. Thus the promoter could stage various scenarios, complete with plenty of ketchup, to fit the computer's "authentic" version; a mock battle between septuagenarians such as Jack Dempsey and Gene Tunney, even with buckets of artificial gore, would have left too much to the imagination.

Some of the most beneficial scientific discoveries came in medicine. After World War II the United States experienced severe epidemics of poliomyelitis. Between 1947 and 1951 this disease, which generally crippled those it did not kill, struck an annual average of 34,000 Americans, mostly children. (Between 1938 and 1942 the annual average had been only 6,400, a figure that rose to 16,800 between 1942 and 1947.) In 1952 doctors reported some success using gamma globulin as a preventative, and three years later Jonas Salk pioneered the first truly successful vaccine. A nationwide program to inoculate people with this and the later Sabin vaccine resulted in the virtual elimination of polio by the 1960s. After World War II doctors also introduced a series of "wonder drugs." Penicillin, an antibotic discovered by Alexander Fleming in the 1920s and refined during the war, came into general use between 1945 and 1952; a powerful set of antibiotics—streptomycin, aureomycin, terramycin, and magnamycin—appeared after World War II; and antihistamines, which proved important in the treatment of allergies, became available in the late 1940s. These drugs and new surgical techniques allowed many Americans to lead longer and sometimes more comfortable lives. Also, they encouraged more determined research into cures for cancer and heart disease, two afflictions that became more common as the United States became more urbanized and industrialized.

New developments in medicine, however, did not automatically bring better health care to all Americans. Exotic new drugs, complicated treatment procedures, and lavish hospital facilities increased the costs of medical care. The very poor and many elderly people simply could not afford the new "wonder" cures; many rural areas and small towns, unable to compete with metropolitan areas for younger physicians, found themselves short of competent doctors as well as of up-to-date hospital facilities. Largely as a result of this maldistribution of medical services, the United States actually lost ground, compared with other industrial nations, in its infant-mortality rate. Between 1950 and 1970 the United States' infant-mortality ranking dropped; by 1970 the world's richest nation stood only fifteenth, slightly behind England and significantly behind Scandinavian countries such as Sweden.

In addition to the unequal distribution of the new developments, advanced medical technology created other problems. Increased specialization produced considerable dissatisfaction with the disappearance of the family doctor—the general practitioner celebrated in some of Norman Rockwell's paintings—and with the proliferation of specialists—doctors trained to diagnose and treat only a limited number of conditions. Indeed, after World War II new medical technology meant that large hospital complexes, with their costly array of machines and their large staffs of specialists, did replace the home and the doctor's office as primary treatment centers. Fewer and fewer doctors made house calls; more and more people went to hospital emergency rooms or outpatient centers. At the same time, people who needed extensive medical care found that the new medical discoveries often meant a costly stay in the hospital. In 1946 only 1 of every 10 Americans was admitted to a hospital for inpatient care; twenty years later the figure had risen to 1 of every 6.5 persons. Unfortunately, a hospital visit did not always result in either an instant cure or, in some cases, even the proper treatment. A number of prominent physicians have contended—and several studies have substantiated their claims—that perhaps half of many common surgical operations, particularly those performed upon women and children, are unnecessary.

Other critics of the medical establishment have gone further: citing information in medical journals, they claim that a sizable percentage of people suffer from iatrogenic illnesses, ailments brought on by the "treatment" for some other malady. Many iatrogenic illnesses, these critics argue, result from some doctors' naive faith in new medicines, from improper testing and regulation of supposedly effective drugs, and from the popular belief that doctors possess a miracle cure for every ache and pain. Although such critics point to some undoubted failures of modern medicine, their indictments tend to neglect the new discoveries that have aided millions of Americans. Certainly, breakthroughs in the treatment and prevention of diseases such as tuberculosis and polio were positive gains. Assessing the impact of new medical technology would prove increasingly difficult.

Agriculture

Postwar science and technology affected all segments of American society. Perhaps no one group saw more changes than farmers, supposedly the slowest people to alter settled ways. Farming became more mechanized and scientific than ever before. Sophisticated biological knowledge resulted in new types of seeds, such as hybrid corn. Introduced in some areas during the 1930s, hybrid corn had spread to all parts of the country by the 1950s. Equally important to grain producers, the chemical industry provided the knowledge to make cheaper fertilizers and pesticides. Farmers quickly turned to these chemicals to boost output: they used three times as much fertilizer in 1950 as they had ten years earlier. Farmers also began to adopt labor-saving machines on a massive scale. Between 1940 and 1960, for example, the number of tractors increased by more than 200 percent, and the number of grain combines rose nearly as much. Meanwhile, engineers were increasing the size of these machines, boosting their horsepower with higher-compression engines, and offering a variety of attachments. The new machinery and chemicals drastically reduced the number of farm laborers needed to bring in key crops (see Table 1).

As a result of all the new developments, American agriculture changed significantly after World War II. For many years agricultural production had been increasing, but now—with hybrid seeds, better equipment, cheaper fertilizers, and new irrigation facilities—output rose at a much faster rate than before. Farmers could cultivate hitherto unproductive land and areas once set aside as pastures for horses and mules. (In 1920 farmers had used more than 90 million acres of potential croplands to graze draft animals; by 1960 they needed less than 10 million acres for pasturage.) In addition, the new agricultural methods permitted farmers to utilize their old land more effectively, and the yield per acre rose substantially after World War II.

Ironically, postwar changes probably created as many problems as they

Table 1   Declining demand for farm labor accelerated the rush to urban areas and left pockets of rural poverty.

Mechanization of agriculture: Man-hours per 100 bushels of selected crops			
Crop	1945 – 49	1955 – 59	1962 – 66
Corn for grain	53	20	9
Sorghum grain	49	20	9
Wheat	34	17	11
Hay	6.2	3.7	3.0
Potatoes	12	6	5
Sugar beets	6.3	2.9	2.1
Cotton	146	74	39
Tobacco	39	31	25
Soybeans	41	23	20

Adapted from Nathan Rosenberg, *Technology and American Economic Growth* (New York: Harper & Row, 1972), p. 136.

solved. Irrigation required massive amounts of water, and fertilizers and pesticides raised serious health hazards for both farm workers and consumers. Meanwhile, steadily increasing production kept farm prices low: after 1947 agricultural prices leveled off until the sudden rise of the early 1970s. While most of the world's people spent almost half their incomes for food, Americans needed only about 20 percent of their paychecks to feed their families. The majority of farmers did not enjoy the rising incomes of most other Americans, and only the largest and most efficient operations could show substantial profits. Although Washington tried to support farm incomes by using the same basic programs devised during Roosevelt's New Deal—direct subsidies and various plans for restriction of acreage—nothing really solved the problem of low farm incomes. Low prices and steadily rising costs continually plagued small operators. Taking advantage of their private economic power and their ability to secure federal assistance, larger corporate farms gained larger shares of the agricultural market while the number of smaller "family farms" continued to decline. (A report by the Department of Agriculture issued in August 1980 reported that under the influence of government programs favoring concentration of ownership, the number of farms in the United States had dropped from 4 million in 1959 to 2.9 million in 1974 and could dwindle to 1.8 million by the year 2000, if present trends continued.)

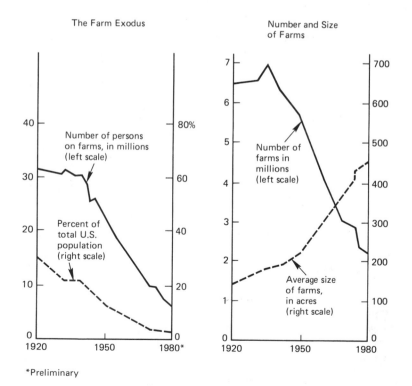

The Farm Exodus

Number and Size of Farms

Number of persons on farms, in millions (left scale)

Percent of total U.S. population (right scale)

Number of farms in millions (left scale)

Average size of farms, in acres (right scale)

*Preliminary

In the post-war period the trends toward fewer but larger farms and toward a much smaller rural population accelerated. By 1980 three of every four Americans lived in a metropolitan area.

A Renewed Conservatism

Despite the widespread postwar optimism, conservatives expressed deep reservations about the direction of American society and called for a return to traditional institutions and settled ways. Arch-conservatives such as Senator Kenneth Wherry of Nebraska and the radio commentator Fulton Lewis, Jr., had long fought a rearguard action against New Deal liberalism, but at the end of World War II American conservatism lacked both a coherent, articulate leadership and a large, attentive following. During the late 1940s and 1950s, however, a new American conservatism began to take shape.

During the heyday of the liberals' "vital center," a fledgling conservative center slowly formed. Seeking to develop the memory of a conservative past, scholars began to search out nonliberal forces in American history. Many found the conservative tradition strongest in the American South, a none-too-novel discovery that oftentimes seemed to place conservatives on the segregationist side of contemporary civil-rights issues. Increasingly, then, conservatives turned their attention away from the South and focused upon the general themes of antimajoritarianism and anticentralism. They praised those individuals such as John Randolph of Roanoke, and those ideas, such as strict construction of the Constitution, that seemed part of a usable conservative past. Conservative scholars generally applauded states rights and condemned national power, praised individual freedom and denounced the "tyranny of the majority." Scholarly activity by conservatives was not limited to the past, especially in the area of cold-war diplomacy. During the 1950s several conservative think-tanks—especially the Foreign Policy Research Institute of the University of Pennsylvania, headed by Robert Strausz-Hupé—called for a stronger anticommunist foreign policy, one that would go beyond the limited goal of containment. Strausz-Hupé, for instance, argued that the United States must combat more actively the communist strategy of "protracted conflict" and "carry the battle to the vital sectors of communist defense."

During the 1940s and 1950s conservative scholars and journalists found new outlets for their writings, especially after the establishment of William F. Buckley, Jr.'s *National Review* in 1955. Conservative writers condemned the growth of "the positive state," the increase in governmental restraints upon private enterprise and individual liberties, the decline of old moral and religious standards, the supposed upsurge in lawlessness, and successive administrations' "no-win" policy toward communism.

The "new conservatives," as many of them called themselves, defied easy categorization. Russell Kirk, one of the most pessimistic of the postwar conservatives, condemned democratic reforms such as universal suffrage and direct election of senators for disrupting social harmony. He urged conservatives to provide voters with a sense of deference to society's "natural leaders." To Kirk, the "creeping socialism" of the Democratic party's welfare state was a giant step toward left-wing totalitarianism. Not all the new conservatives shared Kirk's views. More progressive conservatives, such as historians Peter Viereck and Clinton Rossiter, accepted the idea of political democracy and even praised the

New Deal. Viereck, for instance, saw welfare programs such as Social Security as stabilizing influences and necessary guarantees of economic security. And whereas Kirk favored tight censorship of "dangerous" ideas, the libertarian conservatives displayed a much deeper respect for individual liberties and diversity of opinion.

Despite their growing criticism of the basic direction of postwar society, however, the new conservatives gained little popular support. If Truman and his liberal advisers could not rally the country behind a new crusade for reform, conservatives discovered even less enthusiasm for rolling back the Democratic welfare state. The essence of the conservative movement remained literary and cultural: even during the mid 1950s, when a popular Republican president preached the importance of reviving traditional virtues, militant conservatism still found itself outside the mainstream of American life.

The Taint of Scandal

Although the ultraconservative position remained in the minority, many people did feel uneasy about certain signs of corruption in postwar society. In 1950 and 1951 a politically ambitious senator from Tennessee, Estes Kefauver, dramatically introduced people to the shadowy world of organized crime. Exploiting the still new medium of television, Kefauver brought underworld figures—from top mobster Frank Costello down to petty gamblers and prostitutes—into the living rooms of millions of people. The show held all the drama of a Hollywood production. "It was difficult at times to believe that it was real," said the *New York Times*. For eight days the Kefauver committee kept viewers near their sets; people stopped going shopping or out to eat during the hearings. To sociologists such as Daniel Bell, Kefauver had only revealed the obvious: certain "criminal" activities, particularly gambling, had become big business for their operators and a way of life for many Americans. Like earlier bootlegging operations, the gambling industry provided opportunities that poor boys could not find in "legitimate" enterprises. Discovering plenty of customers clamoring for their products, mobsters had become modern Horatio Algers. Kefauver and most viewers took a less detached view, preferring to see the hearings as a morality play, a confrontation between good and evil.

Other stories of corruption appeared during the early 1950s. In 1950 the United States Military Academy, the citadel of gentlemanly honor and patriotic values, expelled ninety West Pointers, including nine starting members of the football team, for cheating on examinations. That same year, prosecutors in New York uncovered a point-shaving scandal in college basketball. Star players on several top teams—including national champion City College of New York and the University of Kentucky—were found to have taken bribes in exchange for rigging game scores in favor of professional gamblers.

People reacted in different ways to these revelations. Some condemned the commercialism that had invaded college athletics. Some, such as Senator J. William Fulbright of Arkansas, blamed the spirit of corruption on a general decline in moral principles. The National Collegiate Athletic Association banned the basketball players from further competition, and the new professional league, the National Basketball Association, blacklisted them forever. But others were not so quick to accept or to assign moral blame. The West Point cadets eschewed contrition, claiming that they were being punished for a practice followed by most of their classmates. Army's football coach, Colonel Earl Blaik, whose son had been one of those dropped from the academy, refused to condemn his players and publicly reaffirmed his faith in football as a character-building sport.

In the end, the search for corruption reached into the White House. Along with McCarthyite charges of being soft on communism, accusations about "the mess in Washington" drove Truman's popularity lower and lower. During his last years in office, scandals seemed to pop up everywhere. An old crony, Harry Vaughan, was accused of accepting a deep freeze; Senator Fulbright (an old Truman foe known as Senator Halfbright around the White House) uncovered examples of apparent political favoritism in the Reconstruction Finance Corporation; the wife of a former RFC official received a $9,500 mink coat as part of a questionable transaction; the *New Republic* leveled charges of bribery or political favoritism at no less than six federal agencies; the chairman of the Democratic National Committee appeared guilty of influencing a government decision in exchange for legal fees; and Republicans constantly complained that the Truman administration was full of "five-percenters" who traded their political influence for kickbacks on public contracts. Cantankerous and stubborn as ever, Truman lashed out at his critics. Despite clear evidence to the contrary, he proclaimed that "my house is always clean." By the fall of 1951 liberal Democrats as well as Republicans were demanding that Truman take decisive action. He did appoint an investigator to probe the charges in February 1952 but allowed his attorney general to fire the prober two months later. Although no one ever connected any of the scandals with Truman himself, he left Washington with the reputation of being soft on corruption as well as on communism.

SUGGESTIONS FOR FURTHER READING

Eric F. Goldman's *The Crucial Decade—And Afterward* (1960) remains a very readable and useful introduction to the postwar period. A more recent account is offered in the early chapters of Godfrey Hodgson's *America in Our Time* (1976). Harry Truman tells his own story in his *Memoirs* (2 vols., 1955 – 56) and in Merle Miller, ed., *Plain Speaking* (1974); his daughter Margaret Truman Daniel offers her view in *Harry S. Truman* (1972). Cabell Phillips, *The Truman Presidency* (1966) is a readable journalistic account, but Robert J. Donovan's *Conflict and Crisis: The Presidency of Harry S. Truman* (1977) is a more complete work. Barton J. Bernstein, ed., *Politics and Policies of the Truman Administration* (1970) and Richard S. Kirkendall, ed., *The Truman Period as a Research Field* (2nd ed., 1974) offer preliminary assessments of the Truman era by a number of different scholars. Harold F. Gosnell, *Truman's Crises* (1980) offers a later assessment. Alonso Hamby, *Beyond the New Deal: Harry S. Truman and American Liberalism* (1973) provides a generally positive view; more critical is Athan Theoharis, ed., *The Truman Presidency: The Origins of the Imperial Presidency and the National Security State* (1979). See also the relevant portions of Arthur Schlesinger, Jr., *The Imperial Presidency* (1973) and Otis Graham, *Toward a Planned Society: From Roosevelt to Nixon* (1976).

In recent years scholars have produced a growing list of specialized works on the Truman era. These include Susan Hartman, *Truman and the Eightieth Congress* (1971); Richard O. Davies, *Housing Reform during the Truman Administration* (1966); Allen J. Matusow, *Farm Policies and Politics in the Truman Administration* (1967); R. Alton Lee, *Truman and Taft-Hartley* (1966); Maeva Marcus, *Truman and the Steel Seizure Case: The Limits of Presidential Power* (1977); William E. Pemberton, *Bureaucratic Politics: Executive Reorganization during the Truman Administration* (1979); and Monte S. Poen, *Harry S. Truman versus the Medical Lobby* (1979).

On civil rights, see Richard M. Dalfiume, *Desegregation of the U.S. Armed Forces* (1969); William C. Berman, *The Politics of Civil Rights in the Truman Administration* (1970); and Donald R. McCoy and Richard T. Ruetten, *Quest and Response* (1973). See also the relevant chapters of Dorothy K. Newman et al., *Protest Politics and Prosperity: Black Americans and White Institutions, 1940–1975* (1978) and Steven F. Lawson, *Black Ballots: Voting Rights in the South, 1944–1969* (1976).

There is a vast literature on McCarthyism and the consensus mentality of the early cold-war era. Among the best of the older accounts of McCarthyism are Richard H. Rovere, *Senator Joe McCarthy* (1959) and Daniel Bell, ed., *The Radical Right* (1963). For later views, see Michael Rogin, *McCarthy and the Intellectuals* (1967); Athan G. Theoharis, *Seeds of Repression* (1970); Robert Griffith, *The Politics of Fear* (1970); Robert Griffith and Athan G. Theoharis, eds., *The Specter* (1974); Richard Fried, *Men Against McCarthy* (1976); Lillian Hellman, *Scoundrel Time* (1976); John Chabot Smith, *Alger Hiss: The True Story* (1976); and Allen Weinstein, *Perjury: The Hiss-Chambers Case* (1978). The era is viciously lampooned in Robert Coover's controversial novel, *The Public Burning* (1978). A scholarly but nonetheless bitter account is David Caute's *The Great Fear* (1978). On journalism see James Aronson, *The Press and the Cold War (1970).*

Hodgson's *America in Our Time* emphasizes the narrow range of ideas in cold-war America. This theme is also treated in Mary Sperling McAuliffe, *Crisis on the Left: Cold War Politics and American Liberals, 1947–1954* (1978); Norman D. Markowitz, *The Rise and Fall of the People's Century* (1973), a study of Henry Wallace; and Robert Booth Fowler, *Believing Skeptics: American Political Intellectuals, 1945–1964* (1978).

An overview of economic trends, from a variety of different perspectives, can be gleaned from Robert Lekachman, *The Age of Keynes* (1966); John Kenneth Galbraith, *The New Industrial State* (rev. ed., 1971); Paul A. Baron and

Paul M. Sweezy, *Monopoly Capital* (1966); James O'Connor, *The Fiscal Crisis of the State* (1973); Manuel Castells, *The Economic Crisis and American Society* (1980); and Milton and Rose Friedman, *Free to Choose* (1980). Nathan Rosenberg, *Technology and American Growth* (1962) is a standard work.

Political trends are placed in a broad perspective in Walter Dean Burnham, *Critical Elections and the Mainsprings of American Politics* (1970) and in Norman Nie, Sidney Verba, and John Petrocik, *The Changing American Voter* (1976). See also the relevant chapters in V. O. Key, *The Responsible Electorate* (1966) and Angus Campbell et al., *The Voter Decides* (1954). The new conservatism is analyzed in Ronald Lora, *Conservative Minds in America* (1971) and in George H. Nash, *The Conservative Intellectual Movement in America* (1976). Robert A. Taft is the subject of a superior biography, *Mr. Republican* (1972), by James T. Patterson. The seamier aspects of cold-war politics are discussed in Athan G. Theoharis, *Spying on Americans* (1978) and in Michael Belknap, *Cold War Political Justice* (1977).

AFFLUENCE AND AFFABILITY: AMERICA IN THE 1950s

Moderate Republicanism

The friendly smile of Dwight David Eisenhower dominated American politics during the 1950s. "Ike" read little and was noted for neither brilliance nor wit, but his straightforward honesty made him a beloved father figure to many Americans. A successful general in World War II, Ike surely was shrewder than his simple popular image projected. Army promotions and success as a commander required ambition and a politician's keen sense of timing, and Eisenhower put the political skills he had learned in the army to good use during his years in the White House. But to Americans of the 1950s he epitomized down-home common sense. Even his nickname had a folksy ring, lacking the efficient staccato of "JFK" and "LBJ" or the distant formality of "Richard M. Nixon."

The Elections of 1952 and 1956

In 1952, encouraged by the Truman administration's many problems, Republicans anticipated the victory that had slipped away four years earlier. Still, GOP leaders wanted to take no chances, and the desire to pick a winner worked in favor of Dwight Eisenhower.

Some people doubted that Eisenhower would run for the presidency. In 1948 the popular general had firmly rejected the idea of a presidential race because of the "necessary policy" of subordinating the military to civilian rule. And despite a Republican background, his current political affiliation remained a mystery. As late as 1951 Truman had suggested that Eisenhower become the Democrats' standard-bearer. But while president of Columbia University from 1948 to 1951, Eisenhower formed close ties with influential members of the Republican party's eastern establishment. He came to share their belief that another GOP defeat would greatly strengthen the more conservative and the McCarthyite wings of the party. A moderate on almost every issue, Eisenhower did not want the GOP to swing so far to the right. He also believed that the United

States must play an active role in Europe, and he feared that Senator Robert A. Taft, the leading contender for the Republican nomination, was not firmly committed to NATO. When eastern supporters convinced Eisenhower that Taft's reputation as a midwestern reactionary would prove a serious political liability, the old soldier decided that both the GOP and the nation needed him.

Not all Republicans welcomed their party's new savior. GOP leaders and Republican voters from the Midwest and South resented the power of their party's more liberal eastern wing; influential senators such as Everett Dirkson of Illinois supported "Mr. Republican" Taft and strongly opposed Eisenhower. Throughout the Republican nominating convention, speakers proclaimed domestic policies closely attuned to Taft's ideas and trumpeted the militant anti-communist rhetoric of Joe McCarthy. After hearing speeches from McCarthy, Herbert Hoover, and General Douglas MacArthur, one reporter concluded that Eisenhower had walked into the wrong convention. A few Republicans even feared that the party might split apart, as it had in 1912 when Taft's father had battled Teddy Roosevelt for the nomination.

Despite several angry confrontations, the GOP could not pass up a seemingly sure winner: Eisenhower won a first-ballot victory. To soothe ruffled feelings, he selected Richard Nixon, a man with impeccable credentials as a Republican regular and anticommunist crusader, as vice-presidential candidate. The thirty-four-year-old Nixon was also expected to attract younger voters.

During the 1952 presidential campaign, Eisenhower encountered some difficulty in transforming himself from General of the Army to good old Ike. Without his familiar Eisenhower military jacket he looked much like any other sixty-one-year-old politician, and early appearances revealed his inexperience as a stump speaker. In addition, the necessities of campaigning clashed with his personal distaste for the phony familiarity of political life. Gradually, though, Ike developed a more natural style and accepted most of the rituals of American politics. To the displeasure of some, he even made symbolic concessions to right-wing Republicans, holding a highly publicized session with Senator Taft and campaigning alongside several outspoken McCarthyites. In a Wisconsin speech Eisenhower deleted a favorable reference to General George Marshall, his close personal friend but one of McCarthy's favorite targets. And though Ike piously announced, "I shall not and will not engage in character assassination, vilification and personalities," Nixon and other McCarthyites gathered votes by extravagant attacks on communist influence in Washington, corruption in government, and the "no-win" war in Korea. Nixon even reverted to the communist-conspiracy theme when stories about an improper political slush fund threatened his place on the ticket. His televised reply to the charges featured insinuations that the "reds" wanted to deny him the vice-presidency and contained self-pitying comments about his wife's "Republican cloth coat," his worn-out Oldsmobile, and his one political payoff—his daughters' little dog Checkers. The "Checkers Speech" saved Nixon's career and made him an even greater asset to the Republican ticket. It also gave Nixon a reputation as a skilled television performer.

By contrast, Democrats found few bright spots in 1952. Their presidential nominee, Governor Adlai Stevenson of Illinois, won the plaudits of liberal columnists for his cleverly phrased, well-reasoned speeches. But critics in both parties complained that the erudite Stevenson aimed his addresses well over the average voter's head. His image as an egghead, coupled with a recent divorce, became frequently noted handicaps. In addition, Stevenson had to outrun the unpopular shadow of Harry Truman, who insisted upon taking part in the campaign. Political pollsters, who had substantially revised their techniques after the miscalculations of 1948, discovered that many voters simply felt that the Democrats had been in power too long. Election results corroborated their predictions. Eisenhower carried all but nine states, and the Republicans also gained control, though by very narrow margins, of both houses of Congress.

Eisenhower appeared to be a person who could restore old-time American virtues to government, and most voters seemed satisfied with Ike's leadership. Four years later, when the Eisenhower-Stevenson presidential contest was replayed, Eisenhower's popularity as a national hero remained undiminished. Retaining Richard Nixon as a running mate (after several unheeded hints that Nixon might prefer a cabinet post), Eisenhower received almost ten million more popular votes than Stevenson. Ike's popularity, however, did not carry over to the party as a whole. The Democrats had regained control of both houses of Congress in 1954, and they solidified their position in 1956.

The Eisenhower Presidency

Eisenhower promised a "constitutional presidency." Holding great reverence for the traditions of local government and state autonomy, he felt that Democratic administrations had extended national power too far and had spent the public's tax dollars too freely. Eisenhower also believed that Harry Truman, whom he held in very low esteem, had provoked Congress, needlessly embittering relations between the White House and Capitol Hill. Ike came to Washington determined to get along with Congress; such cooperation became a necessity after the Democrats gained control of both houses in 1954. Eisenhower instructed cabinet members to avoid antagonizing members of Congress. The art of leadership, he told one associate, did not require "hitting people over the head. Any damn fool can do that. . . . It's persuasion—and conciliation—and education—and patience. That's the only kind of leadership I know—or believe in—or will practice." During his two terms he received much help from congressional Democrats led by two cagey Texans, Sam Rayburn and Lyndon Johnson. Political moderates themselves, Rayburn and Johnson approved many of Eisenhower's policies; one historian described their version of "loyal opposition" as three parts loyal and one part opposition. Although the executive branch and Congress were not on an eight-year honeymoon, there was little of the bitterness that characterized relations between them during the late 1960s and early 1970s.

Coney Island, 1950. Though the old-style amusement park would not last, prosperity and the baby boom insured that other youth-oriented forms of leisure would flourish.

Eisenhower also tried to promote harmony within his administration. Believing that Democratic administrations had ignored sound managerial practices, Eisenhower filled his first cabinet with Republican businessmen. "Engine Charley" Wilson, secretary of defense, came from General Motors; Treasury Secretary George Humphrey had headed the giant Mark Hanna Company; Postmaster General Arthur Summerfield owned a huge car agency in Michigan. A liberal magazine dismissed Eisenhower's appointees as "eight millionaires and a plumber." The plumber was Democrat Martin Durkin, president of the United Association of Plumbers and Steamfitters. Eisenhower hoped that a union man might smooth relations between his administration and organized labor, but appointment of a Democrat as secretary of labor only angered conservative Republicans. Within eight months Durkin was gone. Eisenhower also drew heavily from business and the military to fill White House staff positions.

The president shrewdly managed his new team. He picked Sherman Adams as his chief aide (some people called Adams the assistant president) and granted him broad authority. Adams acted as the president's gatekeeper, allowing Ike to see people who had important business but blocking those who might waste his time. He also handled many sensitive duties that Eisenhower wished to avoid. Adams soon became notorious for his brusque phone calls—he made more than two hundred every day—in which he barked orders and then hung up without waiting for a reply. This style of operation gained Adams many enemies in Washington, but it also allowed Eisenhower to avoid some ticklish situations. In foreign affairs and in economic policy Eisenhower adopted a similar strategy, letting Secretary of State John Foster Dulles and George Humphrey take the heat while he remained above the battle.

Eisenhower's skillful use of subordinates as political lightning rods reflected his deep conviction that, after all of Harry Truman's troubles, he had to restore the prestige of the presidency. Although he had formed no church ties during his army career, Eisenhower quickly joined Washington's National Presbyterian Church (seven previous presidents had been members) and became a Sunday regular. He opened cabinet meetings with a silent prayer and began the tradition of "prayer breakfasts" at the White House. His inaugural parade contained a hastily constructed entry called "God's Float." Flanked by slogans proclaiming "In God We Trust" and "Freedom of Worship" and topped by a curious structure that was supposed to resemble a nondenominational church, the creation struck one clergyman as "an oversized model of a deformed molar left over from some dental exhibit." But Eisenhower rarely stumbled in his public-relations efforts. Unlike Lyndon Johnson and Richard Nixon, who unsuccessfully used many of the same symbols during their stormy presidencies, Eisenhower apparently convinced most people of his sincerity. Although many journalists questioned the wisdom of Eisenhower's policies, few doubted his integrity or decency. And through his much-publicized addiction to golf and bridge, pastimes that millions of ordinary citizens also enjoyed, he projected the image of the common man.

In recent years, most historians have raised their estimates of Eisenhower's leadership. Once dismissed as a weak president and an incompetent politician, Eisenhower now gains higher marks. Although he lacked interest in some areas of government and party politics, he did demonstrate a sound grasp of many issues. According to his associates, he skillfully presided over cabinet sessions and meetings of the National Security Council. For a long time people believed that strong figures such as Dulles, Humphrey, and Adams dominated Eisenhower and really ran the government. Early in Eisenhower's first term a familiar joke asked, "What if Ike died and we got Nixon as president?" "Yes," went the punch line, "but what if Adams died, and we got stuck with Ike?" But events seemed to demonstrate that Eisenhower retained a firm, though often unseen, rein in those areas he considered critical. During his second term all three of his key advisers resigned (a kickback scandal forced Adams's resignation, Humphrey returned to business, and Dulles fell victim to cancer), yet Eisenhower carried on without any noticeable disruption in the presidential routine.

Still, many questions about Eisenhower's presidency remain unanswered. Did Eisenhower, who left office with an extremely high rating in the opinion polls, defer too much to popular attitudes and exert too little leadership from the White House? Did not the Eisenhower administration ignore crucial domestic problems such as environmental pollution and urban decay? Did Eisenhower's obvious lack of sympathy toward the black civil-rights movement help inflame racial tensions? (See Chapter 5.) And was he as shrewd a president as his close associates claimed, or did he simply have extraordinarily good luck in handling the affairs of state? All these questions and many others await further research and contemplation. But one thing is clear: at a time when many Americans wanted some sign of stability, the former general from Kansas provided a national symbol of old values and traditional virtues.

Economic Policies

Two weeks after taking office Eisenhower announced, "The first order of business is the elimination of the annual deficit" in the federal budget. Guided by Secretary of the Treasury George Humphrey and Budget Director Joseph Dodge, Eisenhower curtailed federal spending whenever possible. To this Republican administration—the first since Herbert Hoover's—mounting unemployment and possible recession were always less frightening than inflation or the "creeping socialism" of big government.

Eisenhower attempted to reduce government's role in the economy. During his first year in office he turned over certain nationally owned offshore oil deposits to the states of California, Louisiana, and Texas for subsequent lease to private oil companies. He also attempted to undercut the federal government's Tennessee Valley Authority by giving the privately owned Dixon-Yates utility a contract to supply power for the Atomic Energy Commission. (Public furor over the questionable circumstances surrounding this deal, however, forced the government to repudiate the Dixon-Yates agreement.) Ike frequently used his veto power against housing, public works, and antipollution bills; after the end of the Korean War he quickly lifted economic controls (too quickly many economists believed); and his secretary of agriculture attempted to lower farm subsidies. Following his vision of moderate Republicanism, Eisenhower did not dismantle New Deal programs—during his eight years as president Congress raised Social Security payments, minimum wage rates, and unemployment benefits—but the president clearly opposed large government expenditures.

One new spending program that Eisenhower did support had a profound effect on the style of American life. The interstate highway program, begun in 1956, committed the federal government to a thirteen-year, $26-billion program to help states construct interstate highways according to a national plan. As the costs mounted to $37 billion in 1961 and $50 billion in 1968, Congress continued to appropriate additional revenues. The program represented a major national commitment to the internal-combustion engine; in effect, it subsidized the trucking industry and those Americans who could afford cross-country travel in private automobiles.

Interstate-highway construction had a host of spin-offs: construction companies boomed; new gas stations sprang up; lines of motels stretched out along the highways. Around big cities the maze of interstate exchanges stood as monuments to human ingenuity, and technology lent its latest techniques to the planning and control of traffic flows. But the positive effects of the interstate-highway program often obscured its drawbacks. Railroads, a less expensive and less polluting means of transportation, could not compete with truckers who used free interstate highways, and rail lines fell into deep financial trouble. In New York City mass-transit facilities decayed; in Los Angeles and many other cities light rail transit was ended, and miles of concrete and asphalt crisscrossed the landscape. Americans became more car-crazy than ever, and the more they drove, the more there was no alternative to driving. Those without cars—the old, the handicapped, the poor—were the losers. The "highway lobby," a loose alliance of auto manufacturers, oil producers, and construction companies, were the winners. The graft sometimes associated with the purchase of right-of-ways and the award of contracts tainted local politics and reminded historians of the railroad corruption of the late nineteenth century.

Despite the interstate-highway program, Eisenhower kept federal spending down, and the economy grew at a slow rate. Moreover, Ike's failure to use government fiscal policy to influence the economy contributed to economic uncertainty. In 1954, after the end of the Korean War, the country slid into a small recession, but Eisenhower's advisers refused to pump in additional federal

Minnesota Historical Society, photo by John Runk

A fleet of urban trolly cars. In the late 1940s many American cities still had extensive light-rail transit systems. Note the extensive overhead electrical network that trolley cars required.

St. Paul Pioneer Press.

The end of light-rail mass transit. Workers rip up streetcar tracks in St. Paul, Minnesota, and a group of photographers record Minneapolis' farewell to streetcars in 1953. Three decades later, under the pressure of soaring gasoline prices, some urban planners lamented the demise of these systems and tried to figure out how to rebuild similar ones.

money to promote recovery. Again in 1957, economic indicators showed an alarming downturn. By spring of 1958, unemployment had reached 7.5 percent, and the recession seemed serious. Even members of the business community, Eisenhower's strongest supporters, began to worry that the Republican administration would not move rapidly enough to stimulate growth. Still fearing an inflationary spiral, Eisenhower opposed tax cuts or increased federal spending, the prescriptions usually favored by Democratic administrations for correcting economic slowdowns.

Liberal economists faulted Eisenhower for his policies of moderate growth and limited spending. America's economic-growth rate, they pointed out, lagged behind the Soviet Union's. Worse still, some economists claimed, the low rate of growth did not expand employment rapidly enough to keep up with population growth. The large baby-boom generation, after all, would soon be part of the job market. In addition, some charged that the lack of new federal programs stemmed not from a dearth of pressing problems but from a determination to ignore them. Pollution, central-city blight, inadequate mass transit, and inequitable health care had not reached the crisis proportions they were to assume in the 1960s and 1970s, but they were nonetheless real problems that might not have become acute if they had been dealt with in the 1950s.

In *The Affluent Society* (1958) liberal economist John Kenneth Galbraith denounced the parsimony of public-welfare programs. He contrasted the personal affluence of most Americans with the lack of decent public services, writing of the travelers who steer their "mauve and cerise air-conditioned, power-steered and power-braked car" through badly paved and littered streets; who "picnic on exquisitely packaged food from a portable icebox by a polluted stream and go on to spend the night at a park which is a menace to public health and morals." Galbraith scathingly attacked the American tax system, which permitted such a disparity between public services and private comfort. He called for higher levels of taxation and greater government spending.

Despite such advice, Eisenhower and his advisers held fast to their economic policies. Defenders pointed out that real wages for an average family had risen 20 percent during Ike's years in office, a gain that meant a great deal to most Americans. In addition, policies of modest growth kept the inflation rate low, and this price stability moderated labor disputes and helped maintain a relatively healthy dollar abroad. If Ike's administration deferred problems until later, many Americans probably wanted it that way. Eisenhower, after all, had not promised to reform and crusade but to soothe and assure. Many years later, Ike proudly remembered his principal accomplishment as having created "an atmosphere of greater serenity and mutual confidence."

But all was not serene and calm during the 1950s. The population was expanding at a tremendous rate; people were flocking to the suburbs in unprecedented numbers; affluence allowed many people to enjoy the products of a booming popular-culture industry; and people at the other end of the economic spectrum, many of them nonwhite, found it difficult to believe that the United States really was a land of affluence.

Social Trends

The Baby Boom

During the ten years after World War II the number of children born each year in the United States rose by nearly 50 percent, the biggest increase in births ever recorded anywhere. Throughout the 1950s, towns and cities busily constructed the brick-and-glass schools that would hold these youngsters until they were about seventeen, socializing them into the American value system and economic structure. Everywhere children of the baby boom turned, they spilled out of conventional facilities. They needed unprecedented quantities of diapers, toys, books, and teachers. Their very numbers gave them a generational identity and tagged them as somehow extraordinary. During the 1950s the pressure of this generation was contained in homes and schools; in the 1960s it would find its way into overcrowded subways, unemployment lines, student revolts, and a "counterculture." Understandably, many of the products of this baby boom would later take up the cry for "zero population growth."

Demographers seeking explanations for the postwar baby boom have arrived at a few tentative conclusions. From 1940 to the mid 1950s couples began marrying and having children at a much earlier age than their parents. There has always been a close correlation between average age of marriage and number of children—the two factors rise or fall inversely—so the extraordinarily high birth rate comes as no surprise. But why did couples marry early and have large families?

Economic security was one reason. The tremendous economic expansion that came with the war opened new jobs and created a general scarcity of labor. The shortage of younger workers throughout the late 1940s and the 1950s meant unusually rapid economic advancement, especially for white males. Not only did pay scales within each job category shoot up, but upward occupational mobility was far greater than in the 1930s or even in the 1920s. Throughout the 1950s business analysts noted a decline in the average age of corporate executives, and older people grumbled at how easily the younger generation could reach positions that had taken them years to attain. Favorable employment and high income levels gave young middle-class couples greater security than ever before.

Certain economic innovations also contributed to the affluence of young, particularly white, couples. Government-sponsored benefits for veterans provided extra sources of income; unemployment compensation made savings seem less necessary. The whole array of New Deal programs—Federal Housing Administration (FHA) home loans, the Agricultural Adjustment Administration soil bank, Rural Electrification Administration energy, Federal Deposit Insurance Corporation insurance, and Social Security payments—particularly assisted middle-income Americans. In addition to these welfare-state measures, wider use of credit allowed families to spend beyond their income. Installment buying, finance agencies, charge accounts, and credit cards helped many Americans buy whatever they wanted, whenever they wanted it. The financial well-being that encouraged early marriage and large families was based upon certain employment, rising income, the new welfare role of government, and the availability of credit.

The baby boom probably also had psychological foundations. Its beginnings in the war years may have stemmed partially from the fears associated with separation as men entered the military. The bright economic picture after the war provided couples with the self-confidence and optimism that are important ingredients in decisions to marry and have children. Then too, Americans had deferred having children throughout the depression. The meteoric rise of the birth rate during the 1950s must always be viewed against the backdrop of its decline during the 1930s.

Middle-Class Domesticity

The baby boom was associated with an upsurge in the ideal of domesticity, the notion that a woman's place was in her home and with her children. Although the employment of women increased during the postwar years, in response to the generally favorable economic situation (by 1960 one third of the women of working age were employed), most women occupied low-paying jobs. The greatest gains in employment came in the field of clerical work, where wages were low. Although women received college educations in unprecedented numbers, fewer women attained advanced degrees, and employment of women in prestigious professions dropped. For the well-educated wives of white-collar professionals, homes seemed more attractive than the low-status careers earmarked for women. The 1950s was a decade of club work, not of crusading for equal job opportunities. In 1949, for example, women who had graduated fifteen years earlier from some of the nation's top women's schools (Barnard, Bryn Mawr, Mount Holyoke, Radcliffe, Smith, Vassar, and Wellesley) were polled to determine what they had done with their college educations. Eighty-eight percent considered marriage more important than a career, and only about 12 percent of the married respondents worked fulltime. One of every four responded that playing bridge was a major activity in her life.

Widely accepted concepts of "scientific" child rearing reinforced the flight into the home. Benjamin Spock's *Baby and Child Care* rivaled the Bible in sales and stood next to it as a guide to appropriate conduct in most middle-class homes. Spock made motherhood a challenging task. Although he cautioned women against becoming too tied to their children and spelled out the consequences of allowing the child to become a tiny tyrant, his book's overall effect was to leave many mothers feeling uneasy about their responsibilities. If a child's budding capabilities depended upon the proper application of "scientific" principles, then the mysteries of child raising deserved a woman's full attention. Any act, it seemed, could have far-reaching consequences upon the child's behavior and psychological makeup. When a mother heard cries, for example, should she ignore them for fear the baby might become spoiled, or attend to them so that the child would not feel afraid and rejected? Spock tried to provide guides to action, but no book could solve every problem. Often he and other child-care "experts" simply left women in a quandary, feeling vaguely guilty about their uncertainty.

Managing the spending for a middle-class family also took much of a wife's time. As incomes rose, as credit facilities became more complex, and as advertisers stimulated demand, women tended to become full-time consumers, deciding what foods to buy and what products deserved priority. Advertisers geared their appeals to women, even for expensive, durable goods such as automobiles. This strategy both reflected and reinforced the role of the woman as prime consumer. *Better Homes and Gardens,* a women's magazine (edited by men) with a circulation of millions, exemplified the trend. Advertisements took up far more than half the space, and the remaining pages contained tips on running a household efficiently and "scientifically"—how to plan quick meals, how to determine what washing machine fit the family needs, how to spruce up a backyard. Women's magazines often emphasized money saving, but their net effect was to stimulate consumer tastes. The word *housewife* less frequently evoked images of sewing and baking and became virtually synonymous with the word *shopper.*

Suburbia

Rising incomes, the baby boom, and the emphasis on domesticity accelerated the flight to the suburbs. Throughout the country the more affluent built new residences further from the center of cities to accommodate their larger families, to flee urban problems, and to achieve new levels of comfort and status. In major cities and even in smaller towns with populations of twenty-five to fifty thousand, neat rows of homes intruded upon the surrounding countryside. Real-estate builders and developers such as Levitt & Company pioneered tract homes, which were cheaply constructed according to a preestablished plan. Building innovations, in addition to the FHA loan program, brought the suburban "paradise" within the reach of millions. One fourth of all the housing that existed in 1960 had been built in the 1950s.

On the surface, suburban living seemed to bring contentment. The predominantly white, middle-class residents aspired to economic success, and although their preoccupation with status often bred rivalries, the shared value system also brought a sense of comfort and community. Conformity was a balm for rootlessness and a cushion against the anxiety of change. But every glimpse of suburban happiness had its darker side of unforeseen problems. Burgeoning residential sections often overcrowded existing facilities, creating the congestion that residents had hoped to escape. Payments for mortgages, autos, and consumer goods sometimes brought new financial worries, and the mounting personal indebtedness among Americans alarmed many economists. Distances to work grew longer and longer; those who commuted in comfortable private cars only contributed to clogged freeways and polluted air.

Suburban life easily lent itself to caricature and derision. The folk singer Malvina Reynolds labeled suburban homes "little boxes made of ticky-tacky" and jabbed at the conformity of men who all "drink their martinis dry" and of children who all "go to summer camp and then to the university." In the 1960s Andy Warhol made the slickly packaged consumer culture associated with surburbia a subject of pop art, creating still-life portraits of monotonous rows of Campbell's soup cans. Upper-class critics of suburbia snorted at its bad taste—the lack of greenery (except for the spindly tree per lot that FHA mortgages required); the cheap construction; the clutter of too many autos, tricycles, lawn mowers, and children. Poor people and nonwhites, trapped in the inner city, also attacked the suburbs, envying the comparative space and quiet while resenting the drain of tax revenue to outlying areas.

Organization Men and Women

The large business organization dominated the lives of many suburban men during the 1950s. The person whom William H. Whyte described in *The Organization Man* (1956) established his primary roots not in a particular town or region but within a corporate structure. The business corporation provided the society in which he defined and understood himself: within its structure he gauged his status; within its values he subsumed his individual morality. He did, of course, withdraw from the corporate world to his home and family each day, but this retreat occupied only a few evening hours. Sociological studies revealed that success as a husband and father and occupational advancement often varied inversely. Home and office were separate and competing spheres, and the organization often won out as the primary frame of reference.

The economic growth and occupational mobility of the 1950s reinforced corporate loyalty. A young executive with dedication was almost sure to rise. But advancement often meant moving around the country at the company's behest. "We never make a man move," one company president explained. "Of course, he kills his career if he doesn't. But we never make him do it." Geographic mobility only strengthened the bond between man and company, for it hindered development of strong ties to a local community and brought the organization right into the family circle as a most important decision maker.

The relationship of women to the large business organization was quite different. Especially to young women, corporate life seemed to promise excitement and independence. But during the 1950s most corporations hired women only for positions in the secretarial ghetto, where pay was low and a woman remained a "girl" no matter what her age. The illusion of glamour and independence darkened into the reality of boredom and bare subsistence. Research showed that illicit relationships between boss and secretary, the subject of endless jokes at corporate conventions, were largely male fantasies seldom duplicated in reality or in the thoughts of the secretaries. For most organization women love for boss or for business did not transcend dollars and cents, and many rapidly deserted secretarial jobs for domestic life. The rapid turnover for women in corporations bolstered the myth that they were poor risks at any level in the business hierarchy. Organization "girls" were entrapped in a vicious cycle of low pay, rapid turnover, and discrimination.

Robert Peterson.

Hat n' Boots Gas. Such examples of oversized pop art disgusted some critics, but others found them an appropriate reflection of American society.

The wives of most corporate employees were also organization women, deriving income and even status from their husbands' jobs. At home, as in the office, the great corporations contributed to female subservience. A wife's identity came through her husband—upon meeting a suburban woman many people did not ask "What do you do?" but rather "What does your husband do?"—and this relationship could limit her sense of personal esteem. Restricted to the sphere of home and children, the model corporate wife was nonetheless supposed to feel devotion to the business world that she seldom saw. But this obligation of loyalty, together with the husband's unfamiliarity with his spouse's domestic routine, drove subtle wedges between married couples. To some women, the organization became a rival for their husbands' attention.

Popular Culture and The Arts

After World War II, middle-income Americans could enjoy an ever expanding array of "popular culture," entertainment aimed at a mass audience rather than a small, highly educated elite. The generally rising level of economic prosperity made this pop-culture explosion possible. As most American workers gained shorter hours, paid vacations, and higher take-home pay, the entertainment business became more profitable than ever before. Farsighted promoters and entrepreneurs refurbished old products, such as popular music, and exploited relatively new ones, such as television and paperback books. By 1950 Americans were spending twice as much money on entertainment as on rent; the total expenditure equaled one seventh of the gross national product.

Travel and Sports

The travel industry, for example, grew tremendously after World War II. For those who could afford the price, travel agencies marketed package tours to Europe. In only two weeks Americans could absorb the culture of the Old World—from Paris, to Brussels, to Geneva, to Rome, to Vienna, to Hamburg, and finally to London. For those who lacked the money to visit Europe (or who had already toured the Continent), the United States provided its own vacation spots. New motels, their quality certified by motor clubs or franchise owners, began to replace the old, independent tourist cabins. When affluent travelers reached destinations such as Southern California, Las Vegas, or Miami Beach, they found luxury-resort complexes that offered expensive nightclubs for adults, professional recreation directors for children, and deluxe kennels for family pets. The vacation and travel industries would continue to grow after 1960, but the basic pattern was already established by the 1950s.

After the reduced schedules of the war years, sports promotions regained their earlier pace. Promoters welcomed back the young men who had served in the armed forces, abandoning the lesser talents and fading veterans who had performed during World War II. (The supply of quality baseball players became so low that during the war the St. Louis Browns employed a one-armed outfielder). Although all levels of professional baseball revived, the late 1940s and early 1950s proved to be the last hurrah for baseball's minor leagues. Before the full impact of competition from network television, many American cities and smaller towns eagerly supported their own professional baseball teams. And with only sixteen major-league clubs, there was a surplus of good players, particularly blacks, to stock the minor leagues. Until the late 1960s black people complained, with much justification, that only outstanding athletes such as Jackie Robinson could play in the majors; white ballplayers generally received preference for jobs such as second-string catcher or reserve infielder. Even talented white players found themselves tied to a monopolistic business system in which major-league teams owned vast numbers of players whom they could freely transfer from team to team, from league to league. Even so, in the patriotic spirit of the cold war, baseball served as a symbol of the openness and equality of American society. Sportswriters, following in the star-struck tradition of Grantland Rice, still lavished praise on the game, celebrating it as an integral part of the American way. One prominent writer-broadcaster, Bill Stern, constantly invented uplifting stories about the national pastime. A dying Abraham Lincoln, Stern solemnly claimed, had told an aide to "keep baseball going: the country needs it."

Professional boxing, plagued by hints of fixed fights and underworld connections, lacked baseball's hallowed reputation but attracted good-sized audiences. Large promotions, battles for world championships, and small neighborhood clubs all made money during the late 1940s and early 1950s. During these years Joe Louis finally concluded his long reign as heavyweight champion; the flamboyant Sugar Ray Robinson captured both the welterweight and middleweight crowns; and a young Italian-American from Massachusetts, Rocky Marciano, battered forty-nine opponents into submission before retiring in 1955 as the undefeated heavyweight champion. Meanwhile, thousands of other boxers toiled in the small clubs, fighting for meager purses and hoping for a shot at the "big money" of a television bout. Professional boxing quickly became one of the staples of network television: at one time during the 1950s, boxing aficionados could watch four nationally televised bouts every week. Such overexposure quickly exhausted both the viewers' attention and the country's supply of good fighters. During the 1960s old-timers lamented the declining quality and quantity of professional matches.

Professional wrestling also claimed prime evening television time during the late 1940s and early 1950s. Obviously contrived and prechoreographed, professional wrestling (as distinguished from the authentic amateur sport) offered a familiar, and very appealing morality play: a stereotyped villain, often posing as a German or a "Jap," abused a long-suffering hero until a dramatic reversal sealed the bully's fate. In the end, justice—and "the American way"—usually triumphed. But a flexible catalog of "rules" allowed promoters to vary the scenario slightly and keep fans coming back for the next contest. Only roller derby, another pseudosport, offered a comparable blend of mayhem and mindlessness. To the uninitiated it seemed like wrestling on wheels, but millions of television viewers eagerly followed the careers of roller derby's kings and queens.

The violence and sadism that generally remained muted in professional wrestling and roller derby too often became explicit in paperback and comic books, two other highly profitable—and often ridiculed—forms of popular culture. The exploits of Mike Hammer, Mickey Spillane's brawny crime fighter, titillated paperback readers; by 1950 Americans had bought more than six million copies of Spillane's potboilers. The Mike Hammer stories, critics charged, reflected the mindless, superpatriotic, vigilante spirit of the cold-war era. With a single-minded devotion to 100-percent Americanism, Hammer loathed communists, sexual perverts, and bleeding-heart libertarians. Spillane's hero expressed only contempt for legal niceties and civil liberties. He relentlessly pursued the forces of evil, judged them according to his standards, and then exacted his special kind of retribution. Scores of communists and thugs fell before Hammer's righteous hands. "He came right at me with his head down," wrote Spillane-Hammer, "and I took my own damn time about kicking him in the face. . . . He smashed into the door and lay there bubbling. For laughs I gave him a taste of his own sap on the back of his hand and felt the bones go into splinters." Hammer was also deadly with women: no female could withstand his charm. The comic-book industry offered similar doses of gratuitous violence and sex. In one of the most notorious examples, comic-book ghouls played baseball with various parts of a dissected human body.

Comic books and cheap paperback thrillers attracted readers of all ages, but they remained firmly identified with young people. Merchandisers of popular culture aimed more and more of their products at the baby-boom generation, the mass of young people who began to come of age during the 1950s.

Rock around the Clock: The Popular Culture of Youth

The 1950s did not seethe with student activism or with talk of generation gaps. But throughout the decade a distinctive youth culture formed, one that did provide a point of departure for the more explosive 1960s. Juvenile delinquency, associated in popular culture with Marlon Brando's *The Wild Ones* and with James Dean's *Rebel Without a Cause,* became both an academic and a journalistic concern. After studying the problems of "the shook-up generation" ("I'm All Shook Up," of course, became a kind of battle cry for Elvis Presley), the journalist Harrison Salisbury concluded that the phenomenon stretched from the nation's worst slums to its most affluent suburbs. In an age of increasing world tensions, Salisbury concluded, the emergence of "the shook-up generation" loomed as "a matter of national security."

Although few people urged the suppression of rock-and-roll on national-security grounds, many custodians of proper culture did express outrage at the popularity of the new music among the young. To most older Americans, the sound of rock was too loud, too raucous; it appeared to be merely gratuitous noise. The lyrics of the songs seemed even worse: "Good Golly, Miss Molly . . . She sure like to ball. . . ." In truth, the early rockers, blacks and whites—Chuck Berry, Little Richard, Carl Perkins, Elvis Presley—were breaking away from the established forms and the settled limits of popular music. In a more profound sense, perhaps, they were exploring the possibility of creating new cultural forms and new life styles in an era dominated by the spirit of consensus. The most innovative rockers, as Greil Marcus has argued, brought a new sense of freedom into popular culture, a "good-natured contempt" for conventional wisdom and for pomposity. Their spontaneity and exuberance contrasted with what many young people considered the drabness and predictability of the popular music produced by the large record companies.

In its earliest days, rock flourished on the smaller record labels and on the smaller AM radio stations. Innovative young producers, particularly Sam Phillips of Memphis' Sun Records, successfully marketed what the major labels hesitated even to record. During the mid 1950s Phillips unveiled the now legendary figures of early rockabilly—Carl Perkins, Charley Rich, Johnny Cash, Jerry Lee Lewis, and Elvis Presley—and realized his hopes of breaking down old cultural barriers, especially the one between white and black music. In other parts of the country, other small producers were also experimenting, releasing songs by both black and white artists that did not fit into the old categories of popular music. Musical purists might break all this down into new pigeonholes—such as "Chicago rhythm-and-blues" and "West Texas country rock"—but millions of young people knew it simply as rock. While many established radio stations and prominent radio personalities steered clear of the new sound, smaller stations and younger DJs hitched their fortunes to rock. The most prominent early rock-and-roll DJ, Alan Freed of Cleveland, soon found himself atop a burgeoning musical empire, a kingdom that collapsed when the federal government prosecuted him for payola—accepting bribes to promote certain records.

Freed's place was soon taken by Dick Clark, host of a popular television show, "American Bandstand." Clark's program gave the emerging rock and dance culture a national audience, but many of the earliest rockers accused Clark of "selling out." Believing that the unruliness of the new music had to be tamed, Clark pushed for "cleaner" lyrics and mass-produced a new generation of singers, such as Frankie Avalon and Fabian, who offered something of a compromise between the wildness of a Jerry Lee Lewis and the blandness of a Perry Como. As one musical critic has observed, rock soon lost its roughness, its regional identity, and its spontaneity. (Clark, for example, insisted that all artists appearing on "American Bandstand" "lip-synch" their songs, a requirement that masked the ineptitude of a Fabian and squelched the artistry of a Chuck Berry.) By the late 1950s the major record companies were absorbing rock, merging it into the mainstream of popular music.

Like rock-and-roll, automobiles became a special passion of the youth culture. Automobiles—especially the increasingly common second car—made young people mobile and provided status symbols, entertainment, and makeshift bedrooms. They provided transportation to teenage gatherings out of parents' sight and gave the freedom of privacy. In the rapidly growing South, stock-car racing became a preeminent sport. Detroit's auto manufacturers vied to contribute innovations that, by giving daredevil drivers an edge on the track, would win loyalties within the vast new youth market. In both North and South, in city and small town, this was an age of souped-up hot rods, of dual exhaust systems, of raked bodies, of rolled and pleated interiors. For many young men, the transformation of one of Detroit's stereotyped products into a special personal creation may have represented a subtle, though tangible, revolt against the mass-produced world of their parents. Although only a small proportion of young people actually owned such a creation, the "Kandy-Kolored Tangerine-Flake Streamline Baby," to use writer Tom Wolfe's phrase, was the envy of the teenage "scene."

The youth culture thrived, especially in the suburbs, where the general affluence trickled down from parents to children. The youth market became a multimillion-dollar business. Sales of the new 45-rpm records and long-play albums exploded, and a teenager's collection of the latest hits became an important status symbol. Other items also tempted teenagers to spend money: record players, the latest in penny loafers or saddle shoes, and charm bracelets displaying pictures of rock idols. The youth generation of the 1950s was a peculiar amalgam: in its crass commercialism and unabashed materialism it mirrored, even caricatured, the rest of society; in its hedonism and stylistic iconoclasm it set itself decisively apart from the 1950s and anticipated the 1960s.

The Critique of Popular Culture

The postwar boom in popular culture disturbed some academicians and social critics. Popular culture, they maintained, glorified all that was ugly and irrational in American life; it represented an assault on good taste, traditional notions of decency, and even common sense. The culture of the masses, its detractors charged, indicated the sorry state of American society.

Popular culture, a diverse group of critics agreed, lacked any artistic value; it represented instead a banal extension of the United States' sophisticated technology and its mass production – mass consumption economic system. Like automobiles and ready-made clothes, the trivial items of mass culture rolled off assembly lines with no concern for quality or durability. In contrast with "high culture," the popular arts made no attempt to increase understanding of nature or to sharpen perception of fundamental human problems. Indeed, popular culture was not meant to be preserved and restudied; like candy and chewing gum, it was to be consumed as rapidly as possible and then quickly discarded. And unlike true folk culture, which ordinary people created from their authentic traditions, popular culture was stamped out by carefully trained manipulators of mass desires. Thus, according to the semanticist S. I. Hayakawa, the folk blues of Bessie Smith, though rough in comparison with classical music, sprang from the lives of poor blacks in the rural South; the pop songs that dominated the Hit Parade contained only the trivial fantasies and sentimental clichés manufactured by the songwriter-technicians on Tin Pan Alley. By its very existence mass culture represented an affront to all that was supposed to be noble and uplifting in human society.

But the effect of pop culture, its most vigorous detractors charged, was even more insidious than this. It acted as a kind of intellectual cancer, eating away at American society and culture. The popularity of mediocre mass culture, some critics contended, inevitably harmed high culture: talented artists succumbed to the monetary rewards of mass culture; popular tastes became too vulgar to recognize good art; and people's senses would become too brutalized to recognize the threat of a corrupt totalitarianism that would employ mass art to manipulate popular opinion. Inevitably, high culture would be destroyed or, at best, be merged with mass culture into some bastard form—a "middle culture."

In addition to eroding artistic values, some writers argued, popular culture undermined American society by diverting attention from real problems and reducing people's intellectual level through constant immersion in junk. Citizens became passive receivers, deferring their critical judgment to the manipulators of mass tastes. Other writers indicted mass culture for fomenting social unrest. The violence of children's comic books, for example, supposedly corrupted young minds and helped produce juvenile delinquents. Some social psychologists hypothesized that the simplicity of any comic-book story, violent or not, hindered young people's emotional development by teaching them to ignore the complexity of life and conditioning them to expect quick, simple solutions for their problems. Pressure groups urged the government to ban comic books or to force companies to censor antisocial material.

Popular culture, of course, had its defenders. Some writers, though finding little that was uplifting in popular culture, doubted that it could cause all these problems. The history of Western civilization indicated that high art had traditionally been the preserve of a small elite and that the "custodians of culture" had always decried the effect of popular and folk arts. Complex social problems such as juvenile delinquency could hardly be traced to comic books or to the novels of Mickey Spillane. Some individuals observed that no amount of sermonizing could retard the growth of popular culture: new technological developments could only increase its influence. Finally, many observers of mass culture found cause for optimism. Gilbert Seldes, a long standing partisan of the popular arts, contended that almost every area of mass culture showed a trend toward more sophistication and artistic craftsmanship. And the history of the movie industry and television after World War II provided some support for the view that the popular arts need not be a cultural wasteland.

The Hollywood Film Industry

Many critics, as well as some filmmakers themselves, expressed particular contempt for the Hollywood motion-picture industry. Director Billy Wilder's 1950 film *Sunset Boulevard* bade a cynical goodby to the old Hollywood. It began with a shot of a corpse floating in a Beverly Hills swimming pool. This dead man, a second-rate screenwriter, narrated the rest of the story. A middle-aged silent-film star, played by Gloria Swanson, lived under the illusion that she would return to the screen in triumph. But a call from a famous director turned out to be only a request for the use of her antique auto, and increasingly she retreated into a fantasy world. The end of the film revealed that the actress had killed the screenwriter and become completely mad. Wilder's message was clear: like the aging actress, Hollywood sustained itself on myths, awaiting an artistic rebirth that would never come. Yet Hollywood survived the 1950s, wounded by the anticommunist witch-hunts of the McCarthy years but still able to ignite the fantasies of millions while making some films of real artistic value.

Between 1945 and 1960 most Hollywood filmmakers did stick to traditional forms. The large studios still relied upon the star system, introducing new celebrities such as Elizabeth Taylor, Kirk Douglas, Burt Lancaster, Marilyn Monroe, Tony Curtis, and Rock Hudson. Most producers operated on the premise, which often proved correct, that the names of popular stars could sell the most mediocre picture. Recognizing the impact of television, moviemakers increasingly tried huge spectaculars. Cecil B. DeMille remade his silent classic *The Ten Commandments* and directed a sprawling circus epic, *The Greatest Show on Earth.* In other efforts to surpass the technical limitations of television, Hollywood developed new visual techniques: CinemaScope, Cinerama, Todd-AO, and 3-D.

Hollywood also managed to offer some films that broke away from tested formulas. A few offbeat films featuring no great stars and eschewing glamor appeared during the 1950s. Adapted from a successful television production, *Marty* told the simple story of a Bronx butcher, played by Ernest Borgnine, who fell in love with a woman who considered herself plain and unexciting. After the decline of McCarthyism several films treated controversial social issues. *Paths of Glory* indicted military leaders for their values and portrayed war as anything but a glorious enterprise. Shot in black and white, *Paths of Glory* did poorly at the box office but gained much critical acclaim for its youthful director, Stanley Kubrick. Kubrick would become recognized as one of the United States' most innovative directors during the 1960s. Racial tension provided the backdrop for several films, the most popular being *The Defiant Ones,* a chain-gang story in which brotherhood triumphed over bigotry. Although the film would seem trite and overly cautious to many later viewers, Stanley Kramer's production appeared at a time when racial prejudice was still considered a dangerous subject in Hollywood.

During the 1950s a prominent school of film criticism, popular in both the United States and France, praised those Hollywood directors who could surmount the restraints of the industry and use their films to make personal statements. These *auteur* critics generally concentrated on so-called lesser films, finding much to admire in the work of directors like Budd Boettcher. A bullfighter turned filmmaker, Boettcher added new dimensions to the most American of all film forms, the western. Traditionally, the western had served as an action-filled entertainment for children (the B westerns of Ken Maynard and Gene Autry) or as a tribute to the glories of the American frontier (the epics of director John Ford). Boettcher's low-budget westerns lacked both the nonstop action of the B Western and the nostalgic qualities of Ford's films. Boettcher concentrated upon a lone hero, skillfully played by Randolph Scott, who drifted through a hostile, or at best indifferent, world. Like a bullfighter, a human in a modern mass society, or a sensitive director in Hollywood, the Boettcher-Scott character found himself constantly forced to demonstrate his individual skill and courage. He rarely initiated a situation but instead reacted to the moves of others. Most of Boettcher's villains, often played by actors who had been or would become leading men, seemed little different from his hero; in Boettcher's amoral world they certainly did not fit the stereotyped role of the western badman. Boettcher carefully selected his locations, and his films emphasized the harsh beauty of the physical world. Boettcher's westerns not only made money but greatly influenced the younger directors, such as Sam Peckinpah, who would create the much-acclaimed antiwesterns of the 1960s.

Television

TV sales soared throughout the 1950s. Before World War II few people had ever seen television; by 1957 there were 40 million sets in the country, and most cities and towns boasted a local station. Within the family, however, the impact of TV was never clear. It did bring popular entertainment into the living room, but it may have become a substitute, not a stimulant, for communication among family members. It may simply have contributed to what Paul Simon called the "sounds of silence. . . people talking without speaking, people hearing without listening." By the 1960s affluent families could afford a set for every member, and each could retreat to his or her room to watch their favorite program.

Expansion of television ultimately revolutionized politics, education, and culture. During the 1952 presidential campaign Richard Nixon used a nationwide television address to defend his beleaguered reputation and save his political career; two years later the televised Army-McCarthy hearings helped expose Joe McCarthy as a crude and irresponsible demagogue; and toward the end of the decade John Kennedy's media image speeded his drive for the 1960 presidential nomination.

The tube had a less immediate impact on education and American culture. Despite hopes that television would dramatically change education, establishment of a separate, nonprofit educational network—and shows such as "Sesame Street"—did not come until the 1960s. Meanwhile, cynics charged, the three commercial networks beamed a steady stream of assembly-line programs that appealed to the lowest common denominator and the widest possible audience. One hit show begat a dozen imitators, and viewers watched endless rounds of standardized variety shows, stereotyped situation comedies, rigged quiz shows, and low-budget westerns. But in its few good moments, television displayed the promise of something better. Sid Caesar's "Your Show of Shows" featured highly sophisticated comedy sketches and utilized the talents of writers such as Mel Brooks, Woody Allen, and Neil Simon; CBS's "Playhouse 90" presented some fine original drama; some of Edward R. Murrow's documentaries rivaled the best products of print journalism; and a few specials even brought highbrow entertainment such as the New York Philharmonic to the small screen.

Some theorists claimed that the media would change people's perceptions. Radio had broadcast the sound of far-off places, but television stimulated visual senses as well. Events seemed more real on TV; viewers became caught up in actual news happenings. Critics complained that television actually manufactured and manipulated news. Some demonstrations, press statements, and human-interest stories might have taken far different shapes had the television camera not been poised to record them. But television's defenders claimed that it offered exciting possibilities: worldwide programming and the instant dissemination of information might ultimately create common values. Just as television homogenized and standardized American culture, it could do the same for the world. Marshall McLuhan prophesied a "global village" in which people of all different cultures experienced a bond of sensory awareness, abandoning themselves to what he called the "cool medium" of television.

The Other Side of Affluence

As city dwellers fled to the suburbs, many people from rural areas flocked in to replace them. These new migrants were usually not white and not middle-class. For them the 1950s did not bring ebullient affluence; their small economic gains came only against a background of oppressive discrimination and entrapment in decaying central cities.

Blacks

Black people from depressed rural areas in the South flooded into northern cities during World War II to take jobs in war-related industries. But even though employment possibilities increased, the overall quality of life remained low. With the nation's resources being poured into national defense, little money remained for housing programs. In Detroit's new black ghetto, for example, one investigator reported that an old converted one-family dwelling might hold over a hundred black people, one family to a room.

Moving into old neighborhoods occupied by white ethnic groups, black newcomers confronted large-scale racial antagonism. Detroit's situation was explosive. Half a million people, including about 60,000 blacks, arrived in three years, and the strain of overcrowding was unbearable. During the hot June of 1943 an amusement-park fight between white and black teenagers escalated into a race war that was not calmed until a contingent of six thousand soldiers occupied the streets. There were 34 people killed and 700 injured; there was $2 million worth of property damage. Race riots occurred in other cities as well.

But overcrowding, discrimination, and harassment by whites did not curb the flow of black people into urban areas. With the new emphasis in the South on corporate farming and mechanized agriculture, many southern blacks who had traditionally hired out as farm laborers found themselves with little hope of employment. Others who had scratched out livings on small farms felt their always marginal existence slip below self-sufficiency. In 1940, 77 percent of the black population lived in the South, mostly in rural areas; by 1960 nearly half lived in the North, and three of every four blacks resided in a city.

Although the gap between the living standards of white and black Americans remained large, the war and northern migration did advance the economic position of many blacks. Between 1947 and 1952 the median income of nonwhite families rose from $1,614 to $2,338 and the gap between black and white narrowed slightly. In 1940, 80 percent of all black workers were employed in unskilled jobs; by 1950 the figure had dropped to 63 percent. Similarly, blacks' life expectancy advanced from 53.1 years in 1940 to 61.7 in 1953 (compared with 64.2 to 69.6 for whites). Throughout the 1950s, the expanding economy and favorable job market helped maintain the economic gains that many black people had made during the war. For many of those who stayed in the rural South or found no jobs in the cities, of course, life remained a constant struggle against hunger and disease.

Puerto Ricans

Thousands of Puerto Ricans moved to New York City in the decade after World War II, transforming that city's ethnic makeup. New York's Puerto Rican community grew by over half a million in twenty years, from 70,000 in 1940 to 613,000 in 1960. A variety of circumstances contributed to this massive migration. Throughout the 1940s Puerto Ricans had experienced increased contact with the United States mainland through mass media, advertisements, and military life (65,000 Puerto Ricans served in the armed forces during World War II). Especially to young and better-educated Puerto Ricans, life in the United States seemed alluring. New York's unemployment rate was lower than Puerto Rico's, and its social services seemed superior. The administration of Luis Muñoz Marín in Puerto Rico encouraged the trend, hoping to raise Puerto Rico's per-capita income by reducing the island's population. Comparatively inexpensive air service between San Juan and New York, begun in 1945, facilitated movement. In addition, United States businessmen encouraged migration; Puerto Ricans provided cheap labor for agriculture and the garment trades. Once a sizable Puerto Rican community existed in New York, it generated its own growth through a high birth rate and the additional migration of friends and relatives.

The Puerto Rican community crowded into East Harlem and then into other ethnic ghettos throughout the five boroughs of New York. Studies showed that the newcomers generally had a higher level of education and skill than the average Puerto Rican, but their Spanish language, skin color, and close ties with the island left them outside the mainstream of city life. During the 1950s most Puerto Ricans could obtain only the lowest-paying jobs, and few entered New York City politics. Puerto Ricans suffered the fate of many groups that lacked economic power and political muscle: discrimination, deteriorating schools, overcrowded housing, and indifference to their problems. Every year around 30,000 people returned to the island, but Spanish Harlem still continued to grow rapidly throughout the 1950s and 1960s.

Mexican-Americans

New immigration from Mexico and the attraction of urban jobs swelled southwestern cities with another Spanish-speaking population: Mexican-Americans, (Chicanos). Before World War II Chicanos, like blacks, lived largely in rural areas, but by 1960, 80 percent resided in cities. According to the 1960 census, over half a million Mexican-Americans lived in the Los Angeles – Long Beach area. Large Spanish-speaking barrios existed in El Paso, Phoenix, and other southwestern cities; and northern industrial centers such as Chicago, Detroit, Kansas City, and Denver attracted growing numbers of Chicano workers.

City life and the favorable job market of the 1950s raised the overall living standards of Mexican-Americans, but racial prejudice kept a lid on opportunity and advancement. Discrimination, coupled with the ethnic awareness that grew in city barrios, produced racial tensions between Chicanos and white "Anglos."

During World War II, for example, street gangs of young Chicanos in Los Angeles defied conventional styles of dress by donning "zoot suits" (or "drapes")—pleated, high-waisted pants with tight cuffs and long, wide-shouldered, loose coats. The ducktail haircut (which would become standard for fans of Elvis Presley in the 1950s) topped off the costume. Many whites, feeling threatened by the display of ethnic separateness, tended to see zoot suiters as hoodlums. In 1943, after a zoot-suited gang reportedly beat up eleven sailors who were strolling through a Chicano neighborhood, large-scale violence erupted. About two hundred sailors, joined by scores of soldiers and marines, cruised through the city beating anyone who wore a zoot suit. The Los Angeles police followed, arresting only the injured Chicanos. The one-sided rioting went on for several days, and similar disturbances quickly flared up in other cities throughout the country.

Despite widespread racial prejudice against Chicanos, the United States government welcomed additional Mexican migrants under the bracero (farm-worker) program. The executive agreement between the United States and Mexico that started the bracero program in 1942 was part of an effort to increase man-power during World War II. But under pressure from large agricultural enter-prises Congress continued to authorize migration of farm laborers long after the war. Throughout the 1950s the number of incoming Mexican workers climbed each year, reaching a peak of almost a million in 1959 alone. Mexican migrants provided cheap, unorganized labor to harvest seasonal crops from Texas to Mon-tana, and growers profited enormously. By the early 1960s, however, the rising unemployment rate among Americans, combined with anti-Mexican predjudice, convinced Congress to discontinue the bracero program. Over the protests of large growers, but to the satisfaction of labor unions that feared competition from cheap labor, the bracero program ended in 1965, although illegal immigration continued.

American Indians

American Indians, like other minority groups, also flocked to urban areas dur-ing and after World War II. Army life and lucrative industrial jobs initially at-tracted Indian people away from reservations, and the federal government's policies during the 1950s substantially increased their flight to the cities. The In-dian policy of the Eisenhower administration, as passed by Congress in 1953, called for the government to end Indians' "status as wards of the United States, and grant them all of the rights and privileges pertaining to American citizen-ship." The plan sought to "terminate" Indians' dependence upon the national government, to liquidate the reservation system, and to permit states to assume legal jurisdiction over Indians. Six bills of termination, applying to tribes who supposedly no longer needed a special relationship with the federal government, passed Congress in 1954.

While pursuing termination, the government also set up a Voluntary Relocation Program (later called the Employment Assistance Program) to coax more Indians into urban areas. Begun in 1952, this program helped Indians move to one of ten cities with "field relocation offices" and paid living expenses until first wages were received. Within about a decade, more than sixty thousand (approximately one of every eight) Indians had migrated from reservations to urban centers.

Termination and relocation greatly disrupted Indian life. Some terminated tribes, now subject to state-tax requirements, fell upon hard times. Others sold tribal lands to private developers. Indians who moved to the cities found themselves ill equipped for the transition from a semicommunal rural existence to the isolation of urban life. Relocated Indians became the most invisible of all urban ethnic groups. Federal officials had hoped that termination and relocation would assimilate Indians into the American mainstream and end federal outlays to support them, but assimilation proved more complicated than a geographical move. The Bureau of Indian Affairs estimated that 35 percent of all relocated Indians eventually returned to the reservations, but other studies suggested that about 75 percent would probably have returned had the reservations offered more job opportunities.

Few Indians favored the federal policy of termination and relocation, and protests mounted against the breakup of reservations and the destruction of Indian culture. Although the Eisenhower administration never abandoned the goal of termination, officials finally promised not to force it upon unwilling tribes. By the 1960 presidential campaign, termination was so discredited that both the Democratic and Republican parties repudiated it. During the 1960s the government reversed the policy and attempted to provide opportunity on the reservation rather than to force Indians to leave.

The "Invisible" Poor

The large-scale migration of poor nonwhites to the cities, coupled with the flight of more affluent whites to the suburbs, transformed urban life. Tax revenues, the lifeblood of a healthy metropolis, drained away, and signs of urban decay appeared everywhere. Sanitation facilities deteriorated, landlords moved out of the neighborhood, and housing became run-down. Hostility developed between largely white police forces and nonwhite citizens. Despite some efforts at reform, city schools especially suffered. Many could barely provide a decent education for English-speaking children, much less deal with the large influx of pupils whose native tongue was not English.

Still, despite urban deterioration, the people who congregated in central-city ghettos were often better off than those who remained on the farm. During the 1950s great agribusiness combinations mechanized operations and engulfed more land. By 1954, 12 percent of the farm operators made nearly 60 percent of total agricultural sales, and this imbalance grew. Unemployment accompanied this agricultural revolution; severe rural poverty became a major, if often unnoticed, problem. Young people often escaped. Throughout the rural Midwest in the 1950s the young left their family farms for cities rather than trying to compete with large agricultural enterprises. A million and a half people left unproductive patches of land in Appalachia. The many old people who remained on the land were the least able to cope with mechanization and changing markets. Whether a person was a black tenant farmer in Georgia, an Indian on an isolated reservation, a white farmer in the hills of Appalachia, or a Mexican-American migrant worker, poverty was an oppressive reality of rural life, and there seemed little hope of escape.

America remained polarized into two cultures: one of increasing affluence and one of persisting poverty. While the medium of television made middle-class comforts highly visible to the poor, poverty and degradation grew more invisible to the affluent. Suburbanites in fast-moving automobiles skirted the slums and rarely penetrated the pockets of rural poverty. A gap grew between the aspirations of the lower sectors and the social consciousness of the affluent. Bitterness mounted in the central city as complacency spread through the suburbs.

Urban Problems

Although the term *urban crisis* did not become a cliché until the 1960s, people who studied urban life recognized severe tensions and strains during the 1950s. Signs of tremendous growth and some examples of positive change, however, helped mask many uncomfortable facts about American cities. Construction of new office buildings and highways, reduction of the number of substandard housing units, and a decrease in population density gave liberals some hope that conditions were improving. In addition, the diversity of urban life in the United States allowed people to cite vastly different information about "the American city." Obviously, problems such as pollution, racial conflict, and crime varied from city to city. But local discomforts increasingly appeared to be variations on a general trend. By 1960 almost every city confronted serious problems that seemed beyond the capacity of established urban institutions.

Most cities were paying the price for more than a century of largely uncontrolled development. Even after the advent of planning and zoning commissions during the early twentieth century, the private decisions of businessmen exerted the greatest influence on the direction and pace of urban change. The needs of business enterprises largely determined what land would be used, how it would be changed, and what groups would pay the highest social costs. All cities faced another problem with a long history. Unlike Europeans, with their long tradition of city living, many Americans continued to view urban life as less natural or virtuous than rural and small-town living. The persistence of this antiurban bias created a curious situation: people moved toward cities to find the economic opportunities located there, while feeling that urban life was not really what they wanted for themselves or their children. (This feeling was not limited to affluent whites: many black and Spanish-speaking parents also feared, with more reason than whites, that urban life might harm their children.)

Whatever their apprehensions about the quality of inner-city life, people still flocked toward urban areas after World War II in search of greater economic rewards. As a result, the urban population grew tremendously during the late 1940s and throughout the 1950s. Sprawling across the landscape, urban areas became more segmented than ever before. After studying cities along the eastern seaboard during the 1950s, a French geographer called this new social organization the "megalopolis." "We must abandon the idea of the city as a tightly settled and organized unit in which people, activities, and riches are crowded into a very small area clearly separate from its nonurban surroundings," wrote Jean Gottman. A city would spread out "far and wide around its original nucleus" until it melted into the suburban neighborhoods of other cities.

Many people blamed this geographical expansion for many of the failures of the modern American city. Larger urban areas made efficient centralized administration difficult, and any decentralized arrangement left less affluent areas saddled with poor schools, inadequate social services, and too little money to solve their problems. Many sociologists also argued that urban sprawl exacerbated people's sense of isolation and contributed to their feeling of being transients rather than part of a community. As long as more affluent urbanites could hope to escape to suburbia, they would hesitate to commit themselves or their tax dollars to projects that aimed at long-range solutions to urban problems.

Ironically, many attempts to meet urban needs seemed only to accelerate fragmentation and a sense of hopelessness. Significant federal aid for construction of low-cost housing rarely reached central cities during the 1950s. Even the modest goal of 810,000 public-housing units by 1955, the target of the Housing Act of 1949, was not achieved until the end of the 1960s. In fact, the Housing Act provided authority for another program—urban renewal—that actually reduced the number of dwellings available to poor people. In theory, urban renewal allowed local governments to obtain federal funds to clear out old and dilapidated buildings and to replace them with new public-housing units or with other projects, including almost anything from new cultural complexes to concrete parking garages. In practice, however, the Eisenhower administration began to permit urban planners and private developers to evade the responsibility of replacing or increasing the supply of living units. Increasingly, urban renewal concentrated upon construction of nonresident facilities. Many people profited from this: building contractors and construction workers enjoyed steadily rising incomes; the more affluent could find a greater variety of cultural and recreational facilities; and city officials gained new sources of tax revenue. But too many poor people, the intended beneficiaries of federal largess, ended up the big losers. In many cities poorer citizens watched their homes bulldozed into rubble and their neighborhoods transformed into business complexes or even into apartment buildings for middle- and upper-income people.

At the same time, creation of a vast network of multilane expressways also brought paradoxical changes to urban life. The new freeways allowed people to travel to work in the privacy of their automobiles rather than on public transportation and enabled those with enough money to live even further from decaying urban centers. In addition to accelerating uncontrolled urban sprawl, the freeways created other problems. The new concrete conveyers contributed to the decay of existing mass-transit facilities and worked against creation of any new ones. The stream of cars creeping to and from the central cities every day also increased air pollution without noticeably speeding the pace of urban transportation. Finally, the new expressways destroyed even more old buildings and further contributed to the fragmentation of urban life.

Despite the national government's ambivalent record in dealing with urban problems, its greater resources required federal officials to take more and more responsibility for the problems of the city. During the presidential campaign of 1960 both Richard Nixon and John Kennedy pledged their support for creation of a new cabinet-level office to coordinate federal assistance to urban areas.

In many ways, then, the ambiguous trends in urban life symbolized the larger ambiguities of the 1950s. Liberals, to be sure, could point to real economic gains and a few genuine victories over social problems. Yet the decade was also marked by clear losses and some outright retreats. Affluence and a sense of affability did characterize the lives of the majority of people, but even many of these Americans found that the supposedly placid 1950s also brought disturbing cultural and social changes, including significant shifts in population and a new spirit of unrest among young people. And despite Dwight Eisenhower's desire that the national welfare state not expand, the old liberal-Democratic approach retained its appeal. There was still strong support, among voters as well as among the problem-solving elites, for greater involvement by the federal government in urban problems as well as in other areas of American life. Recognizing the existence of this support, one of John Kennedy's advisers implicitly dismissed the 1950s when he coined one of JFK's most popular campaign slogans for the 1960s: "Let's get this country moving again." The phrase would, of course, come back to haunt the Fair Deal – New Frontier liberals when the nation began moving in directions that liberals could neither foresee nor ever really control. By the end of the 1960s more than a few people would look back at the 1950s with a touch of nostalgia.

SUGGESTIONS FOR FURTHER READING

There are several good introductions to the Eisenhower presidency: Herbert S. Parmet, *Eisenhower and the American Crusades* (1972); Charles C. Alexander, *Holding the Line* (1975); Peter Lyon, *Eisenhower: Portrait of the Hero* (1974); and Elmo Richardson, *The Presidency of Dwight Eisenhower* (1979). See also Ike's own memoirs, *Mandate for Change, 1953 – 1956* (1963) and *Waging Peace, 1956 – 1961* (1965); Emmet John Hughes, *The Ordeal of Power* (1963);

and Arthur Larson, *The President Nobody Knew* (1968). Richard Nixon discusses his role in *Six Crises* (1962) and in *RN: The Memoirs of Richard Nixon* (1978). A few specialized studies have also appeared, including David Frier, *Conflict of Interest in the Eisenhower Administration* (1969); Gary Reichard, *The Reaffirmation of Republicanism: Eisenhower and the Eighty-Third Congress* (1975); Burton Kaufman, *The Oil Cartel Case: A Documentary Study of Anti-Trust Activity in the Cold War Era* (1978); and Mark Rose, *Interstate: Express Highway Politics, 1941 – 1956* (1979).

Douglas T. Miller and Marion Nowak offer a general introduction to the Eisenhower era in *The Fifties: The Way We Really Were* (1977). Four influential writers who addressed themselves to the quality of American life in the 1950s were John Kenneth Galbraith, *The Affluent Society* (1952); David Riesman, *The Lonely Crowd* (1950); C. Wright Mills, *White Collar* (1951) and *The Power Elite* (1956); and William H. Whyte, *The Organization Man* (1956). Michael Harrington's *The Other America* (1962) remains a revealing analysis of the "new poverty" that persisted in the midst of the "affluent" 1950s.

Popular culture is best approached through the various brief articles that have appeared in *The Journal of Popular Culture*. The debate over the nature of popular culture can be recaptured in two volumes edited by Bernard Rosenberg and David Manning White, *Mass Culture* (1957) and *Mass Culture Revisited* (1971). For later evaluations of popular culture, see Herbert Gans, *Popular Culture and High Culture* (1975) and Michael Real, *Mass-Mediated Culture* (1977). Among the best books on the film industry are Robert Sklar, *Movie-Made America* (1975); Jim Kitses, *Horizons West* (1969); and Michael Wood, *America in the Movies* (1975). See also Andrew Dowdy, *The Films of the Fifties* (1973) and Brandon French, *On the Verge of Revolt* (1978). The early days of rock-and-roll are analyzed in Charlie Gillett, *The Sound of the City* (1972); Carl Belz, *The Story of Rock* (2nd. ed., 1972); and David Pichaske, *A Generation in Motion* (1979). See also Greil Marcus, *Mystery Train* (1976), particularly his chapter on Elvis Presley. The standard histories of television are by Erik Barrouw: *Tube of Plenty* (1977) and *The Sponsor* (1979).

The relevant chapters of Morris Janowitz, *The Last Half-Century: Societal Change and Politics in America* (1978) and Richard Polenberg, *One Nation Divisible: Class, Race, and Ethnicity in the United States Since 1938* (1980) provide a good introduction to the social trends of the 1950s. On the place of women, see the final chapters of Carl N. Degler, *At Odds: Women and the Family in America from the Revolution to the Present* (1980) and the relevant portions of William Chafe, *The American Woman* (1972) and of Peter Filene, *Him/Her/Self* (1975). See also Betty Friedan's *The Feminine Mystique* (1963) and Benjamin Spock, *Baby and Child Care* (1946). Richard Easterlin, *The Baby Boom in Historical Perspective* (1962) remains useful, and Harrison Salisbury's *The Shook-Up Generation* (1958) is an interesting period piece. In addition to Polenberg's study, see the older work by Nathan Glazer and Daniel P. Moynihan, *Beyond the Melting Pot* (1963) for an introduction to racial and ethnic tensions. Specific works include John R. Howard, ed., *The Awakening Minorities* (1970); Manuel P. Servín, *An Awakened Minority: The Mexican-Americans* (2nd. ed., 1974); Dorothy K. Newman et al., *Protest, Politics and Prosperity: Black Americans and White Institutions, 1940 – 75* (1978); The History Task Force Centro de Estudios Puertorriquenos, *Labor Migration Under Capitalism: The Puerto Rican Experience* (1979); Roberto E. Villarreal, *Chicano Elites and Non-Elites* (1979); Alfredo Mirandé, *La Chicana: The Mexican-American Woman* (1979); and Maria Herrera-Sobek, *The Bracero Experience* (1979).

The new relationship between the national government and the nation's cities is treated in Mark Gelfand's *A Nation of Cities* (1975). The highly critical view of suburbia evident in Malvina Reynolds's song "Little Boxes [Made of Ticky-Tacky]" was softened in works such as Herbert Gans, *The Levittowners* (1967) and Scott Donaldson, *The Suburban Myth* (1969). These works have themselves come under scrutiny. See, for example, Samuel Kaplan, *The Dream Deferred* (1976) and Barry Schwartz, ed., *The Changing Face of the Suburbs* (1976). See also Edward Wynne, *Growing Up Suburban* (1977). The car culture of the 1950s is discussed in Tom Wolfe, *The Kandy-Kolored Tangerine-Flake Streamline Baby* (1965) and John B. Rae, *The Road and the Car in American Life* (1971).

PROTECTOR OF THE FREE WORLD

Republican Foreign Policy

Eisenhower and Dulles

President Eisenhower and his secretary of state, John Foster Dulles, contrasted with their flamboyant, controversial predecessors. For years Eisenhower had reconciled diverse opinions into consensus, first as commander of the world's greatest amphibious invasion, the D-Day attack against occupied France, then as president of Columbia University, and from 1948 to 1952 as leader of NATO's vast military apparatus in Europe. Eisenhower harbored no ambitions to be an aggressive president in either domestic or foreign affairs, and he championed conservative economic principles. Aware of the potential for waste, he scrutinized defense expenditures carefully. Congress and the American public placed great confidence in this general who vowed to "wage peace."

John Foster Dulles, the austere corporation lawyer who helped to chart Eisenhower's foreign policy during the 1950s, had the mien of his Presbyterian ancestors. His long face, punctuated by a thin nose and round, wire-rimmed eyeglasses, almost personified the Calvinist ethos. A sense of orderliness, rooted in the certainty of faith, pervaded his ambitions. Containment of communism, a reactive, static policy, grated against his penchant for "getting the job done." He stridently called for a psychological and political offensive against communism, presumably on behalf of "the captive nations of Eastern Europe," extending the position of the 1952 Republican platform that condemned Truman's tactics as "negative, futile, and immoral." Though extravagant rhetoric could not substitute for positive policy, it did make it difficult for right wing Republican senators such as William Knowland, who dreamed of "unleashing" Chiang Kai-shek against Asian communism, to claim that the new administration was not committed to an anti-communist crusade. Dulles never supported preventive wars, but he did sharpen Soviet-American rivalry. Famous for his willingness, at least during press conferences, to risk war in the pursuit of national objectives, Dulles converted diplomacy into apocalyptic posturing. Though Eisenhower discounted the rhetoric of brinksmanship and probably never considered nuclear war a feasible option, his secretary of state broadened containment into an uncompromising, worldwide crusade to determine the pace and nature of change. He saw himself, one biographer wrote, "as the chess master of the free world, daily engaged in a mortal contest against a monolithic adversary."

The New Look

The Republicans had to adjust their philosophies to the realities of a volatile world and to President Eisenhower's desire to balance the federal budget. A cost-conscious president, a messianic secretary of state, and Pentagon generals recast America's strategic doctrines, relying primarily upon the deterrent of massive retaliation. Modern technology could increase American military power while reducing its cost: Secretary of Defense Charles Wilson quipped that nuclear weaponry provided "more bang for the buck." Doomsday bombs, together with sophisticated delivery systems, could protect the United States from attack, since no nation would risk "second-strike" reprisal.

Determined to stake out the boundaries of the "free world" as broadly as possible, Dulles also dramatically expanded the nation's collective-security arrangements. He spent months traveling around the world, signing up allies. A succession of bilateral defense pacts with Taiwan, Korea, and Japan extended America's nuclear umbrella to the shores of China. Even more grandiose schemes shored up Britain's weakness "east of Suez." The Southeast Asia Treaty Organization (SEATO) in 1954 linked Australia, the Philippines, Thailand, and Pakistan with the United States, Britain, and France. The next year Washington sponsored England's Central Treaty Organization (CENTO) with Turkey, Iraq, Iran, and Pakistan. Turkey tied CENTO with NATO; Pakistan connected SEATO with CENTO. Each of these multilateral covenants pledged that an attack against one member, either by overt aggression or, as Dulles put it, "by internal subversion," would bring all into consultation to decide common action. Eisenhower, already skeptical about the military value of large American army reserves, thought that native forces, financed from Washington and linked to a network of alliances controlled by the United States, could contain regional threats and prevent them from escalating into nuclear cataclysm. Although designed to decrease America's obligations, regional pacts could also increase them by involving the United States in local disputes outside the range of its national interests.

Most troubling of all, the New Look policy of the Republicans postulated a communist world of monolithic unchangeability and necessary hostility. The New Look stressed atomic weaponry, but it brought other tools into what Republicans viewed as a global struggle between good and evil: an increase in overseas bases, a larger commitment to foreign military aid, and an active covert program, run by the CIA, to subvert unfriendly governments and even plan assassinations. More and more, the United States' "defense" posture against communism looked like a global offensive.

In Korea, armistice negotiations with the North Koreans and the Chinese had broken down in October 1952, largely because of a complicated impasse over the issue of prisoners of war. The communists demanded that the usual international practice of returning all POWs to their homeland be observed. The United States, however, insisted upon voluntary repatriation. Since most enemy soldiers wanted to stay in South Korea, this formula meant that the South would gain, and the North would lose, an army of as many as 40,000 trained men. Stalemate also continued on the battlefield.

True to his campaign promise, Eisenhower toured the front in November 1952 and then, with Dulles, orchestrated an exercise in New Look diplomacy, which was puncuated by threats and more fighting between the two sides. Armistice talks were resumed in April 1953, after Eisenhower pointedly mentioned retaliation, perhaps with Chiang Kai-shek's aid. (Nationalist bombers did begin peppering the Chinese mainland.) But negotiations broke down almost immediately, again over the POW issue. The president then wired General Mark Clark, the United Nations commander, that the United States might "carry on the war in new ways never yet tried" if the communists remained intransigent. Dulles was more specific: America might drop atomic bombs.

The appeal to apocalypse worked. Within two weeks both sides had initialed armistice terms: Korea would stay divided, as before the war, into a communist North and a pro-West South. Neutral powers were to tackle POW repatriation (an issue eventually settled according to the voluntary formula). However, the South Korean president, Syngman Rhee, certain that only a complete victory could counter leftist discontent with his increasingly dictatorial regime, aborted this compromise: he prematurely released over 27,000 communist POWs, who immediately disappeared into the population of the South. In response, China attacked along much of the front, apparently to demonstrate that it could maintain a balance of power on the peninsula regardless of what South Korea did. Yet neither side wanted the war to continue, and Rhee's action alienated many in Washington. Dulles bluntly ordered him to sign the armistice "or else." So, on July 27, 1953, a truce—not a peace treaty—ended a war that had killed over two million Asians, mostly civilians, and 33,000 Americans.

Superpower Diplomacy

The Bogey Fades: The Soviet Union

New Look calculations about the Soviet Union were predicated on the notions of an international communist conspiracy against American interests and of Stalin's rigid police state. During the 1950s both notions seemed increasingly out of touch with reality. On March 5, 1953, the Soviet dictator died, and his tyranny partially withered. Stalin's theories had proved wrong: world war had revived liberal capitalism, not doomed it. The troika that replaced Stalin—Foreign Minister Vyacheslav Molotov, Defense Minister Nikolai Bulganin, and Nikita Khrushchev, first secretary of the Communist party—went along with Premier Georgi Malenkov's plan to ease tensions with the United States. But internal rivalries soon complicated Soviet diplomacy. Traditionalists such as Bulganin wanted to continue Stalin's defensive priorities and his domestic emphasis upon heavy industry. In contrast, Khrushchev argued for a more flexible approach. Detente with the United States would slow the arms race and permit a higher standard of living in Russia. At the same time, Khrushchev advocated vigorous policies designed to expand Soviet influence in the third world and perhaps break down Dulles's ring of alliances. The clash between expansionism and detente did not much bother the first secretary, who relied on the deterrent of nuclear war to insure American patience. Within three years Khrushchev had triumphed over the others, largely because the Soviet people, tired of fear and poverty, enthusiastically responded to his promises of "peaceful coexistence" and more consumer goods. After Khrushchev denounced Stalin's "Gestapo tactics" in 1956, Russians dreamed of less regimentation, less sacrifice.

This new direction in Soviet policy not only substituted competition for confrontation but also reduced the dangers of massive retaliation. The Soviet Union reduced its armed forces from four million to less than three million men by the mid 1950s. Though primarily an effort to shift economic priorities toward consumer industries, the unilateral gesture did seem to contradict Dulles' hardline premises. It also calmed European fears of a red tide. A change of tactics in the third world brought the Soviets into alliance with anticolonial movements. The Soviets argued that the Russian Revolution was more relevant than the American to the twentieth-century problems of industrialization, and they pushed their model of development, hoping to reap geopolitical advantages from having friends in the third world.

Eisenhower's "Summitry"

While Dulles indulged his preconceptions about the communist menace, Eisenhower turned to new men and different techniques. Working outside the State Department, the president and White House advisers such as C. D. Jackson and Nelson Rockefeller aimed to refashion America's relationship with the Soviet Union, perhaps by easing the nuclear-arms race. During the halcyon months of the Russian thaw, English leaders had urged a conference of heads of state to settle European problems, particularly German reunification. The idea of a summit meeting intrigued Eisenhower, despite Dulles's pessimistic admonitions. Summitry offered not only an alternative to grim crusades but also a new forum for long-stalled disarmament negotiations.

In July 1955 the president traveled to Geneva, where he met with his counterparts among the Big Four: Premier Bulganin and First Secretary Khrushchev, Prime Minister Anthony Eden of Britain, and Premier Edgar Faure of France. The drama of face-to-face sessions obscured otherwise desultory talks about Germany's future and East-West cultural exchanges. Then Eisenhower submitted a unique plan for disarmament. The United States and the Soviet Union would exchange blueprints of all military installations and permit reconnaissance flights over each other's territory. Surprise attacks would become impossible, and each power could assess the other's true intent. The brief summit conference could by itself neither resolve the enormous complexities involved nor convince military leaders in both countries who vigorously opposed the idea. But the "open skies" proposal did counteract recent Soviet propaganda gains and, more important, inaugurated "the spirit of Geneva." Many people sensed that something better than mutual terror and animosity might be possible.

Yet the president's dramatic overture achieved nothing permanent. Later that fall, at a meeting among the Big Four foreign ministers, the Russians gently sidetracked open skies. No one wanted to reunite Germany. Such a change would only upset the European balance of power so painfully achieved during the Stalin-Truman years. Would a united Germany, for example, stay in NATO or leave it? Germans themselves, particularly in the Rhineland and Bavaria, did not want to bear the cost of rebuilding the eastern zones, heavily looted by the Soviets. But even if Eisenhower's efforts solved no problems, Russians and Americans began to see each other as something more than the mirror of their own suspicions. Leaders in the two blocs moderated their intractable rhetoric, and after 1955 culture exchanges eased popular misconceptions. The gains, though small, seemed worthwhile.

The late 1950s became a strange interlude in Soviet-American relations, halfway between cold war and unsteady peace. Both Eisenhower and Khrushchev fashioned innovative proposals for slowing the nuclear-arms race and embarked upon personal diplomacy.

The threat of a nuclear holocaust and the dangers of radioactive fallout from atomic tests frightened many leaders into greater efforts on behalf of arms control. In mid-1958 the Russians unilaterally suspended nuclear testing, presumably to probe American intentions while converting more of their economy to consumer production. Britain and the United States followed later that year, finally responding to growing evidence that atmospheric tests represented a severe health hazard. In the fall of 1958 Khrushchev visited the United States for twelve days. He addressed the United Nations, talked to Iowa farmers, and watched Hollywood stars make a movie. Then premier and president conferred privately at Camp David, a mountain retreat in Maryland. Though achieving nothing concrete, the "spirit of Camp David" moderated the rhetoric of rancor in both countries. At the same time, their leaders embarked upon much-publicized goodwill trips. Eisenhower went to Europe, the Middle East, Latin America, and the Far East, though anti-American riots protesting a bilateral defense treaty forced him to cancel a trip to Japan. Khrushchev appeared in Western Europe, Afghanistan, and India.

But goodwill tours could not erase old problems. Early in November 1958 Khrushchev once again revived unresolved issues regarding Germany. The four-power occupation of Berlin, he announced, must end. Although the enclave could not threaten the Soviet bloc, the showpiece city embarrassed the Russians. Its black market in Western currencies upset financial planning in Eastern Europe. Then, too, Khrushchev wanted to test Eisenhower. Easy concessions could check domestic critics unhappy with the premier's conciliatory approach toward the United States. So the Soviet leader demanded a "satisfactory settlement" within six months; otherwise, he would sign a separate peace with East Germany. The West had no legal claims to the city; its right of access depended upon communist consent, not treaties. Tensions soared, but Khrushchev's bluff failed. The deadline expired quietly only weeks before the premier's visit to the United States.

A more bizarre incident occurred during Eisenhower's last year as president. In early 1959 Khrushchev called for another summit meeting, this time in Paris, perhaps to exchange Berlin for an understanding in the Middle East. The dilemma of German reunification still haunted diplomats, and the paradoxes of nuclear armament apparently required personal solution. Preliminary talks made little progress, however, and on May 1, 1960, the Soviets shot down an American U-2 spy plane over their territory. Each power used the U-2 affair to box the opponent into a diplomatic corner. Khrushchev could have muffled the incident, but instead he trumpeted Russia's injured innocence, demanding an apology and an end to such spy flights. Determined to score as many propaganda points as possible, the premier traveled to Paris, but his diatribes soon angered Eisenhower. After all, the U-2 flights demonstrated that American technology could police any nuclear agreement. Was Khrushchev now trying to back out of serious disarmament talks? Or had he simply lured everyone to Paris not to negotiate but to embarrass the West? Skeptical of Russian good faith, Eisenhower ignored Anglo-French efforts to rescue the summit.

The U-2 incident was a curious epitaph to the oscillating course of Soviet-American relations. Both powers pursued national advantage, at times almost recklessly, but the terrors of nuclear war restrained any ultimate threat. Their rivalry brought neither peace nor war.

Superpower Challenges

Even as Soviet-American tensions eased, discontent fractured the unity of both power blocs. The New Look, based upon America's strategic superiority, communist hostility, and a more efficient globalism, inspired resentment against American dominance. Russia's thaw spread throughout its Eastern European empire, creating unrest—even outright rebellion. The Soviet Union and the United States still sought diplomatic advantage, but without the certainty of subservience. Aligned nations in both blocs rejected crucial parts of their overlords' prescriptions for the future.

The Troubled Alliance

Of all its criss-crossed security pacts, America's alliance with Western Europe was the oldest and strongest. A common heritage and economic ties bound these nations into an Atlantic community. Washington had strongly urged an integrated NATO force armed with conventional weapons. A joint effort would force Europe to finance a larger portion of its defense, increase pressure against the Soviet Union, and rope German power into a regional enterprise. By 1953 Dulles had masterminded the creation of a European Defense Community (EDC), but many Europeans, particularly the French, opposed its transnational approach and its lack of nuclear weapons. In response, Dulles ruminated at a press conference about "an agonizing reappraisal" of America's relations with Europe if EDC foundered.

Dulles's tactics only angered politicians in France and England, who asserted national defense to be the province of their own parliaments, not of foreign statesmen. Specialization—an American nuclear force paired with conventional European armies—would continue Europe's second-class status in the NATO alliance. Would the United States risk nuclear war, and thus its own destruction, to save Western Europe? Conversely, might not Washington and Moscow pull back from direct superpower confrontation after mushroom clouds rose over Paris and, say, Warsaw? When the French National Assembly finally refused to ratify the EDC treaty on August 30, 1954, most Europeans happily approved. Britain and France accelerated their own plans for nuclear rearmament.

More than debates about nuclear warfare fueled Europe's restiveness. By the late 1950s, returning prosperity had repaired Hitler's destruction. Many Europeans, and even Americans, believed that European economic integration would accelerate this revival and discourage Soviet adventures. France, Germany, Italy, Belgium, the Netherlands, and Luxembourg pooled steel and coal production in 1952. The Common Market treaties, signed five years later at Rome, pledged to end barriers to the movement of commerce, capital, and workers among the "Inner Six." Uniform external tariffs gave the Common Market enormous bargaining advantages with other nations. This trend toward economic unity excited the people of Germany and Italy so much that their leaders depended upon its progress to remain in office. The situation in France differed dramatically. Nearly self-sufficient economically, the country's popular president, Charles de Gaulle, could ignore integration. Under French leadership, he believed, Europe should escape the confines of a bipolar world. De Gaulle saw the Common Market as the vehicle for French glory. Clearly, difficult adjustments had to be made among the Atlantic nations in the 1960s, not only between Europe and America but also within Europe itself.

The Suez Crisis

Nowhere were superpower hopes for mastery wrecked more consistently than in the Middle East. Nationalism and charismatic leaders, not economic theories or political systems, defined the contours of change there. In Egypt, for example, military leaders destroyed King Farouk's corrupt monarchy in a 1952 coup, intending to modernize the country and escape Britain's economic domination. Two years later a "colonels' revolt" gave Gamal Abdel Nasser near dictatorial power. The new president dreamed of making Egypt the chief military power in the Middle East so that he could lead Arab nationalism. Popular resentment at Israeli statehood and English control over much of the Middle East's political life encouraged rearmament programs; "positive neutralism" garnered money and technological aid from both East and West. Nasser's successes soon enraptured Arabs but alienated Britain and frightened Israel. Then, after an Israeli raid into Egypt's Gaza Strip, Nasser signed an agreement to buy advanced weapons from Czechoslovakia. Angry with this threat to the Western-dominated status quo, Dulles withdrew American support for loans for the construction of Egypt's Aswan Dam, a huge project that would improve harvests along the Nile River and provide hydroelectric power for Egypt's developing industries. Nasser then seized the Suez Canal on July 25, assuming that its duties could finance the dam's construction.

Britain, France, and Israel resolved to act. Israelis saw the Suez crisis as a pretext for preventive war; Europeans hoped to destroy Arab nationalism in the Middle East. French premier Guy Mollet also reckoned that a militant response would shore up his foundering coalition in the French Assembly. Then too, a blow at Nasser would discourage Arab rebels in Algeria, where France was attempting to suppress an anticolonial guerrilla movement. Meanwhile, the British had created their own domino theory: Nasser was a Hitlerian figure who, if unopposed, would unite the Arab world and confiscate Britain's most valuable investments. When Eisenhower cleverly ducked the Suez crisis during his 1956 presidential campaign, the British Foreign Office chose to interpret his obscure statements as a negative endorsement of their intervention in the Middle East. The United States, they thought, could not abandon its closest ally once military operations began. On October 29 Israel attacked Egypt, and several days later Anglo-French forces retook the Suez Canal.

The war ended quickly, partly because Egypt's armies proved surprisingly inept, but largely because of superpower reactions. The United States angrily reasserted its leadership of the Atlantic community. Opposed to "any aggression by any nation," Eisenhower threatened to support cutting oil shipments to the invaders and to destroy the English pound by opposing renewal of British loans from the International Monetary Fund. Unencumbered by alliances with former colonial powers, the Russians condemned Britain and France more forcefully and even hinted at a nuclear strike. Mollet and British prime minister Eden could only acquiesce in a Canadian-American plan for United Nations troops to police the Sinai Peninsula.

The affair severely damaged America's prestige in most parts of the world. Egyptians did not forget that the "American peace" had stationed foreign soldiers in their country but not in Israel, the aggressor. The Suez crisis ensconced Russia in Egyptian affairs, especially after the Soviets took over financing the Aswan Dam, and insured Nasser's leadership of the Arab world. Neither prospect pleased Dulles. Washington's criticism had also alienated the Europeans. Franco-American relations never quite recovered. Suez convinced most Frenchmen that Washington had sacrificed their national interest; Europe must now chart a new course. The British were stunned. Unwilling to give up their "special relationship" with the United States, English leaders did not know what to do. England increasingly abandoned its former world role to pursue regional interests related to European integration.

Hungary

Strains within the Western alliance during the Suez crisis coincided with a similar emergency within the Soviet bloc. After the war Stalin had backed pro-Soviet regimes throughout Eastern Europe. These "satellites" embarked upon industrial programs designed to complement Soviet reconstruction. Never content with Stalinist tactics and the distortion of national economic needs, some Eastern Europeans challenged these local regimes once the Russian thaw began. Yet how much liberalization would Moscow's new rulers allow? In June 1956 over 15,000 factory workers rioted at Poznan in Poland. Their three-day rebellion set off a popular upsurge in support of Wladyslaw Gomulka, a former minister removed by Stalin when he publicly opposed collectivization and advocated national development regardless of Russian orders. After complicated maneuvers with Poland's old guard and Moscow's politburo, revisionists forced Moscow to accept the unorthodox Gomulka. Events had caught Soviet leaders off guard, but their recognition of Gomulka seemed to indicate the feasibility of economic reform that did not threaten the integrity of the Soviet bloc.

Misunderstanding this subtlety, Hungarians reached for true political independence a few months later. Emboldened by Poland's success and by its own suffering from the same Stalinist exploitation, a huge mob demonstrated on October 23. Students and workers, intellectuals and housewives paraded for hours, demanding the return of Imre Nagy, like Gomulka a former minister disgraced for his liberal views. Nagy formed a new government, but strikes and unrest continued. Protests against subservience to the Soviet Union turned into armed rebellion in the countryside and within days paralyzed the capital as well. Misled by broadcasts from America's CIA-financed Radio Free Europe, the revolutionaries hoped for United States assistance. Nagy pledged free elections and a multi-party system "No nation," he declared, "can intervene in our internal affairs." Although Moscow tried to negotiate, the lure of independence and Dulles' talk of "liberating captive peoples" betrayed the Hungarians into tragic illusions. As violence continued, the Russians sent a huge army into Hungary. Moscow would not tolerate neutrality on its strategic borders. At the same time, however, the Kremlin learned that it could no longer assume passive subservience in Eastern Europe.

Frustrations in the Third World

The pretense of a bipolar world fell apart during the 1950s as superpowers lost more and more control over the course of world events. The focus of international affairs shifted toward Asia, Africa, and Latin America, where charismatic leaders often pursued economic self-determination and control over natural resources no less than political independence. Most nationalists in the third world thought disputes over ideology useless; results alone mattered. The third world took from both Russian and Yankee. If a country came to rely almost exclusively upon one or the other superpower, two alternatives loomed: the giant power might become dangerously involved in purely local issues or disputes in the third world among surrogates could exacerbate tensions between their sponsors. Within the third world, both neutrality and alignment required delicate balancing.

Vietnam

America's most perplexing involvement in third-world politics came in Southeast Asia. Financed largely by Washington, French armies had struggled against the nationalist leader Ho Chi Minh for control of Vietnam since 1945. The French had systematically destroyed much of Vietnamese culture in their eighty-year occupation. Ripped from their villages to work on vast plantations or to serve in colonial bureaucracies, many natives had lost both the will and the means to resist. But Japan's initial victory in 1940 discredited France and galvanized a coterie of nationalist intellectuals into a movement for postwar independence. Ho, an able Marxist scholar dedicated to spreading the class struggle to his country of peasants, assumed leadership of the Viet Minh, a popular front of all revolutionary parties. As Japanese power collapsed at the end of World War II, Ho declared Vietnam's independence (on September 2, 1945). Although his provisional government wanted to negotiate, France almost immediately launched a war of reconquest. Ho and an exceptionally skillful general, Vo Nguyen Giap, countered with guerrilla tactics, seeking to avoid defeat in the field while winning the people over to their nationalist-communist cause.

After nearly nine years and a frustrating succession of French generals, the rebels apparently abandoned their war of stealth and psychology. In early 1954 Giap sent his main force into Laos, resorting to conventional tactics to conquer territory and lure the French away from their coastal supply depots. General Henri Navarre quickly followed. Anxious to provoke the communists into a major assault, he concentrated 25,000 men at a frontier outpost, Dien Bien Phu. Giap surrounded the fort, and the battle became one of attrition. A constant artillery barrage cut off Navarre's reinforcements. Using a complicated system of tunnels and munitions backpacked into the mountains by thousands of peasants, the communists began a slow advance. As the French public watched the sure strangulation of its army, the government under Pierre Mendes-France pledged to end the war, even if that meant leaving Vietnam to nationalist-communists under Ho Chi Minh. The French prepared for a peace conference in Geneva.

Shocked that yet another area might "go communist," Dulles and some Pentagon figures—notably Admiral Arthur W. Radford, chairman of the Joint Chiefs of Staff—proposed an air strike against Giap's army. Some even speculated that American troops could revitalize the French war effort.

Eisenhower did not want to "lose" Indochina so soon after the Chinese debacle, but he was aware of America's limited power in so remote a place and worried about the federal budget. Typically, the president turned to Congress. Its leaders refused to authorize intervention unless the United States first secured foreign support, and Britain quickly refused. After the army outlined cost and manpower estimates, Eisenhower concluded that intervention was impossible. Chief of Staff Matthew Ridgway predicted that a million men, huge draft quotas, and enormous construction might win this political-guerrilla war, but he thought that even then most Vietnamese would still likely support the Viet Minh.

Meanwhile, peace negotiations at the Geneva Conference had reached an odd *demarche*. France wished only to get out of the war. The Russians, afraid of aggravating Washington, and the Chinese, searching for international legitimacy, urged Ho Chi Minh's Hanoi-based communists to accept a compromise. Paris granted Vietnam, Laos, and Cambodia full independence, though none of the new states could join foreign alliances or permit foreign soldiers on its soil. French troops were to regroup in Vietnam south of the seventeeth parallel, communist forces north of it. A nationwide election during 1956 would provide a single government for the reunified country. This solution—a graceful exit for the defeated French and a neutralized Indochina in exchange for a probably communist cabinet for Vietnam—gratified almost everyone concerned.

Everyone, that is, except John Foster Dulles and his followers. He saw a way to "save" at least some of Indochina, though it required unilateral action. The secretary refused to sign the Geneva accords and announced instead that the United States considered North and South Vietnam two separate entities. The State Department hurriedly completed plans for SEATO and gratuitously extended its coverage to South Vietnam, Cambodia, and Laos. After Bao Dai, the legitimate Vietnamese emperor who had served the French, stepped down in 1955, the Eisenhower administration pledged vast amounts of economic aid to his pro-Western successor, Ngo Dinh Diem. Diem, with American backing, called off the scheduled national elections in which a communist victory appeared certain. The Republican administration updated an old doctrine, long applied to Europe, to justify these expedient maneuvers: the domino theory. If South Vietnam "fell," Thailand would be next; then the rest of Indochina, and perhaps even India or Australia. If the West stood firm now, as Britain and France should have stood up to Hitler in 1939, communist subversion would fail. A democracy in Southeast Asia could serve conveniently as an example for the third world. But the connection between Washington and Saigon was so one-sided that Vietnam became more colony than sovereign state. Dependency reinforced the necessity for ever increasing United States intervention.

For six years after the Geneva conference ended the first Indochinese war, Republicans richly supplied South Vietnam's pro-West Premier Diem with economic aid, military know-how, and diplomatic protection. The results at first vindicated their gamble that a limited commitment might yield jackpot gains, not only in staving off another communist victory but also in building a capitalist model for the third world. Between 1954 and 1957 South Vietnam ended wartime economic controls, initiated reconstruction, and began industrial development. Diem redistributed land confiscated from French landlords to peasants in the Mekong River delta. His steadily improving army ended gangsterism in Saigon and forced allegiance from the semifeudal religious sects in the countryside. But Diem could never really centralize the nation, and his Catholicism alienated the predominately Buddhist population. To ensure at least the appearance of popular support, Diem replaced local officials with his stooges. A grandiloquent "population relocation" program degenerated into political purges. Land reform ultimately benefited a new kind of absentee owner, the Saigonese bureaucrat. Corruption diluted American aid, so that little of it helped villagers trapped in the war-ravaged countryside or refugees hounded into inflation-ridden cities. Smiling strangely, clad only in white, Diem retreated more and more into a contracting circle of family members and army generals. The regime's growing isolation and dependence upon the United States frightened nationalists.

To protest such abuses, an odd amalgam of anti-Diem intellectuals, nationalists, harassed politicans, and Viet Minh communists organized the National Liberation Front (NLF) in 1957. Its platform promised a return to village rule, immediate land ownership for the peasants, and a coalition cabinet in Saigon. Discontent in the countryside propelled many recruits into the NLF's makeshift army which communist cadres soon dominated, partly because of their experience during the earlier guerrilla struggle against France. The NLF represented the communal traditions of the village rather than the alien dictatorship in Saigon, which relied on Americans.

A communist-led war for national liberation set in motion a dangerous spiral of escalation. The renewal of serious fighting panicked Washington into supplying Diem with billions of dollars and a growing corps of American advisers—900 by 1960. In response, Hanoi aided the insurgents, training recruits in the North. Then, after a five-year plan had made their country the most heavily industrialized state in Southeast Asia by 1959, the North Vietnamese shipped large amounts of war materiel south along the Ho Chi Minh Trail. Although this primitive line of communications depended as much on human backs as on gasoline engines, it permitted the NLF to make great progress despite America's reinforcements. After all, a little guerrilla action went a long way against conventional armies. Raiders could strike anywhere, shielded behind popular resentments. Their opponents could only garrison the entire country. Thus, the cycle of Saigon corruption and communist rebellion led to American reinforcement and then to more aid from Hanoi.

Washington tried to break this chain by asking Diem to reform his regime. But the premier cared little about generating local popularity as long as he could rely upon Americans to support him. Despite American dissatisfaction with Diem, he seemed the only practical alternative to the NLF. The more isolated Diem became, the more American support he needed; yet the more aid he received, the more corrupt and unpopular he became. Americans began to experience, if only dimly to perceive, the frustration and the long-run dangers of building foreign alliances upon client relationships.

Partly because of larger problems elsewhere, the Republicans avoided final answers in their Vietnamese policy. The secretary of state blurted out during a press conference that "the free world would intervene in Indochina rather than let the situation deteriorate." Once involved, Dulles thought, America's prestige required victory. But the president demurred. A charter member of the Never-Again Club—a group of generals who, after their experiences in Korea, resolutely opposed another land war in Asia—Eisenhower flatly contradicted his chief adviser on foreign affairs. "I can conceive of no greater tragedy," he said, "than for the United States to become engaged in all-out war in Indochina."

Intervention: Iran, Guatemala, Lebanon, Cuba

Vietnam was only one riddle in America's relations with the third world. Disorders in the Middle East, like those in Southeast Asia, were related to the decline of European dominance and the rise of local nationalism. American economic interests in Iran had always been small; Britain held tightly to its petroleum monopoly in that oil-rich land. But in 1951 Iranian Prime Minister Mohammed Mossadegh nationalized Britain's Anglo-Iranian Oil Company. The State Department feared that the precedent of nationalization might ultimately affect America's own holdings in Saudi Arabia or elsewhere and thereby damage the "free world" economy. The CIA, which had previously received explicit orders to make the protection of American-owned supplies of raw materials one of its prime duties, went to work organizing and financing opposition to Mossadegh. Kermit Roosevelt, the grand-nephew of Theodore, orchestrated one of the CIA's most stunning "successes." In an operation costing probably three quarters of a million dollars, CIA agents brought crowds into the streets, forced Mossadegh out of office, and reinstalled their friend, the Shah. Under the terms of a renegotiated oil contract American companies came out holding 40 percent of the Iranian oil concession previously held by British Petroleum, and the Shah launched a "modernization" program closely wedded to American corporate interests.

Events in Iran enabled the major oil companies to convice the Eisenhower administration to drop a large antitrust suit against them. In 1953 Eisenhower told his attorney general that because the giant oil companies supplied an essential commodity to the "free world," the enforcement of antitrust laws "may be deemed secondary to the national security interest." Events in Iran thus proved timely for the American-dominated international oil cartel, a cartel that—in the days before OPEC—controlled the world price of oil.

Success in Iran encouraged the Eisenhower administration to expand its use of the CIA. Headed by John Foster Dulles' brother Allen, the CIA escalated the use of subversion as a tactic against foreign enemies. It became clear that Ike's New Look extended toward the Soviet Union but that in the third world covert action seemed the best substitute for outright military involvement. Guatemala loomed as the next test of what the CIA could accomplish with covert operations.

Guatemalan president Jacobo Arbenz, who had been legally elected on a reform platform, challenged United Fruit Company's longstanding dominance in his country by threatening to nationalize lands that the company had allowed to remain idle and unproductive. And, as in Iran, American business interests and government policymakers easily confused nationalistic reform with communism. Dulles, himself closely connected with the fruit company, saw Guatemala as one more battle in the global struggle to contain communism, and Eisenhower, who knew little about Latin America, probably believed Dulles' oversimplification and incorrectly perceived Arbenz as a communist. Ike authorized and the CIA carried out a covert operation that destroyed the Arbenz government and instituted a dictatorship friendly to the United States government and to United Fruit.

United States-backed repression, however, only aggravated social hatreds in Guatemala and elsewhere. During Richard Nixon's goodwill tour of Latin America in 1958, for example, thousands of Venezuelans mobbed the vice-president's car in Caracas, upsetting not only Cadillac limousines but also American illusions. Once again, Eisenhower reacted belatedly. He supported creation of the Inter-American Development Bank, and the State Department stopped awarding medals to dictator allies and shifted its praises to such liberal reformers as Venezuela's Rómulo Betancourt. But only the image changed. Price supports were ineffective, and judicious American military aid prevented all coups except those staged by approved anticommunists.

As another part of its efforts to contain communist influence, the Eisenhower administration tried to frame a general doctrine that would extend American protection into the Middle East, a region still reeling from the aftershocks of the Suez crisis and the Iranian coup. After weeks of dickering during the spring of 1957, Congress authorized the president to defend countries in the Middle East "against overt armed aggression from any nation controlled by international communism." This new "Eisenhower Doctrine" hardly fit with the political realities of this area, in which older imperial tensions, regional and religious distrust, and the rise of fervent nationalism shaped events more than did superpower contests. But the Eisenhower Doctrine, like the Truman Doctrine before it, forced complex events into simple molds and made it easy to label any challenge to American interests as communist aggression.

During the summer of 1958, when rioting broke out in the small middle-eastern country of Lebanon, the doctrine had its first test. Lebanon's government blamed the riots on saboteurs from the newly organized United Arab Republic (Egypt and Syria), but animosity between Christian and Moslem, city and countryside, Nasserites and moderates had long ago turned the tiny land into a tinderbox. Then nationalists in Iraq murdered King Faisal and his premier, Nuri el-Said. Iraq's new anti-Western leaders renounced ties with Washington and made overtures to the UAR. As violence in the Middle East accelerated, the established elements in Lebanon and Jordan asked the United States and Britain to "stabilize" the situation. Both powers quickly complied, anxious to check Nasserism and protect their dangerously exposed oil pipelines. Over 14,000 marines eventually waded ashore on Lebanese beaches in an intervention notable for its bloodlessness, military polish, and short-range success. American troops set up a new, strongly anti-Nasser government in Beirut, and in Jordan the British restored King Hussein's control over Jordan's army.

Despite its superficial success, the Anglo-American intrusion provoked new fears of Western imperialism. The Eisenhower Doctrine may ultimately have pushed many Arab nationalists toward Moscow. Some Arabs began to turn away from the United States, not because they were procommunist but because they suspected American motives.

American policy did not contain revolution everywhere. In fact, a leftist revolt succeeded in a place long considered a secure outpost of America's informal empire—Cuba. In 1959 a guerrilla leader in Cuba, Fidel Castro, converted his mountaintop rebellion into a social revolution that not only deposed the country's dictator, Fulgencio Batista, but also ended the island's dependence upon the United States. The Cuban revolution at first attracted sympathy from many Americans. The rich sugar crop had benefited foreigners and Cuba's upper class, while the working population had suffered long hours and miserable living conditions. Batista's regime had grown notoriously corrupt. The prospect of honest government, social justice, and land redistribution provided support for the bearded, thirty-two-year-old Castro, like Nasser a charismatic leader. Initially welcomed by many Americans as an alternative to the repressive Batista, Castro soon encountered hostility as he tried to reduce his country's economic dependence on the United States. After a disagreement with some American companies, Castro nationalized their holdings; Eisenhower retaliated by curtailing the amount of Cuban sugar the United States would import; Castro stepped up nationalization and turned toward the Soviet Union for aid. When the spiral of deteriorating relations had ended, Castro had nationalized over a billion dollars worth of Yankee assets, taken reprisals against thousands as "enemies of the people," and frightened most of the Cuban upper-middle class into exile in Florida. During a visit to the United States, Castro appealed to America's racial minorities to follow his example. Later he joined hands with Krushchev at the United Nations.

While many Americans wondered whether Castro was a true communist or had been driven to Moscow by United States intransigence, the Republicans moved methodically to drive him from power. Eisenhower ended American imports of Cuban sugar, which had maintained the island's prices above world market levels. Under great pressure from Washington, the Organization of American States expelled Cuba, thus cutting off all aid to Castro's regime from the OAS. These heavy-handed measures only reaffirmed the Cuban people's belief in Castro and forced him to rely upon the Soviets. Anxious to take advantage of American blunders and, no doubt, to check domestic critics, Krushchev bought up Cuba's sugar crop in 1960 at an inflated price. CIA operatives began training a

Cuban invasion force in Guatemala and plotting other bizarre moves against Castro's regime, but threats of American intervention only justified further swings to the left by Castro. Shortsighted containment in the Caribbean, no less than in the Middle East, produced nationalist reactions often hostile to American goals.

Reevaluation of the New Look

Sputnik

On October 4, 1957, the Soviet Union orbited the first space satellite, Sputnik I; a month later Sputnik II, which weighed over 1,300 pounds and carried a live dog, spent several days in space before landing. The accuracy and large payload of the Russian rockets tilted the symmetry of nuclear stalemate. Some alarmists warned that if the Soviet Union could neutralize America's second-strike deterrent, Moscow might risk a preemptive atomic attack knowing that the United States could not retaliate. Or Soviet military sophistication might be such that conventional operations would suffice, since Washington now could not escalate to nuclear levels. Sputnik ended America's easy confidence in its technological ascendancy and created new, often times exaggerated fears of Soviet strength.

A false sense of vulnerability pervaded American life. Defense planners wondered whether the country should continue to focus on solid-fuel missiles such as the Minuteman and Polaris or switch priorities toward liquid-fuel rockets, like those the Russians used. Though more economical and reliable, America's rockets required very complicated engineering and more time for deployment. Some experts feared that even if the United States accelerated its liquid-fuel programs, there would be a lag of four, perhaps even seven, years before a balance could be restored. They predicted a "missile gap," especially after Defense Secretary Neil McElroy announced that "the United States does not intend to match the Soviet Union weapon for weapon." The beeping Sputniks did frighten the Pentagon into deploying intermediate-range rockets in Britain, Turkey, and Italy. The Defense Department also channeled more and more money into research-and-development programs. But most high officials recognized that America's manned bombers far outclassed Soviet defense systems. Though spectacular, Sputnik in no concrete way threatened the safety of the United States.

The Eisenhower administration's measured response to Sputnik did more to alarm than to reassure large segments of the American public. Long restive about New Look economies, some military people publicly worried about the emphasis on bombers and carrier-based fighters. General Maxwell Taylor, army chief of staff, argued for "armament in depth" so that the United States could fight "low-level, conventional battles" if nuclear stalemate produced "brush-fire wars on the periphery of the free world." Sensing political advantage, many liberal Democrats saw more military spending as a means to stimulate the lagging economy. Defense intellectuals, gathered into research institutes by governments and universities, explained that atomic armaments required constant technological innovation to keep pace with scientific discoveries. This Alice-in-Wonderland world asked citizens to run faster and faster just to stay in the same place. The Korean War had spawned an industry dependent upon arms contracts. Research-and-development money produced ever more complicated weapons. Powerful interests in such politically important areas as Long Island, Texas, and Southern California pressed to increase lucrative defense production. This combination of American generals, Democratic politicians, and enterprising businessmen coalesced into a powerful group that lobbied for more and more armaments. Eisenhower's immense prestige, and his skepticism about Pentagon claims, temporarily quieted the clamor. But opponents of the New Look wondered whether Eisenhower's economies had not misled the country.

The Paradox of Power

Eisenhower left the presidency a discouraged man. He confided to John F. Kennedy that "foreign affairs are in a mess" and warned the American people of "a burgeoning military-industrial complex." Eisenhower tried to be cost-conscious and to pursue peace, but he also allowed Dulles to launch an open-ended ideological crusade to refashion the world into a mold compatible with United States' interests.

The more the Republicans tried to control world events during the 1950s, the more events seemed out of control. Massive retaliation did not guarantee security but instead required more and more doomsday weapons. A chain of anti-communist military alliances, the proliferation of bases abroad, and the growing role of the CIA entangled the United States in local complexities around the globe. Prosperity and a mellowing Russia diverted Western Europeans from the cold war and slowly ended their dependence upon Washington. The expansive rhetoric and international complexities of the 1950s heightened Americans' insecurities and set the stage for burgeoning defense spending and exaggerated cold-war crusading in the early 1960s.

SUGGESTIONS FOR FURTHER READING

The foreign policy of the 1950s can be approached through many of the volumes on the Eisenhower administration cited at the end of Chapter 3. More specialized memoirs include George B. Kistiakowsky, *A Scientist at the White House* (1976); Henry Cabot Lodge, Jr., *As It Was* (1976); Mark W. Clark, *From the Danube to the Yalu* (1964); and Matthew B. Ridgway, *The Korean War* (1967). In the later years of the Eisenhower administration some members-to-be of the Kennedy administration offered their critiques of Republican foreign policy. See, for example, Walt Rostow's *The United States in the World Arena* (1960) and Maxwell Taylor's *An Uncertain Trumpet* (1960). A young Harvard professor named Henry Kissinger offered his critiques in *Nuclear Weapons and Foreign Policy* (1957) and *The Necessity of Choice* (1961). For criticisms from the far right, see Robert Strausz-Hupé et al., *Protracted Conflict* (1959).

The role of John Foster Dulles is assessed favorably in Michael Guhin's *John Foster Dulles* (1972) and much more critically in Townshend Hoopes's *The Devil and John Foster Dulles* (1975). See also Louis Gerson, *John Foster Dulles* (1967); Herbert Finer, *Dulles over Suez* (1964); and Leonard Mosley, *Dulles* (1978). Ronald Steel's *Pax Americana* (1967) and Robert A. Divine's *Eisenhower and the Cold War* (1981) contain excellent analyses of foreign policy during the 1950s.

Robert A. Divine's *Blowing in the Wind: The Nuclear Test Ban Debate, 1954 – 1960* (1978) is a superior study. It can be supplemented with Michael Mandelbaum, *The Nuclear Question: The United States and Nuclear Weapons, 1946 – 1976* (1979). Other studies of specific events or subjects include Stanley D. Bachman, *The Committee of One-Million: "China Lobby" Politics* (1976); Samuel Baily, *The United States and the Development of South America* (1977); John C. Campbell, *Successful Negotiation, Trieste* (1976); David Wise and Thomas B. Ross, *The U-2 Affair* (1962); and Robert F. Randle, *Geneva 1954: The Settlement of the Indo-China War* (1969). Many of the volumes on Vietnam listed at the end of Chapter 6 cover American policy during the Eisenhower years.

Although many foreign-policy papers remain classified, *American Foreign Policy, 1950 – 1960* (1957 – 64) is a valuable documentary collection covering the Eisenhower years.

THE LIBERAL PROMISE: JFK AND LBJ

The President We Hardly Knew

The Making of a President

A 1973 bestseller by one of John Kennedy's former aides expressed a general sentiment: *Johnny We Hardly Knew Ye.* The title was revealing. The Kennedy administration was always shrouded in legend, and books by his associates helped the myths grow larger. Only recently have historians begun to peek through the clouds of adulation that surrounded the thirty-fifth president.

Few fathers groom their sons to be president, but wealthy Joseph P. Kennedy wanted one of his sons to gain the nation's highest office. When his oldest boy died during World War II, his other war-hero son picked up the family colors. Young John Kennedy attended an elite prep school and then graduated from Harvard, all the while refining his social graces and developing a tough-minded view of public affairs. He learned to listen well, to absorb the ideas of others, and to make decisions independently. He also displayed an intolerance for those who did not share his pragmatic approach. People who could not say what they had to say quickly, who moralized or digressed, irritated a busy man like John Kennedy. Sentimental liberals—Adlai Stevenson, for example—seemed suspect: how could people who took so long to make up their mind do great things? John Kennedy always surrounded himself with bright, ambitious young men who shared his distaste for sentimentality. The "public" Kennedy—idealistic, inspirational, and sometimes emotional—was very different from the calculating politician from Boston.

Kennedy's narrow victory over Richard Nixon in 1960 capped a rather unimpressive political career. In 1946 JFK won election to the House of Representatives and six years later ousted a distinguished scion of the Boston aristocracy, Henry Cabot Lodge, Jr., from the United States Senate. Like many other ambitious young men, Kennedy considered the slow-moving, tradition-bound Senate undemanding and often boring. Kennedy usually supported generous expenditures for social-welfare programs and championed a strong anticommunist policy, but he sponsored no important legislative measures. During these years Kennedy did marry an attractive wife, who proved to be an important political asset, and he wrote a prize-winning book—*Profiles in Courage*. Between 1956 and 1960 Kennedy took full advantage of the new age of jet travel, personally visiting people in the Democratic party hierarchy and accumulating political debts that he could cash in during the 1960 presidential campaign. He and his close associates (the Irish Mafia, some called them) put together a smooth-running organization that included pollster Louis Harris, speech writer Theodore Sorenson, his two younger brothers, and a coterie of Harvard intellectuals.

The Election of 1960

The energetic Kennedy dominated the presidential campaign of 1960. As a politician Kennedy did few new things; he simply did the old ones better than most other candidates. His speeches covered the traditional themes—the cold war with the Soviet Union, prosperity at home, and sacrifice for country—but they were cleverly phrased and, after some speaking lessons, effectively delivered. Although he brought his wife and baby daughter into the political spotlight, he used them less frequently and with more taste than most other politicians. Kennedy's operatives employed blatant arm twisting to gain political favors, but they generally knew just how much leverage to use and exactly where to apply it. Unlike Adlai Stevenson, who had let the convention choose his running mate in 1956, JFK made a highly political choice: Senate Majority Leader Lyndon Johnson of Texas. Even Kennedy's much-discussed "charisma" was not a new phenomenon; throughout the 1950s political observers had analyzed the charisma of President Eisenhower. But Kennedy's most distinctive qualities—his youth, good looks, and energy—did distinguish his political image from that of the much older, more deliberate Eisenhower.

The Republican candidate, Eisenhower's vice-president Richard Nixon, tried to contrast his supposed maturity and experience with Kennedy's rather insubstantial political record. The tactic backfired in the widely heralded television debates: TV made the sharp-featured Nixon appear old and tired while it accentuated Kennedy's best qualities. The harsh lights highlighted Nixon's famous five o'clock shadow, leading some viewers to see him as "Tricky Dick" and to compare him to "the man you wouldn't buy a used car from." Most important, Kennedy's confident manner during the first debate undercut Nixon's claim about his opponent's immaturity. And though Nixon scrupulously avoided any hint of anti-Catholicism during the campaign, some of his supporters, particularly the Reverend Norman Vincent Peale, did not. Catholic voters tended to be Democrats anyway, and JFK piled up large Catholic majorities in several key states. The election of 1960 was very close: Kennedy won by only 120,000 popular votes, and small shifts in several large states would have made Nixon president. The unexpectedly narrow victory probably increased Kennedy's political caution.

Although he could hardly claim a popular mandate, Kennedy quickly built an imposing image for his administration—the "New Frontier," the energetic successor to the New Deal and the Fair Deal. First, JFK assembled his version of Roosevelt's brain trust. He appointed his brother and campaign manager, Robert Kennedy, attorney general; Robert McNamara, president of Ford Motor Company, became secretary of defense; Harvard's McGeorge Bundy assumed the important role of national-security adviser to the president; and Dean Rusk, head of the Ford Foundation, got the coveted position of secretary of state. Even the secondary jobs claimed top individuals. (A promising young intellectual named Henry Kissinger found himself outgunned in such fierce competition and took over Bundy's courses at Harvard, awaiting an administration that would better appreciate his talents.) Few of these advisers had much political experience, but they had all been eminently successful in other areas. Vice-President Johnson left the first cabinet meeting dazzled by the intellect that Kennedy had assembled. "You should have seen all those men," he told his old political mentor, House Speaker Sam Rayburn. "Well, Lyndon, you may be right and they may be every bit as intelligent as you say," replied Mr. Sam, "but I'd feel a whole lot better about them if just one of them had run for sheriff once."

The Kennedy White House became a center of art and culture. A telegram that invited people from the arts to attend the inauguration announced that

> During our forthcoming administration we hope to effect a productive relationship with our writers artists composers philosophers scientists and heads of cultural institutions stop. . . .

Jacqueline Kennedy, a well-educated woman who spoke several foreign languages, became the special guardian of culture: she invited artists such as cellist Pablo Casals to perform at the White House, redecorated the old mansion, and then conducted a tour of it for millions of television viewers. Kennedy parties were lavish productions in the grand style; I. F. Stone, the radical journalist, complained that the atmosphere resembled that of "a reigning monarch's court." Such a comparison probably did not disturb Kennedyphiles. Many of the president's followers reveled in the reputation of the Kennedy White House as a modern-day Camelot.

In addition to intellect and style, the New Frontier emphasized toughness. As John Kennedy noted in his inaugural address, he and his advisers were all young men "born in this country, tempered by war, disciplined by a hard and bitter peace." Facing the challenges of a dangerous world, they believed that they could not afford to appear soft. In defending his space program, for example, JFK bragged that Americans would accept the challenges of space "not because they are easy but because they are hard." The Kennedy team displayed its toughness during impromptu touch football games; here the president's brother Robert gained the reputation as the most hard-nosed New Frontiersman. After Floyd Patterson lost his heavyweight boxing title, the attorney general removed the ex-champ's picture from his office.

All the Kennedy people prided themselves on their ability to handle any foreign or domestic crisis. They seemed almost to welcome one. In 1962 Kennedy massed the full power of the national government to combat a price increase by United States Steel and several other large firms. JFK denounced the companies as unpatriotic, contrasting their actions with the sacrifices of servicemen who were already dying in Vietnam and reservists who had been called up to meet a feared confrontation with the Soviet Union in Berlin. The president coupled his verbal assaults with a massive legal offensive: the Justice Department began to seek evidence of price fixing; FBI agents started to investigate possible illegal activities by steel corporations; the Federal Trade Commission threatened to look into the same questions; and administration sources even hinted at possible antitrust actions to break up the steel giants. At the same time, the Defense Department refused to buy from companies that raised prices, and Kennedy aides pressured corporate friends to resist the lead of U.S. Steel. Confronted by this counterattack, Big Steel retreated and rolled back prices. Throughout the short skirmish the president viewed the controversy as an extension of foreign affairs, claiming that price increases threatened national security. It was the type of problem, he believed, that required crisis management.

The president's critics viewed the situation differently. Many businessmen predictably denounced Kennedy for using "police state" tactics, but even some foes of large corporations expressed concern. A young law professor, Charles Reich (who would later gain fame as author of *The Greening of America*), concluded that it was "dangerously wrong for an angry president to loose his terrible arsenal of power for the purposes of intimidation and coercing private companies and citizens." Other observers contended that Kennedy's actions reflected a dangerous crisis mentality and indicated the administration's lack of any consistent domestic policies. Within a year the steel firms raised prices twice, and the Kennedy administration did nothing.

Although JFK was more interested in foreign policy than in domestic affairs, he did have some broad goals for his New Frontier at home. The new Democratic administration revived many of Harry Truman's old Fair Deal proposals: federal aid to education, a national health program, and expansion of other welfare-state programs. Kennedy never saw his education program or Medicare pass Congress, but he could take some credit for several less spectacular measures. Congress extended Social Security coverage to more American workers, covered more people by federal wage standards, raised the minimum wage to $1.25 an hour, appropriated nearly $5 billion for public housing, established the manpower-training program, and passed an area-redevelopment act for West Virginia and other improverished areas in Appalachia. These measures reflected JFK's preference for moderate, gradual reforms and his political caution. Like his intellectual-in-residence, Arthur Schlesinger, Jr., John Kennedy remained committed to "the vital center."

In addition to updating the Fair Deal's social-welfare programs, the Kennedy administration tried to redefine the techniques of Truman's liberal economists. In his first state-of-the-union address, JFK promised that the sluggish economy would soon show both "a prompt recovery" and "long-range growth." Kennedy, of course, blamed the country's economic problems on the Eisenhower administration: the GNP had risen slowly during the late 1950s while the unemployment rate had climbed to around 6 percent. Although Kennedy shared with Eisenhower a limited background in economics—JFK had received a C in his introductory economics course at Harvard—he gathered a distinguished group of economic advisers, including John Kenneth Galbraith of Harvard and Walter Heller of the University of Minnesota. According to these advocates of the "new economics," the national government could use its power over federal expenditures and its controls over monetary policy to "fine-tune" the economy.

The Kennedy administration adopted a number of strategies for stimulating production and creating new jobs. Increased government spending pumped vital funds into the economy and brightened the general economic picture. In 1962 the White House persuaded Congress to give businesses a 7-percent tax credit for investments in new machinery and plants. At the same time, the administration granted one of business's top requests—the readjustment of depreciation schedules for corporate taxes. This action encouraged purchases of new equipment by allowing businesses to write off assets more quickly. Taken together, the investment tax credit and the revised depreciation schedules reduced business taxes and theoretically increased corporate spending by about $2.5 billion; the total tax cut amounted to almost 12 percent.

Although the economy picked up considerably, many liberal economists called for further steps to boost production and employment. John Kenneth Galbraith, who had become ambassador to India, suggested massive government expenditures for social-welfare programs. Kennedy rejected this as politically impossible but did consider further tax cuts. A cut in tax revenues would increase the federal deficit; it would also, however, expand purchasing power for both consumers and businesses. Walter Heller, chairman of the Council of Economic Advisers, and Paul Samuelson, an influential economist at MIT, were among those who urged an immediate tax reduction to ward off a possible recession. But advocates of a balanced federal budget, particularly Treasury Secretary C. Douglas Dillon and Federal Reserve Chairman William McChesney Martin, rejected this example of the new economics, and Kennedy finally shelved the proposal for 1962. The following year, however, the administration unveiled a comprehensive revenue bill that did include a $10 billion tax cut and tax reforms.

Kennedy's carefully calculated approach to social and economic problems reflected his basic assumptions about the new role of liberal government in America. The "old sweeping issues have largely disappeared," he told Yale's graduating class in 1962. Basic domestic problems were now "more subtle and less simple": how to manage a complex economy; how to ensure increasing productivity and rising prosperity for all citizens. The "sophisticated and technical questions involved in keeping a great economic machinery moving ahead" required "technical answers—not political answers." Rational bureaucrats, the cool technicians who could manage complex institutions, held the keys to effective government. Although his tenure in office tempered some of his early optimism, John Kennedy died confident that his view of government remained correct and that Camelot's bright young men could solve most problems.

Assassination

On November 22, 1963, the presidential motorcade was winding its way past unexpectedly friendly crowds in Dallas when a volley of shots—some claimed three, others four or five—raked Kennedy's open-topped limousine. Texas Governor John Connally was seriously wounded, and one shot ripped away the top of Kennedy's head. Within an hour doctors at Parkland Hospital pronounced the president dead; the thousand days of Camelot were over. Aboard Air Force One, Vice-President Lyndon Baines Johnson took the oath of office.

News of the president's death stunned the nation. Most people dropped everything and dashed for the closest television set or radio; Walter Cronkite hurried on camera, covering the story in his shirt sleeves. The wire services quickly sent out the stark, grim details. For two days the nation watched an elaborate memorial, and most people's respect for their fallen leader grew. Pictures of Kennedy's coffin, his riderless horse, and his grieving family clashed with scenes from Kennedy's past. Images of a vibrant JFK—sailing off Cape Cod, laughing with his children, or facing down the Russians in Cuba—made his death seem all the more tragic. The Kennedy mystique grew.

The television spectacle also began to raise doubts about the cause of JFK's death. Within hours after the assassination, Dallas police officials announced the capture of a young man named Lee Harvey Oswald. A former marine who had lived in the Soviet Union for a short time, Oswald refused to confess and steadfastly proclaimed his innocence. On Sunday, November 24, while Dallas police were transferring Oswald to a different jail, millions of television viewers witnessed the assassination of the alleged assassin. A local night-club operator, Jack Ruby, fatally shot Oswald at close range in the Dallas police station.

Oswald's bizarre death raised further doubts about his guilt. Was he part of a larger conspiracy? Was Kennedy's death somehow tied to pro- or anti-Castro forces? Was Ruby a hit man sent to silence Oswald? Were the Dallas police, or the CIA, or the FBI, part of the "plot"? Wanting to squelch such rumors quickly, President Johnson persuaded Chief Justice Earl Warren to head an official inquiry. After a ten-month investigation, the Warren Commission named Oswald the lone assassin and reported no credible evidence of any broader plot. Conspiracy buffs, however, were already offering an amazing variety of scenarios, and the Warren Report merely gave them twenty-six volumes of evidence to piece through. More sober critics of the commission pointed out serious flaws in the hastily researched and sloppily documented report. Despite an intensive "sell" campaign conducted by the Johnson administration through the mass media, many Americans refused to accept the Warren Commission's version of what had happened in Dallas. Proponents of a conspiracy theory received some vindication when, in 1979, a special committee of the House of Representatives concluded, on the basis of evidence not available in 1964, that JFK had "probably" fallen victim to some kind of plot. But despite the expenditure of several million dollars, the committee could offer no hard evidence about the alleged conspiracy.

The Great Society

LBJ

When Teddy Roosevelt succeeded an earlier slain president, William McKinley, a conservative Republican expressed fears about "that damn cowboy"; sixty-two years later, many liberal Democrats felt much the same way about Lyndon Baines Johnson. Except for being a rich Democrat, LBJ had little in common with the cool, urbane Kennedy. Unlike JFK, Johnson loved the Senate, and during the 1950s he had dominated that body as its majority leader. John Kennedy always remembered how, as a senator, he had to beg Lyndon Johnson for favors. But despite years in Washington, Johnson never lost the earthy exuberance of "a good old boy from the ranch." (In his early White House days, Johnson showed a homemade film of deer mating and contributed his own coarse sound track.) In contrast with Kennedy, who had inherited his wealth, the self-made Johnson often was haunted by the hint of scandal. Critics snickered about "landslide Lyndon's" suspicious cighty-six-vote triumph in the 1948 senatorial primary, about his close association with convicted influence peddler Bobby Baker, and about his mysterious financial dealings throughout the Southwest. Lyndon Johnson came to Washington as an ambitious young politician attracted to Roosevelt's New Deal; he left as a former president and a multimillionaire. To some people LBJ looked too much like Jay Gould in a Stetson hat.

Johnson constantly worried about his public image. People would not give him "a fair shake as president," he often complained, "because I am a southerner." But even Johnson realized that his problems lay deeper. "Why don't people like me?" he asked visitors to the White House. One elderly caller, who felt that his advanced years protected him, replied honestly: "Because, Mr. President, you are not a very likeable man." Defensive about his provincial education in southwest Texas and perhaps still burdened by the conflicting childhood demands of his tough, hard-drinking father and his refined, intellectual mother, Johnson seemed to require constant reassurance. He also demanded unswerving loyalty from his subordinates. Among those around Johnson, no one wanted to be the bearer of bad news. He often flew into sudden rages, publicly berating staff members or arbitrarily summoning them at all hours of the night. He appeared to need the LBJ brand on everything. (His wife inherited the name Lady Bird, but LBJ christened his daughters Lynda Bird and Lucy Baines.) White House employees whom he suspected of antiwar sentiments dropped from favor, and only a few loyalists, such as Walt Rostow and Dean Rusk, stayed until the end. A critical reporter might receive the "Johnson treatment"—a private audience during which Johnson conducted a nonstop monologue on the glories of his presidency. A big man, the president liked to get close to his listeners, overwhelming them with his bulk.

Johnson smoothly handled the transition from the Kennedy administration, but after 1964 he watched his popularity decline steadily. Johnson often blamed the media for what became known as his "credibility gap." Stories about Johnson's pettiness, his vanity, and his duplicity entered the media and colored people's perception of the president. Most reporters had genuinely liked Kennedy and had sometimes pigeonholed unfavorable stories about his policies. But Johnson, like Richard Nixon after him, considered himself the target of unfair reporting by large segments of the Washington press corps. In truth, some journalists did compare Johnson unfavorably with the still untarnished image of JFK as well as with the vigorous reality of the Kennedy family. John Kennedy's youngest brother, Edward, represented Massachusetts in the Senate, and in 1964 Robert Kennedy overcame charges of being a carpetbagger to win election to the Senate from New York. The Kennedys only thinly veiled their distaste for Johnson, and many reporters expressed more sympathy for "Camelot-in-exile"—the intellectuals and politicians who swarmed around Bobby's home at Hickory Hill or the family compound on Cape Cod—than for Lyndon Johnson's entourage.

Toward the end of his presidency, as controversy over Vietnam obsessed both the president and the press, many people forgot Lyndon Johnson's accomplishments and admirable qualities. He could take much credit for the Great Society legislation passed between 1964 and 1968, and even most critics conceded his sincere commitment to social reform and racial justice. For all his faults, Johnson was an intelligent, complex, sensitive man. The American people, particularly the opinion-making elites, probably misunderstood Lyndon Johnson as much as he misunderstood them. He was, according to one observer of his last years, a tortured man torn between his fervent, populist hopes of extending the American dream and his meaner, less noble impulses.

The Johnson Program

Lyndon Johnson moved to fufill JFK's promise of rapid economic expansion. Aided by a reduction in taxes (the Tax Act of 1964, of course, was originally a Kennedy proposal) and by increased federal spending (particularly for the expanding war in Southeast Asia), the economy built upon gains begun under Kennedy. Between 1960 and 1964 the gross national product increased by 24 percent while corporate profits went up by 57 percent; the next year the GNP climbed by almost

7 percent and corporate profits by 20 percent; and by 1965 the nation achieved what most economists considered "full" employment, an unemployment rate less than 4 percent. The boom lasted throughout Johnson's second term: unemployment never exceeded 4 percent, and the GNP expanded at a rate of almost 5 percent a year. The median family income, measured in constant dollars, increased from $8,543 in 1963 to $10,768 in 1969.

Not everyone was impressed by the Kennedy-Johnson boom. Some economists correctly warned that the expansion was too rapid and that the Johnson administration was ignoring the threat of inflation. Others argued that LBJ's economic wizardry was largely a fraud. Truman's old advisor Leon Keyserling contended that the Tax Act of 1964, which came out of Congress without most of its original reforms, primarily assisted the wealthy. According to Keyserling's calculations, the average taxpayer in the $10,000 income bracket received only a 3.5-percent increase in disposable income; in contrast, the taxpayer who earned $100,000 enjoyed a boost of 16.5 percent and the very wealthy, those in the $200,000 category, got a 31.1-percent windfall. Keyserling charged that the nation's basic economic problem remained an inequitable distribution of income. Radical economists such as Marxist Paul Sweezy concurred. They complained that economic growth was still too slow, unemployment too high, and the gap between rich and poor too wide. Citing the tremendous rise in corporate profits during the Kennedy-Johnson years, many people noted that large corporations were the main beneficiaries of the high-growth policies of the "new economics."

Lyndon Johnson, the man who sincerely wanted to be "president of all the people," saw the situation differently. Of course, large businesses would benefit from economic expansion, but so would middle-income workers and small entrepreneurs. And galloping prosperity enabled the country to advance beyond the limited goals of Truman and Kennedy and extend greater assistance to the very poor in the best LBJ style—with great breast-beating and with promises of much government money. Buoyed by his early successes and the economic boom, LBJ claimed that there was a consensus—what he later called "a broad, deep, and genuine consensus among most groups within our diverse society"—on behalf of social reform. If only everyone would "sit down and reason together," Americans could realize the Great Society. Speaking in the spring of 1964 before an outdoor crowd of almost 100,000 people, LBJ heralded the coming of America's golden age, a society "where the meaning of our lives matches the marvelous products of our labor. . . a place where men are more concerned with the quality of their goals than the quantity of their goods." Even John Kennedy's speech writers might have blushed at this rhetoric, but then JFK never approached the carload of legislative measures that LBJ rolled through Congress in 1964 and 1965.

In the wake of Kennedy's death and his own landslide triumph over Republican Barry Goldwater in 1964, Johnson broke what he called "the legislative logjam," a congressional stalemate that had dated back many years. Never in recent memory had Congress done so much so quickly. When Johnson left

Washington in 1969 his cabinet gave him a plaque commemorating the more than two hundred "landmark laws" passed during his administration. In LBJ's first full year alone, Congress approved the Tax Act of 1964, a new civil-rights act, federally sponsored recreation programs, funds for urban mass transit, and the Economic Opportunity Act (the measure that signaled the beginning of Johnson's War on Poverty). And this was merely the prelude to the Great Society, a program that Johnson took to the nation in the 1964 presidential race.

The Johnson Landslide

The Republicans graciously handed Johnson the election. Militant conservatives, most of whom lived in the "rim states" from southern California to Florida or in isolated enclaves in the Middle West, temporarily gained control of the GOP. Bragging that they would offer the nation "a choice, not an echo," they successfully nominated Senator Barry Goldwater of Arizona. The hero of most conservatives, Goldwater gained a reputation as an injudicious right-wing extremist. During a series of bitter primary campaigns, some of his overzealous supporters reinforced this image by vehemently attacking more liberal Republicans, particularly New York's Nelson Rockefeller. When Rockefeller rose to address the GOP's 1964 convention, for example, Goldwaterites in the galleries shouted him down. Goldwater's acceptance speech only increased the apprehension of many moderates. "Extremism in the defense of liberty," he challenged his critics, "is no vice. . . . Moderation in the pursuit of justice is no virtue."

Goldwater ran squarely against Johnson's brand of liberalism. Ever since the New Deal, Republican candidates had campaigned against the central government in Washington, but Goldwater really seemed to mean it. His strategists—highly disciplined professionals who borrowed many techniques from JFK's campaign—hoped that a militantly conservative approach would bring millions of alienated people to the polls and attract a backlash vote from whites who were frightened by the civil-rights movement. A Goldwater administration, the senator from Arizona appeared to say, would sweep away all the baneful welfare programs established since the New Deal: agricultural subsidies, pro-labor union legislation, civil-rights laws, and all the other "socialistic" laws. "I will give you back your freedom," he promised his followers. On several occasions he even suggested making Social Security voluntary, a position that Democrats falsely translated into the charge that Goldwater planned to abolish the entire system. Along with some missile-rattling statements about the need for a quick victory in Vietnam, his domestic program enabled Democrats to paint Goldwater as a trigger-happy Neanderthal.

With the moderate center of the American electorate deserting the Republican party, Johnson and his running mate, Senator Hubert Humphrey of Minnesota, recorded a landslide victory. The Democratic presidential ticket gathered 61.3 percent of the popular ballots and the electoral votes of all but six states. At the same time, Democrats gained thirty-nine seats in the House of Representatives and gained more than five hundred new seats in state legislatures across the country. Johnson celebrated his "politics of consensus," and some nervous Republicans wondered if the "Goldwater caper" would destroy the GOP.

The Great Society

After his smashing victory, LBJ pushed more Great Society measures through the new Eighty-ninth Congress. Medicare and Medicaid programs fulfilled Harry Truman's goal of some government-sponsored health care for people over sixty-five and for the very poor. Two other long-debated measures, the Elementary and Secondary Education Act and the Higher Education Act, extended federal funds to schools at all levels of the educational hierarchy. The Civil Rights Act of 1965 eliminated barriers against black voters in the South: it suspended literacy tests and authorized use of federal inspectors in areas where the attorney general suspected chicanery in voting procedures. To deal with the problems of urban decay, Congress passed the Housing Act of 1965, which created the new Department of Housing and Urban Development (HUD), and the Demonstration Cities and Metropolitan Development Act of 1966, which provided federal money for local "model city" projects. Prodded by advocates of automobile safety, Congress passed several bills dealing with highway and traffic safety. One measure, the Motor Vehicle Safety Act (1966), inaugurated federal safety standards for the auto industry and established a uniform grading system for tire manufacturers. As in the case of urban problems, Congress also created a new cabinet department—that of transportation—and gave its secretary the tasks of coordination and enforcement. Finally, Congress passed a number of "minor" pieces of legislation such as a new immigration act, which admitted newcomers primarily on the basis of their economic skills rather than their national origin, and the Truth in Packaging Act, which provided consumers with some protection against deceptive advertising practices.

Most Americans readily accepted these programs, measures once considered "socialistic," as integral parts of the American welfare state. Controversies still erupted over details—how much Medicare patients should pay from their own pockets, or how quickly automakers should comply with safety standards—but few people suggested repeal of these Great Society laws. Much to LBJ's displeasure the loudest complaints came from social activists who charged that the programs required only minimal sacrifices from wealthy special-interest groups and provided too little assistance for needy citizens. Ralph Nader, for example, claimed that auto manufacturers blocked truly effective safety laws while using the cost of minimal improvements as an excuse to raise their prices. And despite all Lyndon Johnson's promises, basic needs such as better mass-transportation systems and effective urban-housing programs remained only dreams.

The War on Poverty

In addition to completing the Fair Deal, Johnson launched a crusade of his own—elimination and prevention of poverty in America. Because of their material abundance, middle-class Americans had largely forgotten that one-fourth to one-fifth of the population, mostly white people, still lived in substandard housing and subsisted on inadequate diets. Michael Harrington's *The Other America* helped spark concern for the poor, and Johnson declared his War on Poverty. At first glance, the array of programs seemed impressive: federal funds for public-works projects, particularly new highways in Appalachia; a Job Corps to train young people who lacked marketable skills; Work-Study, a program to supplement the incomes of college students; Volunteers in Service to America (VISTA), which would send young volunteers into impoverished areas; and Head Start, a program designed to provide compensatory education for preschoolers from "disadvantaged" families. Although these measures went beyond any previous national efforts, even the programs' supporters conceded their traditional approach to social problems. In providing federal money and another federal agency (the Office of Economic Opportunity, or OEO), the Great Society borrowed the techniques of the New and Fair Deals.

One part of the War on Poverty, the Community Action Program (CAP), did represent a significant change in federal policy. Under Title II of the Economic Opportunity Act, Congress authorized funds for local groups—either private nonprofit or public organizations—that developed innovative programs to cure the symptoms of poverty. Sounding a theme that Richard Nixon would later adapt to his own purposes, President Johnson argued that CAP rested upon "the fact that local citizens best understand their own problems and know best how to deal with these problems." At first, many people praised CAP as an attempt to check the extension of federal power into local affairs. Many poor people looked forward to being able to plan their own improvements.

Like the conflict in Vietnam, the War on Poverty brought Lyndon Johnson few clear-cut victories. Many Republicans and blue-collar Democrats denounced the poverty program for giving money to people allegedly too lazy to help themselves. ("Yeah, I helped the War on Poverty," went one lame joke of the mid 1960s. "I threw a hand grenade at a bum.") Actually much of the available money went to middle-class bureaucrats or into expensive equipment. After their stints in public service, some antipoverty workers established consulting agencies that received government contracts for "expert" advice on the problems of poverty. Early in the fight, some social critics declared that the "poverty-industrial" complex was a far bigger winner than the poor.

The widely heralded CAP, for example, produced mixed results. Established welfare agencies and local political leaders opposed grants of funds to new community groups. Since some of the CAP organizations espoused militant demands such as income redistribution, OEO's bureaucrats often sided with the vested interests and against poor people themselves. Even radicals, after all, could hardly expect the "establishment" to finance its own overthrow. In time, OEO placed more emphasis on "prepackaged programs" from Washington, such as Head Start, community-beautification projects, and legal aid, and employed local CAP groups as administrators rather than innovators. Yet, the Great Society also helped to stimulate the growth of local self-help organizations. The results were not always immediately apparent, but the idea of local action had become a reality.

Though Lyndon Johnson would not admit it, the nation could not wage both a war in Vietnam and one against domestic poverty without increased taxes. As a result of his determination not to hike taxes, the entire nation soon faced a rising rate of inflation, and the poor saw funding for social programs slowly level off. Federal expenditures for social programs, measured in proportion to the country's GNP, did increase between 1965 and 1975, but the sums appropriated never matched those LBJ had once projected, or those needed to conquer poverty.

More than a decade and a half after Lyndon Johnson sounded his battle cry, scholars continued to disagree about the exact results—and the larger meaning—of the conflict. Defenders of the basic premises behind the antipoverty war, such as the economist Sar Levitan, have insisted that LBJ's goals were realistic, that the antipoverty programs were managed with reasonable efficiency, that they provided tangible benefits to the poor, and that Johnson's Great Society demonstrated the untapped potential of liberal welfare programs. Critics from both the left and right of liberalism, Levitan maintained, have been far too pessimistic about what was accomplished and about what could be done by another Great Society.

Levitan's optimistic conclusions did, in fact, clash with the views of the poverty program's numerous critics. To the conservative social scientist Edward Banfield, author of the highly controversial *Unheavenly City,* continuation of the programs begun under the Great Society could do little to deal with hardcore poverty, with the people Banfield called "the underclass." Social reforms by "guilt-ridden" liberals, Banfield claimed, only raised the expectations of the poor to "unreasonable and unrealizable" levels. Although critics from the left rejected Banfield's critique of the "underclass" as a classic example of blaming the victims for their plight, many did share his distrust of those liberal reformers who were committed to "doing good," even after it became clear that benevolence from above would not really liberate the poor. Liberal reformers, the radical critics of the Great Society argued, wrongly assumed that with a helping hand from the national government most poor people could work their way out of poverty. But bureacratic programs, VISTA volunteers, and other "service strategies" were of minimal help, radicals claimed. The only sure cure for inequality, contended the sociologist Christopher Jencks, was a program for redistributing income.

But despite their rhetoric about curing poverty and achieving equality, the Great Society's liberals opposed any serious talk of income redistribution. Their solution to what they themselves conceded was economic injustice remained essentially the same as Harry Truman's: use the machinery of government to promote economic expansion. The promise of an ever-growing economic pie could postpone, as it had in the 1940s, discussions about how large a slice should go to each citizen.

With the nation fighting a lengthy war overseas and a battle against inflation at home, an antipoverty program predicated upon an ever-expanding economy and upon steadily increasing expenditures for social welfare could not run its charted course. Some gains were made; even the program's severest critics allowed this. Yet even the Great Society's most enthusiastic supporters had to confront the cold realities: the government's own figures on income distribution and various independent studies on the distribution of individual and family wealth suggested that the gap between the rich and the poor narrowed very little during the 1960s. Johnson's program did not change the basic socioeconomic structure, nor was it intended to do so. But neither did the Great Society approach its stated goal—to deal seriously with the problems of poverty and social injustice.

The Warren Court and Liberal Reform

The Supreme Court also discovered the difficulties of reform from above. Chief Justice Earl Warren, appointed by Dwight Eisenhower in 1953, and his activist colleagues believed that they could forecast the path of social progress and hasten the coming of justice and equality. The result was a flood of landmark decisions during the years of the Warren Court.

Even before Lyndon Johnson became president, controversy surrounded the Supreme Court and Chief Justice Warren. The famous desegregation decision, *Brown* v. *Board of Education* (1954), in which all nine justices held that racially segregated schools were "inherently unequal," angered segregationists throughout the country. In a series of decisions handed down in 1956 and 1957, a divided Court also affirmed the rights of alleged communists. Anticommunist crusaders denounced the Court, and the ultrareactionary John Birch Society erected billboards that demanded, "IMPEACH EARL WARREN." And when the Court appeared to reverse itself on the communist issue in the late 1950s, civil libertarians criticized the justices, particularly Felix Frankfurter, for caving in to popular pressures. Because it was almost equally divided, the Warren Court established no clear pattern during the chief justice's first years on the bench.

During the 1960s, however, the liberal "activists" gained ascendancy. Led by Chief Justice Warren and two veteran justices, William O. Douglas and Hugo Black, the Court began to require state and local governments to conform to the specific guarantees of the Bill of Rights. The activists recognized that effective legal protection remained largely a matter of one's income and social standing. Rich people could afford good lawyers and thereby gain valuable legal protection. Poor people rarely employed attorneys, and they faced powerful government institutions with inadequate knowledge of their rights. In *Gideon* v *Wainwright* (1963) the Court held that states must furnish indigents with lawyers in felony cases. Such decisions expressed the activists' commitment to a single standard of due process and to the principle of equality before the law.

In addition, the Warren Court attempted to invigorate the democratic process. Beginning with *Baker* v. *Carr* (1962), a majority of justices held that malapportioned electoral districts deprived some voters of equal protection. *Baker* v. *Carr's* "one man, one vote" rule aimed at correcting situations in which rural districts with comparatively few people had the same legislative representation as populous urban districts. Hoping to encourage more vigorous scrutiny of public officials, the Court made it more difficult for politicians to sue their critics for libel (*New York Times* v. *Sullivan,* 1964). In a series of highly controversial decisions, the majority declared that Bible reading and prayer in public schools violated the First Amendment's prohibition against establishment of religion. Earl Warren was declaring God himself unconstitutional, grumbled conservatives. Their mood remained sour when the same Court struck down laws against pornography. Despite all the criticism, however, the Court seemed to have consolidated its new position by the mid 1960s. The Kennedy-Johnson appointees—particularly Arthur Goldberg, Abe Fortas, and the court's first black justice, Thurgood Marshall—offset the increasing conservatism of Justice Black and appeared to ensure an activist majority for years to come.

Then, after 1966, the liberal majority collapsed. One of the Court's decisions did much of the damage. In *Miranda* v. *Arizona* (1966) the Court held that once a police investigation focused upon a particular suspect, the authorities had to inform the defendant that he or she could remain silent, have a lawyer present during questioning, and request a free attorney provided by the state. More than any other decision, *Miranda* angered the Court's critics and united them around one emotional issue. The decision coincided with rising fear of "crime in the streets," and advocates of law and order blamed the Warren Court for handcuffing the police. Although criminologists easily demonstrated that such charges were without foundation, popular criticism and pressure from within the legal establishment increased. Congress considered legislation to overturn the *Miranda* decision, and politicians such as George Wallace and Richard Nixon promised to appoint new justices who would "interpret the Constitution strictly." (This meant, of course, judges who favored *less* strict protection of individual liberties.)

Amid all this controversy, the chief justice announced his impending retirement. President Johnson wanted to replace Warren with his old friend Fortas and then appoint another crony, Homer Thornberry, to the Court. Anticipating a Nixon victory in the 1968 election, Republicans and many conservative southern Democrats tried to block Johnson's reshuffling. Their job became easy when *Life* magazine uncovered what appeared to be evidence of official misconduct by Justice Fortas. Johnson had to withdraw his nomination, and Fortas eventually resigned in disgrace. Newly elected President Nixon thus gained two vacancies on the Court—the chief justice's post (which went to Warren Burger) and Fortas's old seat (which was ultimately filled by another Minnesotan, Harry Blackmun).

Even before the demise of the activist majority, however, legal scholars were beginning to question the impact of the Warren Court's decisions. Obviously they had eliminated some gross inequities in the American legal system and had established stricter standards for law-enforcement officials. But the Court lacked the means—as it always had and always will—to enforce its rulings to the letter. Police departments could effectively evade the *Miranda* decision; publicly appointed lawyers often acted more as agents of the prosecutor's office than as representatives of their clients; and local pressures made restrictions against formal pornography laws superfluous. In an even more fundamental sense, decisions by five well-meaning activists were not always effective tools for social engineering. Broad interpretations of the law of libel, for example, could not make every journalist into a vigorous crusader for the public interest, and reapportionment of state legislatures would not automatically produce more effective legislative bodies. On the most explosive public issue of the late 1960s the Court took no position at all: it avoided ruling directly on cases that challenged the legality of the undeclared war in Vietnam. And though the Warren Court played a vital role in the early movement for legal and political equality for black people, the justices had no independent power to effect the sweeping social and economic changes that black militants came to demand. When the black revolution turned away from legal issues in the late 1960s, the judiciary could play only a limited role.

Civil Rights to Black Power

Civil Rights during the Eisenhower Years

In 1954 almost every area of southern society had segregated facilities for blacks and whites. "Jim Crow" extended to public transportation, rest rooms, drinking fountains, even parking lots and cemeteries. Often required by law and always demanded by custom, these separate, but rarely equal, facilities reminded black people of the inferior status assigned them by white society. The National Association for the Advancement of Colored People (NAACP) financed a series of legal challenges; their success in *Brown* v. *Board of Education* (1954) marked an important victory. All nine Supreme Court justices agreed that legally sanctioned segregation of public schools violated the equal-protection clause of the Fourteenth Amendment. In a simple, straightforward opinion, Chief Justice Earl Warren argued that separate schools were "inherently unequal" and deprived black children of equal educational opportunities. But one court decision, by itself, could not produce a revolution in race relations. Bowing to political pressures and recognizing the practical problems of education, the Supreme Court later ruled that school integration need not be immediate; it should proceed "with all deliberate speed." Ten years after the *Brown* decision only about 1 percent of black children in the South attended desegregated schools.

Resistance to desegregation hardened after the *Brown* case. Most white southerners protested this "invasion of states' rights"; some denounced the ruling as part of a communist plot to destroy "the white race"; many pledged massive resistance to school integration. The Ku Klux Klan revived, and a new organization, the White Citizens Council, became a powerful force in many areas of the deep South. Not all members of the KKK and Citizens Council endorsed violent resistance, but some did use force against blacks who "didn't know their place." In 1954 a crowd of whites lynched a young black man, Emmet Till, for allegedly whistling at a white woman.

Southerners also used legal and political stratagems to delay integration. In 1957, 101 congressmen and senators signed the Southern Manifesto, a protest against "federal usurpation" of states' rights, and southern senators employed the filibuster to block civil-rights legislation. A segregationist image was essential to political survival in many southern states; after a moderate young lawyer, George C. Wallace, lost badly to a segregationist, he announced that he would never be "outnigraed again." The most spectacular example of official resistance came in 1957 when Arkansas governor Orval Faubus defied a federal court order to desegregate Little Rock High School and used helmeted national guardsmen to keep black children out of the building. With national authority openly challenged, the Eisenhower administration could not avoid the issue. Although never a firm supporter of integration, Eisenhower placed the Arkansas National Guard under federal control, augmented it with regular Army troops, and enforced the court order. The following year Arkansas officials tried to block desegregation through the courts. Meeting in emergency session, the Supreme Court rejected Arkansas' claim that the state need not obey national court orders and buried once again the states'-rights argument. After the Little Rock incident the Supreme Court declared unconstitutional the evasive tactics of closing down public schools and gerrymandering school districts, and it pressed for realistic desegregation plans.

Desegregation of public facilities in the South gained the support of influential people. Fighting a war against Nazi racism and crusading against "atheistic communism" had made American liberals more sensitive to injustices at home. The success of American institutions, they argued, required a greater commitment to racial justice. Policymakers, competing with the Soviets for the goodwill of third-world nations, found it difficult to explain away discrimination against nonwhites in the United States. When diplomats from the new African states experienced segregation firsthand, the whole system of Jim Crow became highly embarrassing to influential whites. Many religious leaders and scientists also lent their prestige to the civil-rights cause.

At the same time, the migration of northern-based corporations and industries to the southern states was producing important socioeconomic, and ultimately cultural, changes: in many ways the South was becoming more like the North. To a new generation of white southern leaders, this process of "northernization" made old patterns of racial domination, such as Jim Crow and political exclusion, seem both embarrassing and anachronistic. This new group of "white southern liberals" lacked a deep-seated commitment to segregation and possessed some genuine impulses to change settled ways.

The introduction of new industries and new technologies also affected black southerners. With the rise of white-owned agribusinesses, patterned on northern models, and the use of new agricultural techniques, the largely rural southern black population came under severe pressure. Old living patterns were disrupted: slowly at first, and then at a much more rapid rate, black people found themselves pushed off the land. Many moved to cities within the South or to urban areas in the northern states. During the 1940s and 1950s, it should be recalled, more than three million black people left the South. This disruption helped to break old deferential patterns and to encourage a new spirit of militancy among younger blacks. By the mid 1950s white leaders found it impossible to ignore black demands, for within the black community new leaders and new organizations were spearheading the fight for equality.

New Organizations and New Tactics

A young Alabama minister, Martin Luther King, Jr., eventually gained recognition as the most influential black leader. Certainly not a radical, King nevertheless went beyond the courtroom tactics of the NAACP and the calm lobbying of the Urban League. While still in his twenties he led a successful boycott against segregated public-transportation facilities in Montgomery, Alabama. King's tactics of nonviolent civil disobedience and economic pressure soon became the civil-rights movement's newest weapons. Citing the success of Mahatma Gandhi's passive resistance in India, King preached the importance of laying one's body on the line and of loving one's enemy. "If we are arrested every day. . . if we are trampled over every day, don't ever let anyone pull you so low as to hate them. We must use the weapon of love." In 1957 King and other black ministers formed the Southern Christian Leadership Conference (SCLC), which quickly became the most active civil-rights organization in the South.

King and the SCLC worked primarily through churches and drew their heaviest support from middle-class black people. The son of a prominent Atlanta minister, King had enjoyed a sheltered childhood and a good education at Morehouse College before going north to get a doctorate at Boston University. He spoke in the measured cadence of the black preacher, the man who traditionally led the black community, but he also had the oratorical power to move white audiences and touch their consciences with his message of Christian love. Whether he sought the role or not, King became the spokesman for the nation's entire black population. Such a position gained him the enmity of angry whites and of more militant black spokesmen.

Several other groups tried to work with the SCLC in the early 1960s. The Congress of Racial Equality (CORE) had employed nonviolent civil disobedience as early as the 1940s; led by James Farmer and later by Floyd McKissick, it became more active during the early 1960s. Another group, the Student Nonviolent Coordinating Committee (SNCC), evolved from demonstrations in North Carolina during the winter of 1960. Black college students, polite and neatly dressed, unsuccessfully tried to eat at a dime-store lunch counter. Braving hostile whites—who tossed lighted cigarettes, dumped ketchup, and threw punches—the young blacks remained seated, patiently waiting for service. The sit-in movement quickly spread to other kinds of public facilities as thousands of young activists, both white and black, joined the protests. In April 1960 a group of these students formed SNCC and accepted King's approach—nonviolent protest. Some of the early "freedom songs" expressed their optimism:

Freedom's Comin' and It Won't Be Long

We took a trip on a Greyhound bus,
Freedom's comin' and it won't be long
To fight segregation, this we must
Freedom's comin' and it won't be long.

Violence in 'bama didn't stop our cause
Freedom's comin' and it won't be long
Federal marshals come enforce the laws
Freedom's comin' and it won't be long.

On to Mississippi with speed we go
Freedom's comin' and it won't be long
Blue-shirted policemen meet us at the door
Freedom's comin' and it won't be long.

Judge say local custom shall prevail
Freedom's comin' and it won't be long
We say 'no' and we land in jail
Freedom's comin' and it won't be long.

Civil Rights: The Kennedy Years

The election of John Kennedy in 1960 seemed to offer hope of greater support from Washington. During his campaign JFK criticized the Eisenhower administration's reluctant support of integration and promised a new frontier for blacks. Once in office, he appointed a number of prominent black people to federal positions, filed more desegregation suits than his predecessor, and supported a new civil-rights act. (The previous civil-rights laws of 1957 and 1960 had dealt primarily with voting rights; Kennedy supported a measure that would ban discrimination in public accommodations and give the attorney general authority to file desegregation suits.)

Kennedy's political caution, however, tempered his campaign rhetoric. During the campaign he had denounced Eisenhower's refusal to issue an executive order ending discrimination in housing—Ike could do it with "a stroke of the pen," claimed Kennedy—but he delayed his own order for two years. Desiring good relations with southern congressmen, Kennedy often deferred to them on patronage questions, appointing several outright racists to the federal bench. (One Mississippi judge referred to black civil-rights workers as "monkeys" and consistently demeaned black defendants.) Kennedy also refused to cross J. Edgar Hoover, permitting the FBI leader to set his own rules in civil-rights cases. In effect, this meant that Hoover, no friend of civil-rights groups, would do as little as possible to help blacks and to jeopardize his close relationship with law officers in the South. Without thorough background investigations by the FBI, the Justice Department often lacked evidence to prosecute cases of alleged discrimination.

But a series of dramatic events in the deep South took the initiative away from the Kennedy administration; civil-rights activists, not the government in

Washington, began to determine the pace of change. In 1961 young activists from CORE and SNCC defied Jim Crow laws on interstate buses and in southern terminals. Angered by these "freedom riders," segregationists used iron bars, clubs, and finally explosives against the nonviolent invaders. Increasing violence finally forced the government to respond: Attorney General Robert Kennedy dispatched a team of Justice Department troubleshooters and a corps of federal marshals to protect the demonstrators. He also asked the Interstate Commerce Commission to issue an order banning segregation in interstate facilities, a request that the ICC honored in the fall of 1961. The use of federal personnel to protect the freedom riders established a pattern, and the following year President Kennedy reinforced the marshals with United States Army troops to quell violence that followed the enrollment of one black student, James Meredith, at the University of Mississippi. Kennedy's actions probably prevented bloodshed on other campuses—two people died during disorders at Ole Miss—and a confrontation at the University of Alabama in 1963 ended differently. After symbolically "standing in the schoolhouse door," George Wallace—the man who had once proclaimed "segregation now and forever"—stepped aside and watched Justice Department officials integrate the university without serious incident.

In the spring of 1963 the focus of integration struggles shifted from southern campuses to the streets of Birmingham, Alabama. The drive to desegregate public facilities in this Alabama industrial center marked an important turning point in the struggle for racial equality. Police violence escalated into savagery, and many people expressed outrage at the tactics of Birmingham's law-enforcement officials. Police Commissioner Eugene "Bull" Connor, who fit perfectly the northern stereotype of a red neck southern sheriff, turned fire hoses and dogs upon black demonstrators, including small children. Club-swinging policemen rounded up thousands of protestors and threw them into makeshift lockups. White vigilantes unleashed a terror campaign that culminated in the bombing of a black church; four Sunday-school children died in the blast.

Covered extensively in both the print and electronic media, the events in Birmingham had a significant impact on the black movement. Appalled by the violence, liberal opinion in the North and in Congress swung decisively in favor of new civil-rights legislation. Ultimately, then, the police and segregationist violence in Birmingham rebounded against Bull Connor and his allies. Equally as important, the rising militancy of Birmingham's young blacks gave a new urgency to liberal efforts, in both Birmingham and Washington, to deal with racial conflict. Seeking to avoid further violence and bloodshed, the leaders of Birmingham's white business community agreed to compromise with King's forces: three thousand imprisoned demonstrators were released, and the city's white power structure agreed to begin desegregation efforts. In Washington, John Kennedy told the nation that the "rising tide of discontent that threatens the public safety" could not be calmed by "repressive police action"; it was time, JFK urged, for members of Congress to act on the issue. He would press them, he pledged, to enact a strong civil-rights program.

Calm returned to Birmingham but the events there presaged important changes within the black movement. Some people who lived in crowded urban slums had never really accepted the rhetoric of nonviolence, and many young blacks began to express their displeasure with Dr. King's stated philosophy. In retrospect, Birmingham began the long period of urban violence that affected both the black movement and its white supporters. On the other hand, Birmingham also brought a subtle change to the nonviolent approach of Dr. King and the SCLC. He and his associates recognized that the violent white response ultimately rebounded to the benefit of the black movement. Although members of the SCLC never admitted it, their organization turned increasingly toward a strategy of "nonviolent provocation," a strategy designed to take advantage of coverage by the media and to exploit racist violence in the cause of civil rights. The SCLC relied upon this approach during their 1965 crusade in Selma, Alabama, a voter-registration drive that helped push Congress to enact the Voting Rights Act of that year.

But in August 1963, the violence that lay ahead remained hidden in a glow of optimism and a temporary spirit of cooperation that climaxed in the March on Washington. Following closely after the disorders in Birmingham, the march produced much favorable publicity for the civil-rights movement. Most northern newspapers and magazines praised the neat appearance, politeness, and commitment of the estimated 200,000 marchers. The unity within the movement also seemed exemplary: young activists from SNCC shared the platform with the NAACP and the Urban League as well as with white church and labor leaders. The speakers effectively captured the attention of participants and television viewers. Just when the August sun threatened to wilt the marchers, Martin Luther King revived their spirits with his "I Have a Dream" speech. A carefully structured series of images, but devoid of any substantive proposals for change, the address confirmed King's reputation as the movement's greatest spellbinder. With the formalities completed, civil-rights leaders adjourned to the White House for a coffee hour with the Kennedys.

The Civil Rights Act of 1964: End of an Era

Even though black leaders recognized JFK's limitations, his death seemed a great blow to their movement; it brought a southerner with an even more ambivalent record into the White House. But Lyndon Johnson quickly dispelled any doubts about his commitment to civil rights when he helped push a stronger version of Kennedy's bill through Congress in 1964.

The Civil Rights Act of 1964 outlawed racial, religious, and sexual discrimination in private businesses that served the general public—such as restaurants and filling stations—and in public facilities such as swimming pools. It also authorized the executive branch to withhold federal grants or contracts from institutions that discriminated against nonwhites and empowered the attorney general to file school-desegregation suits at his initiative. To safeguard voting rights, the law contained a section that established a sixth-grade educa-

JFK, RFK, and J. Edgar Hoover. The Kennedy brothers were reluctant to challenge entrenched interests and established power-brokers such as the FBI's long-time head.

March on Washington, 1963. The peaceful mood and optimistic spirit of August 1963 would not survive the turbulent 1960s.

tion as the basic requirement for literacy. This provision, it was hoped, would prevent the use of unfair "literacy" tests against black people seeking to register. (A white voting inspector in Alabama once flunked a black applicant because his test contained "an error in spilling.") When properly enforced, the Civil Rights Act of 1964 produced sweeping changes in the pattern of race relations. The law demanded no less than destruction of a settled way of life, a system of racial discrimination that had evolved after the formal end of slavery. According to the act, blacks could now sleep in any motel, eat in any restaurant, or sit anywhere on any bus.

Although it applied to the entire nation, the law cost many whites very little. Lower- and lower-middle-class whites, particularly in the South and in large northern cities, had to make most of the adjustments on behalf of the larger white society. Racists would lose the psychological security blanket of Jim Crow and might have to sit by, eat near, or work with black people. But such things, important as they were, required no basic alteration in America's socioeconomic structure or in the distribution of political power.

By 1964, however, many black people were demanding more than equal access to public accommodations and government facilities; the victories of the early 1960s had raised the stakes. Black militants complained that the government allowed no compensation for the years of discrimination, provided little immediate economic assistance, and gave no significant political power to black people. Such things, white politicians argued, were clearly impossible; it had taken much bloodshed and a great deal of political skill even to obtain the act of 1964. But young black radicals rejected arguments based upon what older black spokesmen and white politicians considered possible. Some blacks charged that their own leaders were selling out to the "white power structure." After the troubles in Birmingham, white philanthropists, perhaps frightened by the specter of violence moving northward or perhaps sincerely moved by the rightness of the cause, pledged almost a million dollars to the leading civil-rights organizations. Militants viewed this as a payoff and denounced Kennedy's civil-rights program as a sellout of the movement. During the March on Washington, leaders had forced John Lewis, the youthful head of SNCC, to rewrite his fiery address. Lewis had intended to criticize the Kennedy civil-rights bill—"What is there in this bill to ensure the equality of a maid who earns $5 a week in the home of a family whose income is $100,000 a year?"—and to condemn "the cheap political leaders who build their careers on immoral compromises and ally themselves with open forms of political, economic, and social exploitation." To preserve the harmony of the day, Lewis softened his speech, but other blacks did not attend the march or temper their words. One man who had not been invited asked, "Who ever heard of angry revolutionists all harmonizing 'We Shall Overcome Some Day' while tripping and swaying along arm-in-arm with the very people they were supposed to be revolting against?" The angry young man was Malcom X, an eloquent spokesman for militancy and black pride.

A series of disturbing events in 1964 made nonviolence and peaceful political appeals less attractive to some blacks. In Mississippi three civil-rights workers—Andrew Goodman, James Cheney, and Michael Schwerner—were brutally murdered; Cheney, the only black among the three, was apparently beaten to death with chains. That same year a group of activists risked their lives to organize the Mississippi Freedom Democratic Party (FDP), only to watch white liberals join with southern leaders to deny the FDP formal recognition at the Democratic National Convention. And during the Freedom Summer of 1964—a SNCC-sponsored campaign to register voters and establish "freedom schools"—racial tensions within the movement itself increased. Blacks frequently expressed their resentment of "paternalistic" whites and "fly-by-night freedom fighters who were bossing everybody around." As SNCC tried to limp along and to test the viability of nonviolence in the South, some northern blacks expressed their grievances in a very different way.

The Ghettos Explode

In August 1965 a clash between a white highway patrolman and a black motorist touched off four days of rioting, burning, and looting in the Los Angeles ghetto of Watts. Before the disorders ended, authorities had sent in the National Guard, thirty-four people had been killed, and property damage totaled more than $20 million. The trouble in Watts inaugurated several years of urban violence. The year 1967 was the worst, with disorders in 128 cities and major clashes in Newark and Detroit. The Detroit "riots," during which regular Army units were called to assist police and national guardsmen, caused at least forty-three deaths and produced widespread destruction in the black ghetto. In all the confrontations, blacks emerged the major losers: most of the people killed were black, and property damage generally remained confined to ghetto areas. Investigations revealed indiscriminate shooting by the authorities and several incidents of outright murder by white policemen. These disorders left behind burned-out buildings, racial hatred, and feelings of uneasiness among most white integrationists. The violence, after all, came during a time of undeniable progress in race relations. What could explain such destruction?

Official explanations tried to steer between theories of a grand revolutionary conspiracy and black radicals' claims of an incipient revolution against capitalist exploitation. Investigating the Watts disorder, the McCone Commission (headed by former CIA director John McCone) propounded a popular view: the "rotten apple" or "riff-raff" interpretation. A small group of troublemakers, the McCone Report concluded, had precipitated the trouble and fueled the violence. The "riots" were not legitimate protests against substantive grievances but "formless, quite senseless, all but hopeless" outbursts of looting and burning—"engaged in by a few but bringing great distress to all." The commission theorized that most of these "rotten apples" had recently migrated from the rural South and had not yet adjusted to the pressures and demands of urban life. Though it refused to call Watts a ghetto (because it contained mostly single-family dwellings and fairly wide streets) or to concede a serious problem of police brutality, the commission did see some problems in Watts. The black area had inadequate mass transit to jobs, poor educational facilities, and a small number of poorly trained policemen. Suggesting that the situation required no fundamental social or economic changes, the report called for greater job opportunities near Watts, more money for education, and "better understanding" between police and citizens. Throughout the report, McCone and the other commissioners viewed the need to maintain respect for the law-enforcement system as the major issue.

Other investigators quickly challenged the basic assumptions and conclusions of the McCone Commission. These observers sympathized with the people of Watts and considered the disorders to be political protests rather than formless riots. The violence in Watts, they claimed, involved a sizable portion of the black community, not a few misfits. The protesters, in fact, represented a cross section of the community: they had lived in Watts for some time, usually held low-paying jobs, and possessed the best education the ghetto could provide. Disputing the idea that the violence had been senseless, some researchers argued that protesters had tried to avoid black-owned businesses and had concentrated upon white firms that were considered dishonest. Critics of the McCone Commission also challenged the idea that Watts was not a ghetto: much of the housing was dilapidated, many businesses exploited black customers and employees, and police brutality was an everyday occurrence. Many of these writers concluded that the violence stemmed from a rational grasp of deep-seated, legitimate grievances.

Thus, the dispute between "riot" theorists and "protest" theorists involved more than a semantical difference. The former view upheld the quick suppression of such disorders and pointed to the need for changes within the existing system; the latter position at least implied the legitimacy of the protest and supported the need for more sweeping changes in American society. Equally as important, the riot view tended to see the problem as one between good people and bad people, between haves and have-lesses. The protest theory pointed to a deep-seated racial crisis, a conflict that could not be solved through more government-controlled "wars on poverty."

As disorders continued, the official explanation changed very little. The most extensive government investigation, President Johnson's National Advisory Commission on Civil Disorders (commonly called the Kerner Commission), rejected evidence that suggested fundamental problems with the American system. In the end, the commissioners did cite "white racism" as part of the trouble, but not before they had fired 120 staff members who wanted stronger language and had suppressed the staff's radical report, "The Harvest of American Racism." The commissioners' own document recommended a moderate two-pronged approach: increased government expenditures to help black people and more effective use of force to suppress disturbances. Inevitably, the last solution seemed more acceptable to most white politicians, and Congress voted additional funds to beef up local law-enforcement agencies and to train the National Guard in more efficient riot control. Saddled with burgeoning expenditures for Vietnam, the president filed away the commission's other recommendations. Johnson, like most other national leaders, ultimately preferred to ignore the broader implications of the commission's gloomy report.

Black Power

Meanwhile, militant black leaders were already citing white intransigence as a justification for rejecting integration—the traditional goal of the civil-rights movement. An established separatist group, the Black Muslims, suddenly gained prominence in the early 1960s. The Muslims preached the superiority of black people and black institutions, predicted eventual collapse for the decadent white society (including the corrupt Christian religion), planned the creation of separate black areas in the United States, and stressed the necessity for hard work and self-discipline. The sect gained a number of converts during the 1950s, including Malcolm Little, a former dope pusher and ex-convict but a self-educated man with a keen intellect. Rejecting his "Christian slave name," Malcolm X became Muslim leader Elijah Muhammad's top aide and the most eloquent spokesman for anti-integrationist ideas. Malcolm's fiery oratory first attracted national attention to the Muslims, and the conversion of the popular heavyweight boxing champion Cassius Clay (who became Muhammad Ali) gained them headlines in the sports section.

In advocating black pride and separation from whites, Malcolm X and the Muslims revived a powerful strain in the Afro-American heritage. Malcolm ridiculed Martin Luther King's philosophy of nonviolence: "If someone puts a hand on you," he preached, "send him to the cemetery." He advised black people to join together "to lift the level of our community, and to make our society beautiful so that we will be satisfied in our own social circles and won't be running around here trying to knock our way into a social circle where we're not wanted." A series of disputes with Elijah Muhammad led Malcolm to form his own movement—The Organization of Afro-American Unity—in 1963. After leaving the Muslims, he slowly began to temper his separatist rhetoric and to suggest a working alliance with a variety of black and white groups. Such ideas seemed heresy to the more isolationist followers of Elijah Muhammad. In 1965 Malcolm was assassinated by his Muslim enemies. After his death, growing numbers of people read his *Autobiography,* and Malcom became an even greater hero to young radicals. "Black history began with Malcolm X," proclaimed Eldridge Cleaver of the Black Panthers.

By the mid 1960s the doctrines of black pride and black nationalism seemed to be gaining greater support. Southern resistance to the Civil Rights Act of 1964 and the new Voting Rights Act of 1965 produced further bloodshed and death; to some blacks, the urban disorders in the North suggested the possibility that violence might bring more concessions or at least greater psychological satisfaction than nonviolent civil disobedience. In May 1966, SNCC, officially committed to integration, urged blacks "to begin building independent political, economic, and cultural institutions that they will control and use as instruments of social change in this country." Later that summer SNCC joined other civil-rights groups, including the SCLC and CORE, in a protest march through Mississippi, an effort that widened divisions within the civil-rights movement. Stokely Carmichael, SNCC's new chairman, took the spotlight away from Martin Luther King, who was often absent. Carmichael vowed that he would never go to jail peacefully again and declared that "every courthouse in Mississippi ought to be burned down to get rid of the dirt." In the most publicized event of the march, he coined the movement's new slogan: Black Power! The media played up the role of the militants, and older black leaders complained that television reporters pushed a microphone in front of anybody who yelled "Black Power!" or "burn, baby, burn!"

Behind the sloganeering, young blacks were seriously attempting to frame a workable philosophy. The people in SNCC and CORE had tried nonviolence and cooperation with whites, and they believed that these tactics had failed. Integration, wrote Stokely Carmichael, "reinforces among both black and white, the idea that 'white' is automatically better and 'black' is by definition inferior." And to blacks like Carmichael, political and legal equality, the basis of the old civil-rights movement, now seemed less important than immediate economic power. Black people, they argued, had to gain control of their communities and expel the "white power structure"—the "dishonest" businessmen, the "rent-gouging" landlords, and the "crooked" politicians. Get Rid of Whitey! became a rallying cry. Along with independence, young nationalists promoted black pride. Since whites would always see blacks as inferior, they contended, black people must reject the values of white society and seek a cultural identity based upon their Afro-American heritage. As a means of stimulating black pride and cultural nationalism, militants demanded community control of ghetto schools and, where this was not immediately possible, black-studies courses taught and administered by blacks.

There were many variations on the themes of black power and black nationalism. Some blacks, identifying with dark-skinned peoples in the third world, viewed black Americans as colonized people subject to the domination of alien, white masters. Others adopted a Marxist framework, seeing blacks as the most exploited group in an exploitative capitalist society. Violent revolution, a few extremists suggested, offered the best means of redressing grievances. But most others warned against open confrontations with the overwhelming firepower of white America, and most radicals suggested the need to build a base of support before pressing the movement for significant social change.

The history of the Black Panthers, an organization that attracted the media spotlight in the late 1960s, revealed the tensions generated by debates over black power and black nationalism. Formed in Oakland, California, the Panthers gained attention primarily through a shootout with Oakland police and through the literary success of Eldridge Cleaver's *Soul on Ice*. The Oakland group borrowed their name from the short-lived Black Panther party of

Lowndes County, Alabama, an organization sponsored by SNCC. Outfitted in paramilitary garb, the Panthers frightened many whites, and law-enforcement officials denounced the group as a grave threat to American society. Panther leaders Huey Newton (who was convicted of killing a policeman during the Oakland shootout) and Bobby Seale urged blacks to organize "self-defense groups that are dedicated to defending our black community against racist oppression and brutality." The Panthers also demanded a guaranteed income for all citizens, exemption of blacks from military service, government funds for cooperative housing facilities, reparation payments "as retribution for slave labor and mass murder of black people," release of all black prisoners "because they have not received a fair and impartial trial," and use of all-black juries to try black defendants. Such demands borrowed from black nationalist ideas, but they also owed much to a simplistic Marxism and to the rhetoric of American constitutional law. (Huey Newton always carried a stack of law books in his car.) In seeking to advance their goals, Panthers found it difficult to fix a strategy: should they ally with white radicals and prepare for revolutionary action, or should they avoid ties with nonblacks and stress black pride? The Panthers finally did seek ties with both white and black radicals, a course that did not please all of the party's members.

By 1968 neither black power nor black nationalism had carried the day. Most black people—if opinion polls are to be believed—still supported the traditional aims of integration and equal rights, and they considered Martin Luther King the foremost black leader. But the spirit of militancy had prompted black people to reexamine their goals and aspirations. Most saw no real contradiction between greater racial pride and some type of integration with white society, no real conflict between greater political power for blacks and acceptance of the basic American system. Black politicans, gaining crucial white votes to add to their power base, began to obtain elective office in many large cities. Throughout the 1960s the income of black families did rise, though it still lagged behind that of whites. New styles of dress—Afro haircuts and dashikis—appeared to be more than the latest fashions; black studies seemed more than a passing fad. When he was killed in 1968, Martin Luther King was trying to use his Poor People's Crusade as a means of bringing together a coalition of "have-nots." He never used cries of "Black Power!" but he had begun to recognize the limits of the old SCLC approach and to stress black pride.

The Civil Rights Act of 1968, the last major civil-rights measure, indicated the ambivalent attitude of white politicians toward the black revolution. Title VIII of the law prohibited discrimination in the advertising, financing, sale, or rental of most homes and charged the executive branch with acting "affirmatively" to achieve integrated housing. Together with a Supreme Court decision and state open-housing laws, the act seemed an important step toward integration of the largely white suburbs. If coupled with generous funding for inner-city projects, it promised better urban housing for minority families. The urban violence of the 1960s did, therefore, produce some positive responses, in the form of congressional legislation and bureaucratic attention, from the political system.

But in the Civil Rights Act of 1968 the majority of whites in Congress also indicated their fear of the radical implications of black violence. At the instigation of Strom Thurmond of South Carolina, Congress included in the act a section that made it a crime to use the facilities of interstate commerce "to organize, promote, encourage, participate in, or carry on a riot; or to commit any act of violence in furtherance of a riot." In approving this seemingly vague provision, most members of Congress knew exactly what they wanted: a federal law that would stop the activities of black-power advocates such as H. Rap Brown of SNCC. The "Rap Brown section" gave national authorities a catchall statute to halt the travels and organizing efforts of black radicals.

The movement for political and economic power and the renaissance of black pride, then, affected white as well as black people. The sight of young persons shouting "Black Power!" and of black men and women with Afro haircuts represented a threat to settled ways. But many whites recognized the need for greater black pride and self-assertiveness. Potentially at least, the message that black is beautiful could also liberate white Americans from narrowness and old prejudices.

SUGGESTIONS FOR FURTHER READING

Two sympathetic but still highly revealing accounts of the Kennedy presidency were written by close associates: Arthur Schlesinger, Jr., *A Thousand Days* (1965) and Theodore Sorenson, *Kennedy* (1965). Much more critical are Henry Fairlie, *The Kennedy Promise* (1972) and Bruce Miroff, *Pragmatic Illusions* (1976). Two later works—Harrison Wofford's *Of Kennedys and Kings* (1980) and Herbert S. Parmet's *Jack* (1980) seek to provide balanced assessments. *Decade of Disillusionment* (1976) by Jim F. Heath remains a useful synthesis. There are also a variety of specific works, including Grant McConnell, *Steel and the Presidency—1962* (1963); Jim F. Heath, *John F. Kennedy and the Business Community* (1969); Victor Navasky, *Kennedy Justice* (1971); and Carl M. Brauer, *John F. Kennedy and the Second Reconstruction* (1977). In addition, see the evaluations of Kennedy in Garry Wills, *Nixon Agonistes* (rev. ed., 1980) and Godfrey Hodgson, *America in Our Time* (1976). There are many books, most of them dreadful, on the Kennedy assassination. Good places to begin with this murky subject are Edward Jay Epstein's *Inquest* (1963) and *Legend* (1978).

Lyndon Johnson, *The Vantage Point* (1972) is an unrevealing memoir. The best studies of LBJ include Eric F. Goldman, *The Tragedy of Lyndon Johnson* (1969); Doris Kearns, *Lyndon Johnson and the American Dream* (1976); and Merle Miller, *Lyndon Johnson: An Oral Biography* (1980).

The War on Poverty has already attracted a huge literature. Marvin E. Gettleman and David Mermelstein, eds., *The Great Society Reader* (1965) remains an excellent introduction. The most favorable assessment of liberal programs is *The Promise of Greatness* (1976) by Sar Levitan and Robert Taggart.

Edward Banfield's *The Heavenly City* (rev. ed., 1970) and Daniel P. Moynihan's *Maximum Feasible Misunderstanding* (1970) offer critiques from what has become popularly known as the neo-conservative perspective. 'Critiques from the left include Richard Cloward and Francis Fox Piven, *Poor People's Movements* (1978) and William P. Ryan, *Blaming the Victim* (rev. ed., 1976). Michael Harrington, who helped to popularize the crusade against poverty, offers his own assessment in *The Twilight of Capitalism* (1976) and in *Decade of Decision* (1980).

There is an even larger literature on black politics. Good places to begin are Howell Raines's skillful oral history, *My Soul is Rested* (1978); Howard Zinn's *SNCC* (1965); and Martin Luther King's *Why We Can't Wait* (1962). The best secondary accounts include Richard Kluger, *Simple Justice* (1976); Steven F. Lawson, *Black Ballots: Voting Rights in the South* (1976); David L. Lewis, *King: A Critical Biography* (rev. ed., 1978); David J. Garrow, *Protest at Selma* (1978); Elliot Rudwick and August Meier, *CORE* (1972); and William Chafe, *Civilities and Civil Rights* (1980). See also the useful syntheses in Cloward and Piven's *Poor People's Movements* and in Hodgson's *America in Our Time*.

The emergence of black nationalism and black power can be seen in works such as Malcom X's *Autobiography* (1965); Eldridge Cleaver's *Soul on Ice* (1967); Huey P. Newton's *To Die for the People* (1972); and *Black Power* (1967) by Stokely Carmichael and Charles V. Hamilton.

THE PERILS OF POWER: FOREIGN POLICY IN THE 1960s

Kennedy's Foreign Policy

New Programs

Republican irresolution annoyed the men of John Kennedy's New Frontier. In the presidential campaign of 1960, Kennedy charged that the Eisenhower-Nixon team had created a dangerous "missile gap" between the United States and the Soviet Union and had not worked vigorously to eliminate Castro. (Neither charge was true.) Once in the White House, Kennedy charted an activist policy, one that did not question the basic cold-war assumptions of the Dulles years but promised to wage the cold war in a more determined way and with a greater variety of techniques. Kennedy promised that his foreign policy would provide a "flexible response": it would challenge communism on every level, from atomic weaponry to "counterinsurgency units" to economic pressure to enlarged covert capabilities.

General Maxwell Taylor, army chief of staff, told Kennedy, "We must show the Russians that wars of national liberation are not cheap, safe, and disavowable but costly, dangerous, and doomed to failure." Believing that ground combat was still relevant, even in the era of atomic brinkmanship, Taylor and his staff sketched a handy new mission for the army: "nation building." To checkmate guerrilla tactics, highly trained elite forces would teach local troops the techniques of counterinsurgency and instruct them in twentieth-century technology and liberal democracy. Air cavalry and special units such as the Green Berets were to fill the interstices of nuclear stalemate and insure that the third world would be stable and friendly to the United States. For Kennedy even more than for Dulles, the front lines of the cold war were everywhere.

Others in the new administration stressed using moral example or America's wealth to promote development. In a fervor of "can-do" activism, these individuals moved to short-circuit the cycle of poverty, the sense of helplessness that they felt fueled communist appeals to the underdeveloped world. Ironically, while Kennedy found it difficult to secure congressional approval for reform at home, Capitol Hill enthusiastically funded Taylor's experiments, along with new departures in foreign aid, such as the Alliance for Progress and the Peace Corps. Just five months after the new president proposed "a ten-year plan for the Americas," all the nations of the Western Hemisphere except Canada and Cuba signed the Charter of Punta del Este in August 1961. The United States promised $10 million over the next decade to finance social programs, such as health care, housing and education, and economic credits to stabilize commodity prices and boost local rates of growth by 2.5 percent annually. This Alliance for Progress, the New Frontiersmen calculated, would thwart radicalism and ensure compliance: they talked of "judicious grants" that could encourage moderate, reformist leaders while breaking oligarchic or anti-American regimes. The Agency for International Development (AID) operated on a smaller scale in all third-world areas. An even more imaginative program, the Peace Corps, sent volunteers to willing nations throughout the world. Functioning primarily in rural areas, the Peace Corps worked to improve health, education, and economic efficiency. Director R. Sargent Shriver expected no dramatic results, only "cumulative years of goodwill among the common folk." By 1963 volunteers were working in over forty countries as teachers, crop specialists, and construction supervisors.

The Alliance for Progress became a disaster, ultimately leaving Latin America debt-ridden and even more dependent on United States-based multinationals. The Peace Corps also came under attack in many lands. But both reflected the New Frontier's confidence in Americans' ability to shape the world in its own image.

Cuba

A curious constellation of events made foreign-policy innovation not only feasible but almost mandatory. To JFK it seemed, Eisenhower-Dulles tactics had produced perverse results during the early 1960s. Despite his usual skepticism about unlikely schemes, Kennedy continued a CIA project to invade Cuba with a small force of anti-Castro expatriates. The disgruntled population, America's spies predicted, would welcome these rebels as liberators. On April 17, two days after CIA mercenaries had attacked Cuba's air bases with B-26 bombers, approximately 1,400 Cuban exiles waded ashore at the Bay of Pigs. Local peasants ignored the unlikely army, most of them pro-Batista urbanites, and Castro's forces soon surrounded them. Though some in the State Department urged full-scale intervention, Kennedy reluctantly accepted the fact of disaster. "Victory has a hundred fathers," he said, "but defeat is an orphan." The episode only tightened Castro's control in Cuba, reinforced his dependence upon the Soviet Union, and loosed yet another round of Yankeephobia throughout most of Latin America. The debacle also raised Kennedy's anxiety about being perceived as weak-willed and thus increased his determination to "get tough" in future showdowns.

Before Washington officials could recover from this setback, another element of Eisenhower's legacy threatened to spin away. Khrushchev thwarted

Kennedy's hopes for continued détente. Unwilling to accept a strategic balance that would solidify America's great lead in weaponry and industrial development, the Russians hoped first to gain easy concessions from an inexperienced president. At an informal summit meeting in Vienna in June 1961, Khrushchev hinted at war unless NATO abandoned West Berlin. If the United States did not agree, the premier explained, he could secure the same result by signing a separate peace with his East German ally Walter Ulbricht. Determined to uphold America's credibility, Kennedy mobilized the National Guard, accelerated arms production, and tripled draft calls. Khrushchev blustered about "thermonuclear holocaust" but acted much more cautiously. Barbed wire and then a wall of cement blocks sealed off East Berlin from the Western sectors, ending an embarrassing flow of defectors (some three million since 1945) and cutting off a black market in goods and currencies. Kennedy gracefully accepted this compromise, realizing the substance of victory.

Stung by rebukes from domestic critics for his poor showing, Khrushchev quickly took up a fortuitous opportunity for a major strategic victory. Frightened of America's aggressiveness, Castro apparently asked the Soviet Union for military hardware. Moscow replied with massive shipments of sophisticated weapons, including missiles armed with atomic warheads. Kennedy responded with a week of crisis diplomacy. In a televised address on October 22, 1962, he vowed, "The United States will not compromise its safety," and ordered the Strategic Air Command to full alert. Within two days the navy had quarantined the island, its destroyers ready to turn away any Soviet merchant ships carrying missiles. But Kennedy also began searching for compromise: if Russia removed its weapons, the United States would not attack Cuba again. While public prodding continued—United Nations Ambassador Adlai Stevenson urged the Soviets "to save the peace"—secret messages between the Kremlin and the White House soon confirmed Kennedy's offer. Then on Saturday, October 26, amid headlines warning of imminent nuclear war, Khrushchev tried an exchange: Soviet withdrawal from Cuba in return for the dismantling of American bases in Turkey. Not an unreasonable request, it was ignored by Kennedy who forced the Soviet premier to accept his own terms. Russian missiles were crated and sent home, over Castro's protests, within three weeks. Castro's Cuba continued to be harassed by CIA plots, but superpower confrontation there was over.

The Cuban missile crisis highlighted the perils of cold-war diplomacy. The swiftness of nuclear escalation frightened both sides; mutual blackmail, if miscalculated, could easily get out of control. Then, too, both powers had other concerns. In late 1962 China overran Tibet and ostentatiously began atomic tests in Sinkiang, near Russia's border. Mao Tse-tung openly challenged Moscow for leadership of the Communist bloc. The Americans, on the brink of a whirlpool involvement in Vietnam, wanted to experiment with counterinsurgency, "nation building," and the other tactics of flexible response. Superpower rhetoric mellowed, Khrushchev admitting, "If the United States is now a paper tiger, it has atomic teeth," and Kennedy calling for "mutual tolerance." During the summer of 1963 the two countries set up a "hot line," a direct telephone link between their capitals. And on July 25, 1963, America, Britain, and Russia initialed a nuclear-test-ban treaty that ended all except underground atomic explosions. (Russian fears that on-site inspections might reveal too much about its industrial potential made a total ban impossible.) Such gestures did little to ease rivalry between the two superpowers, but they did indicate a mutual desire to harness that competition into nonnuclear—and therefore less deadly—channels.

If Cuba daily reminded Washington officials of cold-war dangers, peaceful coexistence allowed them to act elsewhere in the third world. And most Americans, proud of their ingenuity, did not easily recognize limits to what was possible. Surely, with such riches, such power, such determination, the United States could build nations in the third world like itself: prosperous, democratic, and anticommunist.

Struggle in Vietnam

The End of Diem

Hoping to sharpen the nation's credibility while pushing back a communist liberation movement, the Kennedy administration tested its new flexible approach in Southeast Asia. Diem still blocked reform, despite pressure from American ambassadors, so the Democrats undertook the only other alternative, a military defeat of the NLF. Billions of dollars, tons of sophisticated weapons, and 16,000 American combat troops had inundated the Vietnamese countryside by 1963. At first, the communist effort wavered, seemingly justifying the Pentagon's tactics. But then Hanoi increased its aid to the insurgents, and Kennedy widened the American intervention to include a covert war against North Vietnam. More discouraging, Diem's regime came apart at the seams. Apparently limitless treasure from Washington had brought jolting corruption in Saigon. The scramble for loot hindered normal operations of state. Land reform collapsed. Conscripted soldiers seemed more bent on plunder than on winning popular support away from the NLF.

In May 1963, the Catholic Archbishop forbade the carrying of Buddhist flags, and anti-Buddhist persecution grew strong throughout the provinces. Now, forced either to abandon some religious practices or to face charges of treason, Buddhists organized massive demonstrations, which culminated on June 16, 1963, when a priest martyred himself by setting fire to his gasoline-soaked robes. As if finally convinced of Diem's turpitude, city people paraded in the streets and prayed at pagodas for his downfall. For nearly two months the regime waited for animosities to abate, but more self-immolations and the growing violence of student strikes convinced Diem and his brother, Ngo Dinh Nhu, that only strong measures could restore order. On August 21, detachments from American-trained special-forces units attacked Buddhist sanctuaries in Saigon, Hue, and most provincial capitals. This terrorism, coupled with political arrests, prompted another, even more violent, cycle of protest and repression. Intellectuals and the urban middle class abandoned the Diem regime, which was now consumed in self-destruction.

No one knew what to do, least of all the surprised bureaucrats in Washington watching television reports from Saigon. One obvious reaction was to excise the cancer: Diem must go. The internal chaos of his regime enervated the war effort against the communists and mocked hopes for a democratic example for the third world. Religious persecution bothered Americans, including the president, himself a Catholic. During the fall of 1963 several Vietnamese generals suggested plans for a coup to the American ambassador, Henry Cabot Lodge. They received the encouraging reply that Washington would not intervene in "an internal matter." The CIA also began to work toward Diem's replacement. In October the Kennedy administration unexpectedly canceled the commercial-import program that financed Diem's government and publicly disavowed the rest of his family. Reassured that Washington would support Diem's ouster, the generals wheeled into action, and on November 1 Vietnamese battalions near Saigon captured administrative centers and surrounded Diem's palace. The man whom Americans had vainly tried to turn into the George Washington of Vietnam died that night, murdered while trying to escape his country.

American Goals and Vietnamese Realities

That same month an era also ended in the United States. On November 22, 1963, President Kennedy died in Dallas, Texas, victim of an assassination. Anxious to maintain continuity, Lyndon Johnson did not challenge the policy of growing involvement in Vietnam. The new president wanted to help "those little people." Although Johnson's justification for war later became more sophisticated, the Texan never really seemed to forget the Alamo and the brave men who defied everything there in their will to triumph. White House advisers fleshed out LBJ's emotionalism with new variations on cold-war themes. The United States must repel communist aggression now or face repeated nibbling elsewhere. If Washington faltered, many third-world leaders might question America's ability, even its willingness, to protect their countries against subversion. Russia must understand Yankee determination to contain communism. Walt Whitman Rostow, the president's special adviser on foreign affairs, speculated that American pressure in Vietnam would divert Chinese attention away from the Pacific and toward central Asia, thus aggravating the Sino-Soviet split. Vietnamese problems thus became absorbed into global strategy: a Pentagon expert explained in 1968 that repelling communist aggression in Asia was "only 10 percent" of America's purpose; the war was being fought primarily to reassure allies and frighten enemies elsewhere.

Seeking larger goals, bureaucrats lost sight of their tool, Vietnam, still a very traditional peasant society. Ritual emperors had symbolized universal order for thousands of economically self-sufficient villages. Individuals molded themselves into a historical process that emphasized continuity with the past, not

John F. Kennedy's Press Conference, 1961. Breaking with the practice of his predecessors, JFK held frequent press conferences. But he never completely revealed his administration's policies in Indo-China.

progress toward a different future. The Vietnamese valued harmony and unanimity more than personal freedom or abstract principles. Rigid adherence to authority, they believed, insured the day-to-day functioning of society. Such communal certainty provided psychological security for its members and great tenacity for its primary institution, the village. Then French colonialism ripped away the emperor's "mandate of Heaven"—popular confidence in his right to rule—and warped the agrarian economy. The new masters demanded surplus, not self-sufficiency, so they herded Vietnamese together on rice or rubber plantations. Saigon and Hanoi became parasitic pleasure spas for these *colons* and their upper-class mandarin supporters. Although ethnocentric French teachers tried for decades to "civilize" the natives, they educated only a class of intellectuals, who were thereby alienated from the rest of the people. Despite such changes, the villages' timeless agrarianism remained the basis for both society and ethics.

The first Indochinese war, followed by Diem's ruthless centralism, aggravated the rural-urban split, the tension between old and new, familiar and foreign. Westerners valued development, but the National Liberation Front easily accepted the communal basis of life in Vietnamese villages. Red cadres talked of traditional ways and enacted land reforms immediately. Westerners too often exploited national resources or pursued irrelevant political theories. The communists deferred ultimate goals as they pursued popular changes. In contrast, rulers in Saigon tried to impose forms of democracy, but not its substance, upon an uninterested people. Peasants feared Saigon as a hostile place with novel, disruptive ideas.

Americans never realized that their revolution from above—their effort to replace peasant unanimity with Western pluralism—could never compete with the NLF restoration from below. In one sense, however, Lyndon Johnson had few, if any, options. Only a strong American presence could stave off internal collapse in South Vietnam, now without a leader or even a government. The new president's advisers did not readily abandon old rationales. Johnson accepted their theories about credibility as much as he had earlier theories about dominoes: "The United States must take a strong stand," he said, "or else no one will believe our promises." The lure of big gains at reasonable cost still bewitched Washington. After a month-long inspection tour, Secretary of Defense Robert S. McNamara and Chief of Staff Maxwell Taylor reported on October 2, 1963, that the United States could begin pulling out its troops by early 1964. But one thing escaped these computations: the nature of Vietnam itself. This was the tragic flaw that wrecked the careful calculations of computers and the estimates of Washington's most talented prognosticators.

A Vigorous Beginning, 1964–65

American began the second Indochinese war during the winter of 1964-65, responding to growing chaos in South Vietnam. A revolving door of military juntas undermined the anticommunist effort on the battlefield and only aggravated Diem's legacy of corruption and malaise. The NLF rapidly filled the political vacuum in the countryside, appealing to many Vietnamese frustrated by years of indecisive warfare. By the middle of 1964 they had recaptured many villages and begun preparations for a major assault on provincial capitals, always supported by military aid from Hanoi. Considerably frightened at this prospect, Pentagon officials drew up plans for an air war against North Vietnam. Though this was only a substitute for the accelerating counterinsurgency in the South, no other option seemed feasible, short of an embarrassing disengagement or total war. But escalation required legal, if not moral, justification. The White House drafted a congressional resolution authorizing air attacks and waited for an opportunity.

It came almost too quickly. During his 1964 presidential campaign, Johnson presented himself as a peace candidate, firmly rejecting prescriptions from critics, such as former air-force chief of staff Curtis Lemay for "bombing Hanoi back into the Stone Age." Then in early August of that year came reports of a naval encounter in the Gulf of Tonkin. Just after Vietnamese special forces and their American advisers raided two small islands on August 2, the United States spy ship *Maddox* violated Hanoi's self-proclaimed twelve-mile territorial sea limit. Assuming that the destroyer was part of a larger operation, North Vietnam ordered several PT boats into the area. As these ships closed in, several volleys were exchanged. Two days later the *Maddox* and another destroyer, the *C. Turner Joy,* returned to the Gulf of Tonkin. Anxious naval captains and malfunctioning sonar equipment soon reported—perhaps created—a second attack.

Denouncing such "unprovoked aggression" during a nationally televised speech, President Johnson ordered reprisal raids against North Vietnamese naval bases. The temporary feeling of crisis prompted Congress to pass the so-called Gulf of Tonkin resolution. Its open-ended phraseology authorized Johnson "to take all necessary measures" to repulse communist advances. Unaware of the dubious nature of Hanoi's attacks and, like the chief executive himself, ill informed about Vietnamese complexities, the Senate adopted the de facto declaration of war, 88 to 2. Only two senators, Wayne Morse and Ernest Gruening, questioned the wisdom of this potentially unlimited commitment.

After the 1964 presidential election, United States officials translated reprisal into a sustained air assault. Pentagon bureaucrats argued that the Saigon clique could not reform itself as long as insurgency continued. Guerrilla attacks would go on as long as North Vietnam supplied them. Bombing strikes against the North and elite counterinsurgency operations in the South would defeat this national war of liberation, Washington's best and brightest told each other, and restore America's global credibility. But analysis could not alter reality. Anger and discontent with the Saigon regime, together with carefully cultivated affinities between communist propaganda and Vietnamese traditionalism, fueled the NLF's successes. Forcing North Vietnam out of the war would only weaken, not defeat, guerrilla tactics in the South. The deepening morass of Vietnam frightened other nations. More and more, the immediate problem of destroying insurgents preoccupied Washington's planners. Because no one knew exactly what such a mission required, the treadmill of escalation ground forward. It seemed reasonable: just a little more aid, just a few more soldiers would break the rebellion. Victory remained always so close. Johnson himself believed that a steady, predictable escalation would avoid intervention by China or Russia and at the same time convince the NLF and Hanoi that they would not win.

Determination Becomes Self-Delusion, 1965 – 67

The war slowly intensified. Sustained bombing of North Vietnam began on February 15, 1965, ostensibly in reprisal for an NLF mortar attack against a Marine Corps base at Pleiku. That spring, American combat troops began to aid Vietnamese army units under fire. Johnson authorized the first "search-and-destroy" mission—independent sweeps involving large numbers of GIs—for June 27-30, 1965, several miles northwest of Saigon. Assumptions of American omnipotence soon withered, however, because Washington's overconfident planners underestimated the enemy. Guerrilla methods confused soldiers trained for large-scale wars of maneuver. Most military experts guessed that victory required a ten-to-one numerical advantage over NLF-North Vietnamese troops. But the enemy, recruiting the bulk of their manpower within South Vietnam itself, more than matched, at this ratio, Pentagon escalations.

Washington ingenuity, now thoroughly intrigued by immediate problems, tried to cope with this depressing situation in two ways. Against a backdrop of Johnsonian rhetoric about "winning the hearts and minds of the Vietnamese people," a plethora of bureaucrats inundated the countryside with experiments. AID officials taught the villagers useful skills, health care, and modern agricultural techniques. Combat units built hospitals, schools, orphanages. Government programs assured the farmer of high prices for his crop but low prices for the consumer. The junta in Saigon periodically deployed urban volunteers to counteract the work of communist cadres. Nation-building, however, barely touched communist strength in rural areas. By 1967 frustrated officials adopted still another device for rural pacification: the strategic-hamlet program. To protect villagers from NLF attack and ensure their loyalties to Saigon, American soldiers garrisoned many rural towns, often erecting makeshift forts. Herded into barbed-wire enclosures, living under American machine guns, the peasants were expected to continue their agrarian way of life. Such concentration camps did achieve their military purpose, but they permanently alienated farmers, now isolated from land and tradition.

Bewildered and angered by the failure of their good intentions, Americans came to rely upon more direct and even savage tactics. Computer printouts in Washington explained that improved "kill ratios" could substitute for the elusive ten-to-one formula. Bombs, artillery, and rifles could kill so many enemy soldiers that eventually the NLF and North Vietnamese could not replace them,

Chemical Defoliation. Mangrove forests in Vietnam before and after defoliation.

given their relatively small population base. If such thinking skirted genocide, the nature of guerrilla war made it almost inevitable. The NLF did not wear uniforms. Taking Mao Tse-Tung's advice, the insurgents "swam like fishes in a sea of people," and fought a war of stealth: ambush, booby trap, sabotage, quick mortar barrage.

To many American soldiers, both enthusiastic volunteers and scared draftees, the war became one against the Vietnamese themselves. Murder became at once hideously personal and clinically remote. Search-and-destroy missions created a misconception that "body count" alone mattered. Some West Pointers, realizing that careers depended upon numbers, brutalized

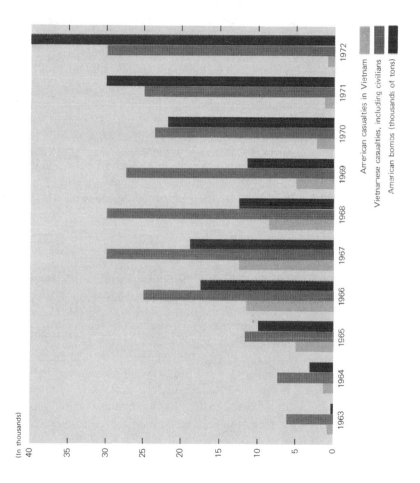

Burner, Marcus, and Rosenberg, America: A Portrait in History, 2nd ed. *Volume 2.*

Casualties in vietnam.

villagers for information and lied to superiors about enemy dead; GIs often tortured NLF suspects, matching the grotesque tactics of their foe. The United States command in Saigon charted "free-fire zones," huge areas in which helicopter gunships strafed anything alive. Chemicals defoliated the earth, and bombers pulverized North Vietnam's industry and South Vietnam's farms. Such devices may have limited communist freedom of movement, but they also destroyed American prestige. In a traditional society whose members valued their ties to ancestral lands and to village communities, terror, free-fire zones, and wholesale murder hopelessly discredited the American cause.

The Americans miscalculated badly, but no one admitted it. Middle-level civilians and field officers reported what higher officials in Saigon wanted to hear, not the actuality of stagnation. America's ambassadors and generals further refined the stylized ritual: we are winning the war, they wired Washington, but send us more money, more men. For many Kennedy Democrats still in the administration, tough-mindedness became not a style but an end. A militant stand ensured approval as a "realistic appraisal" and garnered points in bureaucratic infighting. The Russians and Chinese, bickering over their 4,500-mile frontier, carefully refrained from any cold-war challenge or diplomatic aid that might release their most dangerous rival from the quicksands of Southeast Asia. Such quiescence, in turn, freed America to act in Indochina and convinced its officials that the war somehow promoted communist mellowing. Having shoehorned the conflict into America's global strategy, Johnson isolated himself completely from Vietnamese realities and vowed that "I will not be the first president to lose a war."

Neither Diplomacy nor Reform

Unrealistic calculations scuttled early opportunities for compromise. Johnson and his advisers used diplomacy either to justify further escalation or to secure an American victory. When U Thant, secretary-general of the United Nations, suggested in July 1964 that the Geneva conference reconvene, Johnson righteously refused: "We do not believe in conferences called to ratify terror." But nine months later, the war firmly escalated, the president told an audience at Johns Hopkins University that the United States would discuss peace. He even offered American capital to rebuild "a peaceful Southeast Asia," almost a bribe for surcease. Yet his continued demand for a noncommunist regime in Saigon was unrealistic, tantamount to a Hanoi-NLF capitulation. The enemy routinely rejected such transparent efforts to achieve at the bargaining table what American soldiers had not won in the field. Every rebuff, the president chided his critics, proved communist perfidy.

Johnson used diplomacy more for war-making than for peacemaking. During a thirty-seven-day period in December 1965 and January 1966, he halted the Rolling Thunder bombing raids against North Vietnam and ostentatiously sponsored a far-flung peace initiative. His closest friends applauded his cleverness. The air war had not materially impaired Hanoi's war production, and anyway, few military targets remained. Ho Chi Minh had simply decentralized, then camouflaged his industry in the countryside. Although Ho responded to Johnson's pause with hints about a coalition or neutralist government for South Vietnam, Johnson rejected further talks. Instead he pointed to enemy "truculence" and unleashed a new air war, this one directed against Hanoi's supply routes through Indochinese mountains and jungles. At the same time, Johnson vigorously escalated the ground war. Troop levels jumped from 150,000 in February 1966 to 550,000 at their peak in 1968. For nearly twenty-four months, America saved Vietnam from communism by destroying its land and its people.

Washington bureaucrats also tried to reform Saigon's government. Absorbed in its coups and intrigues but assured of American money, the military junta became not only dictatorial but also useless. Johnson summoned the two most recently installed generals, Nguyen Van Thieu and Nguyen Cao Ky, to a meeting in Honolulu in February 1966. He extracted promises from the quiet Thieu and the more flamboyant Ky that they would redistribute land, end corruption, and rule more liberally. Like Kennedy before him, the president had few levers to enforce the glib assurances from Vietnamese leaders, who were his last option. The junta could always cash in its profits, leaving the country to the NLF. Although the young generals did permit nationwide elections for a Constituent Assembly during 1966, no communist delegates and few neutralists participated in this "constitutional convention." Thieu and Ky, who were elected president and vice-president by suspiciously lopsided victories in 1967, easily took personal control over the new government apparatus. Shielded under America's massive military buildup, they "postponed" reforms and ruled through fiat and secret police. This facade of democracy in Saigon only aggravated discontent in the countryside.

The ugliness of brutal, unending war in Vietnam began to repulse many American citizens. A growing protest movement questioned the country's purposes. Although he had guided the Gulf of Tonkin resolution through the Senate, J. William Fulbright lashed out against what he called "the arrogance of power." "Power," the chairman of the Foreign Relations Committee observed, "tends to confuse itself with virtue." Many thought dangerous the Pentagon's sense of omnipotence and the president's voluble self-righteousness. Perhaps America could not, and should not, graft its domestic institutions onto alien societies. More and more people expressed their moral distaste for the Vietnam adventure. Months of teach-ins on college campuses and media coverage of generally peaceful protest marches culminated October 1967. Nearly a quarter-million students, intellectuals, and ordinary Americans demonstrated against the war during a giant three-day rally in Washington. Thousands more marched in New York and San Francisco. The mushrooming antiwar movement deprived Johnson of part of his natural constituency among liberal Democrats. More ominous, the protests polarized many Americans into "hawks" and "doves"—those who favored victory or peace at any price—which often made intelligent discussion of compromise solutions difficult.

The year 1968 stripped away illusions. Many already doubted whether the United States could ever win in Vietnam at any reasonable cost. But a majority of Americans still believed in American omnipotence. Walt Rostow told reporters that captured documents showed a communist collapse to be "imminent." Then on January 29, 1968, during Vietnam's lunar-new-year celebrations, NLF guerrillas and North Vietnamese armies coordinated a massive attack against Saigon and Hue, the imperial capital of Vietnam, and also against nine provincial capitals. The insurgents overran much of Cholon, the Chinese section of Saigon, and even penetrated the American embassy, killing several guards. In Hue the rebels executed a reign of terror against their political opponents. The attacks on regional cities had the greatest military repercussions. To restore control, General William Westmoreland had to shift troops from northern South Vietnam and from rural areas to take and then garrison places like Tay Ninh, Quang Tri, Pleiku, and other towns. Communist cadres quickly infiltrated the now unprotected countryside.

The United States command saw silver in the lining of the Tet offensive cloud. The NLF had overextended itself, exhausting months of supplies in an unsuccessful effort to end the war. "The enemy is on the ropes," Westmoreland said. "Tet was his last gasp." If only he had 200,000 more men, the American commander promised, he would crush the rural insurgency "once and for all." But Johnson asked Westmoreland whether the communists might not match another American escalation. Yes, said the general. "Then where will it all end?" Johnson wondered. Several civilian advisers had for months counseled diplomatic compromise. McNamara added his columns of statistics, discovered their fabrications, and recommended a coalition government for South Vietnam. Then he resigned. George Ball, the undersecretary of state, repeatedly pointed out the folly of shooting a people into allegiance; the CIA for years had counseled against the effort. But Johnson had, until now, listened more to his generals, relying on their promises of easy victory. After the Tet offensive, the president asked an old friend and much-respected confidant of Democratic presidents, Clark Clifford, to chart a fresh course. As the new secretary of defense, Clifford soon discovered that the military numbers game was relatively straightforward. To send 200,000 men to Southeast Asia and still protect American commitments elsewhere, the president would have to call up the army reserves or triple already high draft quotas. Only new taxes and wide-ranging controls on an overheated economy could ensure war production at a reasonable cost and temper an accelerating inflation. Yet senators privately told their former majority leader what many citizens knew instinctively: the country would reject such steps toward mobilization for war. Clifford urged Johnson to negotiate.

Events, not advice, finally shoved the president toward diplomacy. The Tet offensive had convinced many in Vietnam that the war could never end until the United States left. "Before the Americans came," an old man told a reporter in Saigon, "my home was on the land of my ancestors and my family was honorable. Now I live off my daughter's earnings as a hooch-girl." Morale cracked in the U.S. Army. Helicopter pilots refused to fly during their last four weeks "in country." Some units sought escape in drugs or "fragging"—surreptitious assaults upon their officers. Others lost all restraint, as at My Lai, where American soldiers bayoneted children and old men, apparently without thought or guilt. Both Vietnamese society and the army were coming apart under the strain of a stalemated war of continual and undecided conflict.

The adventure ended abruptly, at least in American politics. So chilling a cold warrior as Richard Nixon, the leading Republican candidate for the 1968 presidential nomination, advocated an end to American involvement in the war, not necessarily a victory. Johnson gradually lost control of his party. On March 14, 1968, Senator Eugene J. McCarthy, an outspoken critic of Pentagon policy, nearly won New Hampshire's presidential primary. The next day, a much more potent challenge to Johnson emerged: Robert F. Kennedy. He announced his candidacy and pledged to stop the conflict. Such startling rebukes to an incumbent president matched the erosion of Johnson's constituency. Liberal Democrats abandoned the man they had so recently praised lavishly. Students and many intellectuals questioned Johnson's ethics, even his sanity. And the president, a great campaigner, could not defend himself publicly on the hustings: the Secret Service considered the security risk too great. Trapped in the White House, losing both nomination and popular respect, Johnson brooded about his nemesis, Vietnam.

On March 31, 1968, Johnson told a nationwide television audience that he had rejected Westmoreland's request for more troops. American escalation would stop. To signal his good intentions and lure Hanoi to the bargaining table, he halted bombing north of the nineteenth parallel. Then, almost as a postscript, Johnson announced that he would not run for reelection. Public sensation at this near resignation clouded a diplomatic tour de force: negotiations would begin, thus defusing domestic demands for immediate disengagement.

Yet the level of violence within South Vietnam actually increased. Thieu promised to conscript another 135,000 men, a figure that together with 55,000 more Americans already in training camps, would almost fulfill Westmoreland's request. Proscribed from the North, American pilots intensified the air war in the South. The president was still attempting to "negotiate from strength." Moreover, he intentionally omitted any reference to a coalition government. Johnson still sought an American peace, a noncommunist South Vietnam.

Diplomatic Cobwebs

Ho Chi Minh, wanting to ensure the bombing halt, took up Johnson's offer for talks, and in private, American and Vietnamese negotiators gradually worked out a practical arrangement that reflected battlefield realities. Since nothing of much military value still existed, America would end all bombing if North Vietnam agreed "by its silence" not to escalate support for the NLF. Both sides might then consider possible coalition governments for South Vietnam.

In this compromise, however, Johnson had not reckoned with his obstreperous ally in Saigon. Thieu thought that the Republican candidate could arrange better terms: "I will win the peace," Nixon had vowed. So Saigon obstructed multilateral talks with the NLF, thus scuttling the compromise. Johnson stayed the bombing anyway, but he could not guarantee Saigon's good faith. If he cut off American aid, the communists would win by default. Thieu could always discipline Washington with threats that he would quit and thereby bring on chaos. Nixon's victory pleased Thieu immensely, but the new president required time to formulate specific policies. Diplomats marked time by haggling over the shape of the bargaining table. By the beginning of 1969, the Republicans faced an extraordinarily difficult situation: stalemated war, ungovernable allies, domestic impatience with half-measures.

Vietnam Fallout: The Atrophy of American Power Elsewhere

Russia and Europe

Washington's fixation with Southeast Asia distorted United States foreign policy. The war in Vietnam simultaneously pleased and worried the Russians; America's burgeoning armies flanked their Chinese rival while it consumed capitalist treasure. Yankee search-and-destroy missions in the Mekong Delta freed the Soviets for attempts to expand their influence in the Middle East. Yet Johnson's very willingness to use force convinced Khrushchev's successors, Leonid Brezhnev and Aleksei Kosygin, that the Americans respected only military strength. Then too, many Russian scientists worried about the implications of the National Aeronautics and Space Administration's mammoth space rockets and plans for orbiting platforms. So the Soviets mass-produced their most sophisticated missile, the SS-9, and accelerated atomic stockpiling. Unable to match this buildup weapon for weapon, given Vietnam's huge drain on available resources, the United States intensified the technology of nuclear war, developing Multiple Independent Re-entry Vehicles (MIRVs), which vastly increased the payload of a single rocket, and "smart bombs," which guided themselves to their target through electronic devices.

But neither power wanted to let cold-war rivalry escalate beyond its control. During June of 1967 Johnson and Kosygin conferred privately at Glassboro State College in New Jersey. Worried that the enormous success of Israel's just completed six-day war might somehow bring on a Soviet-American clash, each promised to respect his rival's vital interests in the crucial Middle East region. Rather than jeopardize the Nuclear Nonproliferation Treaty, finally signed in early 1969, Washington ignored Moscow's brutal repression of Czechoslovak reform efforts in 1968. Such trade-offs symbolized, once again, the high priority both nations placed upon avoiding atomic war.

Though consistently proclaimed as a crusade to reassure its allies, America's adventure in Southeast Asia further fragmented the Atlantic alliance. Western Europe's accelerating prosperity—itself a reflection of American spending overseas—eroded its sense of dependency. Arguments over strategy vitiated traditional comradeship. Determined to build a national nuclear force and, more grandiosely, to break out of "sterile bipolarity," Charles de Gaulle took France out of the NATO alliance, though he did not relinquish its protection. Many West Germans, wanting to normalize relations with their neighbors, chafed at Washington's rigid anticommunism. Even the "special relationship" between Great Britain and the United States withered a bit. As economic obsolescene shoved the English toward the Common Market, they realized more and more their junior membership in the "atomic club." Prime ministers and many other Britons opposed America's policy in Vietnam. If Johnson felt somehow betrayed, England, no less than the rest of NATO, worried that its powerful protector had lost a sense of proportion. The United States seemed so enervated by Vietnam that it could hardly attend to other pressing problems (its balance of international payments, for example). Vietnam became the most visible wedge that drove the Atlantic community apart, Europe's regional interests clashing with America's global visions.

Old Puzzlements in the Third World

The conflict in Southeast Asia resuscitated old devices in American diplomacy throughout the third world. Determined to create an Asian consensus for his policy, Johnson did not challenge oppressive regimes in the Philippines, South Korea, and eventually in Cambodia as long as they supported the American effort in Vietnam. All three countries sent troops to Vietnam, the Koreans' savage fighting noted for its effectiveness. American money once again supported a military oligarchy in Indonesia after General Suharto ousted the increasingly pro-Chinese Sukarno in 1965. Only Japan resisted Johnson's embrace, but regardless of politics, the tendrils of a vast commerce clamped the two nations together. During the late 1960s, then, the United States forced everyone into roles as a free-world leader or communist dupe, ignoring throughout Asia, as in Vietnam, both nationalism and native culture.

Such tactics culminated in Latin America. Once again Washington honored dictators. In 1964 in Brazil, for example, a cabal of generals supported by the United States toppled the popular leftist Joao Goulart, who was showing growing interest in the nationalization of foreign businesses. Panicked by fears of "another Cuba," Johnson's men even reimposed a clumsy overlordship in the Caribbean. In the Dominican Republic, a right-wing coup had ousted the constitutionally elected reformist government of Juan Bosch. But when Bosch's supporters attempted to regain control, American representatives on the island reported that communists had infiltrated Bosch's movement and requested Johnson to send the marines. Some 20,000 troops landed in mid-1965, and despite the quickly discovered inaccuracy of American reports, Johnson left the troops there until September 1966, when carefully supervised elections installed another pro-American leader, Joaquin Balaguer, as president. American gunboat diplomacy and alliances with dictators complemented a geyser of private investment by American corporations looking to Latin America for a quick profit but demanding political stability.

Preoccupied with Vietnam, Johnson either ignored change elsewhere or woodenly enforced the status quo. In this way the Southeast Asian war blinded America to the future, distorting its foreign policies and pushing others into a ready-made mold. The tensions could not be checked for long, but Johnson contained them for the moment.

Johnson's Legacy

If complex, the Democrats' legacy was not unmanageable. Peace talks in Paris provided a continuing structure for negotiation, but Johnson (and his successor) still hoped to win. Native troops, presumably more motivated than America's dispirited soldiers, and sophisticated firepower, Americans hoped, could "Vietnamize" the war while winning it. However plausible in the short run, such tactics could not remedy the flaw of American involvement. Searching for global credibility, Washington bureaucrats still ignored Vietnamese society, its peoples and possibilities. The United States could never impose a solution, either by force or by diplomacy. More years would pass before the nation's leaders abandoned this goal. By then, Johnson's war had become Nixon's.

But the Vietnam conflict was more than a tragic mistake for Asians and Americans. It symbolized the bankruptcy of worldwide anticommunist crusading, of "tough-minded" overresponses, and threw into question the policies of globalism. The United States had overextended itself by 1968, and zealous bureaucrats could not find a route back. Instead, they sacrificed more and more of America's strength elsewhere to justify their rashness. Most people did not immediately recognize another casualty of war—the American economy. To pay for the most expensive war in the country's history, the White House loosed an inflation at home and a dollar crisis abroad that developed their own momentum. By the 1970s America's wealth and self-confidence had visibly atrophied. The adventure in Vietnam, far from protecting American institutions from foreign dangers, helped to bring them under increasing attack from domestic reformers. Opposition to the Vietnam War served to unite the diverse protest movements of the 1960s.

SUGGESTIONS FOR FURTHER READING

JFK left no memoirs, of course, but see the "official" histories written by his two close aides: Arthur M. Schlesinger, Jr., *A Thousand Days* (1965) and Theodore Sorenson, *Kennedy* (1965). In contrast to these books, see Richard J.

Walton's *Cold War and Counterrevolution: The Foreign Policy of John F. Kennedy* (1972) and Richard J. Barnet, *Intervention and Revolution* (rev. ed., 1972). Other members of the Kennedy team, in addition to Schlesinger and Sorenson, have offered their views. See, for example, Roger Hilsman, *To Move a Nation* (1967); Walt W. Rostow, *View from the Seventh Floor* (1964); and Robert McNamara, *The Essence of Security* (1968). RFK's role is discussed in Arthur Schlesinger, Jr., *Robert Kennedy and His Times* (1978). LBJ's *The Vantage Point* (1971) is thin. Warren Cohen's *Dean Rusk* (1980) is a solid study.

Despite its claims of objectivity, *America in Vietnam* (1978) by Guenter Lewy is a carefully-crafted prowar tract. A better place to begin is Leslie Gelb and Richard Betts, *The Irony of Vietnam: The System Worked* (1978). *The Pentagon Papers* (Senator Gravel ed., 4 vols., 1971) is a useful, but incomplete, set of documents; the *New York Times* version is far less useful. The best of the older works on Vietnam include *The Two Vietnams* (rev. ed., 1964) by Bernard Fall; George Kahin and John W. Lewis, *The United States in Vietnam* (rev. ed., 1969); John T. McAlister, *Vietnam: Origins of Revolution* (1969); and Robert Shaplen, *The Lost Revolution* (1966) and *The Road from War* (1970). Older works that criticized American policy from one angle or another include David Halberstam, *The Making of a Quagmire* (1965); Jonathan Schell, *The Military Half* (1968) and *The Village of Ben Suc* (1967); Seymour Hersh, *Cover-Up* (1972); Jeffrey Race, *War Comes to Long An* (1971); and Frances Fitzgerald's widely heralded *Fire in the Lake* (1972). Herbert Schlandcr's *The Unmaking of a President* (1977) traces the downfall of LBJ. George Herring, *America's Longest War* (1980) is a good overview of the entire conflict.

Participants in the planning and execution of the war tell their side in LBJ's *The Vantage Point;* Walt W. Rostow's *The Diffusion of Power* (1972); and William Westmoreland's *A Soldier Reports* (1976). The experiences of participants in the conflict are shared in Charles Coe's, *Young Man in Vietnam* (1968); Tim O'Brien, *If I Die in a Combat Zone* (1973) and *Going After Cacciato* (1978); Ron Kovic, *Born on the Fourth of July* (1976); and Larry Heinemann, *Close Quarters* (1977). Two different but equally gripping accounts by journalists are Michael Herr's *Dispatches* (1977) and Gloria Emerson's *Winners and Losers* (1976). Journalistic coverage of the war, especially the Tet offensive of 1968, is criticized in Peter Braestrup's, *Big Story* (1978).

The history of American involvement in Vietnam cannot be viewed apart from America's policies elsewhere. See the contrasting views in Barnet's *Intervention and Revolution* and his *Roots of War* (1973); Stanley Hoffman, *Gulliver's Troubles, or the Setting of American Foreign Policy* (1968); William A. Williams, *The Tragedy of American Diplomacy* (rev. ed., 1971); Raymond Aron, *The Imperial Republic, 1945 – 1973* (1974); Franz Schurmann, *The Logic of World Power* (1974); David Blake and Robert S. Walters, *The Politics of Global Economic Relations* (1976); Walter LaFeber, *American, Russia, and the Cold War* (rev. ed., 1980); and Gabriel Kolko, *The Roots of American Foreign Policy* (1969). For the relationship between foreign policy and domestic pressures, see Kolko; Barnet's *Roots of War;* David Halberstam's *The Best and the Brightest* (1972); Robert Divine's *Foreign Policy and Presidential Elections, Vol. II* (1975); Seymour Melmon's *The Permanent War Economy* (1974); John C. Donovan's *The Cold Warriors* (1974); and G. William Domhoff's *The Powers That Be* (1978).

For events outside Vietnam during the 1960s see Jerome Slater, *Intervention and Negotiation: The U.S. and the Dominican Revolution* (1970); Phyllis R. Parker, *Brazil and the Quiet Intervention, 1964* (1979); Jack Shick, *The Berlin Crisis, 1958 – 1962* (1974); Stephen Weismann, *American Foreign Policy in the Congo, 1960 – 1965* (1974); Alfred McCoy, *The Politics of Heroin in Southeast Asia* (1973); Philip Agee, *Inside the Company* (1974); David Detzer, *The Brink: The Cuban Missile Crisis, 1962* (1979); and Peter Wyden, *Bay of Pigs* (1979).

THE "YOUTH REVOLT" AND THE "NEW POLITICS," 1960–1968

7 Already, historians and social scientists have waged fierce debates over the nature of society and politics during the years of protest, the period from the mid-1960s to about 1972. A few writers have adopted the viewpoint, expressed in Ben Wattenberg's popular work *The Real America,* that the era was one of broadly distributed material growth and was marred only by the "Cause People, the Movement, the Failure and Guilt Complex and their assorted camp followers." Other interpreters have posed the opposite extreme, seeing the mid-1960s, as a time of glorious revolt against an unjust order, followed by harsh repression under Johnson and then Richard Nixon. Predictably, most scholars have staked out a position somewhere between these two poles. Yet even observers like Wattenberg, who praise the period's tremendous economic and physical growth and who denigrate the radical protests, concede that the outpouring of dissent, particularly among well-educated young people, was one of the central features of the history of the 1960s and the early 1970s.

"The Movement," the term applied to a loose collection of very disparate groups, brought together many different styles of political and cultural radicalism. Members of the New Left urged political solutions for what they considered the failures of liberalism; they believed that through radical political action youthful organizers could change "the system" and bring "power to the people." In contrast, the young cultural radicals displayed little interest in politics. More deeply estranged from American society than most political radicals, devotees of the "counterculture" advocated a more relaxed and sensual style of life as the best antidote for what they saw as the crass commercialism, sterility, and repressiveness of American society.

In the end, none of the radical groups ever discovered any workable strategy for quickly changing the direction of American life. Members of the New Left did gain broader support on specific issues—especially on opposition to American involvement in Vietnam—but radical politics too often tailed off into ineffectual gestures—demonstrations, manifestos, and random acts of violence—against "the system." Cultural radicals left a more ambiguous legacy. Many young people did adopt the trappings of revolt, such as drugs and ragged blue jeans, but most retained a desire to find some place within the existing social and economic structure. The goal of cultural liberation, in many ways, proved perfectly compatible with the ethos of a consumption-oriented society. Increasingly, both political and cultural protests became staples of the mass media; as Todd Gitlin, a veteran of the 1960s has argued, television and the popular press helped to trivialize and to co-opt radical tendencies.

Still, the revolt against liberalism was one of the most important phenomena of the 1960s and early 1970s. For better or for worse, the loosely structured political and cultural radicalism touched almost every area of American life and left a significant impact upon institutions and ideas.

The Revolt of "Youth"

Young people's enthusiasm for John Kennedy led most supporters of the New Frontier to expect that the 1960s would be a decade of steady liberal reform. But even before JFK's death, some young people were becoming disillusioned with his administration and with liberalism itself. The young radicals, almost all of whom were white and from relatively affluent, middle-class homes, began to denounce American institutions and values and to seek their own alternatives to the highly rationalized world of big-government liberalism. The potpourri of sources from which disaffected young people sought insight and inspiration reflected the diversity of this new radicalism. Unlike the "old left" of the 1920s and 1930s, which looked primarily to Marxism, radicals of the 1960s sampled a variety of social theories. "Beat" writers, Eastern mystics, academic mavericks, and folk-rock songwriters helped provide the movement's eclectic intellectual base.

Radicals of the 1950s

While the middle-class protesters of the 1960s were still opening their school day by saluting the flag, the Beat poets and novelists of the 1950s had already dismissed American society as an "air-conditioned nightmare." Jack Kerouac's novel *On the Road* (1957) glorified the drifter, the ever-searching rebel who resisted the temptation to conform. The poems of Allen Ginsberg denounced materialism and middle-class morality and celebrated the satisfactions of marijuana, Eastern mystical religions, and homosexual love. In their best works, Beat poets such as Ginsberg and Gary Snyder displayed a free-flowing style that epitomized their rejection of restrictive forms and too orderly ideas. Part hipster and part huckster, Ginsberg kept alive the spirit of the Beat movement, becoming a revered elder-in-residence to the radicals of the 1960s.

While the Beats protested America's supposed cultural sterility the radical sociologist C. Wright Mills attacked its liberal political system. Although Mills taught at Columbia University, his life style—he would roar up to his office on a motorcycle—and his political ideas clashed with the urbane liberalism that dominated leading colleges. Mills's writings helped popularize theories that became the New Left's central tenets: that an undemocratic "power elite" dominated American society; that liberalism had lost its social consciousness and become an ideology of the status quo; and that most liberal intellectuals merely offered rationalizations for an illiberal society. Mills also condemned United States foreign policy as an extension of the same undemocratic values: he warned that a small group of politicians, military officials, and business leaders enjoyed virtually unchecked power. An activist as well as a scholar, Mills visited Cuba and wrote a short book praising Fidel Castro's social experiments. After his death in 1962, Mills became one of the radical movement's most revered saints.

The critique of American liberalism received greater philosophical development in the works of Herbert Marcuse. A German-born Marxist, Marcuse attacked the sophisticated technology and economic prosperity that liberals praised so highly. The United States, according to Marcuse, was a quasi-totalitarian "technocracy." Real power lay with the "technocrats"—the experts in government, business, science, and other dominant institutions, who ultimately determined social policies and national priorities. In such a one-dimensional society, people became slaves to a technological imperative. The political process offered no real choice: voters could choose only among candidates who endorsed the same social and economic policies and who ultimately relied on the same group of technocrats. Freedom was an illusion. In reality, people had become enslaved to a mass-production, mass-consumption economic system that satisfied only "false" needs—new automobiles, electronic gadgets, and thousands of other products that provided no real sense of happiness or personal fulfillment. Disaffected young people borrowed from Marcuse and his many popularizers, and terms such as *false consciousness* and *technocracy* became parts of the radical vocabulary. Marcuse, like Mills, endorsed the thesis that the liberal "good guys"—including the people who ran the big universities and the big government in Washington—were really the villains. Some young people came to see liberalism as a new form of conservatism; others saw it as a kind of suave totalitarianism, one that enslaved people with images and illusions rather than with guns and concentration camps.

Paul Goodman, a multifaceted social critic, also helped to popularize the theory that supposedly liberal institutions actually repressed Americans, especially young people. In *Growing Up Absurd* (1960) and a variety of essays, Goodman argued that educational institutions stifled young people's healthy natural instincts and subtly indoctrinated them with the values and skills of a badly flawed society. Order and regularity, he claimed, took precedence over spontaneity and creativity; memorization of meaningless data became more important than critical thought; the interests of teachers and administrators outweighed the needs of students. Goodman applied his anarchist critique to all of American society, contending that large bureaucratic institutions run by technocratic "experts" worked against natural human needs and desires. Experience and common sense, Goodman claimed, showed that large, centralized institutions rarely performed their appointed tasks. And by bringing ever more areas of daily life under the control of inefficient and ineffective bureaucrats, Americans only magnified the consequences of centralized bungling. Goodman did not see technology as an uncontrollable demon; the problems, he argued, lay in the way centralized institutions applied technology to society.

Goodman's hopefulness and enthusiasm for change contrasted with Marcuse's pessimism. Goodman claimed that his seemingly utopian ideas—small, volunteer-run radio stations, for example—actually offered highly practical alternatives to centralized structures. In the early 1960s, he believed that young people could remake society by forming decentralized institutions, and he demonstrated his own commitment by taking an active role in the radical movement. He picketed his publisher, participated in campus demonstrations, and taught at decentralized "free universities." As much as any older radical, Paul Goodman understood the younger dissidents' search for greater personal involvement and closer community with others. Though Goodman ultimately became disenchanted by what he came to consider the dangerous antirationalism of the counterculture, efforts to establish alternative institutions owed much to his early influence.

Their own experience in the civil-rights movement of the late 1950s and early 1960s also propelled some young people, white as well as black, toward an open break with liberalism. Lacking great financial resources, the early civil-rights movement relied upon youthful volunteers who could perform time-consuming jobs: preparing leaflets, running mimeograph machines, and marching in demonstrations. All of these activities brought young people together in a common cause. Often travelling long distances and sleeping in makeshift accommodations, civil-rights workers discovered a camaraderie and commitment that seemed to be missing elsewhere in America. Working together, young people found personal fulfillment in a crusade that they hoped would change the entire society.

At the same time, many of these young activists began to view the American political system as hopelessly corrupt and liberal political leaders as impediments to real social change. Attending school during the era of the cold war, young volunteers had been brought up on idealized descriptions of American democracy, and the realization that black people suffered all types of legal discrimination and racist harassment proved disquieting. Seeking immediate solutions, civil-rights workers inevitably confronted hostile or cautious political leaders. Segregationists in Alabama and Georgia would make no concessions, and even liberal politicians such as John Kennedy stressed the need to move slowly and to avoid sudden changes in race relations. On many occasions southern crowds beat up civil-rights workers while FBI agents simply looked on and took notes. After confronting the racial hatred of Oxford, Mississippi, or Cicero, Illinois, many young activists charged that liberals offered Band-Aid solutions for deep national wounds. Segregation and racism, young civil-rights workers charged, were evils that no decent society would tolerate.

Not all young people protested, and the new radicals constituted only a minority of those between eighteen and twenty-five. Others remained true to the liberal spirit of John Kennedy, voting for Lyndon Johnson and going off to fight a war for "democracy and freedom" in Vietnam. Many young people bitterly resented long-haired "hippie" protestors, and they embraced the consumer products and the nine-to-five jobs scorned by the radicals. Talk of a "generation gap" obscured the equally large fissure within the youth generation itself and ignored the small yet significant group of older radicals who joined the Movement. But the young people who protested seemed to dominate their peers in much the same way they dominated the media in the 1960s. Deeply disturbed by the direction of American society and convinced that they could find alternatives, the youthful rebels became the symbols of their generation.

What distinguished the young radicals from others of their age? Drawing upon several studies of college students, the psychologist Kenneth Keniston argued that the rebels were "psychological adults" but "sociological adolescents." Contrary to conventional wisdom, Keniston found that protesters tended to be excellent students, usually in the humanities, who suffered no great psychological difficulties. But as the products of affluent or solidly middle-class homes, they possessed the freedom, as well as the desire, to postpone settling into a permanent sociological role. Instead of leaping into an established career pattern, the young radicals wanted to adopt a less conventional role—that of social activist and agitator for political change. The fact that many believed their parents shared many of their ideals, but were forced to compromise them in their day-to-day lives, only intensified their desire to remain free from settled, adult roles.

To the young dissenters, liberalism's failures seemed more important than its admitted successes. Liberals *had* produced greater material affluence, but at a price: most jobs seemed boring; life lacked adventure and excitement; racial discrimination oppressed millions of people; and personal relationships seemed as "plastic" as the products by which "straight" people measured their success. The cool, rational world of John Kennedy appeared to lack genuine feeling and to substitute eloquent rhetoric for meaningful social change. In contrast, a stance of opposition seemed to offer hope for immediate personal fulfillment as well as the chance for basic social change. Through a commitment to radicalism young people could instantly complete Paul Simon's "dangling conversations" or explore Bob Dylan's "smoke rings of the mind." Raised with television at their side, many young people became accustomed to having even the most baffling problems resolved quickly, and they expected similar results from the political system.

During the late 1950s and early 1960s a small group of college students helped to spark a revival of radical politics in the United States. At various universities—especially the University of Wisconsin at Madison, the University of California at Berkeley, and the University of Michigan—youthful graduate students began to explore the relationship between "radical scholarship" and social activism. How could university professors avoid the kind of "scholarly dispassion" that radicals considered a means of justifying a repressive status quo? In time, a number of graduate students came to see themselves as prototypes for a new breed of college teacher: in the style of C. Wright Mills they would awaken campus life and bring new vitality to radical thought. Other university students took more direct action. In the San Francisco Bay area, students from Berkeley joined older radicals to demonstrate on behalf of such causes as dissolution of the House Un-American Activities Committee, abolition of capital punishment, and elimination of racial discrimination. Young people were also active in the South, helping miners fight the large coal companies in Hazard County, Kentucky, in addition to working for various civil-rights organizations. In February 1960 four young black students at North Carolina A and T College, inspired by Mahatma Gandhi's philosophy of nonviolence, attacked segregated dining facilities by "sitting in" at a Woolworth's lunch counter in Greensboro. As young whites joined youthful blacks on the firing line, the sit-in movement spread, oftentimes to the discomfort of older black civil-rights leaders. By April of 1960, young veterans of the sit-in campaign felt the need for their own organization—the Student Nonviolent Coordinating Committee, or SNCC.

The predominately white Students for a Democratic Society, which began as an arm of the old left's League for Industrial Democracy, shared SNCC's activism. SDS's Port Huron Statement of 1962, written largely by Tom Hayden, argued that America needed a dramatically new social and political system in which people "share in those social decisions determining the quality and direction" of their lives. In contrast to the liberal political order—one that "frustrates democracy by confusing the individual citizen, paralyzing policy discussion, and consolidating the irresponsible power of military and business interests"—Hayden and SDS offered the possibilities of "participatory democracy." The search for a true participatory democracy, the Port Huron Statement argued, was "governed by two central aims: that the individual share in those social decisions determining the quality and direction of his life; that society be organized to encourage independence in men and provide the means for their common participation." Though the Port Huron Statement contained clear hints of the radicalism that would soon engulf SDS, the manifesto of 1962 remained essentially a leftist-liberal document. It sounded no call for revolution and endorsed specific political programs only slightly to the left of the Fair Deal-New Frontier tradition.

SDS's leaders initially viewed community organizing as the first step toward participatory democracy. Poor people fell victim to better-organized elites, SDS argued, because they could not exert political pressure commensurate with their numbers. SDS branched out from the college campuses—many of its early leaders came from the University of Michigan—and launched grass-roots programs among the urban poor. By moving into the ghettos SDS hoped to stimulate the formation of new organizations and to channel poor people's discontent into local politics. In cities such as Newark, New Jersey, SDS mounted drives against urban renewal and in support of better housing, more jobs, and school lunch programs. The first SDSers displayed a missionary zeal. While some young people were already sprouting long hair and smoking dope, the SDSers bragged that they were turned on to political organizing. But despite their commitment, they quickly discovered the difficulties of organizing poor people, especially for a group committed to participatory democracy. Drawn mostly from white, middle-class families, young SDS members, unlike veteran organizers such as Saul Alinsky, were too impatient. Seeking a more congenial environment, SDS shifted its emphasis back to the college campus, the heart of the youth revolt in the 1960s.

Campus Protests

The first serious campus protest occurred at the University of California at Berkeley in the fall of 1964. When university officials tried to limit political activity by radical students, protesters charged that the university's administration was bowing to pressures from right-wing business leaders in the Bay Area and destroying free speech on campus. As protests against the new university restrictions escalated and a temporary truce collapsed, mass rallies, takeovers of university buildings, and raids by local police highlighted the Berkeley Student Revolt. A number of campus groups, not all of whom represented New Left factions, joined under the banner of the Free Speech Movement. Thus, the earliest protests represented more of an attack upon the bureaucratic routine of Berkeley than a revolt against the entire university structure. In early December 1964 student protesters began wearing IBM cards as name tags; militants soon called a campus-wide strike. Although critical newspapers pronounced the action a failure, student leaders claimed that almost three-quarters of the student body—and a sizeable portion of the faculty—supported the three-day walkout.

The Free-Speech Movement gradually took a turn toward cultural and political radicalism. A young New Yorker who had drifted West to "check out the scene" arrived with a simple protest sign—FUCK. (Some people claimed that the letters really stood for "Freedom Under Clark Kerr," the president of the University of California.) His example encouraged a group of imitators, the "word-mongers," who helped give Berkeley an even more lurid reputation among the already unsympathetic. By the spring of 1965 many of the issues that had precipitated the first student protests had been largely forgotten or replaced by larger political concerns, especially the war in Vietnam.

The unrest at Berkeley provided a scenario that repeated itself on many large college campuses during the 1960s. Increasingly, the tone and the aims of the protesters grew more militant. In banding together to fight college administrators and their outside supporters—James Kunen, a clever observer of the 1968 disturbances at Columbia, called them "the biggies"—young people often discovered a new sense of community. As the civil-rights workers in Mississippi had done earlier, they developed a kind of garrison mentality, viewing themselves as victims of a faceless power structure. Buoyed by their underdog status, student propagandists proudly announced that they were the "new niggers."

The modern "multiversity" provided a perfect target. Big universities displayed what radicals considered the major sins of modern liberalism: an emphasis on competitiveness, reliance on bureaucratic structures, and an apparent feeling that bigger inevitably meant better. Many nonradicals shared some of these concerns. Sensitive young students, many of whom had been reared in families that stressed openness and concern for their children's feelings, felt especially frustrated by the impersonality and routine of universities such as Berkeley and Columbia. They complained that large, impersonal lectures and haphazard discussion sections exemplified the multiversity's assembly-line approach to education. Many students felt reduced to IBM numbers, subject to the whims of giant computers and dependent on faceless bureaucrats who ran the multimillion-dollar operations. Even the University of California's liberal president Clark Kerr considered himself primarily the administrator of a large "benevolent bureaucracy," a huge enterprise that produced knowledge instead of consumer goods. "The university and segments of industry are becoming more alike," Kerr observed in 1960. Finally, most students resented what they considered invasions of their personal freedoms by university officials. Women, even those who were legally of age, had to observe dress codes and dorm hours on most college campuses during the early 1960s; men at many state universities were required to take two years of ROTC; and faculty-dominated committees censored student publications. Dissidents began to demand that universities abandon or relax these restrictions, reduce the number of required courses, and offer programs "relevant" to mid-twentieth-century society.

When student muckrakers examined the multiversity's role in American society they saw additional crimes. Professors conducted classified research for the Defense Department; Harvard chemists, not Dow Chemical, had developed napalm. Seeking additional space for new buildings, athletic stadiums, and parking lots, universities sometimes expanded into neighboring black ghettos and pushed out the residents. Some private universities, radicals also discovered, owned inner-city properties and qualified as genuine slum landlords. To make the indictment complete, big universities rarely admitted black students; when they did, recruitment efforts centered on talented athletes and a few top-flight students. Viewed from within, the multiversity seemed to offer mind-numbing courses and senseless regimentation. Seen as part of a corrupt liberal society, it appeared to aid war and racism.

Student and faculty pressures brought significant changes and a few strategic retreats by the old guard. Most colleges relaxed archaic restrictions, abolished compulsory ROTC, adjusted curriculum requirements, made special efforts to recruit minority students, and established separate minority-studies programs. A few professors even encouraged social activism by permitting students to substitute "relevant" outside projects for more traditional assignments. Although a number of spectacular "busts" temporarily halted protests at some universities, most campuses continued to serve as staging areas for forays against the outside world. At many urban universities large groups of street people—dropouts, hangers-on, and runaway teenagers—provided additional troops for campus demonstrations and swelled the ranks of the "student" opposition. A radicalized university, many activists began to hope, would be an important tool for changing the larger society.

Teach-ins and Marches

The protests against American involvement in the war in Vietnam demonstrated the value as well as the limitations of the university in radical politics. The crusade against the Vietnam war did not begin on the campuses, but dissent within the academic community gave the antiwar movement an influential forum. Early in 1965, after President Johnson mounted his all-out bombing campaign against North Vietnam, antiwar activists organized a nationwide series of teach-ins, meetings at which supporters and opponents of American participation in the war debated before largely student audiences. Initially some protesters hoped that the teach-ins would spark vigorous exchanges with government officials and that the confrontations might eventually change the policies of the Johnson administration. But by 1966 most militant opponents of the war were charging that teach-ins only wasted precious time. Obviously, the meetings were having little effect on President Johnson's actions, and the novelty of the gatherings was wearing thin. Although teach-ins continued sporadically throughout the 1960s—and even into the 1970s on some campuses—the antiwar movement began to desert the lecture platforms for the streets.

Antiwar demonstrations borrowed from the tactics of the civil-rights movement and the techniques of the teach-in. Beginning with a mass march, demonstrations invariably concluded with a series of speeches and entertainment by folk-rock musicians. Organizers claimed that by bringing large numbers of people into the streets they could dramatize the strength of the Movement, increase "radical consciousness," and pressure the national government to change its policies. Each new march had to outdo the last; organizers struggled to attract more people or to devise new strategems to goad the liberal establishment. During the October 1967 March on Washington, a group of what the *East Village Other* newspaper called "witches, warlocks, holymen, seers, prophets, mystics, saints, sorcerers, shamans, troubadours, minstrels, bards, roadmen, and madmen" tried to exorcise the Pentagon, hurling "mighty words of white light against the demon-controlled structure." Alas, the five-sided symbol of the military-industrial complex hardly budged, but such productions undoubtedly raised the spirits of the protesters.

The difficulties of organizing such demonstrations helped cover up differences over goals and tactics. Negotiations with political leaders, police chiefs, rock entrepreneurs, and portable-toilet vendors sometimes seemed as complex as the government maneuvers to conduct the war itself. By collecting tens of thousands of people at one demonstration, leaders of the movement could reassure themselves that all was going well. Even a fraction of a percent of the baby-boom generation, when gathered in one spot, made a good-sized crowd, and a sprinkling of older people raised hopes that the movement was making converts outside its normal youth market. Such gatherings gradually became ritualized. Protesters sprawled on the grass, half-listening to familiar political rhetoric, and reminisced about previous demonstrations and "hassles." For many people marches served much the same function as revival meetings: the faithful assembled from across the country, exchanged pleasantries, felt their faith renewed, and then went back to plan for the next gathering.

The vast majority of the protesters strongly opposed the war and felt estranged from the liberal society, but many simply lacked interest in sustained political activity. In time, the antipathy that many disaffected young people felt toward the liberal establishment was transferred to the "peace bureaucrats" in the New Left. Most cultural radicals, whom the mass media labeled hippies, preferred to "do their own thing." San Francisco, the old home of the Beats, once again became a mecca, the center of the cultural revolution of the 1960s.

Radical Youth Culture

In the mid 1960s the San Francisco Bay area, especially the Haight-Ashbury neighborhood of San Francisco, became famous, or notorious, as the focus of cultural revolution. "Hip" people from all over the country flocked to northern California, hoping to enjoy the "laid-back" life styles of the "age of Aquarius." Soon, the media highlighted the comings and goings of "the hippies." Many young people were intrigued by the hippies' communal living arrangements, their "liberated" views on sex, their experimentation with drugs, and their fascination with the electrified sound of folk-rock music. Hippies celebrated their emancipation from "hang-ups" such as work and clothing fashions. Attired in America's castoffs, including old military uniforms, the new rebels espoused philosophies that stressed mystical experiences and universal love. Unlike members of the New Left, most devotees of the counterculture showed little interest in political questions and displayed no passion for new political organizations. Following the Beat writers of the 1950s some began to study Eastern faiths such as Zen and Taoism; a few joined Timothy Leary's League for Spiritual Discovery or eclectically sampled all sorts of other cults that emphasized the use of psychedelic drugs; many eschewed any real philosophical base and simply relied upon slogans. "Make Love, Not War" and "Flower Power" became familiar parts of the hippie litany. Sociologists eagerly studied the hippie phenomenon; pop journalists such as Tom Wolfe breathlessly covered it; and most middle-class tourists made a quick tour of Haight-Ashbury an essential part of their visit to San Francisco.

But Haight-Ashbury soon became something other than a quaint haven for the nation's "flower children." San Francisco's political establishment declared war on "this hippie thing," and the city's police chief condemned the young rebels as people without "the courage to face the reality of life." Quickly taking their cue, many patrolmen ruthlessly searched for drugs and often harassed any unkempt young person. At the same time, Haight faced an invasion of petty criminals, drifters who discovered that the hippies were easy prey. The community also developed internal divisions. The radical Diggers, a group that tried to live without any money and according to the Golden Rule, complained that "hip entrepreneurs" had taken control of Haight-Ashbury's economic life and that phony "weekend hippies" had inundated the area. As dope became big business, pushers began to peddle stronger and stronger chemicals. The wiser "heads" warned about the dangers—"Speed Kills," proclaimed posters—but many naive young people became hooked on hard drugs or experienced bad "trips" on powerful hallucinogens. A few died from overdoses. A handbill printed in August 1967 expressed the growing disillusionment with Haight-Ashbury.

> The trouble is that the hip shopkeepers probably believe their own bullshit lies. They believe that dope is the answer and neither know nor care what the question is.
>
> Have you been raped? Take acid and everything will be groovy. Are you cold, sleeping in doorways at night? Take acid and discover your inner warmth. Are you hungry? Take acid and transcend these mundane needs.
>
> You can't afford acid? Pardon me, I think I hear somebody calling me.

Despite the rapid rise and fall of Haight-Ashbury, more and more young people seemed to be joining the counterculture, especially as it became linked to new trends in rock music. By 1966 groups such as the Beatles and the Rolling Stones were reinvigorating rock, and Bob Dylan was augmenting his acoustic guitar with the amplified sound of folk-rock. Groups from San Francisco took the lead in exploring the possibilities of electronic rock. Deploying an awesome array of amplifiers, mixers, and microphones, Jerry Garcia and The Grateful Dead attracted a devoted following in the San Francisco area. The Dead gradually added various kinds of light shows, and the Merry Pranksters (a group of young people attracted to the novelist Ken Kesey) laced the audience with LSD. ("Can you pass the acid test?" the Pranksters slyly asked concertgoers.) The result was "acid rock" and a whole new genre of drug-related, "mind-blowing" sounds. Soon, the new "progressive rock" became a smashing success, financially as well as artistically. Although cautious programmers and disc jockeys generally excluded the new sounds from AM radio's Top-40 play lists, progressive rock spawned its own medium—"free-form" FM radio. The popularity of San Francisco groups—particularly the Dead, Jefferson Airplane, and Big Brother and the Holding Company (featuring Janis Joplin)—rapidly spread across the country.

The union of disaffected youth, drugs, and rock music—the combination that made the Woodstock Rock Festival of 1969 briefly appear to represent the flowering of a true cultural revolution—was consummated. By the late 1960s the counterculture appeared everywhere. Aided by the wonders of modern technology—mass-produced books and magazines, stereo record albums, automobiles, airplanes, and psychedelic chemicals—the radical youth culture became a nationwide phenomenon. The counterculture was difficult to classify: it was variously a state of mind, a way of life, or sometimes merely a style of dress. It developed its own mass media. The success of the *Berkeley Barb* and the *Los Angeles Free Press* encouraged other "underground newspapers," and radical journalists soon formed their own Liberation News Service. Although few of these enterprises survived for any length of time, the proliferation of underground papers did suggest the counterculture's broad appeal. The growing populations of countercultural students and street people created little Haight-Ashburys around major college campuses and in most large cities.

New York's East Village, a run-down area near fashionably radical Greenwich Village, quickly became the East Coast's version of Haight-Ashbury. Here Abbie Hoffman and Jerry Rubin conceived the spurious Youth International party—the Yippies. A free-wheeling attempt to blend political and cultural radicalism and to gain attention from the media, the short-lived Yippie movement made Rubin and Hoffman national celebrities. Yippie philosophy owed more to Groucho, Harpo, and Chico than to Karl Marx. The Yippie program was theater in the streets, an updated, drug-inspired vaudeville of the radical left. With the Yippies, revolution and symbolic defiance became one and the same. In one of their most famous escapades, Yippies invaded the New York Stock Exchange, hurling currency at brokers who were wildly trading their paper securities. Hoffman facetiously suggested that such theatrics would eventually produce upheaval through a mystical process he called "cultural jujitsu": confronted by the taunts of the Yippies in the streets and by its own innate contradictions, corporate America would hack itself to pieces. The Yippies' penchant for playing radicalism for laughs—Hoffman entitled his treatise *Revolution for the Hell of It*—and their adolescent bravado—which oftentimes took the form of media-oriented exhibitionism—only underscored their lack of any serious program for social change, let alone for political revolution.

The Meaning of the Counterculture

From the very beginning, critics of the cultural revolt denounced it as a dangerous and foolish attack against the realities of modern life. The prominent psychologist Bruno Bettelheim dismissed the outcries against technology as the babbling of "obsolete youth" in a technological age that required discipline and order. Zbigniew Brzezinski condemned the youthful protestors as "twentieth-century Luddites." Noting that most college dissidents came from the humanities rather than from the sciences or engineering, Brzezinski claimed that the rebels were blindly attacking the new learning because it threatened their power and prestige. He dismissed both the cultural rebellion and the politics of the New Left as "a reaction to the more basic fear that the times are against them, that a new world is emerging without either their assistance or leadership." The counterculture, Brzezinski concluded, was "the death rattle" of the historically obsolete.

Even people opposed to the dominant liberal order came to criticize the counterculture, especially for its emphasis upon the necessity of "doing your own thing." To the Marxist scholar Peter Clecak, the leaders of cultural revolution rushed forward to be packaged and sold as the media's lastest celebrities. Having been raised on the adolescent television fare of the 1950s, Clecak complained, eternal adolescents such as the Yippies "easily fell into the comic roles" assigned them by the television producers of the 1960s. The result, he concluded, was the trivialization of dissent and the reckless expenditures of mindless energy. Another Marxist writer, the historian Christopher Lasch, has drawn an even broader indictment. The counterculture's infatuation with "finding oneself" and with sampling the wares of all those who promised an "alternative consciousness," Lasch argued, contributed to what he considered the excessive narcissim of the 1970s.

The counterculture, though, had—and still has—its fervent defenders. The historian Theodore Roszak, who first popularized the term counterculture, viewed dissident young people as the vanguard of a reaction against an oppressive technological society. Saturated with the meaningless trappings of misdirected technology, "technocracy's children" sought a society and a level of consciousness that allowed for beauty, mystery, feeling, and love. In *The Making of a Counter-Culture* (1968), Roszak sympathetically explored the counterculture's interest in Eastern religions, Beat writers, anarchist philosophers, and mystics of all kinds. But he warned that the middle-class rebels would have to avoid at least two dangers: losing touch with disadvantaged people, particularly nonwhites who had never enjoyed the temptations of technology; and becoming "an amusing side show" for those swingers attracted to *Playboy* magazine's brand of liberation. Indeed, more than Roszak would allow, elements within the counterculture itself displayed much the same commercial slickness, albeit in different forms, as the entrepreneurs on Madison Avenue. In time, hippie-style clothes and a more casual attitude toward sex became fashionable among many business and professional people; the hippie life style could blend, without much difficulty, into what neo-Marxists condemned as the "pop hedonism" of an advanced capitalist society.

In his later works, though, Roszak continued to insist that the cultural revolt of the 1960s represented the only viable path toward human liberation, and perhaps the only route toward human survival. In *Person/Planet* (1978), for example, Roszak contended that an emphasis on personal self-discovery was not incompatible with the development of a larger, alternative social conscience, one that would lead to Roszak's dominant goal—"the creative disintegration of industrial society." In Roszak's view, "the new consciousness we are gaining of ourselves as people" could lead to a broader recognition of the need to gain an alternative vision of life itself, one that acknowledged the destructiveness of technological society. In an age in which both individuals and their societies face the daily onslaughts of technology, Roszak argued, "the needs of the planet are the needs of the person," and "the rights of the person are the rights of the planet."

1968: The Politics of Confrontation

Yet even the most fervent supporters of the counterculture had to concede that most Americans had not yet reached an "alternative consciousness," especially in the late 1960s and early 1970s. Predictably, a number of politicians joined the attack on "dirty hippies" and "permissiveness." Ronald Reagan, for example, left the entertainment business for good and pledged to "straighten out things at Berkeley" during his successful campaign for the governorship of California in 1966. Reagan and many other politicians took an increasingly hard line against the use of drugs, condemning the growing popularity of marijuana as proof of young people's disrespect for law and authority.

By 1968 the protest against liberalism had become both a political and a cultural issue. The 1968 presidential campaign reflected the diverse tensions within American society and channeled them into the political arena. As events would show, however, the political process offered a poor forum for resolving the deep social and cultural divisions; few national contests have produced as much bitterness and political violence as the 1968 presidential campaign.

The Fall of Lyndon Johnson

Lyndon Johnson became the first casualty of the fierce political wars. After capturing more than 60 percent of the popular vote in 1964, Johnson had celebrated his "politics of consensus." Some Republicans even worried about their party's future. But trapped in an unpopular and unwinnable war, blamed for racial conflict, and assailed by enemies of Great Society liberalism, Johnson saw many of his old supporters desert him. The tall Texan, who had once thoroughly enjoyed his role as "the leader of the free world," now found himself the butt of innumerable jokes. As his standing in opinion polls and his support in Congress steadily dropped, LBJ's enemies gleefully lampooned his outsized image.

Dissident Democrats organized a "Dump Johnson" movement to deny the president his party's nomination in 1968. At first considered hopeless, especially when Senator Robert Kennedy refused to run for president, the anti-Johnson campaign finally coalesced behind an unlikely hero, Senator Eugene McCarthy of Minnesota. An unorthodox, aloof antipolitician—his political critics called him arrogant and exceedingly vain—McCarthy offered a striking contrast to the earthy Texan. He instinctively recoiled from LBJ's rhetorical overkill and promised no great societies. His whole campaign suggested a conservative's doubts about the dreams of liberals like Lyndon Johnson. "All we want is a moderate use of intelligence," McCarthy told his supporters. Gradually, McCarthy's low-key, antiwar campaign caught on, and a small army of college students rallied behind the only "peace candidate" in either major party. When Johnson declined to campaign in the New Hamsphire presidential primary, reporters found McCarthy the most interesting candidate on the road. His "quixotic children's crusade," as the media called it, gained considerable air

LBJ, 1964. In 1964 Lyndon Johnson was widely celebrated as a political genius; by 1968, largely as a result of the Vietnam War, and the growing protests against it, his popularity and his political reputation were in eclipse.

time on the evening news. Meanwhile, the communists' Tet offensive in Vietnam increased popular doubts about Johnson's war policy.

Although McCarthy actually won only 43 percent of the Democratic vote in New Hampshire's March primary, he ran well enough to refute conventional wisdom about the invincibility of an incumbent president within his own party. McCarthy also accomplished something else: he captured media attention for the anti-Johnson movement. (In some ways McCarthy's appeal was as much anti-Johnson as it was antiwar: when asked about their second choice as a Democratic candidate, some McCarthy supporters named Alabama's hawkish governor, George C. Wallace.)

After the New Hampshire primary, Johnson's political and personal problems only increased. Within days, Robert Kennedy announced his intention to enter the race for the Democratic nomination; and, facing certain defeat by McCarthy in the Wisconsin primary, a physically exhausted Lyndon Johnson retired without a fight. On March 31, 1968, the president dramatically announced that he would not seek another term. Coupling his retirement with a serious offer to negotiate in Paris with North Vietnam and the National Liberation Front, he proclaimed that he would not let partisan politics stand in the way of the search for peace.

About to be relieved of the responsibilities of the presidency, Johnson abandoned the spartan routine that his heart condition required. He resumed smoking and began to eat greater quantities of rich, fried food. Within two years he suffered a serious heart attack; within five years he was dead.

The "Politics of Joy" and the "New Politics"

Johnson's retreat brought forth a full-scale charge by Hubert Humphrey, LBJ's vice-president and an unsuccessful presidential contender in 1960. Humphrey enjoyed the full support of party chieftains—labor leaders such as George Meany, political bosses such as Chicago Mayor Daley and Texas Governor John Connally, and LBJ himself. With this backing, Humphrey could ignore the primaries and use his political muscle to line up delegates. At first, he tried to gain support with the unlikely theme "the politics of joy," but even Humphrey came to recognize the foreboding political atmosphere of the 1968 election.

The unrelenting political violence of 1968 made a mockery of Humphrey's politics of joy. In April Martin Luther King was gunned down in Memphis; black ghettos erupted in anger. Disorders rocked more than one hundred towns; thirty-six people died; and public officials deployed more than fifty thousand national guardsmen and federal troops. Many black and white radicals refused to believe that another lone gunman, this one an escaped convict named James Earl Ray, could have killed still another national leader. (In 1979 a special House Committee concluded that some type of conspiracy very likely did surround King's shooting, but it could produce no firm evidence.)

As Americans recovered from the shock of King's death, Eugene McCarthy and Robert Kennedy attempted to use their campaigns to bring alienated Americans back into "the system." McCarthy's brand of "new politics"—a much-abused phrase that suggested no back-room deals with powerful interest groups, reliance on youthful volunteers, and straightforward political speeches—appealed to bright, politically aware college students. (Bobby Kennedy once joked that McCarthy had all the A students while he could attract only those who got B's and B–'s.) Shaving beards and donning skirts to "come clean for Gene," thousands of young men and women canvassed door to door and state to state with their hero. Kennedy's efforts also excited young people, but many idealists complained that his campaign smacked too much of the "old politics." Kennedy tried to make special appeals to a diverse coalition of white ethnic voters, blacks, chicanos, liberals, and even George Wallace supporters. As he vigorously stumped Indiana, assisted by plenty of Kennedy money, reporters dubbed his campaign train the "Ruthless Cannonball."

He has the Poles in Gary,
The Blacks will fill his hall,
There are no ethnic problems on the Ruthless Cannonball.

While Humphrey rested on his safe cushion of nonprimary delegates, Kennedy and McCarthy tried to impress party leaders with their vote-getting ability. McCarthy lost to Kennedy in Indiana and Nebraska, but in Oregon he became the first politician ever to defeat any Kennedy. The Kennedy mystique seemed broken; Bobby battled for his political life in preparing for the California primary. A Kennedy campaign was something special: an array of movie stars, folk singers, athletes, university professors, and even business executives dropped everything to follow Bobby. Ignoring threats against his life, Kennedy waded into crowds wherever he went, with only a few burly friends to shield him from danger.

The night of the California primary, these same supporters stood helplessly nearby as Kennedy was shot at point-blank range in the kitchen of a Los Angeles hotel. Police immediately arrested Sirhan Sirhan, a Jordanian immigrant, whom a jury later convicted of Kennedy's murder. Minutes before the shooting Kennedy had accepted congratulations for a narrow victory over McCarthy in the climatic California primary; twenty-four hours later he was dead. Although McCarthy said that he would continue to fight for the nomination, Kennedy's death took the heart out of his campaign. Humphrey had a clear path.

Miami and the Siege of Chicago

Republican delegates assembled first to choose their presidential candidate. Meeting amid racial violence and protest in Miami (four people were killed during racial disorders there), Republicans chose a face from the past—former vice-president Richard Nixon. Although he had lost the 1960 presidential contest and had presumably retired from politics after his defeat in the California gubernatorial race of 1962, image makers proclaimed a "new Nixon." (Early in the 1968 campaign, a critic complained that "there is no new Nixon. What we have here is the old Nixon, a little older.") In truth, the dogged campaigner fellow law students at Duke had called "Old Iron Butt" simply outlasted the field. Nominated on the first ballot, Nixon surprised the convention by selecting Spiro T. Agnew, the obscure governor of Maryland, as his running mate.

In his acceptance speech, the "new Nixon" suggested peaceful overtures to the Soviet Union and the People's Republic of China and pledged to give black Americans "a piece of the action in the exciting ventures of private enterprise." But the address also contained echoes of the old Nixon. He praised the "forgotten Americans, the nonshouters, the nondemonstrators"; he suggested that Americans had been "deluged" by government welfare programs that had only "reaped... an ugly harvest of frustrations, violence, and failure"; and he promised that his attorney general would "open a new front against crime."

The cry for law and order became stronger after the violence that accompained the Democrats' Chicago convention. Mayor Richard Daley and various security agencies expected trouble. Several peace groups planned demonstrations, and the Yippies promised to stage a "festival of life," an answer to what they called the Democrats' "festival of death." Abbie Hoffman talked about sending ten thousand nude Yippies wading into Lake Michigan, releasing greased pigs in Chicago's crowded Loop area, and slipping LSD into the city's water supply. Mayor Daley took Hoffman's jokes seriously and, in the words of reporters from the *Times* of London, prepared "security in the paranoid style." Although information indicated that the number of demonstrators would fall far below the Yippies' expectations, the mayor readied his twelve-thousand-man police force and had the Illinois National Guard and the United States Army waiting for action. "If you're going to Chicago, be sure to wear armor in your hair," warned an underground newspaper editor.

After several days of skirmishes between youthful protesters and the Chicago police, serious violence erupted on the night delegates selected Humphrey as the Democratic nominee for president. Police beat demonstrators, non-protesting bystanders, and even a few reporters. A special commission eventually labeled the disorders a "police riot." Policemen, the commission concluded, had faced taunts and some random missiles, but they had responded out of all proportion to the provocations. According to one eyewitness, "Some police pursued individuals as far as a block and beat them. . . . In many cases it appeared to me that when the police had finished beating the protesters they were pursuing, they then attacked, indiscriminately, any civilian who happened to be standing nearby. Many of these were not involved in the demonstration." But many people saw events the other way: one poll revealed that nearly 60 percent of the American public blamed the demonstrators and supported the police.

On the question of disorders at the convention and on the war issue, Hubert Humphrey found himself caught in the middle of squabbling Democrats. He dared not openly criticize either Mayor Daley's police or the antiwar forces. Humphrey tried to pretend that the Democratic party would pull together, but his early campaign efforts belied such optimism. Antiwar hecklers confronted the underfinanced and badly advised Humphrey at every stop, and his audiences remained small and generally unenthusiastic.

The Great Race of 1968

Initially George Wallace suffered none of these problems. Running on the American Independent ticket, the former governor of Alabama preached law and order, a slogan that black people and liberals denounced as code words for racism. Wallace's angry denials were, in a sense, correct. The black revolt was only one of the social issues that Wallace hoped to exploit. In his standard address he contended that "there's not a dime's worth of difference" between the two major parties, denounced "pointy-headed professors" who "don't know how to park a bicycle straight," and predicted that all the "intellectual morons" and "theoreticians" were "going to get some of those liberal smiles knocked off their faces." Wallace cleverly linked distaste for big government with fears of the counterculture. "Our lives are being taken over by bureaucrats, and most of them have beards." Campaigning with a variety of county-and-western singers,

Wallace made good his promise to shake up the major parties. As election day neared, however, many northern Democrats, primarily blue-collar workers and ethnic voters, who had been leaning toward Wallace began to return to the Democratic ranks. Aided by their desertion of Wallace, the vice-president nearly caught Nixon.

Richard Nixon and his army of strategists watched Humphrey draw closer until the last polls showed the race a toss-up. Finally deciding that he would have to untangle himself from Johnson's Vietnam policy, the vice-president announced in October that he would risk a bombing halt in hopes of speeding the Paris peace talks. Several days before the November election, President Johnson ordered a temporary cessation of air raids over North Vietnam. These steps induced some antiwar people, including Eugene McCarthy, to announce at least grudging support of Humphrey's candidacy. Despite his late surge, however, Humphrey fell about a hundred thousand votes short, and Nixon captured the presidency with only about 43 percent of the popular vote. The lonely long-distance runner, as Garry Wills called Nixon, had finally won the big race.

Although Nixon and Humphrey had tried to identify themselves with the "new politics," their nominations, and the election of Ike's former vice-president, demonstrated the tenacity of traditional political habits and institutions. Careful studies of voting behavior revealed that people most likely to cast ballots were unyoung, unpoor, unblack, and largely unsympathetic to the exuberance of youthful radicalism. Most voters identified cultural rebellion with ingratitude for the material abundance they associated with "the American way"; they considered left-wing politics, with its stress upon demonstrations and direct participation, socially disruptive. Those who initially wanted to cast a protest vote supported McCarthy, Kennedy, or Wallace, believing that, in their own unique ways, these three had broken with conventional politicians. With Kennedy's death, some of his discontented working-class supporters switched their allegiance to George Wallace. And after McCarthy's virtual retirement from political life following the violence of Chicago, many supporters of the new politics simply stayed home. Others reluctantly joined the other American voters in choosing between two familiar candidates who stood firmly in the center of the American political spectrum. By 1968, then, the youth-inspired rebellion had failed to bring participatory democracy, the age of Aquarius, or even the triumph of the new politics. Although shaken by the agitation of the New Left, the people who dominated the American political system remained committed to the liberalism of the Democratic party or the moderate Republicanism espoused by Richard Nixon. But events would show that the age of protest was not over.

SUGGESTIONS FOR FURTHER READING

The controversial ideas of Herbert Marcuse and Paul Goodman can be traced in their own works. *One-Dimensional Man* (1964) and *An Essay on Liberation*

(1969) were Marcuse's most important works in the 1960s. Among Goodman's many books, *Growing up Absurd* (1960), *People and Personnel* (1963), and *The New Reformation* (1971) are especially recommended. For a critical analysis of the views of both Goodman and Marcuse, see Richard King, *The Party of Eros* (1972). Theodore Roszak is much more sympathetic in his *The Making of a Counter-Culture* (1969). See Roszak's other works, including *Where the Wasteland Ends* (1972) and *Person/Planet* (1978). Charles Reich's *The Greening of America* (1970) and Philip Slater's *The Pursuit of Loneliness* (rev. ed., 1976) offer two different contemporary views of the counterculture. For widely divergent later assessments, see Morris Dickstein, *The Gates of Eden* (1977) and Daniel Bell, "The Sensibility of the Sixties," in his *Cultural Contradictions of Capitalism* (1976). See also Joan Didion's *Slouching Toward Bethlehem* (1968) and *The White Album* (1979).

C. Wright Mills offered his most sweeping critique of American political culture in *The Power Elite* (1956). For a critique of Mills and of other theoreticians on the left, see Peter Clecak, *Radical Paradoxes* (1973). On the history of the New Left, see Irwin Unger, *The Movement* (1974); Kirkpatrick Sale, *SDS* (1973); and George Vickers, *The Formation of the New Left* (1975). *Personal Politics* (1979) by Sara Evans offers a corrective to these male-dominated accounts. Clecak's *Radical Paradoxes* and Todd Gitlin's *The Whole World is Watching* (1980) provide critiques from scholars generally sympathetic to the Movement's ends, though not its means or its analyses of American society.

The social-psychological bases of the "youth revolt" were analyzed by Kenneth Keniston in *The Uncommitted* (1965), *The Young Radicals* (1968), and *Youth and Dissent* (1971). Klaus Mehnert's *Twilight of the Young* (1978) provides a transnational perspective. The literature on the Berkeley Student Revolt has been collected in a book of the same name (1965) by Seymour Martin Lipset and Sheldon Wolin. Although David Zane Mairowitz's *The Radical Soap Opera* (1974) is often too flippant, it can also be very insightful. Members of the Movement have not been reluctant to tell their own stories. See, for example, Abbie Hoffman's trilogy *Revolution for the Hell of It* (1970), *Woodstock Nation* (1969), and *Soon to Be a Major Picture* (1980). Jerry Rubin's most famous slogan, and work, was *Do It!* (1971). On *Ramparts* magazine's stormy life see Warren Hinckle, *If You Have a Lemon, Make Lemonade* (1974). See also Raymond Mungo's *Famous Long Ago* (1970) and *Cosmic Profit* (1980).

Although Tom Wolfe does not suit everyone's tastes, his views of the 1960s are well worth sampling. See *The Pump House Gang* (1968), *The Electric Kool-Aid Acid Test* (1968), and *Radical Chic and Mau-Mauing the Flak-Catchers* (1970). Daniel Yankelovich, *The New Morality* (1974) offers a preliminary assessment of the impact of the 1960s; less satisfactory is Rex Weiner and Deanne Stillman, *Woodstock Census* (1979). In *Thy Neighbor's Wife* (1980) Gay Talese explores the new sexual morality.

The opposition to the war is the subject of Thomas Powers, *The War at Home* (1973); Norman Mailer, *Armies of the Night* (1967); Ken Hurwitz, *March-*

ing Nowhere (1971); and Sandy Vogelgesang, *The Long Dark Night of the Soul* (1974). See also Louis Menashe and Ronald Radosh, *Teach-Ins, U.S.A.* (1967).

The political events of 1968 are detailed in *An American Melodrama* (1969) by Lewis Chester and several other reporters for the *Times* of London. See also Norman Mailer, *Miami and the Siege of Chicago* (1968); Jeremy Larner, *Nobody Knows: Reflections on the McCarthy Campaign* (1970); and Ben Wattenberg and Richard Scammon, *The Real Majority* (1970). The best book on Richard Nixon and the meaning of the 1968 campaign remains Garry Wills, *Nixon Agonistes* (rev. ed., 1979).

PROTEST AND THE SEARCH FOR POWER, 1968–1976

The Violent Years, 1968-1972

Violence in Southeast Asia

Despite the years of antiwar protest and Richard Nixon's talk of a secret peace plan, the war in Vietnam continued, even accelerated, in the late 1960s. After a thorough review of war policy Nixon and his national-security adviser, Henry Kissinger, made several crucial decisions. As quickly as possible the United States would turn the ground war over to the South Vietnamese and begin a gradual withdrawal of American forces while stepping up the air war. At the same time, the United States would try to enlist Soviet help in wringing concessions from Hanoi. In July 1969 the president placed his Vietnam policy within a grander design—the so-called Nixon Doctrine—pledging that the United States would continue giving military assistance to anticommunist governments in Asia but would have Asians, not Americans, do the fighting. In later statements Nixon made it "perfectly clear" that the United States would not "bug out" on its commitment to Saigon. The president was promising peace but still hoping to design the military victory that had beguiled, and eluded, his predecessors. Essentially "Vietnamization" of the war was a formula for stepping up the war while diffusing domestic dissent by ending the involvement of American draftees.

Nixon looked primarily to Henry Kissinger rather than to his cabinet to help construct his policy of Vietnamization. In fact, the foreign-policy-making process was so thoroughly centralized in the White House that Secretary of State William Rogers and Secretary of Defense Melvin Laird often remained peripheral to important decisions. Kissinger, a Harvard professor and protégé of Nelson Rockefeller, saw world politics as a global geopolitical confrontation between Soviet and American power. According to Kissinger, America's primary duty consisted of foreclosing Soviet opportunities for expansion; conflicts anywhere in the world had to be viewed in light of how they "linked up" to the central concern of American policy. It was through his crucial concept of linkage that Kissinger justified his hopes for an early and favorable settlement in Vietnam. Kissinger hoped, he later wrote in his memoirs, to make "progress in settling the Vietnam war something of a condition for advance in areas of interest to the Soviets, such as the Middle East, trade or arms limitation."

The "secret plan" for ending the war by enticing the Soviets to pressure the North Vietnamese went nowhere. It made at least two faulty assumptions: one, that the Soviets could easily influence Hanoi; and two, that the Soviets would be persuaded to pull their strings on America's behalf. Neither proved true, but Kissinger continued to pursue Vietnamization.

To Kissinger, the dilemmas of war abroad and resistance at home simply required a tactical adjustment in strategy: begin bringing the ground troops home, and compensate for their withdrawal by new air offensives. The military once again labored to revise the English language by labeling this new variety of escalation "accelerated pacification" and "protective reaction strikes." Although Nixon and Kissinger honored Johnson's bombing halt over North Vietnam, they increased targets in the South and launched a full-scale war against Cambodia.

In May 1970 Nixon announced on national television that he hard ordered an American-led invasion of Cambodia, supposedly a neutral country. In making this decision, he ignored the advice of his secretaries of state and defense and neglected to consult (or even inform) Lon Nol, America's Cambodian ally who, less than two months before, had successfully overthrown the neutralist regime of Prince Norodom Sihanouk. North Vietnamese forces had been using various parts of Cambodia as staging areas, and Pentagon strategists had long pressed the White House to clear out the sanctuaries and destroy a mythical Vietnamese guerrilla headquarters. A quick strike, it was hoped, would throw the enemy off balance, capture valuable supplies, and buy time for Vietnamization to shape South Vietnam's army into an effective force.

American troops met surprisingly little resistance in Cambodia during the April invasion and found no guerrilla headquarters, but the president's defenders nevertheless considered the maneuver a success. They claimed that it upset North Vietnam's plans and allowed the United States more time to prepare for their withdrawal. But widening the war into Cambodia ultimately had disastrous consequences. America continued to wage a secret air war in Cambodia long after the April strike, and the heavy bombing destroyed large portions of what had been a peaceful, agricultural country, creating a large refugee population and a devastating decline in food supplies. Cambodians rallied in resistance. The Khmer Rouge, the native communist guerrillas, transformed themselves from a disorganized force of 5,000 in 1970 to a fierce army of 70,000 in 1975; Lon Nol found support only in the capital city. Subsequent American defeat and withdrawal would leave communist regimes in both Vietnam and Cambodia, fulfilling the domino effect the war had initially been staged to prevent.

Antiwar forces at home severely criticized the accelerating violence in Southeast Asia. Public revelations of the My Lai massacre (which had occurred in March 1968) intensified criticism of American involvement in Southeast Asia.

The slowly unfolding story of what had happened in the hamlet of My Lai shocked most Americans. American servicemen testified to the killing of unarmed civilians, including women and children, by a company under the command of an ineffectual young lieutenant named William Calley. After bungling an attempt at a cover-up, the army finally prosecuted several officers, but only Calley was convicted. A member of another unit testified to similar activities by his outfit. "I used to think my company was a bad-ass one until I started seeing others," he said. "Sometimes you thought it was just my platoon, my company that was committing atrocious acts. . . . But what we were doing was being done all over."

The Cambodian invasion of 1970 polarized opinion about the war in Asia, especially on college campuses. Students mounted protest marches and strikes at more than four hundred schools; demonstrations at Ohio's Kent State University led to the killing of four students. Many colleges abruptly ended the spring semester early and closed their doors. The reaction to the invasion of Cambodia did produce a small tide of approval in Nixon's direction—according to one poll, the percentage of people who approved of the way the president was handling his job increased by six points—but it also hardened antiwar sentiments. Most important, the widening of the fighting into Cambodia clearly stamped the conflict as "Nixon's War."

Violence at Home

Paralleling the bloodletting in Vietnam (or growing out of it, according to some social scientists) was a violent new direction in the radical movement at home. The Weathermen—later called the Weatherpeople or the Weatherfolks in response to the feminist movement—pledged to "bring the war home to Amerika" in order to help the National Liberation Front. To the tune of the Beatles' "Nowhere Man," this small but highly publicized faction of SDS sang,

> He's a real Weatherman/Ripping up the mother land,
> Making all his Weatherplans/For everyone;
> Knows just what he's fighting for/Victory for the people's war,
> Trashes, bombs, kills pigs and more/The Weatherman.

Predictably, the Weatherpeople gained considerable attention from the media and met with almost no political success. Their much-publicized Four Days of Rage, an invasion of Chicago in 1969, proved a disaster. After smashing some windows, almost all of the helmeted Weatherpeople were overwhelmed, beaten bloody, and arrested by Mayor Daley's police.

After this fiasco most of the prominent Weatherpeople went underground. Some were seeking to avoid arrest for previous activities. Some joined other desperate young people in a bombing campaign against various symbols of "Kapitalist oppression." Between September 1969 and June 1970 there were more than 170 bombings and attempted bombings on college campuses.

An explosion at the University of Wisconsin killed a graduate student, and other campuses endured non-lethal attacks. Universities gradually adjusted to the threat of violence, and cautious scholars began keeping valuable materials and manuscripts at home. Bombers also struck off campuses, hitting targets such as the Bank of America, the Chase Manhattan Bank, and even the United States Congress. Three Weatherpeople blew themselves apart when their bomb factory in a fashionable Greenwich Village town house exploded in 1970. In the end, though, few of the attacks did major damage—corporation bathrooms, the easiest place to hide explosives, suffered the brunt of the onslaught—but they contributed to an increasingly ugly mood throughout the country.

President Nixon and Vice-President Agnew sanctimoniously upheld the rule of law. "You see these bums, you know, blowing up the campuses," the president grumbled after students protested (in most cases nonviolently) the invasion of Cambodia. "We cannot afford to be divided or deceived by the decadent thinking of a few young people," fumed Agnew. We could, he argued, "afford to separate them from our society—with no more regret than we should feel over discarding rotten apples from a barrel."

Some law-enforcement people shared these sentiments. More violence, in the final analysis, came from the upholders of law and order than from outgunned students and radicals. In early 1968 state troopers killed three protesting black students at Orangeburg State College in South Carolina. During a 1969 confrontation at Berkeley, state patrolmen indiscriminately dropped tear gas from helicopters and fatally shot one long-haired bystander in the back. In December of 1969 Chicago police stormed the Illinois headquarters of the Black Panthers and killed two persons. In May 1970 white police officers opened fire on a women's dormitory at Mississippi's Jackson State College, an all-black institution; two unarmed students were killed. And in the most celebrated incident, Ohio national guardsmen shot thirteen students, four of whom died, at Kent State.

A "Law-and-Order" Administration

The persistence of political disorder, along with the rising crime rate, encouraged the Nixon administration to emphasize its commitment to restoring "law and order." To many Americans, the young antiwar protesters seemed a band of troublemakers. After the killings at Kent State, public-opinion polls showed that most people believed that the National Guard had fired on the unarmed students in self-defense; Nixon and Agnew continued their tough talk; and Attorney General Mitchell strengthened the Justice Department's internal-security division. Moreover, as subsequent investigations would reveal, the White House, the FBI, and the CIA all continued—or intensified—various illegal activities against domestic radicals. The FBI, for example, did not limit itself to surveillance of groups espousing violence but mounted numerous efforts to infiltrate and to harass groups and individuals who favored significant, and peaceful, social change. In one celebrated case, the bureau circulated vicious rumors about the personal life of a prominent actress who had expressed support for the Black Panthers. Similarly, some of the FBI's undercover agents operated as *agent provocateurs* and actually urged violent action by protesters. Commenting on the FBI's notorious COINTELPRO operation—which extended from 1956 to 1971 and was cancelled only after stolen FBI documents revealed its existence—a committee of the House of Representatives made a sweeping indictment: "Careers were ruined, friendships severed, reputations sullied, businesses bankrupted and, in some cases, lives endangered."

While engaging in massive lawbreaking of its own, the Nixon administration was mobilizing the national legal system against dissidents. In the most celebrated political prosecution since the 1940s, the Chicago conspiracy trial of 1969, Attorney General Mitchell pressed for indictments against eight leading radicals. (Mitchell's predecessor, Ramsey Clark, had decided not to prosecute, because of insufficient evidence.) The government charged the group—which included Tom Hayden, Bobby Seale, Abbie Hoffman, and Jerry Rubin—with conspiracy and with crossing state lines to encourage violence at the 1968 Democratic convention. The defense team, led by attorney William Kunstler, hoped to make a serious constitutional challenge, but some of the defendants viewed the affair as a countercultural "happening" rather than a legal battle. Goaded by Judge Julius Hoffman's obviously prejudicial rulings, the defense never mounted a coherent counterattack. At the end of the trial Judge Hoffman unexpectedly cited all of the defendants for various actions in contempt of court. Concluding the sorry affair, the jury rendered obviously what was a compromise verdict: it acquitted all the defendants of the more serious conspiracy charge but convicted the most famous—including Yippies Rubin and Hoffman—of crossing state lines to incite a riot. After a lengthy appeal process all of the defendants escaped jail, but the Chicago conspiracy trial hardly cast much credit on the American legal system.

Other such trials—including prosecutions of antiwar priests Philip and Daniel Berrigan, of Bobby Seale, and of various lesser-known radicals—produced few convictions, but they did help to focus public attention on the political "criminals in the streets." Simply by filing charges, the Nixon administration and state officials encouraged public fears of the radical "menace" and increased the disarray of the left.

The Violence Wanes

Richard Nixon continued to pose as the president who would listen to the "forgotten American." From 1969 to early 1972 Nixon and Agnew plied "middle Americans" with one theme: a small group of New Left "hooligans," aided and abetted by "radical liberals" within the Democratic party, threatened the country's stability. For two years Agnew assailed the "biased liberal" media, which "slandered" the president; the "nattering nabobs of negativism," who scorned traditional American values; the "curled-lip boys in the eastern ivory towers," who thumbed their noses at ordinary people; and those, such as Benjamin Spock, who encouraged the "growing spirit of permissiveness." As the off-year elections of 1970 neared, Agnew stepped up his attacks on the New Left and "radical liberals," proclaiming that it was "time to sweep that kind of garbage out of our society."

Despite energetic campaigning by Nixon himself, the Republicans failed to make any gains in the 1970 elections. The GOP did add a few members to the Senate but dropped about a dozen seats in the House and lost no fewer than eleven governorships. The electoral results clearly revealed that the Democrats, though badly divided and somewhat demoralized, remained the majority party. The apparent lesson of 1970 was not lost on the White House. Nixon's political strategists abandoned grand theories about "an emerging Republican majority" and began to plan a presidential reelection campaign that divorced the president, as much as possible, from the rest of the Republican ticket. Nixon's image makers left all the invective to a slightly more subdued Agnew, organized more subtle campaign tactics for 1972, and accentuated the president's role in foreign affairs.

By 1972 a good deal of the passion—indeed paranoia—of domestic politics seemed to have vanished. By reducing American ground forces in Vietnam, promising an end to the draft, and helping to lower the voting age to eighteen, the Nixon administration removed three highly visible irritants. Although many other causes of the New Left remained, especially the conflict in Southeast Asia itself, they failed to ignite the old passions. The Movement was beginning to run out of momentum.

During the early 1970s the New Left, for example, was in disarray. Seeking militant allies and fresh sources of inspiration, a few young radicals looked to prison inmates, particularly articulate blacks, as the new vanguard of revolution. This desperate turn—alliance with the most powerless group in American society, one heavily infiltrated by police informers and perhaps even *agent provocateurs*—proved suicidal. George Jackson, who became a New Left celebrity after the publication of some of his prison letters, was eventually gunned down (assassinated, insisted his admirers) during an alleged escape attempt from San Quentin Prison in 1973. A small group of young white radicals who had worked closely with prison militants met a similarly violent end. Calling themselves the Symbionese Liberation Army (SLA) and led by an escaped black prisoner who called himself Cinque, the group briefly gained national attention in 1973 by kidnapping Patricia Hearst, daughter of a prominent San Francisco newspaper publisher. The SLA converted their captive and evaded police and FBI pursuers for several months. Then in May 1974 six members of the group perished after a furious shootout, carried on television, with Los Angeles police. In September 1975 Patty Hearst and two remaining SLA members were finally apprehended. Long before the rise and fall of the SLA, however, most young people had lost interest in both radical and revolutionary politics. By the early 1970s the New Left, though not the movement for political change, was through.

The "youth revolt" had ended. But the basic impetus for social change persisted. A movement based so heavily upon young people and upon confrontation tactics only accentuated the traditional weakness of the American left—its

Robert Peterson.

The New Homesteads. Construction of condominiums and conversion of older apartment buildings into condominiums became a major new trend in housing during the 1970s and contributed to the disruption of old neighborhoods and to ethnic antagonism.

lack of a mass base of support. As disappointed rebels, no longer so young, came to realize, all the paths toward significant social change were (in Peter Clecak's words) crooked ones. There were no shortcuts—through rock music, drugs, the mass media, or any other magical potion—to a more just society. Yet despite the dominant presence and the apparently growing power of Richard Nixon, there were a variety of groups struggling to gain greater power for themselves and hoping to change the old order that Nixon and his Republican successor Gerald Ford represented.

The Search for Power, 1968 – 76

Although the Nixon administration's constant fears about the power of the left were undoubtedly overstated, the forces of dissent did seem to grow in breadth, if not in strength, during Nixon's first term. At the beginning of the 1970s a number of different groups were demanding more power—more "power for the people" and more power for their own special constituencies. Few of these groups achieved stunning victories, but they all laid the groundwork for what they expected would be new gains in the future.

Black Power

After 1968 the black movement went in many different directions. No leader replaced Martin Luther King, and his own SCLC lost most of its prestige when the much-publicized Poor People's March of 1968 bogged down in the spring rains of Washington, D.C. Dr. King had hoped that poor people might establish an ongoing presence in the nation's capital and lobby for new social-welfare measures. But the marchers' waterlogged tent camp, Resurrection City, broke into squabbling factions, and most protesters slowly deserted the capital. The government finally expelled the few survivors, and the SCLC never recovered from the debacle. Other black groups suffered similar fates. CORE, the organization that had begun the freedom rides in 1961, gradually lost influence and visibility. H. Rap Brown, Stokely Carmichael's outspoken successor—he once defiantly justified black violence as being "as American as cherry pie"—kept SNCC in the headlines and on the evening news for a short time, but he finally dropped from sight after a grand-jury indictment. (In 1972 Brown was apprehended in New York City after holding up a black social club in Harlem.)

In 1972, in an attempt to create a new organizational structure, advocates of black power formed the National Black Political Assembly. In March, more than ten thousand delegates and observers met in Gary, Indiana, to hammer out a "Black Agenda." A militant statement that bothered older integrationists, the Black Agenda charged that white politicans "offer no real hope of real change" and that the "crises we face as black people. . . are the natural end-product of a society built on the twin foundations of white racism and white capitalism." In retrospect, the Gary meeting represented the high point of black-power unity; within months, deep fissures developed within the National Black Political Assembly as Marxists tilted with liberals, as integrationists battled cultural nationalists. While activist-intellectuals debated theories of cultural and political change, the black scholar Manning Marable has argued, the mass of black workers, students, and unemployed tended to lose interest. As the remnants of the movement clashed with one another, they lost any hope of gaining a mass base of support. As a result, black social and political movements became more fragmented than before.

In this situation, the Nixon administration moved cautiously and obliquely on racial questions. Gaining only five of every one hundred black votes in 1968 and doing no better in 1972, the president had most of his political capital invested elsewhere. "Watch what we do, not what we say," suggested John Mitchell, who as Nixon's chief political strategist was closely identified with efforts to attract white southerners but who as Nixon's attorney general was responsible for enforcing civil-rights laws. The Nixon administration gave the greatest priority to finding better jobs for black workers with skills and more opportunities for "black capitalists." In these areas real gains were made. The number of black-owned banks, for example, more than doubled between 1970 and 1975, and the number of small businesses, especially "mom-and-pop stores," increased dramatically.

In almost every other area, though, critics denounced what Nixon's people did as well as what they said. Criticism was not limited to that by blacks. Bishop Stephen Spottswood, a leader of the NAACP, accused the administration of deliberating adopting an antiblack posture; Father Theodore Hesburgh, president of Notre Dame and head of the United States Civil Rights Commission, denounced the president's reluctance to enforce existing civil-rights measures; and Leon Panetta, head of the Civil Rights Division of the Department of Health, Education and Welfare (HEW), resigned in protest against Nixon's opposition to school busing as a means of desegregating public schools.

From the outset, the administration braked the drive toward school desegregation. In deference to its white southern supporters, the White House initially ordered HEW to revise the Johnson administration's tough desegregation guidelines and to exempt schools "with bona fide educational and legal problems." And in a dramatic sign of the administration's attitude, Nixon's Justice Department broke with a long tradition and argued *against* implementation of a desegregation plan for Mississippi. In March 1972 the president himself went on national television to ask for a moratorium on busing.

The administration's record in other areas proved equally disappointing to the vast majority of blacks: the gap between black and white incomes increased during the Nixon-Ford years; the government did little to help register black voters in the South; despite the hopes of the Department of Housing and Urban Development's George Romney, attempts to push integration in federal housing programs got almost nowhere; and the administration failed even to provide adequate funding for its own pet project, black capitalism. Daniel Patrick Moynihan, a former official in the Kennedy administration and Nixon's own domesticated Democrat, best summarized the administration's attitude toward black America when he urged a policy of "benign neglect." If blacks expected little or nothing from the national government, Moynihan reasoned, disappointments over the lack of significant change would generate less frustration and violence.

Moynihan's proposal, whatever its merit as a public-policy position, did represent a shrewd appraisal of the nation's ambiguous record on racial progress. Change on both the economic and the political fronts was occurring, but the immediate results were seldom dramatic. Aided by favorable rulings from the Supreme Court and by pressure from Democratic holdovers in HEW, a number of young blacks were finding greater educational and economic opportunities. On the issue of education, a majority of the Supreme Court gradually moved beyond a narrow reading of *Brown* v. *Board of Education* and held that the Constitution demanded that schools be "racially mixed." Although the Court did not apply this principle in every case, its new rulings generally required considerable busing of children from their old neighborhood school districts to other schools in order to provide "racial balance." Officials in HEW, citing the small numbers of nonwhites and women in the professions, began to press graduate and professional schools to take "affirmative action" and recruit a student body that was not overwhelmingly white and male. College-educated blacks stood to gain from such pressure, but many universities hesitated to overemphasize their affirmative-action programs, which were often denounced for establishing quotas and for denigrating merit. Working-class blacks encountered even more obstacles, especially from labor unions whose largely white memberships considered the government's efforts to increase minority employment a direct attack on their traditional seniority system. In 1970, for example, only 3.3 percent of the nation's sheet-metal workers and 1.7 percent of its tool and die makers were black.

In the area of politics, the drive for black power also produced mixed results. The continued migration of blacks to northern cities (together with the flight of many whites from those cities) virtually ensured the election of greater numbers of black political leaders. In 1955, for instance, only the black ghettos of New York and Chicago sent a representative to Congress; in 1972 fifteen blacks were elected to the House of Representatives. A number of cities—including Cleveland, Gary, and Newark—selected black mayors, and several northern states, including Michigan and New York, had more than 100 elected black officials.

But the creation of this new black political base failed to inaugurate sweeping changes. Those cities that elected black officials generally had a large (and largely poor) black population; their urban problems involved, but also transcended, racial issues. The new black officials were not miracle workers. Moreover, the new black leadership often faced a difficult dilemma: their efforts to reach out to powerful interest groups, in order to obtain private and public funds for necessary urban projects, did not always please all parts of their black constituency. In Detroit, for example, leaders from poor black neighborhoods charged that Mayor Coleman Young (elected in 1973) catered to the corporate and political elites' desire to rebuild the Motor City's business center while generally ignoring the plight of Detroit's poorest black residents. Young countered that Detroit's citizens desperately needed a viable business environment and that his policies addressed the needs of the entire population. In the ghettos themselves a new cynicism about all politicians, black as well as white, set in. Despite the black-power movement, for example, the percentage of northern blacks who bothered to register and to vote actually declined between 1964 and 1972.

Meanwhile, the Voting Rights Act of 1965 (renewed in 1970) and pressure from black groups gradually produced some tangible results in the South. In the election of 1970 more than 100 black candidates gained office in the South; by the end of that year more than 700 black people held political office in the southern states. At the same time, black voters gained more leverage in contests involving only white candidates. Openly seeking the support of blacks, most white candidates moderated their stands on racial issues.

Such gains, however, did not automatically bring radical changes to the South. In many heavily black counties and towns, black candidates still failed to gain office. More important, even the triumph of black politicians could not solve longstanding social and economic problems. Changing the skin color of mayors and county officials could not rejuvenate those rural areas plagued with limited resources and antiquated public services. Even the most energetic black officials often found it difficult to run all the bureaucratic roadblocks and obtain state or federal funds for their communities. By 1973, a decade had passed since Martin Luther King had shared his dream with those who had marched on

Washington; after surveying the changing status of blacks during that decade, King's vision of a truly just and equitable society remained a dream.

Brown Power

Although the black movement captured more attention, other nonwhite ethic groups displayed new cultural pride and growing political militancy. Throughout the 1960s, Mexican-Americans and Indians emulated the tactics of the black movement to organize their supporters and to attract the attention of the national news media. "Brown power" and "red power" made white Americans increasingly aware of the nation's pluralistic culture. They also dramatized the price that nonwhite minorities had paid—in economic deprivation and loss of self-respect—for their cultural and racial differences.

Mexican-Americans often confronted the type of discrimination with which black people were too familiar. Especially among migrant farm laborers, wages were low, housing inadequate, and education virtually nonexistent. The language barrier and the proximity of Mexican culture kept many Mexican-Americans far outside the mainstream of American life. During the 1960s the average Chicano child had only a seventh-grade education; nearly nine of every ten Chicanos dropped out of Texas high schools before graduation. Yet the problem was not inadequate motivation or low intelligence. As one teacher put it, "Our kids don't drop out; they are pushed out by poverty." Children could not concentrate on their studies if they were hungry, and many young people left school to help support their families.

Even if poverty did not force Chicanos out of school, the attitudes of officials often did. In some California school districts students could be expelled for speaking Spanish, even on the playground. Bilingualism, a quality highly valued among middle-class white children, was a badge of inferiority among Mexican-Americans. Standing on the edge of two cultures, many Chicano youths had severe identity problems that contributed to high dropout rates and low scholastic achievement. Advancement for Mexican-Americans, it seemed, had to proceed along two fronts—lifting their economic status and creating a positive cultural identity.

Cesar Chavez launched a drive to raise wages among Mexican-American farm workers. Chavez, who had grown up in California migrant camps during the late 1930s, recalled his family's first grape-picking job. "Each payday the contractor said he couldn't pay us because the winery hadn't paid him yet. At the end of the seventh week we went to the contractor's house and it was empty—he owed us for seven weeks' pay. . . . We were desperate." Chavez never forgot his people's poverty, and when the federal government's bracero (farm-worker) program ended in 1964 he began to unionize workers in the grape fields. With the source of new, cheap labor from Mexico diminished, unionization had a chance. The outlook grew even brighter when Chavez's United Farm Workers Union (UFW) attracted support from the powerful American Federation of Labor. During the grape pickers' strike in Delano, California, in 1965, Walter Reuther of the United Auto Workers joined Chavez on the picket lines, carrying a sign reading *HUELGA* ("STRIKE") and reminiscing about his own organizing fights during the 1930s. Robert Kennedy also visited the scene and became the UFW's most influential political supporter. But the growers held out, always finding enough hungry and jobless people to replace the strikers. Finally, Chavez adopted the technique that would bring the UFW some success and make him famous—the nationwide boycott. Dramatizing his personal commitment, Chavez went on a lengthy fast, an act that damaged his frail health.

Chavez's appeal to boycott California grapes captured the sympathy of liberals and radicals during the mid-1960s. For over a year, millions of Americans refused to buy grapes (the army bought them in great quantities to send to Vietnam, however), and growers finally signed with the UFW. Chavez, always a favorite of the media, became the first Mexican-American to receive sympathetic national coverage, and many reporters hailed him as a Spanish-speaking Martin Luther King. When lettuce growers signed what Chavez considered "sweetheart contracts" with the Teamsters Union, he appealed to Americans to boycott lettuce. By the early 1970s, however, the novelty of boycotts had worn off, and Chavez's victories grew fewer and fewer. Still, the UFW stayed alive through the years of trouble.

While Chavez worked to improve economic conditions among field workers, a charismatic minister in New Mexico, Reies Lopez Tijerina, attempted to organize a separatist movement and reopen the Mexican-American War of 1846-48. His organization, the Federal Alliance of Land Grants, reclaimed southwestern land, water, and grazing rights that whites had usurped over the previous hundred years. In 1967 he declared the area an independent republic. Guerrilla bands supporting Tijerina formed in northern New Mexico in the late 1960s and seized control of a portion of Kit Carson National Forest. When authorities arrested some of his followers, other disciples of Tijerina raided the courthouse in Tierra Amarilla to free them. The desperate action, which killed one deputy, catapulted Tijerina into the national news and caused widespread fear among Anglos in the area. Rumors swept New Mexico that Cuban-trained guerrillas were hiding in the mountains, and the National Guard patrolled the area for a time. But Tijerina seemed to be fighting for an idealized and irretrievable past of small, independent peasant communities untouched by modern America.

More practical leaders and organizations, not the Federal Alliance of Land Grants, appealed to most Mexican-Americans. Jose Angel Gutierrez's political party, La Raza Unida, raised hopes among Mexican-Americans in Texas. In 1970 La Raza captured a majority of seats on the school board in Crystal City, Texas, and began to remold the educational system according to the needs of the Spanish-speaking population. Soon La Raza gained control of all other political offices in Crystal and turned the town into a showcase of Chicano government, hoping to spread the party's popularity into barrios throughout the Southwest.

Despite the rising level of Chicano militancy, national officials devoted little serious attention to the problems of Mexican-Americans. Some Southwestern school systems did begin to teach some basic skills in Spanish and at the same try to improve children's use of English; on some college campuses Chicano-studies programs quickly followed the inception of black studies. But Chicano problems remained largely invisible on the national level. In 1969 Senator Joseph Montoya of New Mexico introduced a bill to extend the life of the President's Inter-Agency Committee on Mexican-American Affairs, a group that studied Chicano problems. The bill passed the Senate and went to the House, where it was "lost." After months of delay searchers finally found the bill, misfiled in the Foreign Affairs Committee.

Red Power

"Red power" did not really break into the national news until a cold November morning in 1969 when a group of militant Indians seized Alcatraz Island in San Francisco Bay. On the basis of an 1868 Sioux treaty that gave Indians possession of any unused federal land, the group argued that they could legitimately claim the abandoned prison on Alcatraz. Hundreds of Indian supporters soon joined them, demanding that the government convert the island into an Indian cultural center and appropriate funds for a Thunderbird University. Few white people took the Indians' proposals seriously. News reporters played up the announcement that the Indians would create a Bureau of Caucasian Affairs and would pay the government twenty-four dollars in glass beads for the property, but they largely ignored the more serious issues. For many Indians, nevertheless, the occupation had a symbolic significance. "Not just on Alcatraz, but everyplace else, the Indian is in his last stand for cultural survival," explained Richard Oakes, one of the elected leaders of the Alcatraz community. Many Indians saw Alcatraz as an important step in the formation of a pan-Indian cultural consciousness that would preserve the native American heritage. The Indians on Alcatraz represented tribes throughout the United States. They hoped that Indians could begin to use their separation from white society to instill pride rather than breed inferiority. And Alcatraz provided a particularly apt location for protest; the Indians claimed that its uninhabitable buildings, bad water and sanitation, and certain unemployment resembled conditions on most Indian reservations.

Although the seizure of Alcatraz—which continued until 1971—gave the "Indian problem" brief national headlines, white injustice and Indian protests were hardly new. The vast majority of Indians missed out on the great affluence of postwar American. After two-and-a-half decades of tremendous national "progress," the per-capita income of Indians was 60 percent less than that of whites; Indian life expectancy was only forty-seven years; half of all Indian children never completed high school; and the unemployment rate for Indians was 40 percent (on most reservations it exceeded 50 percent). But statistics told only a small part of what it meant to be a native of America. The Indian was the arch-villain of western movies, the embodiment of a cruel stereotype of sloth and incompetence, the obstacle to "civilization" in history textbooks. (Indian leader Russell Means said that historians "have to realize that Columbus was a honkie half a world off-course, and that *we* discovered *him*.") Discrimination against Indians was everywhere. La Nada Means, one of the original occupiers of Alcatraz, remembered the "meanness of the small towns around the reservation. Blackfoot, Pocatello—they all had signs in the store windows to keep Indians out. . . . There were Indian stalls in the public bathrooms; Indians weren't served in a lot of the restaurants; and we just naturally all sat in the balcony of the theaters." What were the effects of such treatment? "It becomes part of the way you look at yourself," she explained.

After Alcatraz, taking a cue from the tactics of other activist minorities, Indians became more militant. Chippewas in the Minneapolis-St. Paul area organized the American Indian Movement (AIM). In 1973 two AIM leaders, Russell Means and Dennis Banks, began protesting the disparity in law enforcement for Indians and whites. In Custer, South Dakota, officials charged a white with second-degree manslaughter for fatally stabbing an Indian, while in nearby Rapid City an Indian accused of killing a white women was held for murder without bail. Means and Banks led protests in both cities, and the hundreds of Indian demonstrators eventually clashed with police. AIM then seized a trading post at Wounded Knee, South Dakota, the place where the Seventh Cavalry had brutally crushed the last substantial pan-Indian resistance movement in the 1890s. AIM leaders believed that this small community on the Pine Ridge Reservation offered an appropriate place for launching a revival of "Indianness."

The occupation of Wounded Knee, highly publicized by the media, shattered the image of the passive, downtrodden Indian. AIM members vowed to hold the town until the Senate Foreign Relations Committee reviewed broken treaties with Indians, until the government investigated corruption in the Bureau of Indian Affairs, and until the Oglala Sioux tribal chairman, Dick Wilson, was removed from office.

AIM's bold tactics split the Indian community. Some Indians condemned AIM's members as outside agitators who wreaked physical destruction on an Indian town and repudiated Indian ways by attacking tribal elders. Others, including many older traditionalists, sympathized with AIM's opposition to Dick Wilson, criticizing him for corruption and for his cozy relationship with the Bureau of Indian Affairs. After federal marshals cleared Wounded Knee, the next tribal election reflected the division. Although Wilson was reelected, Russell Means received only several fewer votes, which indicated the hollowness of the outside-agitator theme.

The siege of Wounded Knee did not end Indian militancy: AIM then shifted its focus into the courts. Indicted on various counts, Banks and Means began a spectacular trial in St. Paul, first trying to have United States treaties with Indians (they contended the government had systematically violated them) admitted into evidence on their behalf. After a nine-month trial the presiding judge dismissed the indictments and charged the government prosecutors with serious misconduct. By the mid-1970s other Indians throughout the country were launching legal challenges and threatening direct action to redress grievances. Although militant tactics did not gain support from the entire Indian community, red power, like black power, had a far-reaching impact. It promoted a new pride in Indian culture, a fresh concern with preserving an ancient heritage, and a stronger determination to make whites live up to past promises.

Woman Power

In 1955 Adlai Stevenson told graduates of Smith College that their job in politics should be to use the "humble role of housewife" to influence their husbands and sons. The advice neatly fit the then current emphasis on domesticity. A woman's discontented women to their "natural," passive, home-centered roles. Some ad- dull and unchallenging life but from a psychological disorder resulting from a failure to accept her feminine character. These "experts" believed that advocates of women's rights were maladjusted and neurotic, that their frustrations derived from unfulfilled sexual desires or unsatisfactory relationships with their fathers. The stereotype of the feminist who "just needed a good man" to cure her anxieties remained firmly implanted in the minds of many American males.

Most psychologists recommended individual therapy to "readjust" discontended women to their "natural," passive, home-centered roles. Some advocated programs that would channel the need for self-expression into "proper" areas, such as cooking, childbearing, and interior decorating. Mass-circulation women's magazines responded with a repetitious array of articles that pictured cookery, decoration, and crafts as truly challenging and creative pursuits. Despite the burgeoning women's liberation movement and the growing numbers of working women, articles on home-centered women's activities remained the standard fare of women's magazines.

Some women, however, began to argue that the answer to female discontent lay not in molding errant women into the female stereotype but in reforming society so that women could escape the traditional female role without feeling guilty. These spokespeople presented evidence that wives who worked felt greater self-esteem and related better to their husbands and children than women who lost their personal identity amid the confines of home life. It followed that women should have the choice, without suffering any social stigma, to pursue careers outside the home. Betty Friedan's *The Feminine Mystique* presented a full-blown critique of the sex-role conditioning that, from birth, channeled women into a position of inferiority. From dolls and dainty ruffles through teenage dating conventions to myths of married bliss, women were contained within a mystique that prevented them from developing their full potential as human beings. Women had to break through the social conditioning to gain true equality and self-esteem.

Friedan's book appeared at a propitious time and helped launch a new feminist movement. Concern with civil rights for blacks was at a high point, and women began to realize that issues of equal opportunity, equal pay, and full acceptance applied to them as well as to blacks. In addition, the stereotype that white society had of blacks—childlike, irresponsible, emotional, and intellectually inferior—became a mirror in which women also saw themselves. Too many white males expected both women and blacks to be docile and to "know their place."

The black people's struggle also provided organizational and tactical models for the women's-rights movement. In 1966 Friedan and other women founded the National Organization for Women (NOW). Similar to black civil-rights organizations, NOW campaigned against institutions that practiced sex discrimination, lobbied for the creation of child-care centers, and publicized the cause of women through the media. NOW created local chapters and encouraged "consciousness-raising sessions," small groups of women who would discuss their lives, vent their grievances, and come to recognize their inferior status. Consciousness-raising would, feminists hoped, enable women to lead fuller, more satisfying lives.

The black movement also fought legal battles that ultimately benefited women. The Civil Rights Act of 1964, passed mainly in response to racial inequality, prohibited discrimination on the basis of sex as well as color. (Southern congressmen inserted the provision hoping that the specter of female equality would quash the bill.) The Civil Rights Act provided the principal legal tool that women's groups used to force government and business to stop sex discrimination. By the late 1960s the government was requiring corporations receiving federal funds to adopt nondiscriminatory hiring practices and equal pay scales; in the early 1970s the government required affirmative action to recruit more women and minority-group applicants.

The antiwar and radical movements of the late 1960s also contributed to the feminist upsurge. Demonstrating against racial injustice and war made women more conscious of their second-class roles; men dominated the podiums and the news while women typed circulars and brewed coffee. The development of a radical critique of American society provided women in the "movement" with a full-blown explanation of injustice and finally led them to militant feminism.

The development of a radical feminist position splintered the women's movement. NOW, consisting largely of middle-class professionals, sought to obtain equality through legislatures and courts. Political radicals such as SDS's militant Bernardine Dohrn, who joined the FBI's ten-most-wanted list after her alleged connection with bombing incidents, attacked the same capitalist system in which members of NOW wanted to work. Cultural radicals sought to abolish marriage, which they considered a sexist institution; some rejected male companionship entirely and embraced the growing "gay-pride" movement as well as feminism. As all these feminist groups received publicity, those women who recoiled at their radical philosophies began to organize their own groups. Movements of housewives—who resented the feminists' implications that they were ignorant, useless, and discontented—rallied in support of the old family values. These women claimed that passivity, motherhood, and devotion to their husband should continue to be the hallmarks of the true woman.

One of the most bitter battles pitting women against women came over the long-proposed Equal Rights Amendment to the Constitution. The amendment, granting equal rights specifically to women, passed Congress in early 1972 and was quickly ratified by more than half of the states. But the necessary approval from three quarters of the states did not come, and the amendment's progress stalled. NOW lobbied intensely on its behalf, but vigorous opposition from people such as arch-conservative Phyllis Schlafly and organizations such as the Christian Crusade more than counterbalanced NOW's efforts. Opponents charged that the amendment would not only undermine the stability of the traditional family but that its effect on alimony, protective labor laws, and eligibility for military service would positively harm women themselves. (In response to such arguments and to the growing identification between the political right and antifeminism, the Republican party reversed a position it had held for the past forty years and dropped support of the ERA from its 1980 platform.)

Abortion became an even more controversial feminist and legal issue than ERA. What feminists called "the struggle for reproductive self-determination" received legal support when in 1973 in *Roe* v. *Wade,* the Supreme Court struck down state laws prohibiting abortions. But, as feminists quickly realized, *Roe* v. *Wade* was an ambiguous victory. In some cases it encouraged public officials to force abortions upon poor women. At the same time, the false claim that women could now "enjoy abortion on demand" helped to fuel a growing "right-to-life" crusade. Feminists charged that the "right-to-life" movement—which drew much of its support from traditionalist Catholics, from fundamentalist Protestants, and from ultraconservative political groups—really represented a counterattack by antifeminists. In response, prolife groups denounced abortion as legalized murder and championed "the rights of the unborn." Feminists countercharged that most antiabortionists did not adopt such a strong "moral" position on other questions involving the right to life. Prolife groups, for example, often espoused a militant (if not militaristic) foreign policy and opposed social programs, such as subsidized child care and sex education, that might offer alternatives to abortion.

The right-to-life crusade, like the anti-ERA movement, gained strength throughout the 1970s. A number of political candidates found that the prolife issue could overshadow all others, even in races for city councils or county commissions. (The right-to-life cause gained an important legal victory when, in 1980, the Supreme Court upheld the constitutionality of the "Hyde Amendment" and ruled, in a controversial five-to-four decision in *Harris* v. *McRae,* that Congress could ban the use of Medicaid payments to fund abortions for poor women. Already encouraged by this decision, antiabortion forces gained further ground when the Republican party platform of 1980 pledged support for a new constitutional amendment, one that would overturn *Roe* v. *Wade* and outlaw most abortions.)

If clear-cut legal victories were elusive, women found it even more difficult to achieve fundamental changes in social mores. By 1970 more than 40 percent of all women held full-time jobs, a figure that reflected the growing number of women who had entered the once exclusive male sphere over the preceding two decades. But women continued to occupy the traditional, home-centered female role as well. Women were changing, but a male-dominated society was not.

True sexual equality seemed as far away as ever. One study showed that when a wife took on full-time employment the husband usually assumed only a few domestic chores: on the average, husbands of working wives did about one fourth of all work around the house. Men continued to expect certain supposedly male prerogatives: another study revealed that among husbands with wives who worked full time, 38 percent still believed that women should be paid less than men for the same work; 32 percent still felt that sexual intercourse should occur whenever they desired it (regardless of the woman's feelings); 71 percent thought that men had no obligation to help around the house "all the time"; and 80 percent said that they would not be willing to make sacrifices for their wife's career. (Husbands of nonworking women expressed these attitudes of inequality even more frequently.) The study showed that although a wife's employment might increase her self-esteem, it by no means brought her equality, even in her husband's eyes. Certainly, employment was unlikely to bring most women equality at the pay window: the median income for women who worked full time was less than 60 percent of the median income for men. (The difference actually increased during the 1960s and 1970s: the ratio had been 63 percent in 1956.)

By the 1970s it was clear that men, much more than women, needed their consciousness raised if sexual equality were to be achieved. The women's movement did begin to broaden its appeal to reach the male half of society, and "men's liberation," or "human liberation," gained some supporters. Some men, often the partners of feminist activists, began organizing consciousness-raising sessions patterned after those of NOW. But gains for women depended upon economic conditions as much as attitudes, and the up-and-down job market of the 1970s limited alternatives for women even as governmental pressure opened them. Then too, as radical politics went out of fashion, militant feminism also receded. Still, the 1960s and early 1970s had their impact: concern for equal opportunity and affirmative action seemed a lasting feature of American life.

Blue-Collar Power

During the 1960s the crusades of women, blacks, and other nonwhite minorities tended to dominate the discussion of social problems by the media and by academicians. By the early 1970s, however, it had become evident that other Americans believed that they too needed more visibility and more power. Spokespeople for blue-collar workers of all backgrounds and for white ethnics complained that liberal reformers were too anxious to advance others, especially blacks, at their expense. Despite optimistic theories about the emergence of a "postindustrial" society and despite many years of faith in America's fabled melting pot, the working class and ethnicity remained important realities in American life.

Members of the working class often complained, with some justification, that cosmopolitan liberals unfairly dismissed them as bigoted, ignorant obstacles to progressive change. A much-publicized attack in New York City by pipe-wielding "hard-hats" on antiwar demonstrators and the popularity of television's Archie Bunker were oftentimes considered indicators of general working-class attitudes. Although blue-collar America contained its share of Archies and hawkish militants, any broad indictment was unfair. One study of the attitudes of manual laborers, for example, revealed that they opposed the war in Vietnam more strongly than suburban businessmen. And examinations of racial views indicated that a good many white workers supported the movement for black equality. The working-class discontent of the late 1960s and early 1970s defied simple explanation.

One thing, however, seemed clear: despite generally rising real wages, most blue-collar workers felt that they were not doing as well as they should be. Blue-collar families complained that their neighborhoods had been "invaded" by blacks and destroyed by urban-renewal projects, their streets "overrun" by criminals, their savings and paychecks undermined by inflation, their take-home pay cut by rising taxes, and their sons shipped to Vietnam. Many of these grievances were authentic. The small increase in real income, for example, never quite covered all the new expenses. In 1968 an urban worker with two children, according to figures from the Bureau of Labor Statistics, needed almost $10,000 a year to live at "a moderate but adequate standard of living." Yet even well-paid workers made less than $8,000, and more than 60 percent of white middle-class families required two or more breadwinners to boost their living standard into the "moderate" range. Only through the miracle of installment buying could most families afford new appliances and late-model cars; in 1969 the nation's total installment debt reached almost $90 billion.

In addition to concern about money, many American workers expressed dislike for their jobs and their lives. (A government study revealed that lower-

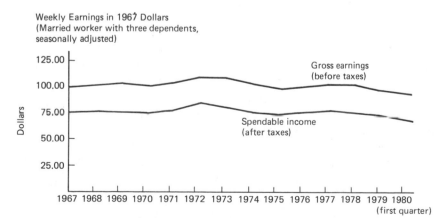

Weekly Earnings in 1967 Dollars
(Married worker with three dependents,
seasonally adjusted)

status white-collar workers—file clerks, salespeople, and computer programmers, for example—shared most of the complaints of blue-collar workers.) Trying to escape the tedium of factory work or the boredom of manual labor, growing numbers of workers turned to alcohol and drugs; many told interviewers that daydreaming provided the best way to make the work day pass less painfully. Employers and labor leaders began to warn that low morale and high absenteeism threatened to undermine American industry. But workers themselves voiced more concern about the declining quality of their lives. Labor-union officials, many rank-and-filers claimed, cared little about lax safety standards or bad working conditions.

Workers complained that home life offered little escape from the rigors of their jobs. Rising early in the morning or working the last shift at night, they returned home exhausted, lacking the energy and the money for the leisure activities that business and professional people took for granted. For a blue-collar family, dinner at a good restaurant and an evening at the movies were rare treats. Vacations rarely involved two-week rests at a posh resort. Blue-collar families generally visited nearby relatives or jammed into a small trailer or camper, their answer to lakeside cottages and deluxe mobile homes.

Many blue-collar workers felt that other people looked down on them. While many workers had no use for hippies, dissident young people generally expressed undisguised contempt for working class lifestyles. Workers themselves felt uncomfortable with better-educated business leaders or professional people. Talking to a sociologist, a house painter complained that "whenever I'm with educated people, you know, or people who aren't my own kind... um... I feel like I'm making a fool of myself." When he went to a social gathering, "there were all these people in suits and I had on a jacket.... Somehow people were introducing themselves to each other all over the place, but nobody was introducing themselves to *me*. So that's how it is."

Ethnic Power

In some ways the new ethnicity reflected the general militancy of blue-collar workers—many workers came from ethnic backgrounds—but in more profound ways the new assertiveness of white ethnics represented a complicated response to the black movement. White ethnics, like militant proponents of black pride, extolled the traditional values of their cultures and emphasized the deep significance of the old country to them and to their children. The fabled American melting pot had only singed the people whom Michael Novak, a Catholic philosopher of Slovak background, called the "unmeltable ethnics." For decades, for example, employers insisted that ethnics not "bring their culture to work," that Jewish-Americans or Serbian-Americans work the same hours and dress in roughly the same fashion as their fellow workers. But most efforts at "Americanization" had never extended into the private realm, into the close-knit, family-oriented communities of the white ethnics. As a result, large numbers of ethnic families devoted much of their leisure time to social and cultural activities that were closely linked to their Old World past. Thus, the new ethnicity was an old phenomenon; the novelty came in the pride and the self-confidence with which younger Polish-Americans, Slovak-Americans, and other "unmelted ethnics" defended their cultural heritage and their present way of life.

The new directions in the black movement had much to do with the surfacing of the new ethnicity in the late 1960s and early 1970s. Deeply rooted in clearly identified neighborhoods, ethnic groups felt threatened by the influx of black newcomers, many of them from the South, into northern industrial cities. Tied less securely to the American economic structure, many ethnics also felt challenged when nonwhite minorities, and their white allies, pushed for greater employment opportunities. Ethnic workers, for instance, regarded hard-won union seniority systems as forms of social insurance and were not ready to sacrifice them for "affirmative action." Their resentment only increased when white and black integrationists labeled ethnic groups barriers to social progress.

The ethnic awakening, though, represented more than a white backlash. Although there were many points of conflict between blacks and white ethnics, there were also, as the 1970s would reveal, equally important common interests. Poor schools, decaying transit facilities, inflation, and all the other problems of the 1970s affected both blacks and white ethnics. Even more important, the new assertiveness among blacks and the "unmelted ethnics" could be traced back to the oversized, corporate-dominated society that the United States had become in the second half of the twentieth century. There was a recognition by many ethnic and black leaders that their interests and their cultures had been too long ignored.

The tremendous popular response to the television version of Alex Haley's *Roots* and to the film *Rocky* suggested the depth of this feeling. Haley's tale was not exactly the story of a Polish-American's or an Irish-American's "roots." Yet the dominant theme *was* the same: the search for a tradition that could provide links to the past and a sense of stability in a time of ceaseless, often misdirected change. If blacks found their special heroes in Haley's characters, many white ethnics found theirs in *Rocky*. Never patronizing the working-class culture of Philadelphia's Italian-American neighborhoods, the popular motion picture depicted the ethnic's version of the American dream—a decent place to live; a life of understandable scale; and, above all, respect for one's own accomplishments. As the film developed, the battle between Rocky and Apollo Creed was not really a fight between whites and blacks. The conflict pitted the old, expansive American dream of fame and success in the marketplace—represented by Creed, the cosmopolitan corporate promoter—against a scaled-down, community-based version of that dream—represented by Rocky Balboa, the Italian Stallion. In this latter version, the promise of wealth and fame was less important than the immediate reality of security and mutual respect.

An Assessment

None of the groups seeking greater power came close to achieving gains that matched the grandoise rhetoric so often heard during the late 1960s and early 1970s. Cynicism and outright despair were sometimes the only results. Writing after the death of two black students, killed during protests at Southern University in 1973, the black poet June Jordan confessed,

> *I'm tired*
> *and you're tired*
> *and everybody's goddam tired*
> *tired*
> *students tired*
> *Liberals tired*
> *Revolutionaries tired....*

Yet in retrospect, the years in which Richard Nixon and Gerald Ford occupied the White House witnessed the continuation, not the repudiation, of movements begun during the 1960s. All of the various movements did set in motion new political and social forces, ones that could not be halted easily.

Of course, by organizing themselves to challenge the liberal order directly, dissenters encountered certain problems. The more radical ones ran the risk—a considerable one, as members of the Black Panther party and the American Indian Movement discovered—of government action, both legal and extralegal, against them. Moreover, the search for power could produce fierce divisions. As militant feminists and black activists found, new strategies and tactics could lead to confrontations with liberals who had long supported social change and with "sisters" and "brothers" who also believed that the older, gradualist path was still the best road to improvement.

Yet, in a more fundamental sense, all of the groups seeking greater power rejected, to one degree or another, the old gradualist, progressive ethic that had characterized the liberalism of the Fair Deal, the New Frontier, and the Great Society. Prior to the late 1960s, for instance, the leaders of most black and women's groups had accepted the need to operate within structures dominated by white males. Because of the appealing vision of an ever expanding economy and because of the promise of continued assistance from progressive-minded elites, there had seemed no reason to go outside the "system" and challenge it. The United States appeared to be a basically open, essentially progressive society. Although the vast majority of protesters did not give up entirely on America's structure of power, by the late 1960s many had come to believe that they could not rely exclusively upon the benevolence of progressive reformers. Increasingly, activists argued that they had to gain control over their own lives by building power in their own communities. Only after they mobilized their own constituencies could they bargain effectively with entrenched political and economic interests.

SUGGESTIONS FOR FURTHER READING

On the escalation of violence in Southeast Asia, see Seymour Hersh, *Cover-Up* (1972) and Williams Shawcross, *Sideshow* (1979). Kissinger defends his policies, especially against Shawcross's attacks, in *The White House Years* (1979). Many of the volumes on foreign policy listed at the end of Chapter 9 are also relevant here.

Kirkpatrick Sale's *SDS* (1973) surveys the final days of the Weatherpeople. An anthology from *Rolling Stone, The Age of Paranoia* (1972), recaptures the mood of the late 1960s and early 1970s. See also I. F. Stone's, *The Killings at Kent State* (1971); Joseph Kelner and James Munves, *The Kent State Coverup* (1980); Jessica Mitford, *The Trial of Dr. Spock* (1969); and Jason Epstein, *Conspiracy* (1970). For the illegal activities of the Nixon administration, see the works cited at the end of Chapter 9.

On the search for power by various minority groups, consult the studies listed at the end of Chapter 3. See also J. Harvie Wilkinson III, *From Brown to Bakke: The Supreme Court and School Integration* (1979); James Button, *Black Violence: Political Impact of the 1960s Riots* (1978); Ray C. Rist, *The Invisible Children* (1978); William B. Gould, *Black Workers in White Unions: Job Discrimination in the United States* (1977); Thomas Blair, *Retreat to the Ghetto* (1977); and Arthur F. Corwin, *Immigrants—and Immigrants: Perspectives on Mexican Migration to the United States* (1978).

On the struggles of feminists, see Sara Evans, *Personal Politics* (1979); Robin Morgan, ed., *Sisterhood is Powerful* (1970) and *Going Too Far* (1977); Jo Freeman, *The Politics of Women's Liberation* (1975); William Chafe, *Women and Equality* (1978); and Janet K. Boles, *The Politics of the Equal Rights Amendment* (1979).

On blue-collar workers, see Andrew Levison, *The Working-Class Majority* (1974); Irving Howe, ed., *The World of the Blue-Collar Worker* (1972); Richard Sennett and Jonathan Cobb, *The Hidden Injuries of Class* (1972); Richard Pfeffer, *Working for Capitalism* (1979); Irving Louis Horowitz et al., *The American Working Class: Prospects for the 1980s* (1979); Richard Edwards, *Contested Terrain* (1979); and E. E. LeMasters, *Blue-Collar Aristocrats: Life-Styles at a Working-Class Tavern* (1975).

Natives and Strangers: Ethnic Groups and the Building of America (1979) by Leonard Dinnerstein, Roger Nichols, and David Reimers offers a broad historical survey of the place of various ethnic groups in American society. See also Richard Polenberg's *One Nation Divisible* (1980). Specific studies of the new ethnicity include Michael Novak, *The Rise of the Unmeltable Ethnics* (1973); Richard Krickus, *Pursuing the American Dream* (1976); and Andrew Greeley, *Ethnicity in the United States* (1974).

THE POLITICS OF THE 1970s

9

Domestic Politics under Three Presidents

Richard Nixon made the American people a simple promise: he would head a law-and-order administration that would give the nation political calm in the 1970s. Instead, his reckless and lawless presidency only produced more political turbulence and a constitutional crisis that Nixon never seemed fully to understand. The president's close circle of advisers—including his "Berlin Wall" of John Ehrlichman and H. R. (Bob) Haldeman—barely knew the techniques of politics, certainly not the art of government. They shielded the president from dissenting views and reinforced his worst instincts, especially his tendency to see political battles in personal terms. Nixon had spent his entire political life tilting at enemies, so it was not surprising that the Nixon White House would have its own "enemies list" and order illegal surveillance of people the president deemed dangerous to the nation. Only after it was too late did Nixon even begin to recognize the depths of his Watergate problems, and even then he proved unwilling, or unable, to fight his way clear.

Nixon's forced resignation failed to bring political calm. The nation's political culture—including popular attitudes toward public policy and America's entire governmental structure—remained unsettled. Both of Nixon's successors in the 1970s, Gerald Ford and Jimmy Carter, came to the same realization that their ousted predecessor had: the American presidency, though still an office of great power, could not really command. Belying the notion of "an imperial presidency," the chief executives of the 1970s faced a loss of effective authority. The presidency, like the other institutions of American politics, was hamstrung by ongoing debates about the proper role of government and by continuing struggles for effective political power. The politics of the 1970s did not mark a repudiation of the battles of the 1960s but rather a continuation of the same attempts to define America's role in the world and to settle the meaning of equality at home.

Richard Nixon and Family. In the happy days of his presidency Richard Nixon relaxes with his wife, Pat; his daughters, Julie and Tricia; and his son-in-law, David Eisenhower. In his final days, Nixon retreated into a closed circle of his family and a few close friends.

Politics in a Media Age

Using the slogan "Four More Years," Republicans reanointed President Nixon as their standard-bearer in 1972. George McGovern, an apostle of the "new politics," captured the Democratic nomination. With the political retirement of Eugene McCarthy, who left the Senate in 1970, Democrats who wanted to move their party leftward rallied around McGovern. So, ironically, did the Nixon administration. Various Nixon operatives, particularly a young lawyer named Donald Segretti, mounted an extensive program of "dirty tricks" designed to undermine the image of Maine's Senator Edmund Muskie and McGovern's other challengers, candidates whom the White House considered more formidable than McGovern. It is difficult, of course, to gauge the impact of such tampering by the Republicans, and there was no doubt that McGovern possessed his own political assets. Capitalizing upon party-rules changes enacted after the 1968 convention, supporters of the South Dakota senator skillfully lined up delegates in the nonprimary states. Meanwhile, McGovern himself developed an effective campaign style and outlasted more centrist candidates, notably Senators Muskie and Hubert Humphrey, in a series of bitter primary fights. Overall, though, McGovern won only a handful of primaries.

By the time Democratic delegates gathered in Miami for their 1972 convention, a number of familiar faces, including Mayor Richard Daley of Chicago, were absent. Outmaneuvered by McGovern's strategists, many Democratic regulars watched the convention on TV. The Miami gathering, complained one veteran labor leader, contained too many women, too many long-haired young men, and too few cigars. McGovern easily captured the nomination on the first ballot, but a number of old-line Democrats, such as Chicago's Daley and labor's George Meany, were less than enthusiastic about the "prairie populist." Many leaders of traditionally Democratic groups gave McGovern only tepid support or left him to stumble on by himself.

And stumble he did. Almost immediately McGovern was forced to jettison his running mate, Senator Thomas Eagleton of Missouri, when it was revealed that Eagleton had undergone electric-shock treatment for nervous exhaustion. McGovern was further embarrassed when several prominent Democrats (including Edward Kennedy) declined to become Eagleton's replacement. McGovern eventually did find a partner (Sargent Shriver, a brother-in-law of Ted Kennedy and LBJ's ambassador to France), but he never discovered a means of bringing large numbers of voters to accept his theme of "Come Home America." His central issue, a speedy withdrawal from Vietnam, angered those Americans who endorsed Nixon's call for an "honorable" peace, and McGovern failed to convert his reformist stands on domestic issues into popular support. Calls for higher taxes on large inheritances and for "demogrants" of $1000 to every citizen, for example, appeared to alienate some traditionally Democratic voters without attracting significant numbers of new supporters.

The Nixon campaign, on the other hand, enjoyed plenty of support, much of it in the form of illegal financial contributions from large corporations. While importuning various corporations, Nixon's "bagmen" warned of the antibusiness tone of a McGovern administration and hinted of the advantages contributors would gain from a second Nixon administration. When various interest groups, such as milk producers in the Middle West, came forward with illegal contributions, the Nixon camp was happy to accept them. The Committee to Re-Elect the President collected a huge war chest, some of which was eventually used to finance the White House's campaign of harassment against the Democrats.

Not even the arrest, in mid-June of 1972, of the "Watergate burglars"—political spies with close ties to the Republican campaign and to the White House itself—could slow Richard Nixon's reelection drive. Ronald Ziegler, the president's press secretary, quickly dismissed the illegal entry into Democratic headquarters, by people who had links to the CIA and FBI and who were equipped with sophisticated wiretapping equipment, as a "third-rate burglary." Ziegler was soon forced to retract this statement, but the media generally gave the Watergate break-in little attention during the electoral campaign. Certainly it had no discernible effect on Nixon's or McGovern's political fortunes in 1972. In November the McGovern-Shriver ticket carried only one state, Massachusetts, and the District of Columbia. Richard Nixon, dismissed only six years earlier as a political has-been, climaxed his comeback by capturing nearly 61 percent of the popular vote and all but a handful of the electoral ballots.

Subsequent analysis of voter statistics only confirmed what was apparent in November 1972: the American electorate perceived George McGovern as too far outside the political mainstream, while Richard Nixon managed to occupy a broad centrist position, as LBJ had done against Barry Goldwater in 1964. In some ways such a view was accurate. On a number of issues McGovern did stand to the left of Fair Deal–Great Society liberalism. Yet McGovern's basic position hardly qualified as a radical one; he probably did not lean as far to the left in 1972 as Goldwater had to the right in 1964.

Although McGovern, like Goldwater, sometimes failed to explain his position as clearly as he might have, the mass media also failed to provide even-handed coverage of the campaign. The established press utterly failed to break through the protective shield that surrounded the Committee to Re-Elect the President. The problem, it should be emphasized, was not that most members of the press secretly favored Nixon; the reality was probably the opposite. Nor was it that Nixon and his aides skillfully managed events and the media that covered them. The real difficulties transcended "dirty tricks" and Madison Avenue tactics. As close observers of the media noted, the traditional rules of "objective" reporting generally worked in favor of the incumbent, who relied upon traditional themes, and against his challenger, who tried to interject new issues and to attack Nixon's performance as Chief of State. It seemed a revolutionary departure from journalistic ethics, for example, when Catherine Mackin of NBC reported that Nixon was distorting McGovern's positions on defense expenditures, welfare policies, and changes in the tax laws. For most of the campaign, the "boys on the bus" (as *Rolling Stone's* Timothy Crouse called the press corps) took statements by Nixon or by his press secretary at face value. Thus, McGovern generally "alleged" while the president and his supporters "announced." Such a perspective proved particularly helpful to Nixon—and damaging to McGovern—when the administration was "announcing" the impending "end" of the war in Vietnam or ridiculing charges about Watergate and other "dirty tricks" by the Nixon forces.

Most of the investigative reporting about Watergate came from a single newspaper, the *Washington Post,* and from two reporters, the *Post's* Bob Woodward and Carl Bernstein. Even these reporters, persistent as they were, did not uncover a great deal of new material about the Nixon administration by themselves. In developing their stories on Watergate, Woodward and Bernstein had to rely upon "Deep Throat," an unnamed informant (or perhaps several informants) within the government bureaucracy.

Table 1   Levels of Confidence in People Running Key Institutions, 1973*

Percentage of Respondents Expressing
Various Levels of Confidence
As far as the people in charge of running ____ are concerned, would you say you have a great deal of confidence, only some confidence, or hardly any confidence at all in them?

Institutions	High	Medium	Low
Major companies	29%	44%	20%
Organized religion	36	35	22
Higher education institutions	44	37	15
U.S. Senate	30	48	18
Organized labor	20	41	32
The press	30	45	21
U.S. House of Representatives	29	49	15
Medicine	57	31	10
Television news	41	43	14
Local tax assessment	19	40	30
U.S. Supreme Court	33	40	21
Local government	28	49	19
State highway systems	34	43	17
Local public schools	39	36	18
State government	24	55	17
Local police department	44	36	18
Executive branch of federal government	19	39	34
Local United Fund	35	35	20
Local trash collection	52	27	12
The military	40	35	19
The White House	18	36	41
Law firms	24	49	20

*Opinion polls revealed significant public distrust, during the Watergate era, of many major institutions; political pundits talked of a "crisis of confidence," especially in light of the low ratings given to the White House and to Congress.

Source: U.S. Congress, Senate, Committee on Government Operations, Confidence and Concern: Citizens View American Government, 93rd Cong., 1st Sess., 1973.

Although the media may not have played the dramatic role pictured by journalists themselves or by the film *All the President's Men,* it finally became a force in Watergate politics. If the press lacked the power and resources to discover many dark secrets by itself, journalists could give widespread coverage to the taint of scandal spreading around the Nixon administration. Using information developed by federal prosecutors and relying upon leaks by various anti-Nixon individuals within the vast federal bureaucracy, some members of the press assumed an aggressive, adversary relationship toward the administration. For their part, Nixon and his close advisers, who had been castigating the press for several years, issued vague hints about reprisals against "irresponsible" journalists.

In retrospect, threats against the media by the Nixon administration represented only part of an increasingly desperate "game plan," one that was being diagrammed in the Oval Office. As transcripts of taped conversations between the president and his aides later revealed, Richard Nixon found that he could not halt or even slow the leaks to the press about the "underside" of his administration. In the late summer of 1973 rumors of wrongdoing began to envelope Nixon's vice-president, and in October Spiro T. Agnew pleaded no contest to charges of accepting kickbacks. With Agnew forced to resign in disgrace, Nixon chose Gerald Ford, the minority leader of the House, as his replacement. The man who held the office generally considered to be the most powerful in the world confronted the limits of his ability to control events or even employees of his own executive branch.

The Underside of the Nixon Administration: Leaks and Plumbers

Indeed, many of Nixon's Watergate troubles actually stemmed from his earlier doubts about the reliability and loyalty of various government agencies and officials. Although many details cannot be known until scholars have greater access to tapes of Nixon's presidential conversations and to printed documents, it does appear clear that the Watergate "burglary team" was originally formed as part of an attempt to provide the White House with its own covert intelligence unit. As early as the summer of 1970 a young White House aide, Tom Charles Huston, unveiled an ambitious plan to improve the administration's ability to conduct wire taps, mail covers, and "surreptitious entries" (i.e., burglaries). Although Nixon approved the "Huston Plan" in July, this effort to coordinate covert activities under the control of the White House ran into stiff opposition from the already established arms of America's "secret government," the CIA and the FBI. Claiming the Huston Plan threatened to lead to serious violations of civil liberties, J. Edgar Hoover offered especially strong resistance, and the president was forced to drop the plan. While some top officials at the White House began to leak information critical of the aging but still powerful Hoover, others began to search for a new means of accomplishing Huston's objective.

According to the files of Egil Krogh, who worked for Nixon in several lower-level positions before serving a prison term for his White House activities, the administration finally decided to use the issue of drugs to cover the creation of a secret strike force controlled by the White House. Expanding earlier discussions about the need for a private "Republican detective agency," one that could undertake jobs considered too sensitive to be handled by agencies "infested" by Democrats, the White House searched for a way to restart the Huston initiative. G. Gordon Liddy, a former FBI agent then working for the Treasury Department, played a key role in formulating plans for a new antidrug squad within that department. Once operational, the unit could not only handle the type of covert work once envisioned for the private detective agency but could also draw upon the resources and talents of the national government itself. In addition, Nixon's domestic strategists hoped that the drug issue could be used to hide the unit's covert activities: if any of its illegal activities were ever discovered, the administration could explain that the indiscretions were only part of the vital war against drugs. In fact, the administration had already been lining up support from its friends within the media for an all-out crusade against drugs, and a presidential declaration of a national "heroin emergency" was slated for delivery in late June 1971. But on June 13, 1971, the *New York Times* began to publish excerpts from the Pentagon Papers, a hitherto secret history of American involvement in Vietnam.

Enraged at the appearance of this classified report, which had been prepared by the Defense Department during the Johnson administration, Nixon's inner circle shifted their attention from drugs to security "leaks." Nixon's antidrug speech was canceled, and the national heroin emergency was never declared. Instead, the administration mobilized to stop further publication of the Pentagon Papers and to plug the leaks within its own executive branch.

Almost immediately, it obtained a court injunction that barred further publication of the Pentagon Papers. Responding to the unprecedented use of a prior restraint against the press—censorship in its classic form—the *New York Times* carried an appeal to the United States Supreme Court. By a vote of six to three the justices lifted the injunction, holding that the First Amendment barred prior restraints in instances such as this. Although many people, particularly in the media, celebrated this victory for the cause of "open government," the administration was already mounting a much more extensive, and more covert, crusade for executive secrecy.

Using some of the personnel assembled for the antidrug crusade, the White House formed its own leak-stopping crew, the self-styled Plumbers. The group soon included Gordon Liddy, E. Howard Hunt (a former CIA agent), and several Cuban exiles with close ties to the CIA. After it became known that Dr. Daniel Ellsberg, a former analyst for the Defense Department and for the Rand Corporation, bore primary responsibility for leaking the Pentagon Papers, the Plumbers began a campaign to harass and discredit him. Over the Labor Day weekend of 1971 a team led by Liddy and Hunt burglarized the office of Ellsberg's psychiatrist in search of any information the White House could use to discredit Ellsberg. The secret strike team conducted similar activities against other "enemies" of the White House, including the columnist Jack Anderson. This group, with the significant addition of James McCord, another former CIA operative, formed the nucleus of the group that made the badly bungled entry into Democratic headquarters at the Watergate.

Nixon's defenders have consistently contended that these kinds of activities did not start with Watergate. Indeed, careful studies relying upon official documents obtained under the Freedom of Information Act have shown that the development of secret government preceded the presidency of Richard Nixon. John Kennedy, for instance, took a particular interest in expanding the executive's covert capacities, both overseas and at home, and Robert Kennedy, his attorney general, gave the FBI nearly carte blanche in wiretapping and bugging operations.

Thus, the Nixon administration did not invent domestic spying, but it did significantly expand the scope and purposes of covert activities. During Lyndon Johnson's second term, for example, successive attorneys general had moved to limit FBI wiretaps, and the number of taps did decline from 233 in 1965 to only 9 in 1968. The next year, however, Nixon and his attorney general, John Mitchell, began to use taps on a much greater scale. They claimed that the chief executive could order wiretaps, without having to obtain a court order, upon any group or individual considered a threat to "national security." (In 1972 the United States Supreme Court held that the president could not order, on his own authority, electronic surveillance of purely domestic organizations.) Reports on some of these taps, such as ones on government employees and on several journalists suspected of having sources inside the Nixon administration, were forwarded not only to officials concerned with "national security" but also to Nixon's primary political strategist, H. R. Haldeman.

Haldeman's involvement in the Nixon administration's earliest wiretaps established the pattern that would lead to Nixon's downfall: the attempt to centralize power within the president's inner circle. As Garry Wills has noted, Nixon and his close aides operated a kind of counterinsurgency presidency. Seeing themselves as the lonely defenders of the American way, the Nixonites waged war not only against the New Left but against the very same establishments that the protesters attacked—the press, J. Edgar Hoover's FBI, and even the CIA. In the end Nixon became ensnarled in his clumsy efforts to create a secret government of his own, one that could spy on the people in the streets and on various elites in Washington.

The same concern for centralizing control within the White House affected the conduct of foreign relations. Nixon and Henry Kissinger, his national-security adviser, saw the regular foreign-policy agencies—including the departments of state and defense and the CIA—as oftentimes uninformed and as consistently unimaginative. Worse, Nixon and Kissinger believed, these branches of government were filled with individuals who would obstruct presidential initiatives or, as in the case of Daniel Ellsberg, leak sensitive and secret material to the press. As a result of their fears and their desire for greater White House power, Nixon and Kissinger began to conduct their own secret foreign policy—secret not only from the American people but from other government officials as well. Their decision in 1970 to begin heavy bombing of neutral Cambodia, for example, deliberately bypassed high officials in the state and defense departments.

Nixon's Last Battle

In the end Nixon's secret war in Cambodia—like his other attempts to bring foreign and domestic "dirty tricks" under the control of the White House—

became public knowledge and then part of the legal case accumulating against the president and his administration. Despite various attempts to "cut off" the trail of criminality—at the Watergate burglars, then at high officials within the Committee to Re-Elect the President, and finally at top-ranking members of the White House staff—Nixon's pursuers pressed on. In May 1973 a special Senate committee headed by North Carolina's Sam Ervin began televised hearings into charges of misconduct during the last presidential election. Ervin, who liked to call himself a simple "country lawyer," quickly became a media celebrity, and his folksy image contributed to the panel's public credibility. Equally as important, Ervin maneuvered the committee and its staff through the inevitable partisan and personal jealousies and kept the direction of the hearings moving inexorably toward the Oval Office. Throughout the summer of 1973 witness after witness offered tantalizing hints about involvement by the White House in a series of unseemly activities. Even Senator Howard Baker of Tennessee, a Republican loyalist, came to ask a familiar question: "What did the president know and when did he know it?" Then, in mid-July, what had begun to seem like an unanswerable query suddenly had a most unlikely source of verification—Richard Milhaus Nixon.

"Nixon Bugged Himself!" proclaimed the newspaper headlines of July 16 and 17. Apparently called to testify about relatively minor issues, an obscure White House official named Alexander Butterfield revealed that Nixon had secretly taped the bulk of his presidential conversations and his phone calls. Clearly, these tapes could provide the "smoking pistol" that Nixon's defenders challenged his accusers to produce. The Ervin Committee and the special Watergate prosecutor, Archibald Cox of Harvard Law School, immediately sought access to the tapes. Claiming an absolute "executive privilege," Nixon flatly refused.

Ringed by lethal celluloid strands, Richard Nixon vainly struggled to survive the Watergate fight. Although some advisers urged him to destroy the tapes, Nixon tried to battle his way free while still clutching the damning evidence. A veteran political club-fighter who had a deep faith in his ability to survive any scrap, the president bobbed and weaved and occasionally even tried to counterpunch. But his opponents clearly had the heavier weapons. In October 1973 a desperate attempt to knock out the special Watergate prosecutor backfired: Nixon's dismissal of Archibald Cox, for his refusal to accept Nixon's formula for limited access to nine crucial tapes, only led to the departure of Elliot Richardson and William Ruckelshaus, two of the most respected figures remaining in the Nixon administration, and to the arrival of another prosecutor, Leon Jaworski. It also forced Nixon to surrender the tapes, one of which contained an 18½-minute gap that was later found to have been the result of deliberate erasing, most likely by Nixon himself.

The Saturday Night Massacre, as Nixon's dumping of Cox was called, represented his last real attempt to take the offensive. Slowly the president retreated, trying to stave off impeachment with his own version of Muhammad Ali's "rope-a-dope" strategy. By early 1974 Nixon could do little more than continue his cover-up, hoping that his opponents would run out of energy and that he could somehow survive the remaining years of his presidency.

Throughout the year, though, Nixon's difficulties only increased. On March 1, 1974, a federal grand jury indicted seven of Nixon's top aides for their alleged involvement in the cover-up of Watergate; only Leon Jaworski's insistence that the law barred an indictment against a chief executive saved Nixon from becoming defendant number eight. Instead, the grand jury secretly named Nixon as an unindicted co-conspirator. Although news of this unprecedented action remained unknown to the public and members of Congress, the decision to link Nixon to the indictment did give Jaworski new leverage as he sparred with White House lawyers over access to more of the tell-tale tapes.

Increasingly, the fight narrowed down to one between a badly confused Nixon, comforted in the final days of his presidency only by his immediate family and a handful of loyal aides, and the combined power of the other branches of the national government. In April Nixon tried one last desperate gamble: he released his own edited version of forty-two taped conversations that were being sought by Jaworski and by the House Judiciary Committee. The bowdlerized transcripts, so often sanitized by the phrase "expletive deleted," only raised new doubts about the president's honesty and his competence. More important, the Nixon tapes failed to satisfy either the House committee or Jaworski; both sought additional tapes and transcripts.

Nixon's defenders in Congress and his lawyers before the Supreme Court had no better luck than their chief. By early summer the issue was not whether the House Judiciary Committee would support Nixon's impeachment but how many Republicans would join the Democratic majority and how many articles of impeachment they would vote against the president. On the other side of Washington, the Supreme Court, which had expedited the appeal of Nixon's refusal to honor a subpoena for additional tapes, voted unanimously to reject the president's sweeping claim that tapes needed for a criminal investigation were protected by "executive privilege."

At nearly the same time, the House Judiciary Committee completed its deliberations on articles of impeachment. On July 27, 1974, three days after Nixon's rebuff by the Supreme Court, the committee passed, by a margin of twenty-seven to eleven the first article of impeachment against the president. It charged Richard Nixon with obstruction of justice for his efforts to impede the investigation of Watergate. Subsequently, the committee voted two other articles. One charged Nixon with abuse of presidential power by trying to use agencies, such as the IRS and the FBI, for partisan purposes, and the other charged him with violating his constitutional duty to enforce the law by refusing to turn over subpoenaed tapes. (Significantly, the committee rejected an article that would have cited Nixon for his clearly illegal bombing of Cambodia.)

Although Nixon remained publicly committed to a floor fight in the House and to a last-ditch battle in the Senate, efforts were already under way within the president's shrinking entourage to ease him out of office. On July 24, while waiting for the Supreme Court to hand down its decision on Nixon's tapes, a presidential aide finally found, in these same tapes, the elusive "smoking pistol." The tape of a conversation between Nixon and Haldeman on June 23, 1972, was unequivocal: the president and his then chief of staff had plotted from the very beginning to use the CIA to halt the FBI's investigation of the Watergate break-in. The tape contained proof, in clear language, that the president himself had orchestrated the cover-up, had conspired to obstruct justice, and had been systematically lying about his complicity in the whole affair. Even Nixon's special Watergate defense counsel, James St. Clair, had been misled, and he in turn had consistently misinformed the House Judiciary Committee about his client's activities.

In late July and early August, aides to Nixon and to Vice-President Gerald Ford began cautiously discussing plans for terminating the Nixon administration and inaugurating a Ford presidency. Unyielding to the end, Nixon insisted that the conversation between Haldeman and himself contained no fatal admissions. But his current chief of staff, General Alexander Haig, flatly contradicted this claim and went ahead with plans for the transition to a new presidency. Once the transcript of the June 23 meeting became public, most of Nixon's remaining supporters vanished. Finally, on August 5, Richard Nixon gave up his loneliest battle of all and surrendered, if only temporarily, to political reality. Four days later he resigned, and Gerald Ford became the nation's first nonelected president.

The Lurching Economy

The Watergate scandal paralyzed the national government just when complex economic problems required new policies. Richard Nixon faced two alarming new economic trends—"stagflation," a concurrence of recession and inflation; and a growing deficit in the United States balance of payments.

Conventional economic wisdom held that inflation resulted from an "overheated" economy in which demand far exceeded supply; dampening demand by inducing a mild recession would thus reduce inflation. In attacking inflation early in his presidency, Nixon acquiesced to policies that raised interest rates in order to slow spending and that brought more unemployment. The recession came. Skyrocketing interest rates nearly ended residential construction, forced barely solvent businesses such as the Penn Central Railroad into bankruptcy, brought a decline in industrial production, and raised unemployment to 6 percent. Yet, contrary to expectations, prices continued to gallop forward. Big business and big labor continued to layer higher wages and higher costs upon an economy now slumping into recession. By 1971 pundits

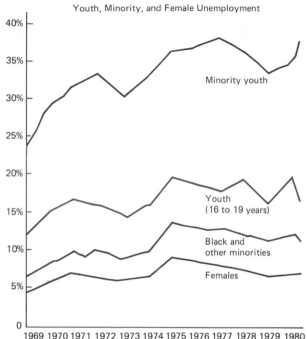

Youth, Minority, and Female Unemployment

Minority youth

Youth
(16 to 19 years)

Black and
other minorities

Females

1969 1970 1971 1972 1973 1974 1975 1976 1977 1978 1979 1980

Bureau of Labor Statistics

Unemployment remained a persistent problem throughout the 1970s. For young people, especially minority youth, the job situation was bleak, if not desperate.

were speaking of "Nixonomics"—a new economic condition of stagflation in which unemployment and the spiral of inflation crept upward simultaneously.

After experimenting unsuccessfully with these anti-inflation measures, Nixon decided that inflationary prosperity was better than an economic slowdown that might, as it had done in 1960, jeopardize his next presidential campaign. He began devising policies to correct the recession he had earlier induced. After telling a startled group of journalists, "I am now a Keynesian," Nixon took up that favorite tactic of liberal Democrats, deficit spending financed by government borrowing. This dramatic about-face prompted a television commentator to quip, "It's a little like a Christian crusader saying 'All things considered, I think Mohammed was right!'" But antirecession spending scarcely dented unemployment, and, under renewed stimulus, prices spurted ahead even faster. Measures taken against either inflation or unemployment seemed only to make the other problem more severe. Some advisers within and without the administration began to advocate an across-the-board governmentally imposed freeze on wages, prices, and interest rates as the only sure way to hold down inflation, but Nixon shied away from "artificial controls which could only foul things up."

Worrisome foreign-trade statistics soon changed the president's mind. For eighty years the United States had exported far more than it imported, but after World War II huge military expenditures and corporate overseas investment created deficits in the balance of payments. The country paid some of this debt with gold; by 1972 America's prewar hoard of bullion had shrunk by half, to $10 billion. For the rest, foreign creditors accepted paper dollars, pleased with the stimulating effect of this large new source of capital that could be used for domestic investment. By 1970, however, the Vietnam War had brought ever larger deficits, and inflation had crippled America's ability to sell its high-priced goods abroad. More and more paper flooded Europe's money markets, inevitably jolting prices. United States Treasury officials, hoping to avoid devaluation of the dollar—an act that would undermine the dollar's position as the preeminent international currency—quietly urged England, West Germany, and Japan to revalue their currencies upward to discourage American buying. Only the Germans complied. Then, at the end of June 1971, the Commerce Department announced a trade deficit, the first since 1890. As fears rose about the nation's solvency, speculators attacked the United States dollar, dumping vast amounts on world currency exchanges to avoid the losses that would result from a widely expected devaluation of the dollar.

After a hurried meeting with his financial advisers at Camp David in August 1971, Nixon dramatically responded to the international monetary crisis and to the larger problems—including inflation and the new trade deficit—that fueled it. First, the United States ceased to value the dollar in terms of gold. Instead, American currency would "float" on the exchanges, supply and demand determining its worth. Second, a 10-percent tariff surcharge was instituted, which significantly reduced imports into America. Nixon later removed the surcharge in return for obtaining new world monetary agreements. The new arrangement terminated the system of fixed exchange rates established in the Bretton Woods Conference of 1944, and it effectively ended the dollar's career as the most privileged medium of international exchange. The dollar became just another currency whose value fluctuated. By substantially altering the system of international exchange, Nixon had given Americans more room to manipulate currency values in the fight against the trade deficit, but he had also led the United States and the world into the uncharted waters of floating exchange rates.

Nixon's advisers also plotted a new anti-inflation program for the domestic economy. The president froze wages and prices for ninety days, an interim measure called Phase I, while he worked on a comprehensive program to attack inflation and the trade deficit. On November 15, 1971, the White House announced its new program, Phase II. This plan cut government spending (slashing $5 billion from foreign aid and the federal civil service) but focused far more on stimulating business through a tax credit aimed at promoting modernization of American enterprise. To stimulate the crucial automobile industry, Congress repealed the 7-percent excise tax on American-made cars.

Such measures ensured greater production and higher profits and, together with the certainty that Nixon would not risk retrenchment in an election year, perked up the sluggish economy. Consumer spending increased, and public confidence blossomed in the spring of 1972. Meanwhile, the new Cost-of-Living Council attacked inflation by banning wage hikes of more than 5.5 percent and supposedly limiting retail-price increases to 2.5 percent. Though inflation continued, especially in the uncontrolled food and farm commodity markets, public confidence improved enough for Nixon to defuse the economic issue during the 1972 campaign.

Nixon's tactics were thus to give the economy a mild stimulus while holding down inflation through government controls. The strategy lasted just long enough to aid Nixon's reelection. Once settled in his second term, Nixon replaced Phase II price ceilings with voluntary restraints. Predictably, consumer prices shot upward, compensating for the time they had spent under controls. Within six months, Treasury Secretary George Shultz candidly admitted, "Phase II is a failure." So, in midsummer Nixon again froze prices, this time for sixty days, while his advisers again debated alternatives. Finally, in April 1974 Nixon again reversed course, canceling all government restraints. Convinced that "artificial bureaucracies" could never substitute for the "free" marketplace, Nixon was unwilling to take steps more drastic than economic controls that were just voluntary or temporary. When it became clear, in 1974, that such mild controls did not work, Nixon—now immersed in Watergate difficulties—effectively abandoned any coherent strategy for dealing with stagflation.

The effectiveness of Nixon's mercurial economic strategies was not helped by the deadlock between the executive and congressional branches. Nixon's economic programs—especially his determination to cut federal spending for social welfare—provoked growing hostility between the White House and the Democrat-controlled Congress. In 1973 the president vetoed nine major bills, even education and antipollution measures. He also calmly announced that he would impound funds, rather than spend them, if Congress overrode his decisions, an action that congressional opponents (and later the courts) condemned as unconstitutional. With prices at their highest levels in history, Republicans talked about "allowing supply and demand to allocate resources." Decrying what they called favoritism for the rich, liberal Democrats struggled to pass alternate plans, but Congress became mired in thickets of complexity and politics. Growing personal hostilities, aggravated by Watergate, soon coalesced into an ongoing adversary relationship between the two branches of American government.

When Nixon left office, economists, like members of Congress, continued to debate what had gone wrong. Had government controls been too severe or insufficient? Should government spending have been cut to curtail inflation or increased to combat recession? Meanwhile, inflation continued at an annual rate of nearly 10 percent while unemployment hovered at just under 6

An Era of Persistent Inflation

Department of Labor Statistics.

According to the "new economics" of the 1940s, high rates of unemployment (see page 210) should have been accompanied by low rates of inflation. But this bar graph demonstrates the "stagflation" that beset the American economy in the 1970s.

percent, a recession rate. After a five-year battle against stagflation and trade deficits, the economic situation was worse than ever, and inflation had become endemic. All of Nixon's remedies had failed, though economists and politicians differed sharply in their diagnoses of the precise reasons for their failure.

The Ford Presidency: The Wounds Remain

The Nixon presidency, coming so soon after the political traumas of the late 1960s, appeared to raise new doubts about the viability of the old liberal political order. Although defenders of postwar liberalism, such as the semi-official presidential chronicler Theodore White, hastened to claim that Nixon's fall dramatically demonstrated that "the system worked," others were not so sure. Less sanguine observers pointed out that the long Watergate battle showed the inflexibility of the American constitutional system and that the affair reached a conclusion only because of Nixon's telltale tapes. These writers have suggested that Watergate represented only one episode in the seamy history of America's "secret state." According to this interpretation, Watergate culminated a long power struggle involving several government bureaucracies and various political and economic elites opposed to the Nixon administration. Investigative reporters, for example, have suggested that Woodward and Bernstein's "Deep Throat" was a CIA operative who had "infiltrated" the White House and that one of the Watergate burglars, James McCord, deliberately sabotaged the ill-fated operation at Democratic headquarters.

For many ordinary voters Watergate appeared to be just another example of political corruption in Washington. Although millions of Americans did retain their faith that the political system worked, a majority of those eligible to vote displayed considerably more cynicism about politics and about the individuals who sought public office. According to reliable public-opinion polls, popular confidence in government officials had been declining throughout the 1960s, the years of Vietnam, and this slide continued both during and after the Watergate period. In the presidential election of 1972, only 56 percent of those eligible to cast ballots did so; in 1976 the turnout decreased once again, this time to 54 percent.

Gerald Ford later claimed that his brief presidency had been a time for healing, but during the years 1974–1976 old political wounds continued to fester, and new ones appeared almost daily. Many people's doubts about how the system really worked were only increased—or simply confirmed—when Ford offered Nixon an unconditional pardon, an act that shielded the former president from prosecution and contributed significantly to Ford's defeat in the 1976 presidential race. Moreover, the Ford years brought new revelations about illegal, or at least questionable, activities that had been undertaken since World War II by the FBI, by successive presidents, and by the CIA. The CIA was already deeply divided over its involvement in Watergate politics and by various internecine power struggles, and the agency could no longer keep its secrets as closely as in the old days of the cold war. Some former agents, such as John Marks and Philip Agee, wrote best-selling books confessing their past misdeeds, and a few aggressive reporters began to find leaks within the agency itself. Throughout 1974 a series of stories revealed various CIA domestic spying operations, clear violations of the agency's mandate to operate only overseas. Ironically, Gerald Ford, who gained considerable popular notoriety for his inability to climb in and out of helicopters or to navigate the ski slopes, sprang the biggest leak himself when he blurted to editors of the *New York Times* the most explosive of all CIA secrets: its involvement in attempts to assassinate various foreign leaders, including Cuba's Fidel Castro. Although the *Times* itself sat on the story, news of Ford's gaffe soon reached reporters who were not bound by the president's claims that his remarks to the *Times* were off the record.

Even before the story about assassination plots broke, President Ford had created a special commission, headed by his newly appointed vice-president, Nelson Rockefeller, to look into allegations of domestic spying by the CIA. In time, committees in both the House and the Senate heard testimony about a wide range of CIA "dirty tricks"—drug-testing projects on unsuspecting subjects, mail covers on private citizens, efforts to "destabilize" the economies of "hostile" nations, and several bizarre plots to murder foreign leaders. Although cynics doubted that the whole story had been told, the hearings did culminate the long process, begun by dissenting scholars and journalists during the 1960s, of rewriting the simplistic history of the cold-war era. Testimony before several congressional committees, especially the lengthy record compiled by Frank Church's Senate panel, left no doubt that American intelligence officials sometimes considered constitutional and legal restraints mere annoyances, paper restrictions that were to be ignored whenever it seemed convenient to do so.

Ford's greatest annoyance may have been the revelations of past misdeeds that undercut the public's faith in government. His most pressing problem, however, was the economy. Like Nixon, Ford aimed his economic remedies alternately at inflation and then recession, and they ended up producing worse cases of both.

During the first weeks of his presidency Ford targeted inflation, rather than unemployment, as the nation's most serious economic problem. The White House organized a belt-tightening campaign against rising prices that Ford called WIN ("Whip Inflation Now"). WIN was accompanied by buttons and ballyhoo, but its primary achievement was to nudge the country into its worse recession since the 1930s. Consumer demand dropped precipitously, especially in the crucial automobile industry, where higher sticker prices and worries about the availability of gasoline frightened off potential buyers. Triggered by large layoffs in Detroit, unemployment quickly spread. Slackening demand closed more and more factories, which in turn further reduced demand.

Faced with a jobless rate averaging 12 or 13 percent and with falling production almost everywhere, the president reversed course within a few months. In late 1974, now focusing on jobs and trying to cure recession, he projected a budget deficit of some $60 billion and asked Congress for a tax cut. This heavily inflationary plan was designed to increase retail spending and to create a demand for manufactured goods. After several months of politicking, Capitol Hill finally passed an act that rebated some taxes already paid in 1974, reduced the withholding rate, and provided tax credits for the purchasers of new homes. Government also forced down interest rates, though the prime level still hovered around 8 percent. Taken together, these measures prompted a modest revival during the summer of 1975. Inflation, however, also resumed, once again rising toward double-digit rates. The economy seemed to oscillate between recession and inflation, both worsening with each swing, and both undermining America's economic position internationally.

While economics bedeviled Americans, other issues widened the gap that had opened between president and Congress during the Nixon years. Afraid that dependence on Arab oil might weaken American foreign policy, Ford wanted to raise the price of domestic gasoline by boosting federal taxes and ending all price controls on oil. The marketplace would "ration" gasoline and, in effect, force down consumption. Democrats in Congress countered that Ford's approach would only accelerate inflation and unfairly hurt poor people, while giving oil companies windfall profits.

Other factors complicated an easy resolution of the differences between the president and Congress. In the 1974 elections voters had sent many younger, more liberal Democratic representatives to Capitol Hill. These freshmen legislators, together with some of their more experienced colleagues, recoiled at some of the business-as-usual politics of logrolling. By early 1975 they had ousted several powerful committee chairs who had long blocked liberal legislation. Then too, many legislators saw an opportunity in the Watergate scandals to reassert their prerogatives. This feisty, heavily Democratic Congress outlined its own energy program. But Ford vetoed bills that would have maintained price controls and allocated funds for mass transit, while publicly denouncing governmental gasoline rationing as unworkable. Lacking unified leadership—more than ten Democratic senators, for example, were maneuvering for their party's 1976 presidential nomination—Congress enacted laws to improve gasoline mileage in American cars and increased taxes on "gas guzzlers." The absence of any coherent response to the nation's economic and energy problems illustrated the drift that beset public-policy making in the 1970s.

Jimmy Carter: "Compassion and Competency?"

James Earl Carter, soon to be known around the globe as Jimmy, capitalized upon popular disenchantment with runaway intelligence agencies, political corruption, political insiders, and economic disarray. Emphasizing his southern roots, his born-again Christianity, and his lifelong distance from Washington, the naval-commander-turned-peanut-farmer promised voters that he would never lie to them or sail a crooked ship of state. Beginning the 1976 race for the White House in 1973, the former governor of Georgia presented himself both as a plain man of the people—"a Southerner and an American . . . a farmer . . . a father and a husband, a Christian"—and as a skillful technocrat—"an engineer . . . a planner . . . a nuclear physicist." These diverse talents, he suggested, made him the ideal person to answer the "two basic and generic questions" facing the nation: "Can our government be honest, decent, open, fair, and compassionate? Can our government be competent?" Thus, Carter campaigned for the Democratic nomination and then against Gerald Ford for the presidency as a kind of honest neo-populist manager, as a man who could balance both the nation's moral accounts and its national budget. He avoided strong stands on difficult issues—such as the government's role in defining social justice or in attacking inequality—and tried simply to project a straightforward, down-home image. (Unlike previous presidents, for example, Jimmy was often photographed wearing blue jeans.)

Carter's meteoric rise was aided not only by his own ability to project a multifaceted image but by his staff's ability to operate in the new political climate of the 1970s. Although popular disillusionment during the Vietnam and Watergate eras had contributed to a decline in party regularity and in voter turnout, the upheavals of the late 1960s and early 1970s had also led to significant changes in the ways in which the two national parties, especially the Democrats, selected delegates to their national conventions. By 1976 the state party machines and prominent party leaders had lost much of their old clout, and Carter's strategists realized that they could appeal directly to party activists, either in person or through the media, and make an end run around most party stalwarts. Thus, Carter was able to outmaneuver more established Democrats, most of whom could not match his energy (holding no political office, Carter could devote full time to campaigning) or his shrewd, young campaign staff. Another outsider with plenty of time to run for office, California's former governor Ronald Reagan, almost snatched the GOP nod away from Gerald Ford, who was even less exciting as a candidate than as a president. Had Reagan only started his charge a little sooner or had the GOP's primary process been as "democratized" as that of the Democrats, some political scientists have argued, Reagan might have pushed aside Ford and captured the Republican nomination in 1976.

Taken together, the new political climate and the new political ground rules made Carter's ultimate victory over Ford somewhat difficult to interpret. On the one hand, the election of 1976 can be seen as less "democratic" than other recent presidential elections if one emphasizes the fact that large numbers of people apparently found neither of the major candidates acceptable. Less than 25 percent of the total electorate cast their votes for Jimmy Carter in November. But viewed in a different way, Carter's victory may be seen as the triumph of new "democratic" trends and the erosion of older elitist patterns. Those party activists who did participate, especially in the Democratic primaries, saw their votes counting for more than they had in previous elections. In 1968, it should be remembered, Lyndon Johnson could virtually hand the nomination over to Hubert Humphrey, and in 1972 George McGovern could gain the nomination by winning only eight presidential primaries. In contrast, Jimmy Carter had to survive nearly four years of caucus battles and primary fights—what one journalist aptly labeled a political marathon—before he could even claim the nomination. Thus, many observers have concluded (some approvingly and others with obvious displeasure) that Carter's electoral triumph owed relatively little to the traditional power brokers and a good deal to the "new politics" of the late 1960s.

But once anointed by the supposedly sovereign voters, Jimmy Carter faced another "election." Events of the past decade may have significantly affected the rules for conducting the presidential sweepstakes, but they did not greatly alter the larger political and constitutional structure, the one in which President Carter had to carry out his promise of a compassionate and competent administration. As the political scientist Theodore Lowi has argued, the "real" American constitutional system (Lowi called it the working constitution of "the Second American Republic") has been dominated by powerful, vested-interest groups. This system has produced very valuable rewards for the organized—including tax loopholes, government subsidies, and lucrative public contracts—but has provided the unorganized only with leftovers. The result, Lowi concluded, is something approaching socialism for the organized and virtual laissez faire for the rest of the citizenry.

The postwar presidents who had preceded Carter, including Richard Nixon, had also had to deal with this reality, but Jimmy Carter's difficulties were compounded by his outsider image and by the new route through which he had arrived at the White House. His overpublicized ties with the Tri-Lateral Commission—a group of "private citizens" who favored closer cooperation among the "industrial democracies" and more comprehensive economic planning by the national government—helped some. Carter selected several key advisers, including his first secretary of the treasury (Michael Blumenthal) and his national security advisor (Zbigniew Brzezinski), from the commission's membership. Even so, a number of political analysts have noted that Carter, more than other recent presidents, had to undergo lengthy scrutiny by important corporation executives, prominent bankers, and other leaders of powerful institutions and interests. To the political scientist Sheldin Wolin, for example, the whole process seemed to represent "a second stage of legitimation" during which the choice of the people had to win the votes of corporate interests. Carter's problems were complicated by the fact that he had to work with a Congress filled with incumbents who had close working arrangements with the very interests that distrusted the new president. Although Carter owed his position to his direct appeal to a shrinking electorate, traditional interest groups, based upon geography and economic self-interest, retained much influence in Congress.

Given this structural backdrop, then, it was not surprising that Jimmy Carter soon found himself under sharp attack for his allegedly weak leadership, political naiveté, and inability to understand the complexities of power in Washington. Yet Carter's situation was not unique: all three men who preceded him—Johnson, Nixon, and Ford—suffered similar problems. In part, such difficulties stemmed from the tremendous expectations placed upon the office and the person who held it. The presidency had become the focus of the national political life, but no modern president possessed the power, formal or informal, to deal with the problems of a system undergoing severe stress.

Overseas, Jimmy Carter and the rest of the American people had to confront the realities of a new world order, one in which American power and influence simply could not be used as they had been in the past. At home, the sluggishness of the economy and new demands by various groups for greater equality produced a political culture significantly different from that of the first two decades of the postwar years. The problems of the Carter years can be understood only against the backdrop of these significant foreign and domestic developments, changes that began to occur even before Jimmy Carter began his dash for the White House.

Nixon, Kissinger, and World Politics

The "Three-Dimensional Game"

Henry Kissinger, Nixon's national security adviser until February 1973 and thenceforth his secretary of state, viewed himself as a master of geopolitical strategy. He talked of détente with the Soviets, but his later memoirs make it clear that his détente was not a policy of passivity, acceptance, or compromise. Instead, it involved "a firm application of psychological and physical restraints and determined resistance to challenge." It was, in fact, a beefed-up form of the old containment policy, which Kissinger viewed as rather weak and limited. Détente, according to Kissinger, was *realpolitik*—political realism exercised forcefully, unrelentingly, and with a great variety of political, economic, and psychological methods.

Arranging America's geopolitical cards to maximum advantage involved introducing a new player—China. Triangular diplomacy might put maximum pressure on the Soviets and gain substantial advantages for the United States as each of the bitter communist rivals courted America's support. Throughout the Nixon-Kissinger years Americans negotiated with the Soviets and opened channels to China. What Kissinger called the "three-dimensional game" of diplomacy was designed to enhance America's bargaining power in all parts of the world.

After 1969, the Soviet Union and the United States intermittently discussed nuclear-arms control—proposals to regulate future growth, not to scrap existing military hardware. In 1969 both powers pledged not to build underwater installations and agreed to begin strategic arms limitation talks (SALT) in April 1970. Such negotiations required intense bargaining over intricate technical issues as well as over broad questions of overall strategic balance. Yet after mid-1971, when the United States formally accepted the principle of nuclear parity, diplomats made rapid progress.

Reassured by the progress of SALT, the Nixon administration took up a more visible but even less familiar task, relations with China. Small courtesies started a chain reaction. Nixon spoke of "the People's Republic," not Red China, and told journalists of his desire to visit "that vast, unknown land." Nervous about their ancient enemy, Russia, and about Japan's surging economy, Chinese leaders reopened Sino-American talks through both countries' ambassadors in Warsaw. Profound differences over Nationalist China and America's future in Asia persisted, but so did diplomacy. Nixon eased trade restrictions against China in early 1971, and the Chinese reciprocated with an invitation for a ping-pong tournament. Then in July Kissinger made a secret trip to Peking to arrange a presidential visit for 1972. The announcement of Nixon's trip startled both liberals and conservatives in the United States and refashioned world politics. The United Nations admitted the People's Republic three months later, rejecting the American two-China proposal, which was designed to preserve membership for Chiang Kai-shek's regime on Taiwan. The prospect of Sino-American détente apparently pushed the Soviet Union into some technical concessions at SALT and into an invitation, eagerly accepted, for Nixon to visit Moscow in the spring of 1972.

On February 21, 1972, one of America's most celebrated anticommunists traveled to Peking to shake hands and bow gently with Mao Tse-tung, the world's archetypal anticapitalist. President and First Lady walked atop the Great Wall, mingled with communist dignitaries, and ate a twenty-two-course state dinner. But public goodwill, carefully televised, could not dissolve long-standing animosities. Four days of negotiations with Premier Chou En-lai produced primarily a list of postponements. The United States agreed that Taiwan's future was "an internal matter," but China pledged to settle with Chiang "peacefully." Nixon reminded Chinese leaders of America's friendship with Japan, and Chou broached the subject of "Tokyo's militarism." Mao voiced sympathy for "the people's struggle" in Indochina; Kissinger responded with references to "self-determination" and America's "eventual withdrawal." Though the new contacts went on—especially scientific exchanges, token shipments of grain from the United States, and relaxation of trade and travel restrictions—movement toward compromise on fundamental differences remained slow.

Nixon's visit to Moscow in May 1972 continued previous negotiations. The two countries agreed to extensive technological cooperation in medical research, space exploration, and environmental protection. Some months later, technical experts polished off several important trade agreements. Most important, Nixon and Soviet leader Leonid Brezhnev initialed two arms-control treaties, the first fruits of SALT, called SALT I. A year later Brezhnev visited the United States, and Nixon returned to Moscow in mid-1974. The regularity of such high-level visits gave substance to détente and seemed to prove the advantages of triangular diplomacy.

As the Watergate scandals unfolded, Nixon increasingly sought redemption by stressing his international accomplishments. His personal diplomacy with China and Russia rated high in domestic opinion polls, and Kissinger was the only prominent member of Nixon's inner circle who emerged unscathed from the Watergate scandals.

Vietnam

Despite such triumphs, Vietnam still threatened the president's reputation and sapped America's strength. In 1971 Nixon continued negotiations in Paris while fighting in Vietnam, Cambodia, and Laos. Still hopeful for a South Vietnamese victory, President Thieu and his American ally attacked Laos under a massive shield of American air power. But the North Vietnamese counterattacked, and the invaders were routed. Terrified South Vietnamese dangled from helicopter skids, trying to escape; American advisers reported wholesale desertions. After the failure of this attempt to give Saigon more "breathing space," Nixon concentrated upon his other hope, Kissinger's intermittent peace talks.

After several months of secret diplomacy in Paris, Kissinger and North Vietnam's Le Duc Tho had made some progress, but their meetings failed to achieve a final formula for peace. Encouraged by their opponents' misadventures in Laos and Cambodia and already planning their own military offensive, leaders in Hanoi insisted that Thieu and his followers must go. For its part, however, the Nixon administration saw Thieu's presidency as the symbol of South Vietnam's self-determination. Patient bargaining amid the luxuries of Parisian town houses could not unravel the basic puzzle: if Thieu stayed on, he would subvert any "free" election; without Thieu and his political organization the country would easily fall under communist control, for the NLF was its only other organized political force.

Apparently stalemated at the bargaining table, both sides yet again reached for a military solution. In late March 1972 North Vietnam attacked along a broad front, aiming to occupy as much strategic territory as possible. Communist units drove frighteningly close to Saigon, capturing An Loc, a gateway city only thirty miles away. Thieu's listless troops fell back on all fronts, as American air power, by itself, failed to check the communist ground advance. Nixon resumed bombing raids against North Vietnam almost immediately after the attack began, but the communist offensive continued week after week. Many in the Pentagon again predicted a humiliating defeat. Nixon angrily told the nation that the United States would not "become a pitiful, helpless giant," and on May 12 he ordered the navy to mine North Vietnam's harbors and escalated bombing raids against the North and in Cambodia. Few military targets remained untouched, and civilian casualties and numbers of refugees mounted.

The violent spring spurred diplomacy. Painfully, Kissinger and Le Duc Tho fashioned another cease-fire and peace plan. On October 26, several weeks before the end of the 1972 presidential campaign, Kissinger announced that a short, final round of talks would settle minor issues. "Peace," he said, "is at hand."

Despite Kissinger's election-eve optimism, all sides still sought victory at the table. As so often in the past, conflicting aims produced a fateful, familiar cycle of events. In mid-December 1972 Nixon ordered an armada of B-52s to attack North Vietnam twenty-four hours a day "until they are ready to negotiate." Despite heavy losses, American bombers attacked North Vietnam's factories, ruined rice fields, and, too often, destroyed schools, hospitals, and other civilian facilities. This so-called Christmas attack was the heaviest bombing in history. It caused an international uproar and a determination in Congress to end the war. North Vietnam returned to the bargaining table in early January, and the two sides quickly settled on a makeshift cease-fire.

The Paris Accords, signed on January 27, 1973, ended formal hostilities between North Vietnam and the United States. Washington promised to withdraw its remaining 50,000 men, dismantle its military installations, and deactivate mines in North Vietnam's harbors. No foreign soldiers were to remain in Laos or Cambodia, but Hanoi's troops could stay "in place" within South Vietnam. North Vietnam agreed to release American prisoners of war and to cooperate in national elections in the South. A complicated, two-tiered bureaucracy—observers from Canada, Hungary, Poland, and Indonesia and a second team from the four belligerents themselves—would police the cease-fire. Later, an international conference would guarantee a long-term peace, presumably by neutralizing all Indochina and imposing coalition governments in Laos and Cambodia.

Yet the new Paris Accords did not bring peace, only American withdrawal. The war in Vietnam between communists and Thieu's dictatorship dragged on, 48,000 soldiers dying during the first eighteen months of the "cease-fire." In Cambodia, the radical Khmer Rouge guerrillas penned the pro-American regime of Lon Nol in its capital, Phnom Penh. For the next two years, Kissinger and Nixon could only hint at reviving large-scale military assistance to South Vietnam. Having promised an end to the war at last, they were keenly aware of congressional and public restraints on their actions. Yet by the summer of 1974 war had again returned to most of South Vietnam.

Meanwhile, Hanoi's almost legendary general, Nguyen Giap, was organizing a coordinated assault by all his forces for the spring of 1975. Disintegration and demoralization in the South aided his plans. Thieu arrested opponents, banned opposition political parties, and closed down most newspapers. His corrupt rule alienated all but those who profited from it. To consolidate his military position and possibly frighten the United States into sending more hardware, Thieu suddenly withdrew his armies from the three northernmost provinces of South Vietnam. But the planned retreat turned into a disorganized rout when Giap's troops took the opportunity to attack. Unwilling to fight for Thieu's self-serving clique and deprived of American air support, the dispirited South Vietnamese troops raced southward, pillaging their own villages as they went. The North Vietnamese followed, scarcely having to fight, while hundreds of thousands of civilian refugees crowded highways. Only at the gateway to Saigon itself, the provincial capital of Xuan Loc, did the South Vietnamese make a stand. But Thieu's regime collapsed, and the communists overwhelmed the city in less than a week. On May 1 North Vietnamese and NLF forces entered Saigon, while the last American officials were frantically escaping from the United States embassy by helicopter. Lon Nol's regime in

Cambodia had already succumbed to communist Khmer Rouge rebels under Pol Pot. The long second Indochina war ended in defeat for America and its allies. So great had been the devastation of the war that the suffering of South-east Asians would continue for years.

Most Americans accepted defeat, though several weeks of face-saving maneuvers followed. Military airlifts flew over 100,000 South Vietnamese, mostly those closely identified with the United States, to new homes in America. Meanwhile, Kissinger and the new president Gerald Ford blocked the diplomatic and psychological consequences of the communist victory. Quietly reassuring allies in Western Europe, the secretary of state denied that his country would yield to "neo-isolationists" at home. The administration also successfully countered congressional efforts to reduce the numbers of American soldiers stationed overseas and to pare military spending. To regain an image of diplomatic initiative, Kissinger gave a green light to a CIA project to supply and bankroll friendly forces in the Angolan civil war. (America's secret intervention in Angola prompted large-scale Soviet and Cuban aid to the other side; when Congress discovered and terminated this CIA adventure in Africa, the Soviet-backed faction came to power.)

In late May 1975 the new Khmer Rouge regime in Cambodia seized an American merchant vessel, the *Mayaguez,* and imprisoned its crew for alleged-ly carrying contraband within Cambodia's territorial waters. President Ford, determined to flex American muscles and recoup his sagging popularity at home, dispatched a naval task force and some two thousand marines to rescue the thirty-nine-man crew. Critics denounced the gunboat diplomacy that cost America thirty-eight dead and fifty wounded, but most Americans supported their president. Clearly, although the communist victory in Vietnam may have marked the limits of United States power, America still had a worldwide reach.

The long struggle in Vietnam proved more costly than anyone had im-agined. It provoked bitter divisions at home and ended the consensus of the post–World War II period. It also raised a preoccupation with secrecy within the government. The Watergate scandals and the revelations of CIA activities gave mere glimpses into the "secret government" that had grown during the war. At the international level, the war strained the American balance of payments and built up pressure on the dollar. Defeat hurt the credibility of American commitments abroad, chipping away still more at the dollar's strength. Through Vietnam, Americans discovered the consequences of power used unwisely and indiscriminately.

The Middle East and Latin America

As Americans disentangled themselves from Southeast Asia, the Middle East exploded in war. In the fall of 1973, on the Jewish holy day of Yom Kippur, Egyptian and Syrian armies attacked Israel. With United States diplomatic support and vast donations from American Jews, the Israelis first weathered the assault and then drove deeply into Arab territories. By the middle of October, Israeli units had isolated Egypt's Third Army and were shelling suburbs around Damascus, Syria's capital. Egypt's oil-producing supporters embargoed shipments of crude oil to Western powers who backed Israel, principally the United States. Then escalation stopped. Anxious to defuse Arab-Israeli hostilities, Kissinger argued that the United States could best help Israel by negotiating with its enemies, not fighting them. After nearly two years of dramatic shuttle diplomacy the secretary achieved a tentative settlement: Israel would pull back from part of the Sinai, and America would grant military aid to Israel and Egypt. Nixon's week-long trip to the Middle East during the summer of 1974 again showed the President trying to diffuse the Watergate controversy by polishing his image as an international statesman.

Despite behind-the-scenes maneuvering by the United States, Tel Aviv demanded near absolute guarantees for its future security, Cairo insisted upon an Arab-dominated Palestine carved out of strategic Israeli territories, and the future of the territories Israel had captured still caused dispute. Yet there were also hopeful signs. Egypt's Anwar Sadat, Nasser's successor, seemed ready to abandon his predecessor's ambitious dream of uniting the Arabic world in favor of reviving his country's economy and easing its authoritarian politics. In Israel, although militants claimed that only armed force could ensure survival of the Jewish state, moderates believed that compromise would best achieve that end. Best of all, according to Kissinger, was that his shuttle diplomacy had eased the Soviets out of the picture altogether. In March 1976 Sadat even canceled the Soviet's rights to use Egyptian ports.

Kissinger's efforts to jockey for geopolitical advantage and reduce Soviet influence throughout the world translated into a simple formula: support "friends" and punish "enemies." In pursuing this policy, Kissinger did not worry much about the character of his friends' internal policies. Kissinger's realpolitik held that as long as these countries provided a regional bulwark and were hospitable to American economic interests, issues of morality were beside the point. Kissinger's grand design for world stability through regional policemen aligned America's global interests with some of the most oppressive dictators in the world: Shah Reza Pahlavi in Iran, Park Chung-Hee in South Korea, Ferdinand Marcos in the Philippines, and the military leaders of Brazil. In Africa, Kissinger's "tar-baby" report of 1969 concluded that black African insurgent movements were not "realistic or supportable" alternatives. The Nixon-Kissinger policy was therefore to continue to look primarily to South Africa (which received 40 percent of United States investments in Africa) and European colonialists to provide stability in the region and to form close ties with the military regime in oil-rich Nigeria.

In Chile, the United States demonstrated the punitive measures it could employ against a regime that tried to pull out of America's sphere of influence. In 1970 Salvador Allende, a Marxist, was elected president of Chile, a country with a strong tradition of civilian government and an apolitical military establishment. Greatly alarmed by Allende's campaign pledges to nationalize

American-owned copper companies and move the country toward socialism, Nixon and Kissinger met with CIA chief Richard Helms, who emerged from the Oval Office with these notes:

One in 10 chance perhaps, but save Chile!
worth spending
not concerned risks involved
no involvement of Embassy
$10,000,000 available, more if necessary
full-time job—best men we have
game plan
make the economy scream
48 hours for plan of action

With an unlimited budget and full authority for any maneuver to "save Chile" from its elected ruler, the CIA first attempted to arrange a military coup to prevent Allende from taking office. This plan ran against the Chilean military's traditions and thus, at that point, failed. CIA encouragement did, however, lead to the assassination of one of Chile's most respected generals, a man who persistently opposed a military takeover. Next, Helms urged an economic offensive: the government ceased its aid to Chile; the World Bank cooperated by dropping Chile's credit rating; private banks suspended loans; and International Telephone and Telegraph (ITT) and American copper companies, which Allende had nationalized, worked tirelessly to promote his downfall. As chaos overtook the Chilean economy (Chile had huge foreign debts because of the large loans extended under JFK's Alliance for Progress), CIA dollars helped finance a trucker's strike that brought distribution to a halt. Shortages mounted, and the middle class increasingly blamed Allende. In 1973 the military finally decided to intervene. The leaders of the coup killed President Allende and thousands of his supporters and installed a regime so oppressive and barbaric in its use of torture that it quickly became an embarrassment to many in the United States government. Over Kissinger's protests, Congress subsequently suspended aid. And after the new Chilean government managed to assassinate Allende's former ambassador to the United States, right on the streets of Washington, D.C., relations between the two countries broke down almost completely—at least on an official level. On a private level, however, United States enterprise and investments again flooded Chile, attracted by the ironfisted stability.

Foreign Affairs under Jimmy Carter

The Human-Rights Policy

The Kissinger-Nixon-Ford years saw stunning breakthroughs, such as the opening of a dialogue with China, but the government's willingness to shrug off glaring violations of human decency by its allies provoked growing outrage abroad as well as at home. Jimmy Carter's promise, as a presidential candidate, to press human rights in international affairs won him popularity. Forming alliances with hated despots, Carter argued, was neither morally right nor strategically sensible: opposition to terror and despotism in many countries had, under Kissinger's policy, become identified with opposition to United States influence. Once America lost its image as a benevolent power, Carter claimed, it lost its major strength in international affairs and its most powerful weapon in the cold war.

The human-rights policy proved difficult to effect. President Carter appointed a full-time officer to oversee implementation of the policy, supported the weighing of human-rights records in the granting of foreign aid, and stopped America's role as a supplier of instruments of torture. But rapid changes could not help but affect America's global position. In fact, Carter quickly assured many of America's dictator-allies that United States national-security commitments would continue to take precedence over their internal conduct. Thus, governments, such as those in Iran, South Korea, and the Philippines felt few punitive measures under the new human-rights policy, but they did feel increasing pressure to ease up on flagrant violations. Countries less strategically exposed, such as Chile and Argentina, felt the new administration's disapproval much more dramatically.

As Carter's critics had predicted, the human-rights policy gave heart to popular liberation movements in several countries and brought dilemmas to Carter's policymakers. The contradiction between the emphasis on human rights and the geopolitics of Henry Kissinger surfaced most notably in Nicaragua and Iran. In these countries popular uprisings swept the hated regimes of Anastasio Somoza and Shah Reza Pahlavi out of power. Despite severe pressure from domestic Republican allies of both regimes, the Carter administration, after a few attempts at compromise solutions, did not intervene to save the despots.

If Washington was not enthusiastic about the new government in Nicaragua, which contained a number of nationalists of Marxist orientation, at least it tolerated it and tried to find common ground for future relations. Through promises of aid (most of which Republicans in Congress eventually prevented from being fulfilled), Carter tried to co-opt the Nicaraguan revolution onto a moderate, pro-United States course. He hoped to work with reformers rather than repeat the disaster of Nixon's Chilean policy. In doing so, however, he risked opening the door to more revolution in Central America, as oppressed Salvadoreans and Guatemalans also began to work to overturn their socioeconomic systems. Rising violence and even civil war threatened Nicaragua's neighbors, and the Carter administration was left trying to find supportable democratic reformers at a time when politics became increasingly polarized between reactionary despotism and left-wing revolution. After so many years of profiting from a close alliance with dictators, Americans could not hope to create suddenly large groups of popular and friendly middle-class democrats.

In Iran, Carter faced even more difficult choices, as Americans reaped the whirlwind of Kissinger's tight alliance with the hated Shah. A long-exiled religious leader, the Ayatollah Khomeini, established an Islamic Republic dedicated to wiping out the influences of Americanization. In late 1979 a group of Islamic revolutionaries entered the compound of the American embassy and seized about sixty Americans. The Iranian government demanded the return of the Shah, who had been admitted into the United States to undergo medical treatment for cancer, in exchange for the release of the hostages. Iran also talked of gaining possession of the Shah's personal fortune and of placing some of the American hostages on trial for spying, using evidence captured in the embassy takeover. Despite the Shah's departure from the United States and various attempts at mediation, U.S.–Iranian relations worsened. Iran cut off oil shipments to the United States; the American government froze Iranian assets, instituted full economic pressure against the Ayatollah's regime, and attempted—against the advice of Secretary of State Cyrus Vance—an unsuccessful military mission to rescue the hostages. In this climate of extreme tension, even the Shah's death in the summer of 1980 did not bring swift release of the hostages. Finally, in a frantic round of diplomacy in the closing days of the Carter administration, freedom for the hostages was exchanged for complex economic settlements, but relations between the two countries remained poor.

Despite the many difficulties spawned by the human-rights emphasis, redressing the long drift toward alliances with repressive, unpopular regimes was healthy for America's world position in the long run. Old allies began to respond to new American expectations and, more important, to their own people. Nigeria and Ecuador elected new civilian governments that replaced military regimes; the military president of Brazil announced policies of amnesty for exiles and some internal liberalization; and in South Korea, there was a brief easing of government repression between the assassination of President Park in October 1979 and the ascension of a new strongman, Chun Doo-Huan, the following spring. Carter engineered a rapprochement with black Africa. United Nations ambassador Andrew Young, a black veteran of civil-rights struggles in the South, gained African trust as had few high-ranking Americans before him. Young was forced to resign in 1979 after he lied to the State Department about engaging in talks with representatives of the Palestine Liberation Organization (PLO), a group with which the State Department had forbade dealings, but the new look in African policy continued anyway. For example, President Carter stood strongly behind British efforts to force the white-minority government in Rhodesia to effect a peaceful transition to black rule, a transition that signaled the end of an important bastion of white rule in Africa. If the Carter presidency seemed to usher in a particularly unsettled period in American foreign policy, this was less a consequence of what some critics charged was a lack of leadership than of the very difficult task of trying to reduce America's reliance on oppressive tyrants and attempting to build a more positive image abroad.

In addition to a gradual shift of emphasis toward human rights, Carter believed that he could point to other solid accomplishments during his term of office. Unlike the human-rights policy, most of the major negotiating achievements from 1976 to 1980—those in Panama, the Middle East, and China—built upon the initiatives of his Republican predecessors. Carter's foreign-policy advisers directed these efforts. Secretary of State Cyrus Vance, a low-key, experienced diplomat, and National Security Adviser Zbigniew Brzezinski, a noted political scientist, seemed effective even though they generally stayed away from the glare of the mass media, unlike their predecessor Henry Kissinger.

In September 1977 the United States and Panama signed two treaties covering the ownership, operation, and defense of the Panama Canal. United States control over the Canal Zone, a strip of 550 square miles slicing through the middle of Panama, had caused bitter resentment for years and brought serious riots in 1964. Denounced in Latin America and throughout the third world for still holding this land acquired in the days of territory-grabbing imperialism, the United States under President Johnson committed itself to the negotiation of a new treaty. Talks took place over the next thirteen years. After heated debate and a full application of presidential leverage, the Senate ratified the new treaties in 1978. Under their terms, the Canal Zone ceased to exist, and Panama assumed general jurisdiction; the United States retained primary responsibility for operating and defending the canal until the year 2000 but with ever increasing Panamanian participation; and Panama agreed that the canal should be permanently neutral—open to all vessels with no discrimination on tolls. In addition, Panama would receive a share of canal revenues and a substantial commitment of American loans (not grants).

Although critics charged that the treaties represented a rollback of America's strength, the Carter administration stressed that ratification removed a major obstacle to building closer hemispheric ties and deflated charges of colonialism. Moreover, bolstering America's image in Latin America took on increasing importance as Mexico discovered enormous reserves of petroleum and as Ecuador and Peru also became major oil exporters.

Fresh from the battle for the Panama treaties, the president turned his full attention to the Middle East. Kissinger's efforts at shuttle diplomacy between Tel Aviv and Cairo had stalled after the breakthrough of partial Israeli withdrawal from the Sinai in 1975. Carter at first hoped that involving the Soviets in the promotion of a general settlement at Geneva might put negotiations back on track. But the necessary preliminary agreements still eluded everyone. Then Anwar Sadat surprised the world by traveling to Jerusalem. The unprecedented and improbable sight of Egyptian and Israeli heads of state smiling and talking with each other about peace provided a major psychological advance. Sadat's visit also indicated the economic exhaustion that ongoing confrontation had brought to both nations. The time again seemed right for progress. President Carter once more interjected American power and persistence. This time, following Kissinger's strategy, he carefully excluded the Russians from any mediating role. For thirteen days in 1978, Carter, Menachem Begin, and Anwar Sadat remained in near isolation at the presidential retreat at Camp David. When they emerged, they issued for television audiences an emotional three-way statement that outlined the beginnings of a negotiating process. To many, it seemed that Carter had accomplished only somewhat less than the parting of the Red Sea: the reconciliation of irreconcilables.

Over the next year Egypt and Israel negotiated and ratified the treaty that the Camp David accords had promised. It was still the framework, not the substance, of settlement: future negotiations would agree upon the "modalities" for establishing an elected governing authority in the West Bank and Gaza that would bring autonomy to that area. The goal was vague enough to provide ample room for failure. Israel categorically forbade any official participation by the Palestine Liberation Organization in the negotiations, even though the PLO was the major representative of the Arab Palestinians in the West Bank and Gaza. The PLO and most Arab states charged that Sadat had sold out the Palestinian people and had negotiated matters that were not his to negotiate. The split within the Arab world widened as Israeli-Egyptian divisions narrowed. Some domestic critics, observing that the exclusion of the PLO and the antagonism of other Arabs made substantial solutions even more difficult than before, wondered whether Carter, Begin, and Sadat had created the illusion of settlement to raise their images at home. But optimists argued that the importance of the 1979 peace treaty lay in the momentum of negotiation. Clearly, the Egyptian-Israeli peace firmly established United States hegemony and eliminated Soviet influence in Egypt. Carter, like Nixon, dangled the large carrot of American aid and increased arms sales in order to keep the appearance of negotiations alive.

Carter's diplomacy with China had less ambiguous results. On January 1, 1979, the United States and the People's Republic of China established formal relations, and over the next year they signed a number of cultural, scientific, and economic agreements. A joint economic committee, co-chaired by the secretary of the treasury, worked to enhance trade, and the United States zoomed up to fourth place among China's trading partners. In January 1980 Defense Secretary Harold Brown's trip to China (coinciding handily with the Soviet invasion of Afghanistan) signaled the opening of a military relationship as well. The new technocrats who succeeded to Chinese leadership after the death of Mao were bent upon accelerating modernization by borrowing from the capitalist West, and the lure of the China market once again enthralled the American business community.

Toward the end of 1979 the Counselor for the department of state summarized the general view that had initially guided the Carter administration's foreign policy worldwide: "It is not a sign of weakness to recognize that we alone cannot dictate events elsewhere. It is rather a sign of American maturity in a complex world." More negotiation, more compromise, and greater attention to human rights marked Carter's early foreign policy.

External events and political pressures at home gradually led Carter to begin to revise his foreign-policy emphasis. By 1978 policymakers talked more of larger military spending and cold-war dangers. Then in December 1979 the Soviet Union invaded Afghanistan. The Soviet action, the first armed Soviet invasion since the incursion into Czechoslovakia in 1968, probably reflected the Soviets' fear of a unified Islamic movement and their desire to take advantage of the instability in the region to enlarge their sphere of influence. Coming at a time when Americans were exceedingly nervous about the security of Middle Eastern oil supplies due to the Iranian revolution, the Soviet invasion touched off feverish cold-war rhetoric reminiscent of the 1950s.

Critics of Carter's foreign policy leaped to their election-year podiums, denounced America's presumed weakness, and clamored for a response. The Carter administration warned Americans that "overreaction" was as dangerous as "underreaction," but announced reprisals against the Soviets. Carter ordered a halt to exports of grain and high technology to the Soviet Union, began to arm Pakistan, publicly highlighted the secretary of defense's trip to China, organized a boycott of the Olympic Games held in Moscow in the summer of 1980, withdrew the SALT treaty from the Senate, and reinstituted registration for a military draft. Despite such measures—the strongest response possible short of some type of military action—more and more Americans began to charge that Carter had presided over an erosion of American power that had opened the way for the Soviet invasion of Afghanistan. Neo-conservative groups such as the Committee on the Present Danger constructed a litany of signs of America's weakness: the Shah's ouster in Iran, the Soviet-Cuban presence in Africa, the growing power of Soviet-aligned Vietnam in Southeast Asia, and the revolutionary ferment in the Caribbean. Many of Carter's critics looked nostalgically back to when, during the Truman era, America supposedly talked tough and held tight rein over most of the world, and they wanted such control restored. Such was the promise held out by Ronald Reagan in the presidential campaign of 1980.

Carter knew the political perils of soft-line diplomacy. Afghanistan, he claimed, had shattered his previous illusions about Soviet behavior, and he promised to lead the nation in more forceful directions. A rift became increasingly apparent between Secretary of State Vance, who believed in rationality and the negotiating process, and National Security Adviser Brzezinski, a hard-liner who held a bipolar view of world politics and who viewed the Soviets with deep suspicion. After Carter ordered his ill-fated military mission to rescue the hostages in Iran (whose lengthening captivity had become a major political lia-

230

bility for Carter), the secretary of state resigned his post. Vance indicated that he was out of sympathy not only with what he considered a rash and risky military incursion into Iran but with the new confrontational policy in general. The new secretary of state, Edmund Muskie, had neither the experience nor the stature of Vance, and Carter continued to develop his harder-line policy and to allow Brzezinski to articulate it. With Republicans goading the administration about a weak defense, Carter complemented cold-war rhetroic with promises to revitalize America's strategic posture. He began refurbishing military bases throughout the world and beefing up American military capabilities in critical areas, such as the Indian Ocean and the Caribbean; he increased defense spending and promised more emphasis on new high-technology weapon systems (satellites and lasers); and he strongly backed the controversial and extravagant MX missile system. His advisers even began to blur the traditional distinctions between "nuclear" and "conventional" military action, leaving the Russians to speculate publicly that Americans no longer considered "limited" nuclear strikes unthinkable.

Although the new cold warriors drew alarming pictures of an expansionist Soviet Union, the Soviets were themselves feeling embattled. Suffering major economic problems, threatened by growing dissent at home, and wary of a resurgent and hostile China, Soviet leaders also faced a decline in geopolitical power. Kissinger and Carter had both outmaneuvered the Soviets in the Middle East and effectively excluded them from influence in that area. Signs of discontent in Eastern Europe—especially the successful strike by Polish workers in August 1980—highlighted strains even within the Warsaw Pact itself.

If both American and Russian leaders felt increasingly insecure about their global roles in the early 1980s, it was because the rest of the world was struggling to avoid the tight grip of bipolar alliances and to build new power blocs. OPEC; the movement of "nonaligned nations"; the Committee of 77, which represented the South in the so-called North-South debate; the new power of Islam; a variety of regional pacts—all illustrated the growing intricacy of world politics. Yet, as in the era of the first cold war, the leaders of the superpowers appeared tempted to resort to the simplistic slogans of "communist aggression" and "capitalist encirclement" to explain away the complexities of neutralist or nationalist aspirations. America's foreign policy in the 1980s would, in part, be shaped by whether or not most Americans would accept the proposition that strength derived from recognizing limitations as well as from asserting power.

The New Egalitarianism

The Meaning of Equality

One of the most perplexing issues facing the nation in the 1970s was the meaning of equality. Nearly all of the Republic's sacred documents—including the Declaration of Independence and the Constitution's Fourteenth Amendment—affirmed the idea of equality. Yet one of the undeniable realities of the American experience had been the persistence of inequality—political, legal, and economic. Even in the late 1960s, as the need for the Voting Rights Acts of 1965 and 1970 confirmed, many black people in the South still lacked the same political rights as whites.

The attention given the search for greater equality during the 1960s and 1970s revealed some fundamental differences over the meaning of equality and over the desirability of making it one of the goals of a free society. As the nation approached and then passed the bicentennial of its birth, debates about equality became more heated. In the late 1970s, polarization over the issue of equality, though less visible than a decade before, was no less intense, especially in journalistic and academic circles.

Throughout most of American history, "equality" meant "equality of opportunity," the ability of every citizen to join in the great American race for success. The sweetest victories and the largest rewards, it was assumed, should go to those who ran the swiftest. But everyone should have a chance to get to the starting line, and no one should have to jump hurdles while more fortunate competitors sailed along an obstacle-free track. Yet even equality of opportunity, though much celebrated, remained a dream for many Americans. Liberalism in the United States had worked as well as it had, it might be argued, because so many people never really got into the race at all. Women, black people, ethnic minorities, gay people—these and other groups carried "handicaps" that prevented them from getting very far out of the starting blocks. The famous blues singer Big Bill Broonzy summarized the way many black people saw the great American race:

If you're White, you're all right,
If you're Brown, stick around,
But if you're black, O' brother,
Get back! Get back! Get Back!

Many of the political and legal battles of the 1960s and of the 1970s aimed at preventing people from being "moved back," at rehandicapping the race, and at removing old hurdles. Thus, the earliest demands of the black movement involved elimination of various obstacles, such as segregation laws and discriminatory hiring practices, that prevented blacks from entering the gates of American institutions. Similarly, women's groups channeled their energies toward passage of the Equal Rights Amendment, an attempt to end discrimination through legal and constitutional change.

While the struggle to eliminate obstacles to equality of opportunity was still proceeding, the victories that had been achieved in this area began to change the perspective of many activists. As they looked at the old American race for success, these "new egalitarians" began to argue that efforts to allow everyone to enter the race and to remove the old system of hurdles were not enough. Renewed commitment to the principle of equality of opportunity would not likely change the fact that only a few people were leading the race for economic success, that many people were bunched in the middle of the pack, and that a sizable portion had fallen permanently behind. In the distribution of both income and wealth, the United States in 1980 remained a very unequal society: at the top of the scale, 5 percent of the population received 20 percent of the nation's income and owned more than 50 percent of its wealth; the lowest 20 percent, in stark contrast, gained 3 percent of the income and held less than .5 percent of the wealth. According to the new egalitarians, such inequality of condition and of results meant that there were all sorts of subtle and hidden handicaps in "the system." If the United States were to be a truly egalitarian society, there must be vigorous and affirmative action to achieve greater "equality of condition" rather than simply a spurious equality of opportunity.

In the late 1960s and especially the early 1970s, the agenda of egalitarianism changed. Not only should black students be protected from discriminatory procedures that barred them from educational institutions, the new egalitarians argued, but there should be affirmative action programs to ensure their admittance and their graduation. In the area of employment, proponents of affirmative action argued that there must be pressure to ensure that women and minority applicants were not simply interviewed but were then hired and promoted on an "equal" basis. Proof of substantial progress toward greater equality of results was increasingly measured by comparing the percentage of women and minorities in educational or business institutions with their percentage of the total American population, a process that opponents condemned as inevitably leading to the institution of quotas.

The quest for greater equality of condition involved more than pressure for affirmative-action programs in educational and corporate institutions. Looking at the gross inequality of wealth and income, the sociologist Herbert Gans argued that the nation must confront the issue of income redistribution. After surveying the problem in *Inequality* (1971) and resurveying it in *Who Gets Ahead?* (1979), another sociologist, Christopher Jencks, found that social-science data showed that attempts to equalize people's "personal characteristics," especially their educational backgrounds, was an "unpromising way of equalizing incomes." If the American people truly wanted a more equal economic order, Jencks concluded, efforts to "redistribute income itself" offered the "most effective strategy."

But as Senator George McGovern discovered during his ill-fated presidential campaign, proposals to redistribute wealth and income were difficult to sell to voters. Although many of Nixon's "forgotten Americans" would have benefited from McGovern's proposed changes in inheritance laws, for example, most voters saw his ideas as too radical. "They must think they're all going to win a lottery," complained McGovern. In fact, many ordinary citizens did consider redistribution as hostile to their interests. It seemed to strike at the deeply rooted American commitment to "propertarianism" and at the faith that no matter how unjust the general economic system might appear something would turn up for them. (Public-opinion polls taken in the late 1970s revealed a similar phenomenon: people expressed considerable pessimism about the general social situation but a striking optimism about their own prospects.)

Yet the movement for equality spread, and some of the new egalitarians went beyond purely economic issues to argue that all Americans should have an equal opportunity to enjoy, without risking penalties, their chosen style of life. Some of the most bitter battles in the struggle for equality were fought over the issue of homosexuality. During the late 1960s and throughout the 1970s more and more homosexuals "came out of the closet" and joined a growing "gay-rights" movement. Gay-rights activists first wanted acknowledgment of their right to privacy, their right to satisfy their own sexual preferences with other consenting adults. Increasingly, they also demanded that gay people be treated, in their public roles, in exactly the same way as heterosexuals. The gay-rights movement pushed for state and municipal laws ending traditional patterns of discrimination and sought greater police protection against physical abuse. Although the gay-rights movement won significant support, especially from civil-liberties elites, it also produced a considerable backlash among those who feared the spread of what they considered an immoral way of life.

Efforts to create greater equality for women also raised controversy. Here, it was the American family, the bedrock of the social order, that became the issue. Proposals to expand government funding for day-care centers—necessities for most women who wanted both children and a job—angered those who claimed that the state should stay out of private matters and those who argued that more day-care facilities would only upset an already unstable family structure. In addition, most employers displayed little enthusiasm for ideas such as flexible work hours and job sharing, egalitarian arrangements that could benefit both men and women who wanted families and careers.

The New Right

Fervent opposition to the new egalitarianism helped unify the conservative coalition of the 1970s. Although some commentators had predicted that the "Goldwater caper" of 1964 signaled conservatism's imminent collapse, conservative leaders inside and outside the GOP smoothly regrouped their forces. As conservatives gained new visibility and greater self-confidence, the New Right emerged as an important political force.

Several things distinguished this New Right from the conservative movement of the 1940s and 1950s. First, conservatives now gained broad popular support, especially through their alliance with rapidly growing evangelical religious groups. Conservatives, who had once had to search for roots in

America's distant past, could now join the Christian right in rallying around contemporary institutions such as the American family. (For the emergence of the religious right see Chapter 10.) In addition, conservatives mastered the latest media and organizational techniques. Conservative speakers, such as William F. Buckley and Milton Friedman, became skilled television performers, and conservative fund-raisers mounted highly sophisticated direct-mail appeals for donations. And following the lead of Goldwater's 1964 campaign, conservative political strategists were oftentimes more innovative than their opponents on the political left.

The merger of evangelical religion, media, and new political techniques converged in the 1978 senatorial compaign of North Carolina's Jesse Helms. Helms was a creation of the media, a former editorialist for a Raleigh television station, and he collected more than $7 million, much of it from direct mailings to conservatives across the country, for his successful reelection drive. Helms's campaign was the most expensive in the history of the Senate, and it quickly became the prototype for other conservative political efforts, almost all of which supported Republican candidates. Although many members of the GOP had opposed the changes in campaign-finance laws that grew out of Watergate, Republican-oriented pressure groups on the right skillfully used loopholes in the new measures, especially the provision allowing unlimited spending by independent "political-action committees"—PACS. In 1980 a variety of right-leaning PACS distributed millions of dollars to Republican candidates and successfully targeted key Democrats, such as senators George McGovern and Frank Church, for removal from office.

Finally, the New Right developed a much livelier and broader intellectual base than the conservatism of the 1950s. Buckley's *National Review* remained the most popular conservative journal, but it was joined by a number of other widely read, scholarly publications, many of them sponsored by the American Enterprise Institute (AEI), a new conservative think-tank in Washington, D.C. Many of the people associated with the AEI—the much-heralded "neo-conservatives"—were actually newcomers to the conservative ranks.

Many of the most prominent neo-conservatives were fugitives from the cold-war liberalism of the "vital center"; they espoused a more cautious and extremely nervous version of the thoroughly cautious liberalism of the late 1940s and the 1950s. Many of the neo-conservatives' enemies of the 1970s had been the foes of cold-war liberalism—especially international communism, Marxism, and domestic radicalism. Their favorite causes—particularly gradualism, capitalism, and economic growth—had been the hallmarks of Truman's Fair Deal. But the neo-conservative movement also represented a strong reaction to the leftward drift of liberalism and the emergence of a new radicalism during the 1960s. Norman Podhoretz, editor of *Commentary* magazine, proudly pointed out that he had first published Paul Goodman in the early 1960s and had only broken ranks after realizing the "sinister" implications of the Movement. The counterculture, Podhoretz claimed, was winning, and sober intellectuals had to take a firm stand against "irrational" ideas and "dangerous" values.

Critical of what they considered a cowardly appeasement of communism overseas and a soft-headed tolerance of cultural and political radicalism at home, chastened liberals like Pohoretz, Irving Kristol, Daniel Bell, Nathan Glazer, and Daniel Patrick Moynihan formed the intellectual core of neo-conservativism. In addition to their own numerous publications, they helped to popularize some of the more conservative social-science literature, especially the work of Edward Banfield and James Q. Wilson. The resulting battles between the neo-conservatives' set of academic "experts" and those of the left were fierce. Many of the leading neo-conservative theorists possessed backgrounds in both academia and journalism, and they combined these talents to produce sprightly polemics for *Commentary* and more scholarly pieces for *The Public Interest,* an influential periodical edited by Kristol and Glazer.

Although neo-conservatives found the United States—indeed, Western civilization—entering a period of profound crisis, the specter of the new egalitarianism frightened them nearly as much as did the Soviet Union. Some neo-conservatives were disturbed by the new efforts to achieve the traditional goal of equality of opportunity, at least when such equality was sought by militant feminists, cultural radicals, and gays. Irving Kristol and the political scientist Walter Berns, for example, endorsed more vigorous censorship of "pornographic" materials, and Ernest van den Haag warned that the new militancy of gays threatened traditional values based on heterosexuality.

The neo-conservative attack on the new egalitarianism, however, centered on the demand for greater equality of results—what neo-conservatives denounced as "equality of outcomes." Nathan Glazer condemned affirmative action as an insidious form of reverse discrimination, a doctrine that discriminated not simply against white males but against all people of true merit. When applied to black Americans, the political scientist Robert Sasseen argued, affirmative action really affirmed an "arrogant contempt" for blacks: it disguised a "paternalistic policy" that consigned its purported beneficiaries to "perpetual inferiority" and to a life as "special wards of the state." Midge Dector (Norman Podhoretz's wife and an influential book editor) denounced militant feminism as a revolutionary attack on motherhood, as a sign of deep-seated self-hatred, and as the manifestation of the "desperately nihilistic idea" that there were no "necessary differences between the sexes." Irving Kristol blamed most of the controversy over equality on "an intelligentsia" that despised liberal capitalist society and "that is so guilt-ridden at being implicated in the life of the society that it is inclined to find even collective suicide preferable to the status quo."

The National Government and the Riddle of Equality

The struggle over the true meaning of equality was not, of course, limited to rhetorical clashes in the academy and political journals. The egalitarian currents of the 1960s and 1970s, as wary neo-conservatives recognized, touched most areas of American life, especially educational and corporate institutions. Did affirmative-action programs that set aside a specified number of classroom seats or jobs for certain minorities constitute reverse discrimination against others who claimed they were more deserving of the places on the basis of their individual merit? Should, for instance, blacks or Hispanics be admitted to a law school, while whites with higher test scores and better academic records were rejected? (Such questions became especially difficult and emotional when the persons rejected came from ethnic groups, such as the Jews and the Italian-Americans, who had once suffered from discrimination themselves.)

The controversy over affirmative action and reverse discrimination raged throughout the 1970s, and the United States Supreme Court finally entered the lists. In the much-discussed *Bakke* case of 1978, a deeply divided Court struck down a plan that set aside a certain quota of seats at a California medical school for "minority" applicants. But, more significantly, a majority of justices also indicated that they were not willing to invalidate all affirmative-action programs. This stance became clear when the Court upheld a private affirmative-action plan, devised by Kaiser Aluminum in order to upgrade the positions of minority workers, and approved a congressional requirement that 10 percent of all contracts awarded under a public-works program go to "minority business enterprises." These decisions—*Steelworkers* v. *Webber* (1979) and *Fullilove* v. *Klutznick* (1980)—made *Bakke* appear to be a minor setback. Both *Webber* and *Fullilove* applied to areas—the personnel practices of large corporations and the awarding of government contracts—in which affirmative action would produce more immediate results than in higher education. More important, a majority of the Court accepted plans that included specific quotas. According to Chief Justice Warren Burger, the Court's majority accepted affirmative-action quotas in the *Fullilove* case because they rejected the contention that in remedying past discrimination the "Congress must act in a wholly color-blind fashion."

The *Webber* and *Fullilove* cases, no more than any other Supreme Court decisions, "settled" a complex issue, one with social, economic, political, and moral dimensions. But these decisions meant that the new struggle for equality, like the black civil-rights movement two decades earlier, could proceed with the moral force of law on its side. In 1980 even a divided Supreme Court could be a welcome ally; the new egalitarianism had never possessed much support in Washington, especially at 1600 Pennsylvania Avenue.

Following the retirement of Lyndon Johnson, no president gave the issue of inequality much attention. Richard Nixon and his domestic strategists offered the poorest one fourth of the population "benign neglect," while they underscored their concern for the "forgotten American"—middle-class and lower-middle class citizens who obeyed the laws, worked hard, and paid more than their share of taxes. Nixon also promised to slash national welfare expenditures and to inaugurate revenue sharing, a plan to dispense federal money in the form of discretionary block grants rather than as a part of pre-packaged, nondiscretionary programs from Washington. The idea, part of Nixon's broader concept of a new federalism, was supposed to encourage decentralization of authority in both planning and administration and to revitalize state and local government.

Not unexpectedly, reality lagged behind rhetoric. Although the Nixon administration finally shut down Johnson's Office of Economic Opportunity and never did emphasize spending for social welfare, many of the Great Society's programs already enjoyed strong support from many members of Congress and from a variety of interest groups. As a result, expenditures for social welfare, measured as a percentage of the GNP, actually continued to rise under Nixon and then under Gerald Ford. By this standard, the growth was faster under two Republican presidents than under Lyndon Johnson, though these funds generally failed to alleviate deeply rooted inequalities. Meanwhile, Nixon's promises to the "forgotten American" went largely unfulfilled as soaring inflation rates eroded most workers' real income.

As his presidential campaign suggested, Jimmy Carter was not interested in even promising great changes in government policies. Despite the vigorous debates among neo-conservatives, true believers in Great Society liberalism, and advocates of more radical approaches, Carter seemed most interested in procedures and planning, not in broad policy arguments or political philosophy. The small-town populist, who had broken tradition by strolling down Pennsylvania Avenue with his wife on inauguration day, was soon replaced by the nuclear engineer-technician from Annapolis. Carter's first proposals for national action sounded no clarion calls for social justice but stressed managerial and technical issues—reorganization of the executive branch, streamlining of existing welfare programs, and new budget procedures. When confronted by energy problems, Carter did talk about energy as "the moral equivalent of war," but his "wartime" strategy followed rather conventional paths. Most important, all of the Carter administration's plans assumed that the old liberal *deus ex machina*—real economic growth—could be restored and could provide, as it had in the past, a means of avoiding a direct confrontation with the problem of inequality. If, through the magic of new energy-producing technologies, the economic pie could once again expand, even the smallest slices would be bigger.

The Carter administration, however, was no more successful than the Nixon or Ford administrations in promoting real economic growth. Throughout the 1970s, under Republicans and Democrats, the American economy failed to perform as well as it had done in the 1960s—or even in the 1940s and 1950s. Although the United States still produced more than any other nation, the gap narrowed as America's economic productivity—its output per worker—grew more slowly than that of other industrial nations. Even Britain and Italy, countries with serious economic problems, could boast of higher productivity rates than the United States. These countries simply proved more effective in marketing new products and in improving the processes for manufacturing their old ones. At the same time that productivity languished, inflation flourished. The inflation rate for 1979 stood at nearly 14 percent, and the monthly rate for early 1980, when figured on a yearly basis, ran as high as 20 percent. According to one study, a family of four that had earned $13,200 in 1970 would have required an income of more than $25,000 to maintain the same standard of living in 1980. Although the salaries of most upper-income professionals kept pace with inflation, most American workers suffered a decline in their real income.

The nation's economic difficulties contributed to the unsettled political climate. In 1976 Jimmy Carter had exploited the popular distrust of political institutions; as president, he found that he could become the victim, rather than the beneficiary, of popular cynicism about government. And in charting his political course he had to deal with a party structure that was undergoing constant shifts and sags. Just as the Goldwater defeat had proved only a temporary setback for the Republicans in the late 1960s, Watergate marked merely a momentary downturn for the GOP in the 1970s. While the Republican party regrouped behind Ronald Reagan and the banner of the GOP's right wing, the Democratic party splintered into even more factions than it had in the late 1960s. Carter and his strategists successfully built their own faction, but powerful members of the old Democratic coalition, especially social activists, expressed little enthusiasm for Carter's domestic policies.

Even if he had been blessed with a treasure chest of political assets and burdened with no liabilities, Jimmy Carter would still have found it difficult to discover easy answers to the nation's economic woes. On economic questions there was no longer any firm "conventional wisdom" to which Jimmy Carter —or any president—could turn. The economist-social critic Herman Daly, for example, spoke for many advocates of the "small-is-beautiful" approach when he urged abandoning the old goal of economic growth in favor of a "steady-state economy," one that aimed at "sufficient wealth efficiently maintained and allocated, and equitably distributed—not maximum production." Other social critics also advocated major departures from the old liberal economic formulas. After surveying the growing pressures on the supplies of resources in the United States and in other nations, Richard J. Barnet predicted the onset of "the lean years." He urged greater government planning, reliance upon "soft" rather than "hard" energy technologies (solar energy in preference to nuclear energy, for example), and greater democratization of the national and international marketplaces. The socialist writer Michael Harrington joined Barnet in insisting that most of America's problems resulted from the misuse of power by the giant multinational corporations. In the age of monopoly capitalism, Harrington argued, unemployment, inflation, and a stagnant economy were all products of decisions made in corporate board rooms and accepted by political leaders. America's economic ills, Harrington contended, reflected underlying structural problems, conditions rooted in the very nature of an oversized capitalist economy.

Other observers offered a much different analysis. According to neo-conservative theoreticians such as Irving Kristol, traditional economists such as Milton Friedman, and representatives of large business corporations, the problems of American capitalism could be traced back to the national government's interference in the marketplace and to "crushing" levels of taxation, especially upon businesses. They blamed huge government deficits, unnecessary environmental restraints, ill-advised safety regulations, and the general burden of governmental-required paperwork for preventing American capitalism from reaching its full economic potential. (As the economist Lester Thurow pointed out, though, those countries with higher productivity *all* had much *more* governmental regulation than the United States.) These conservative writers promised no easy solutions, but they urged that the only paths to economic growth involved massive government deregulation and substantial tax cuts, both measures to stimulate the "supply-side," that is the productive infrastructure of the American economy. They also called for tighter control over the money supply and a sharp reduction of government borrowing to finance deficits which, they claimed, deprived private business of necessary loans for research and expansion. They insisted that their proposals were good not only for business but for all Americans. Even conservatives could not ignore the issue of greater economic justice for the poor and for various minority groups, but the problems of the poor could only be solved, conservatives argued, through the unleashing of American capitalism.

Even the more conventional liberal economists, to whom Carter ultimately turned, offered him a variety of approaches to the key problems of productivity and inflation. Although the president endorsed the Humphrey-Hawkins bill, which pledged that the White House would reduce unemployment to 4 percent by 1982, he and his economic advisers placed their primary emphasis on fighting inflation. First, they bowed toward the arguments of the deregulators and sought to lower prices by ending federal regulatory structures, such as those in the transportation industry, that supposedly raised prices. And though the Carter administration rejected calls for a thoroughgoing system of wage and price controls, it did establish voluntary wage and price guidelines. Finally, Carter and his economic aides pursued a policy of tightening credit (thus raising interest rates) and of "cooling down" the economy. Carter's monetary policies did drive down the inflation rate—though it still hovered near double digit levels—but they generated rising unemployment and increased social tensions. By the summer of 1980 the nation had slid into one of the worst recessions since the 1930s.

The Election of 1980

Lacking a strong base of political support and any real experience in government, Carter seemed confused in his approach to domestic affairs. As Nixon had done with his "Berlin Wall," Carter isolated himself behind a small group of fellow Georgians, individuals who were skillful political tacticians but who seemed to lack any broad vision of national priorities. Confidence in Carter's performance, as measured by various public-opinion surveys, steadily plummeted. By the time of the Democratic convention in August 1980, only 23 percent of the Gallup Poll's sample thought he was doing a good job. Carter's showing was even more dismal than that of Harry Truman during his final months in office or of Richard Nixon during the dog days of Watergate.

Yet several different circumstances allowed Carter to amaze most political pundits and recapture the Democratic nomination. First, as the incumbent and the nation's commander in chief, Carter gained support as a result of the United States' foreign-policy problems. With Iranians occupying the American embassy in Teheran and the Soviets invading Afghanistan, many Democrats felt that they should stick with their leader, even when his own policies—such as admitting the Shah of Iran into the United States—had contributed to some of the problems. Second, Carter benefited from the liabilities of his major Democratic rival, Senator Edward Kennedy of Massachusetts. Although Kennedy gained generally favorable media coverage before he declared for the presidency—and after his capitulation to Carter—many members of the press dug relentlessly at the senator's vulnerabilities, especially his old personal problems, while he was an active candidate. At the same time, Kennedy did little to erase nagging doubts about his involvement in the death of Mary Jo Kopechne at Chappaquiddick or to answer new questions about the viability of his social and economic proposals. Many Democrats, as pollsters discovered, distrusted Kennedy more than they disliked Carter. Even many who thought that the president was something of a bumbler still considered him a decent and honest man. Finally, Carter effectively (ruthlessly, claimed the Kennedy camp) capitalized on his position as the incumbent and used federal patronage to build strong ties with local Democratic officials. Although the White House failed to devise clear strategies for meeting domestic ills, it did dispense federal grants, both large and small, to Democratic mayors and governors. Thus, the Democratic National Convention of 1980 produced a curious result: delegates warmly embraced the man they had rejected for the presidency, Edward Kennedy (and incorporated many of his proposals into their party's platform), and unenthusiastically renominated a candidate, Jimmy Carter, who seemed a sure loser in November.

Although the president appeared to have gained "momentum" (a favorite term of political reporters in 1980) during the fall campaign, election day proved a disaster for Jimmy Carter and a serious setback for the Democratic party. The GOP's presidential ticket of Ronald Reagan and George Bush carried 44 states, including most of those in Carter's native South and captured 486 electoral votes. (Independent candidate John Anderson gained enough of the popular vote, 7 percent, to qualify for federal funds but failed to win any electoral votes.) Post-election analyses revealed that Reagan and Bush had cut into almost all of the traditionally Democratic voting blocs, especially union members, Jews, and white ethnic voters. According to one survey, 25 percent of those Democrats who voted supported Reagan. The oldest person ever elected to the presidency—Reagan was only a few months short of seventy on November 4, 1980—the former Governor of California even outpolled Carter among voters under thirty years of age.

At the same time, Reagan's Republican party showed that it had recovered from Richard Nixon and Watergate. The GOP gained 12 Senate seats and took control of the upper house of Congress for the first time since 1954. A number of prominent Democratic liberals—including George McGovern, Frank Church, Birch Bayh, and Gaylord Nelson—were turned out of the Senate. Although the Democrats managed to hold onto the House of Representatives, the GOP still picked up 33 seats in the lower house.

Some pundits, especially those associated with the GOP, hastened to call the results a "mandate" for Reagan and a signal that a new "conservative majority" was about to take control of national politics. Upon reflection, most observers hesitated to attribute such significance to the 1980 elections. In many ways, the presidential result represented more of a repudiation of Jimmy Carter than an affirmation of Ronald Reagan. Nearly half of the eligible voters did not vote for any presidential candidate so that Reagan's 51 percent of the popular vote gave him the support of little more than one-quarter of the potential electorate. Similarly, the defeat of most of the Democratic senators could be traced less to their liberalism than to their difficulties disassociating themselves from the unpopular president who headed their party's ticket. Almost all of the defeated senators ran far ahead of Jimmy Carter. Even without Carter's troubles, Reagan's victory had its ambiguities. In his choice of a vice-presidential running-mate and in many of his subsequent cabinet selections, for example, Reagan veered away from the New Right and moved toward the center of the GOP. And in contrast to the outsider stance maintained by Jimmy Carter and suggested in Reagan's own campaign, the new president quickly moved himself, his family, and his followers into the Washington social scene. One prominent columnist even suggested that the Reagans would bring "a little class for a change" to the White House.

Reagan and his inner circle of wealthy advisers also brought with them a set of plans to reverse the domestic political trends that had dominated the postwar political era. In contrast to Carter, for example, Reagan pledged not to reorganize governmental agencies but to dismantle at least some of them. His secretary of interior promised he would not even listen to environmental "extremists," and Reagan's new budget director, David Stockman, was on record as suggesting that most governmental welfare programs should be eliminated. The "new egalitarianism," Reagan's conservative supporters hoped, would be a thing of the past.

A master of political symbols, Ronald Reagan won rave reviews from those who analyzed presidential image-making. The lavish inaugural proceedings, generously sprinkled with designer gowns, rented limosines, and Reagan's old Hollywood friends, recalled the early days of the Kennedy administration; Reagan's speeches, which called for rebuilding "the American dream" and for overcoming fears of new approaches, suggested the self-confident optimism of Franklin Roosevelt; and the president's narrow escape from an assasin's bullet a few months after taking office placed him in the fearless western mold of John Wayne, a pop culture hero often invoked by Reagan himself. But acting out a saleable political script would prove much easier than mapping out a workable political program. Ronald Reagan, like the postwar presidents who preceded him, confronted a complex web of social and political institutions. Although some of Reagan's enthusiastic backers claimed that the GOP had forged a new conservative consensus from a variety of disparate groups, the very complexity of American society suggested the superficiality of such a view. No single election, no single political movement could hope to roll back the postwar trend toward an "oversized society."

SUGGESTIONS FOR FURTHER READING

On the Nixon administration, see the "insider" accounts of Richard Nixon, *RN: The Memoirs of Richard Nixon* (1978) and *The Real War* (1980); William Safire, *Before the Fall* (1975); H. R. Haldeman, *The Ends of Power* (1978); and Henry Kissinger, *The White House Years* (1979). The best journalistic accounts include John Osborne's various volumes entitled *The Nixon Watch*; J. Anthony Lukas, *Nightmare* (1976); and Jonathan Schell, *The Time of Illusion* (1975). Theodore H. White's *The Making of the President 1972* (1973) is hopelessly uncritical, but the early chapters of his *Breach of Faith* (1975) partially redeem his infatuation with the "new" Nixon. Timothy Crouse's *Boys on the Bus* (1973) and Hunter S. Thompson's *Fear and Loathing on the Campaign Trail* (1972) provide iconoclastic views of the 1972 presidential campaign.

White's *Breach of Faith* offers a general overview of Watergate and the downfall of Richard Nixon. In *Power Shift* (1976) Kirkpatrick Sale links the sleazy side of the Nixon administration to the "rimsters" from the Sunbelt areas. Various participants have told their stories. See, for example, John Dean, *Blind Ambition* (1976); G. Gordon Liddy, *Will* (1980); John Sirica, *To Set the Record Straight* (1979); and Leon Jaworski, *The Right and the Power* (1976). Bob Woodward and Carl Bernstein detail their own chase of the Watergate story in *All the President's Men* (1974) and the story of Nixon's downfall in *The Final Days* (1976). Edward J. Epstein's *Agency of Fear* (1977) is much better in seeking out what "Watergate" was really about; he links the emergence of the plumbers to the Nixon administration's crusade against drugs. Peter Schrag's *Test of Loyalty* (1974) tells of Daniel Ellsberg's problems; and in *The Papers & The Papers (1972)*, Sanford J. Unger examines the legal battles over the Pentagon Papers. "Dirty tricks" and various illegal activities are detailed in Athan Theoharis, *Spying on Americans (1978)* and two books by David Wise—*The Politics of Lying* (1974) and *The American Police State* (1976). See also Frank J. Danner, *The Age of Surveillance* (1980).

The story of "dirty tricks" overseas has been at least partially revealed. See, for example, William Shawcross's controversial *Sideshow* (1978) on the not-so-secret war in Cambodia. See also Noam Chomsky and Edward Herman, *The Political Economy of Human Rights, Volume I: The Washington Connection and Third World Fascism* (1979); Thomas Powers, *The Man Who Kept the Secrets: Richard Helms and the CIA* (1979); Michael Klare, *Supplying Repression* (1977); John Stockwell, *In Search of Enemies* (1978); and *The Secret Report of the House Select Committee on Intelligence* (chaired by Otis Pike), published in *The Village Voice*, February 16 and 23, 1976.

The Nixon-Ford-Kissinger foreign policy is the subject of Kissinger's memoirs, cited above, and the following critical studies: Stanley Hoffman, *Primacy or World Order* (1979); Roger Morris, *Uncertain Greatness* (1977); John G. Stoessinger, *Kissinger: The Anguish of Power*; and Tad Szulc, *Illusion of Peace* (1978). *Kissinger* (1974) by Marvin and Bernard Kalb is useful for its factual survey, but is not sufficiently critical. Gerald Ford's account of his brief presidency, *A Time for Healing* (1979), is not very revealing.

On the 1976 election and Jimmy Carter, see Jules Witcover, *Marathon* (1977); James Wooten, *Dasher* (1978); and Carter's own *Why Not the Best?* (1976). The Carter presidency is critiqued in Clark Mollenhoff, *The President Who Failed* (1980) and Haynes Johnson, *In the Absence of Power* (1980). A more substantial study is Betty Glad's *Jimmy Carter: In Search of the Great White House* (1980). Several broader studies place the Carter administration into a larger interpretive structure: Theodore Lowi, *The End of Liberalism* (2nd ed., 1979); Bertram Gross, *Friendly Fascism: The New Face of Power in America* (1980); Richard Fagen, ed., *Capitalism and the State in U.S.–Latin America Relations* (1979); Chomsky and Herman, *The Political Economy of Human Rights, Volume II: After the Cataclysm: Postwar Indo-China and the Reconstruction of Imperial Ideology* (1979).

On the issue of egalitarianism, see J. R. Pole, *The Meaning of Equality* (1978); Christopher Jencks, *Inequality* (1973); Herbert Gans, *More Equality* (1973); Richard F. Curtis and Elton F. Jackson, *Inequality in American Communities* (1977); Paul Blumberg, *Inequality in an Age of Decline* (1980); and the relevant portions of Lester C. Thurow, *The Zero-Sum Society* (1980). See also John Livingston, *Fair Game?* (1979).

On the rise of neo-conservatism, see Peter Steinfels, *The Neo-Conservatives* (1979). *The New Egalitarianism* (1979), edited by David Lewis Schaefer, is a collection of essays by leading neo-conservatives. Nathan Glazer, *Affirmative Discrimination* (1977) is a book-length attack on the new egalitarianism. Irving Kristol's *Two Cheers for Capitalism* (1979) and Norman Podhoretz's *Breaking Ranks* (1979) and *The Present Danger* (1980) can also be consulted.

On the rise of the New Right as a force in the politics of the late 1970s, see Richard A. Viguerie, *The New Right: We're Ready to Lead* (1980); Alan Crawford, *Thunder on the Right* (1980); and for historical background Michael W. Miles, *The Odyssey of the American Right* (1980).

THE OVERSIZED SOCIETY: LIFE DURING THE 1960s AND 1970s

10 The post-1960 era was a time of giantism and excess. Lyndon Johnson, the extravagant Texan who dominated the middle of the 1960s, provided an appropriate symbol: he drove too fast; he threw gargantuan barbecues for his political friends; and in one well-publicized incident he pulled his dog's ears until the puppy yelped. Restraint seemed a quality of the past. The era throbbed with raw power and extremes. American involvement in Vietnam seemed to escalate uncontrollably; presidents Johnson and Nixon roared at their critics; huge business conglomerates formed; rock singers grew old before they turned thirty; football replaced baseball as the national sport. The 1970 census reported that three of every ten homes had more than one television set and that only three of a hundred had no TV at all. The post office, assisted by its new zip-code numbers and electronic equipment, delivered a yearly average of 400 pieces of mail to every man, woman, and child. Book publishers issued more than 35,000 titles a year, double the number put out just ten years earlier. The 1980 census and other surveys showed jumps in scale that were just as staggering. According to one study, the average American threw away four pounds of garbage per day, and the nationwide total amounted to 150 million tons a year—enough refuse to fill three lines of garbage trucks extending from New York to Los Angeles and enough potential energy to light the United States for an entire year.

Clearly, growth did not necessarily bring satisfaction. To many people, American life had become nearly incomprehensible. Who could understand a trillion-dollar economy, trace lines of responsibility through the sprawling federal bureaucracy, or gain redress from an impersonal, computerized corporation? Summing up the misgivings of many, the journalist Kirkpatrick Sale argued that American life had come to exceed any meaningful "human scale."

The Economy: A Gathering of Giants

The Military-Industrial Complex

In his famous farewell speech of 1961, President Dwight D. Eisenhower described one of the most important trends affecting American life: a permanent government-supported weapons industry. No longer, he explained, did Americans mobilize civilian industries for war and reconvert them after the peace. Cold-war pressures had kept the economy on a perpetual war footing and had created "a permanent armaments industry of vast proportions." The old general warned that "we annually spend on military security more than the net income of all United States corporations," and he expressed fear that the resultant military-industrial complex held the "potential for the disastrous rise of misplaced power."

The military-industrial complex grew even larger during the Vietnam war. This national defense structure consisted, at the top, of politicians, military men, business contractors, and university researchers, and, at the bottom, of workers in defense industries. All of these groups were mutually dependent. Government grants for research and development constituted a significant portion of many university budgets; huge corporations, such as General Dynamics and Lockheed depended almost exclusively on government contracts; and by 1967 the salaries of nearly three million people came from defense-related work. But the government was beneficiary as well as benefactor: without this complex of research, industry, and manpower, policymakers could not have pursued their idea of national security, which in postwar years required large-scale military capabilities.

The interests of the military-industrial complex cohered perfectly; the system demanded ever larger expenditures, always rationalized in patriotic language. If the air force wanted a new plane, Boeing wanted a lucrative contract and the people of the Pacific Northwest wanted more jobs. Taxpayers who shouldered the bill had little control over spiraling costs, for few could evaluate the need for a new weapons system. Sophisticated weaponry made the concept of democratic policymaking increasingly obsolete. America's defense complex ran counter to other old values as well. In 1971 Congress took the unprecedented action of extending governmental loans to a private corporation—Lockheed, a leading defense contractor—in order to save it from bankruptcy. How could Americans honestly extol the virtues of free enterprise and a free-market economy when the Pentagon directed the largest planned economic system outside the Soviet Union?

The end of the Vietnam war brought little decrease in military production. So important had continued prosperity for defense industries become that the Nixon administration assiduously sought new customers abroad. During the 1970s American arms sales to foreigners boomed, providing one of the few bright spots in a dreary picture of deteriorating trade balances. There were always customers for arms—always friends, such as the Shah of Iran and the generals in Brazil, who believed they needed to beef up their military establishments. Between 1972 and 1978 the Shah purchased nearly $20 billion worth of military equipment in the United States. For America, arms sales supposedly brought two blessings—profits and the development of strongly militarized allies who could police their particular region and relieve the United States of direct involvement in the maintenance of the status quo.

The main drawback to arms sales was the rising level of violence throughout the world in the 1970s, as countries in Southeast Asia, the Middle East, Latin America, and finally Africa began to engage in mini-arms races. As sophisticated weaponry saturated the world, the toll of death and destruction from regional rivalries or civil war increased immeasurably. But this appalling development went scarcely noticed by the American public. Even President Carter, who had promised in his 1976 campaign to curtail America's role as a merchant of death and encourage human rights abroad, proved unwilling to accept the consequences of canceled contracts, reduced exports, and discontented allies. The flow of arms sales under the Carter administration continued unabated, changing not its volume but only its channels. After the Shah's ouster in 1979, for example, the huge amounts of advanced weaponry formerly sold to Iran found buyers in Israel, Egypt, and elsewhere. And in January 1980 Carter took the unprecedented step of giving the go-ahead for production of America's first armament manufactured solely for export—the FX fighter plane.

Brisk military spending also continued at home during the 1970s. One might have expected that a decade marked by the end of conflict in Vietnam and by the SALT talks with the Soviets would have deemphasized the arms race, but the reverse was true. The lengthy SALT negotiations, which produced an interim agreement called SALT I in 1972 and the more comprehensive accord, SALT II, in 1979, actually inflamed military rivalry as both sides hurried to develop new weapons that could be traded off for concessions from the other side. Furthermore, as the Senate debates over SALT II slowly progressed, it became clear that even if ratification resulted, SALT II would signal a new beginning, rather than a slowdown in military spending. In an attempt to attract the votes needed for ratification, Carter agreed to a large increase in the defense budget. In addition to its acceptance of larger defense budgets, the Carter administration gave a green light to exotic new post-SALT weapons such as the controversial MX, a missile system projected to cost at least $33 billion. When the Soviet Union invaded Afghanistan in early 1980, Carter temporarily withdraw SALT II from Senate consideration, recognizing that the Senate would kill anything that even sounded like a limitation on defense capabilities. In the presidential campaign of 1980 both Carter and Ronald Reagan, the Republican nominee, promised increased spending for defense, more sophisticated weaponry, and a revitalization of America's strategic capabilities worldwide. The military-industrial complex would continue to be a major feature of American life in the 1980s.

Government research money also accelerated new developments that spilled out of the defense sector and transformed American life. The 1950s and 1960s marked a transition to what Zbigniew Brzezinski termed a "technetronic age," an age based upon computers and communications networks. In the technetronic era science and technology, not haphazard experimentation, became the major agents of change: important discoveries seldom came from a lonely basement tinkerer but from the collective work of huge laboratories that depended increasingly upon government funds.

In the 1970s the emphasis of government research-and-development funds shifted somewhat. Physics and engineering drew proportionately fewer federal monies, and health, environment, and energy attracted more than before. The scientific community complained of declining federal commitment, but statistics showed otherwise: in 1979 the National Science Board reported only a small decline in federal money (in real dollars) compared with the late 1960s, years when federal research funds supported spectacular space programs and military research for the Vietnam war.

The electronics industry was a chief beneficiary of well-funded research, and during the 1960s and 1970s various sectors of the economy underwent a computer revolution. Everything from police records to life-support systems in hospitals to office typewriters were plugged into computers. File cabinets eased towards obsolescence, while "information managers" and "word processors" replaced old-fashioned bureaucrats and secretaries.

The American space program—which depended upon the interrelationship of university research, government funding, and industrial production—was also a child of the new technetronic age. Shortly after the Soviet Union launched its first Sputnik satellite in 1957, Congress created the National Aeronautics and Space Administration (NASA), and in 1961 President Kennedy committed the nation to landing a man on the moon by 1970. The space program, often compared to the Manhattan Project, which developed the atomic bomb during World War II, organized scientific and technical bureaucracies into a crash effort to surpass the Soviet Union in space exploration.

Critics of the program's expense called it a "moon-doggle" and compared it to ancient Egypt's pyramids—a feat of much grandeur but little practicality. To counter such charges NASA projected a highly utilitarian image, stressing the spin-offs of space research for civilians, such as heart pacemakers and miniature electronic components. NASA officials also liked to compare their feats to the solo fight of Charles Lindbergh in 1927. (Lindbergh celebrated his achievement as a union of man and machine in a book entitled *We*; the original astronauts issued a ghost-written account of their adventures called *We Seven*.) But Lindy's flight rested largely upon private discoveries and a few financial backers; the Mercury and Apollo programs, products of government-managed technology, relied upon thousands of people in aerospace industries, "operation teams," and recovery forces. Even the small Mercury program required nearly 200 managers.

Despite its wide publicity, enormous pool of employees, and spectacular technological achievements, the space program seldom attracted broad popular enthusiasm. After the much-celebrated moon walks, NASA's other activities attracted little attention, until in the summer of 1979 an old space station—Skylab—came crashing down to earth. But the importance of NASA's programs continued to grow. Satellites brought a quiet revolution in international communications, increasing America's worldwide dominance over radio and television transmission. And joining satellite technology with weapons research spurred an arms race in space, a race characterized by bizarre, deadly instruments and enormous costs. When the space shuttle Columbia finally lifted off in 1981, the Pentagon was firmly entrenched in the space program.

The Great Business Boom

During the 1960s, the huge infusion of government money into the economy, together with a rising level of consumer spending, brought rapid business expansion and consolidation. Growth seemed to be the key to economic survival, and the fastest way to expand was to merge with or purchase other firms. In the banner year of 1968, large corporations acquired ten times greater assets than the amount that had changed hands in 1960. This growth of huge enterprises further centralized economic power. By the late 1960s the two hundred largest United States companies controlled 58 percent of all manufacturing assets in the nation.

New companies most often were not purchased by competitors in the same field but were absorbed by business empires that managed a wide variety of unrelated industries. Financial daredevils could no longer legally corner the market in any one product (horizontal monopoly) or establish control over all the steps of production in the manufacture of any one item (vertical monopoly). Modern entrepreneurs, however, pioneered conglomerates, businesses that minimized overall risk by diversifying holdings. Gulf and Western and Transamerica Corporation, two of the wonder children of the 1960s, acquired companies as fast as they could find them; they owned Hollywood studios, auto-parts distributorships, land-development corporations, insurance companies, and sports arenas.

The secret of conglomerate growth lay in the acquisition of investment institutions, such as insurance companies. These businesses dealt in capital rather than in goods and could funnel a steady stream of investment money into the conglomerate's coffers. With one subsidiary borrowing from another, conglomerates could internally finance their expansion. International Telephone and Telegraph (ITT), in an out-of-court antitrust settlement in 1971, was willing to sell two of its well-known properties, Levitt Construction and Avis Rent-A-Car, in return for government permission to purchase Hartford Fire Insurance Company. Later investigations suggested a link between

Robert Peterson.

Auto Row. Every city had its own automobile row, but rising gasoline prices and foreign competition meant lagging sales for Detroit's gas guzzlers.

the Justice Department's willingness to settle with ITT and the company's contributions to the Nixon reelection campaign.

Under pressure to grow rapidly, some businesses fell into shady dealings and unsound financial practices. The decade was spiced with the kinds of abuses associated with periods of full-throttle expansion: bribed officials, defective products, defrauded consumers, and ineffective government regulations. But Americans of the 1960s did little on a small scale, and, true to form, one of the most daring frauds of all time racked the business world. A relatively new California insurance company, Equity Funding Corporation, built a phenomenal growth record on the basis of more than $2 billion worth of phony insurance policies and more than $120 million in nonexistent assets. Caught up in the Southern California boom mentality, the company's officials systematically fabricated two thirds of the firm's policies, sending its insurance in force soaring from $54 million in 1967 to $615 billion just five years later. Government auditors never caught the fraud because they did not check the computers; an associate finally exposed the scheme in 1973. The Equity Funding scandal, probably the biggest computer crime ever, was a "simple perversion of a simple computer system," one data processor at Equity Funding later commented. The *Wall Street Journal* headlined the revelations with a warning:

250

"Crooks and Computers Are an Effective Team." By the 1980s, computer-assisted fraud had become a major problem of corporate life.

As American enterprise expanded at home, it also moved into other lands at a pace that astonished and alarmed many foreigners. A variety of motives led American business to establish operations in foreign lands: cheaper labor, lower interest rates, favorable tax laws, proximity to new markets and raw materials. Whatever the precise constellation of motives in particular cases, the net result was an unparalleled outflow of American investment dollars in the 1960s. IBM, for example, provided 70 percent of all computers in the noncommunist world and maintained research labs in most of the developed nations; Standard Oil of New Jersey drilled and distributed oil throughout the globe; Pepsi-Cola was a universal refreshment, admitted even into Russia.

The financial power of these multinational companies often exceeded that of the nation in which they operated. One official for the American Agency for International Development reported in the late 1960s that if the gross national products of nations were ranked with the gross annual sales of corporations, half of the top hundred would be corporations and two thirds of these would be American-based. Devaluation of the dollar in 1971 slowed the flight of American enterprise abroad, and other multinational competitors—especially Japanese companies—began to challenge Americans, but problems between American firms with a global reach and smaller nations persisted.

Rapid business growth and new technological discoveries changed the way Americans lived. Natural materials, such as wood, wool, cotton, and natural rubber gave way to man-made substitutes—plastics, acrylic fibers, and synthetic rubber. In 1968 the quantity of synthetic fibers surpassed the output of natural fibers, and doubleknit cloth soon revolutionized both the men's and women's clothing industries. Middle-class Americans could be distinguished anywhere in the world by the doubleknits they wore.

All kinds of new products flooded the marketplace. During the 1960s drug and grocery stores stocked six thousand new products every year; the rate for the introduction of new items nearly doubled during the 1970s. More than half the items stocked by supermarkets in the 1970s did not even exist in 1960, and nearly half of the products available in 1960 had been withdrawn from the marketplace a decade later. Stiff competition for the buyer's dollar often made packaging and advertising more important than a product's content. Critics of the highly competitive breakfast-food industry, for example, claimed that the quality of some products was so low that the flashy packages had more nutritional value than the overprocessed grain inside. Even cereals with solid nutritional content often contained excessive amounts of sugar. The variety of new products grew so rapidly that finding an unused brand name could be a problem. Some large companies set their computers to work providing printouts of letter combinations that sounded attractive—Exxon and Pringles were just two of the results.

Entrepreneurs devised new methods to market these products. Throughout the 1960s, independently owned, locally operated shops found their customers turning to large chain or franchise operations that offered greater volume at lower prices. What McDonald's did for hamburgers, Holiday Inn did for travel, K-Mart for retailing, and 7-11 stores for neighborhood groceries. Every American city of any size had a "miracle mile" or a "strip" nearly identical to that of every other: a string of discount houses, supermarkets, and fast-food chains (Kentucky Fried Chicken, Arby's Roast Beef, and half a dozen hamburger palaces). Shopping became easier when the Bank of America introduced BankAmericard (renamed Visa). This new kind of credit card, quickly imitated by New York banks, tempted consumers to spend and borrow more, channeled large amounts of consumer purchasing through a few large banks, and threatened to make currency nearly obsolete.

For some companies the uncertainties of the 1970s ended the great business boom. Giants, such as the Penn Central railroad, Franklin National Bank, and W.T. Grant slid into bankruptcy. One of America's largest employers, Chryster, survived, but only with the aid of federally guaranteed loans. Bethlehem Steel posted large deficits, and U.S. Steel announced the closing of sixteen plants in thirteen cities, signaling the fact that the American steel industry, which had let its domestic plants run down while investing in new facilities abroad, was no longer competitive in the world market.

But if many of the old industrial-age companies faired poorly, the technetronic age brought boom in other sectors. Demand accelerated for consultants of all sorts; cable television became a major industry; industrial-aircraft manufacture flourished; and sporting-goods and leisure companies chalked up large gains. (In 1979 American joggers spent $400 million on running shoes and warm-up suits.) Perfection of the so-called silicon chip, a tiny microprocessor that for $10 could do the work of a $100,000 computer, revolutionized electronics, opening the way for new products, such as computerized cash registers and video games. With the increase in women working outside the home, fast-food chains also continued their growth. McDonald's, always the frontrunner, erected four thousand new outlets during the 1970s.

As inflation pushed interest rates well into two-digit numbers, the world of finance began to experience a revolution. The stock market languished during the 1970s, and many brokers diversified their services so that people could easily put their money in a variety of investments. Americans in all walks of life began speculating in "futures" or in gold and silver; international bullion prices rose more than 1000 percent during the decade. Inflation and economic uncertainty called into question the steady investment practices of the past and made the game of high finance much more complex and variable.

Energy and Ecology

Galloping growth came at the expense of the environment. To achieve a high living standard, Americans used the country's water, air, minerals, and timber

Price Increases for Oil, Gas, and Coal
1965 to 1978

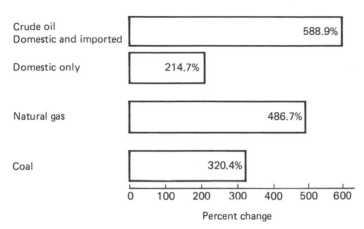

Crude oil Domestic and imported	588.9%
Domestic only	214.7%
Natural gas	486.7%
Coal	320.4%

0   100   200   300   400   500   600

Percent change

DOE Monthly Review, API Basic Petroleum Data Book, and EEI Statistical Yearbook of the Electrical Utility Industry.

Soaring energy costs helped to fuel inflation, forced many poor people to choose between fuel and food, and provoked fierce debates over the proper course for public policymakers.

as if they were unlimited, and they purchased more and more resources from foreign lands. In 1970, one expert calculated, Americans constituted less than 6 percent of the human race but used 40 percent of the resources consumed worldwide each year and produced 50 percent of the physical pollution.

Cheap energy was one basic ingredient in America's rapid industrial growth, and its use multiplied at an astonishing rate. Gasoline consumption rose from one billion barrels in 1950 to two-and-a-quarter billion barrels in 1971; production of electricity increased 500 percent between 1950 and 1971. By 1979 the United States was using 18.4 million barrels of oil a day, of which 8.2 billion were imported; Americans were consuming nearly 30 percent of all the oil produced in the world.

New products were partly to blame. Aluminum, for example, an excellent substitute for steel and tin in certain cases, was dubbed "congealed electricity" because of the enormous amount of energy required to produce it. Americans processed twenty times more aluminum in 1971 than they had before World War II, and each year production figures climbed higher. Aluminum beer cans, aluminum pipe, aluminum siding, all treasured for their light weight and noncorrosiveness, contributed to the pressure on the environment.

Where would Americans find the energy required to fuel their economy in the future? The question became more urgent after the Organization of Petroleum Exporting Countries embargoed oil in 1973 and sent prices skyrocketing. For the rest of the decade, OPEC price increases and Middle East turmoil, such as the Iranian revolution in 1979, made it clear that the days of

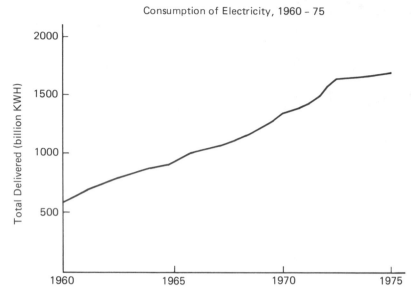

Consumption of Electricity, 1960 – 75

Federal Energy Administration.

The rising demand for electricity reflected America's economic expansion during the 1960s and early 1970s. This same demand also suggested how quickly nonrenewable sources of energy—such as the coal and oil used to produce electricity—were being depleted.

cheap energy were over. In January 1971 the average price of a barrel of OPEC oil was $1.80; by the end of the 1970s it was $20.00 and going up.

Advocates of unrestricted domestic development of energy sources had some answers. Increased strip mining and relaxation of environmental regulations would enhance the nation's ability to use its enormous coal deposits. Accelerated oil drilling in offshore beds would bring new supplies hitherto blocked by environmental safeguards. Development of atomic-power plants and strip mining for uranium fuel would increase America's energy self-sufficiency. And production of "synfuels," liquid fuels made through a high-technology process from deposits of coal and oil shale, might also make effective use of native resources. These full-throttle measures were endorsed in the Republican party platform of 1980 and by the Reagan administration.

Environmental groups questioned many of these plans, and their organized strength grew steadily throughout the 1970s. In April 1970 environmentalists held Earth Day, a carnival extravaganza of booths and speakers designed to spawn the same kind of nationwide concern that civil-rights and antiwar causes had generated during the 1960s. Subsequently, scientists, such as Barry Commoner, author of *The Closing Circle,* became popular on the college lecture circuit. Commoner warned that damage beyond a certain point to ecological systems was irreversible, and that we were rapidly approaching, if we had not already reached, that critical moment. The obsession with careless material growth, he argued, had strained the environment to the breaking point. Commoner and others popularized the word *ecology,* the natural balance necessary to sustain life on this planet, and tried to put distance between the new environmental movement and the "Don't Be a Litterbug!" and "beautification" campaigns of the past. By the 1980s, supporters of the movement claimed, environmentalism involved not simply the quality of life but the continuation of life.

Still, environmentalists could show few stunning victories. In the early 1970s, halting construction of the Alaska pipeline became a *cause celebre* among environmentalists, who claimed that an oil pipeline would upset the ecology of the frozen tundra and adversely affect plants and animals. For several years groups such as the Sierra Club and the Friends of the Earth successfully blocked the pipeline, but the energy crisis of 1973, produced by the boycott of the United States by Middle Eastern oil suppliers, brought rapid congressional approval for construction. The Alaska pipeline, together with relaxation of various environmental regulations, showed how quickly many Americans might dismiss ecological considerations when faced with energy shortages. Meanwhile, business pressure groups and political conservatives tried to make environmentalism a dirty word. Affluent environmentalists, it

Robert Peterson.

Chemical Dump. Haphardly stored toxic chemicals such as these near downtown Seattle constituted a new potentially lethal environment hazard.

was charged, opposed the kind of economic development that would allow middle-class Americans to maintain their present living standard and poorer citizens to improve their lives.

Environmentalists and industrialists continually clashed over the issue of pollution. The rising material standards that Americans thought would enhance their comfort bore price tags—brownish skies, strangely colored rivers, dying lakes, aggravated respiratory problems, and a sharply rising cancer rate. Urban areas suffered most visibly in the 1960s; cities, such as Los Angeles, New York, and Gary, Indiana, became health hazards. Breathing New York's air for a day, one study reported, was the equivalent of smoking four packs of cigarettes. Throughout the nation, once sparkling trout streams turned into sickly trickles of industrial waste. Strip mining, which had doubled during the 1960s, raised the specter of permanent destruction of land.

Industrialists, of course, did not favor dead lakes, wasted land, toxic subsoil, and unhealthy air. But charged with the duty of running their companies at a profit, they could not afford to take the long-range view of many environmentalists. Most wished to postpone or to compromise environmental concern in order to keep their businesses profitable, and they often had the support of their workers and anyone else dependent upon their products. Environmentalists, it was charged, had simply lost their nerve; it was impossible to live in a risk-free society. In addition to stressing the need for continued economic growth, industrialists and their supporters emphasized two other points: stringent regulations would put an even greater stress on America's apparently dwindling energy reserves by making it difficult to use high-pollution fuels, such as coal, and the cost of meeting tough environmental standards would make American industry uncompetitive with foreign enterprises.

Trying to steer a course between environmental hazards and tolerable costs was the government's Environmental Protection Agency. Established in 1970, it became the government's largest regulatory body, employing 10,000 people and striving to enforce the barrage of new statutes enacted by Congress. The new environmental legislation of the 1970s aimed at regulating the use of pesticides, protecting endangered species, insuring occupational safety, controlling strip-mining practices, and establishing maximum levels of emission of certain chemical and bacteriological pollutants into the air and water. Predictably, the EPA came under sharp attack from both industrialists and environmentalists: industry charged it with obstructionism; environmentalists assailed its laxity. But the EPA's efforts did improve safety in the work place, dissipated much of the urban smog of the 1960s, and cleaned up at least the surface of many of the nation's waterways.

With visible pollutants and some gross violations of nature under control by the late 1970s, even graver problems emerged. The higher smokestacks that had helped eliminate smog merely elevated pollutants, spread them over wider areas, and altered their chemical composition. The resultant acid rain, which threatened cropland throughout the country, constituted a less visible but more serious hazard than smog. Safe disposal of toxic wastes presented another significant problem. In the early 1980s people began to discover that many industries had for years haphazardly dumped toxic chemical wastes. These substances, some of which were capable of promoting genetic defects and cancer, sometimes even became landfill for housing projects, as was the case at Love Canal in New York. Critics warned that if there were not stronger safeguards against chemical wastes and other toxic pollutants, cancer might become the epidemic disease of the future. Unlike the pollution problems of the past, those of the 1980s tended to be invisible; toxic effects were more long-term and were not immediately apparent. Any increased rate in environmentally caused cancer, for example, might take twenty years to detect. The 1970s may have been an "environmental decade" of new concern and legislation, yet the environmental problems of the 1980s seemed even more severe than previous ones.

Toward the end of the 1970s, environmental groups increasingly directed their primary attention to the issue of nuclear power. Ralph Nader and others argued that atomic-power plants presented unacceptable risks, and a New England group, the Clamshell Alliance, attempted direct action to halt construction of an atomic facility at Seabrook, New Hampshire. In 1978 the "antinuke" movement received a boost from the popularity of a film about a nuclear melt-down—*The China Syndrome*. Just as the power industry launched barbs at the implausibility of the movie, a real-life accident in the spring of 1979 raised fears about nuclear energy to new heights.

A malfunction in the nuclear reactor at Three Mile Island, near Harrisburg, Pennsylvania, touched off a near disaster. Residents living near the facility evacuated their homes, and the confusion and conflicting reports surrounding the several days of crisis ballooned public doubts about technicians' abilities to handle this deadly new technology. According to power-company supporters, the Three Mile Island accident proved that the ultimate disaster of melt-down could be avoided and that even a fairly serious accident could result in no loss of life. Critics, however, pointed out the lack of established safety procedures revealed by the accident, highlighted the escape of radiation into the surrounding atmosphere and water, and calculated the huge costs of clean-up. The official reports of a special presidential commission and of the Nuclear Regulatory Commission came down hard on the power industry. The NRC's investigation concluded that without "fundamental changes" in the nuclear industry "similar accidents—perhaps with the potentially serious consequences that were avoided at Three Mile Island—are likely to recur." The expenses of new designs, more elaborate safety procedures, and possibly even future damage suits exploded the myth that nuclear energy would be cheap. With seventy-two atomic plants in operation and another ninety-one in various stages of construction in 1980, the United States was not likely to abandon the nuclear alternative. But Three Mile Island did deliver a blow to utility companies' credibility and made an all-out rush to a nuclear future unlikely.

By the early 1980s most Americans agreed that they should meet the energy crisis with some sort of common action. But what? Environmentalists favored federally assisted crash programs to encourage decentralized production of power through solar, geothermal, or wind-generated systems. Ralph Nader, Barry Commoner, and Tom Hayden all pressed the argument that the energy debate, in fact, involved fundamental issues of economic control: it pitted decentralized, "democratic" energy sources against those that the utility and oil companies could continue to monopolize and run from a centralized facility. Supporters of the power industry, however, considered solar, geothermal, and wind power to be marginal sources at best, unable to satisfy America's voracious appetite for energy. They urged Washington to cut the red tape of environmental regulations and open some long-delayed offshore oil developments, and they continued to tout coal, synfuels, and atomic power.

One thing seemed clear: the concentration on energy production needed to be matched by an emphasis on energy conservation. Carter advised conservation, utility companies "advertised" for it, and the American people responded to higher prices by cutting their consumption of crude oil from 7.15 million barrels in 1979 to 6.8 million in 1980. But the precarious state of the national economy in the early 1980s militated against any serious, coordinated effort by government to dramatically change Americans' buying habits or life styles.

Land and Real-Estate Hustlers

A great land boom that began in the mid-1960s added to environmentalists' concerns. Huge land-development corporations began subdividing tracts at an alarming rate, focusing their efforts on the "sunbelt states" of Florida, California, New Mexico, and Arizona but also operating in northern recreational states, such as Colorado and Maine. The National Association of Home Builders estimated that Americans built ninety thousand *second* homes in 1971, although the *overall* number of homes constructed that year was lower than it had been a decade earlier. But these fishing huts, mountain cabins, seaside bungalows, and retirement villas represented only a fragment of the land that had been cut into parcels and put up for sale as potential homesites; 97 percent remained close to its original state, with no improvements or structures. In the late 1960s, it seemed, Americans just wanted to own a piece of land, whether they intended to build on it immediately or not.

Why this obsession with land buying? To begin with, the 1960s provided a perfect climate for a land boom. The new affluence brought second homes within the reach of millions; faster automobiles and new interstate highways made distant vacation homes practical; increased leisure time and earlier retirement raised the demand for recreation. And in a decade of fast economic growth it was easy to appeal to people's spirit of adventure, to convince them that they could afford the monthly payments and that land was always a good investment. One company's sales pitch asked, "Do you know any big rich man who doesn't own real estate?...Wouldn't it be wise to buy land somewhere—anywhere—before prices get out of reach?" Land hustlers rolled out (and usually overstated) forecasts of population growth and made land ownership seem like a vanishing luxury.

As soon as businessmen discovered how easily they could sell land, "development" corporations sprang up everywhere. Some created attractive planned communities with good sanitary facilities, nearby employment opportunities, and luxurious recreation areas. But too many others simply bought large tracts of cheap land and resold it in expensive lot-sized packages. A development company in Florida, for example, purchased some swampy land for $180 an acre and quickly resold it for $640 an acre. To make this enormous profit, the company did not drain the land, build roads, plan sanitation facilities, or construct major buildings. It merely hired a high-pressure sales force, ran advertisements in newspapers around the country, and gave the supposed community a fancy name. Word of such profits turned subdividing into a national craze, and most conglomerate enterprises quickly created land-development subsidiaries. By the early 1970s developers in California were buying fifty thousand to one hundred thousand acres a year; subdivided land near Albuquerque, New Mexico was slated to hold a population four times the size of Baltimore; and plots for sale in Colorado would have increased the state's population five times over. In North Carolina, a real-estate salesman and a former lawyer were charged with mail fraud after allegedly trying to sell over 60,000 acres of the Great Smoky Mountain National Park.

Bill Wunsch, The Denver Post.

Colorado Land. An undeveloped development in Colorado.

Table 1   Decline of the Industrial Northeast, Rise of the Sunbelt*

Old Industrial Centers	1970	1980	% Change
New York	9,897,000	9,060,000	−8%
Chicago	6,975,000	7,032,000	+1
Philadelphia	4,824,000	4,696,000	−3
Detroit	4,200,000	4,342,000	+3
Boston	3,849,000	3,848,000	—
Pittsburgh	2,401,000	2,261,000	−6
Cleveland	2,064,000	1,893,000	−8
Buffalo	1,349,000	1,240,000	−8

Rise of Sunbelt			
Dallas-Fort Worth	2,318,000	2,961,000	+28%
Houston	1,985,000	2,887,000	+45
Atlanta	1,390,000	2,004,000	+44
San Diego	1,358,000	1,858,000	+37
Miami	1,268,000	1,574,000	+24
Tampa-St. Petersburg	1,013,000	1,552,000	+53
Phoenix	971,000	1,505,000	+55
Fort Lauderdale-Hollywood, Fla.	620,000	1,005,000	+62

*In response to these demographic trends, public policymakers debated their proper course of action. In 1980 a special presidential commission recommended that the national government allow demographic trends to run their course and that it takes no dramatic action to bail out older industrial centers.

Source: U.S. Census Bureau.

Sometime during the 1970s the land boom abruptly changed location. It moved, in fact, to what most demographers of the 1960s would have considered the least likely place of all—the supposedly decaying central city. The 1970s bred near perfect conditions for a reversal in urban fortunes. Rising gas prices from 1973 on mounted a frontal assault on commuting; the large baby-boom generation strained on the housing market; widespread cultural nostalgia helped generate interest in the renovation of old houses; a temporary decline in crime rate boosted the image of cities. New pollution standards made cities bearable again, and cities also benefited from the demise of some dirty, industrial-age jobs and the rise of clean, service occupations. By 1980 the largest single employer in "steel city"—Pittsburgh—was not U.S. Steel but the University of Pittsburgh. Although New York City and Cleveland hit the headlines for walking the tightrope of bankruptcy in the 1970s, many more urban centers found that federal funds temporarily gave them a surplus. In 1969 few cities received more than 10 percent of their general revenue in the form of federal money; by 1980 many cities received over 50 percent in federal funds.

Such conditions produced a significant urban revival in an estimated 70 percent of American cities. Developers once devoted to mapping out suburban shopping centers began selling designs for urban malls. In "rescued" neighborhoods, renovators attacked any edifice with a brick facade still standing, and prices shot up as speculators quickly acquired an interest in promoting historical preservation. Condominiums became the latest fad for a generation of busy folks who wanted the advantages of home ownership without the disadvantages of single-home upkeep.

This "gentrification"—the return of the gentry class to the inner city—had its flip side. Renewal was, after all, highly selective. "Old towns" of new-old cobblestone streets sprouted where architecture was interesting and sound. But the rise in rents drove the poor out of the best of their neighborhoods and left them in the worst. And where did those in need of cheap housing go? Moving to a more run-down neighborhood only increased the general demand for housing and mercilessly drove up prices for everyone. Speculators began to realize that even nonrenovated areas experienced a boom in prices and brought easy profits. Some evidence suggested that the cheaply constructed suburban housing of the previous two decades might become the slums of the future. For the poor, then, the inner-city renewal of the 1970s was something to oppose and organize against. It brought not only rising prices but the physical disruption and dispersion of older communities. But most city officials were slow to grapple with the adverse results of "gentrification"; they were delighted by the new activity, and they kept busy joining public and private capital in new development projects.

An Out-Sized Culture

The Publishing Industry

The book-publishing industry, once the comfortable preserve of gentlemen-publishers and small booksellers, underwent considerable growth and change after 1960. By the mid-1970s, the number of bookstores in the United States had surpassed, for the first time since the early days of the cinema, the number of movie theaters, and the yearly revenues of the publishing industry outstripped those of Hollywood. Americans bought twice as many books each year as movie tickets. Although small bookstores still held their fascination, especially for people who liked to browse, most Americans shopped in streamlined book supermarkets. Large-scale operations, such as the spectacularly successful B. Dalton chain, increasingly dominated sales figures. Using their own computerized systems, book supermarkets stocked relatively few titles, primarily mass-market paperbacks and hardbacks from the bestseller lists, and aimed for a brisk, steady turnover. In fact, a large order from B. Dalton could ensure a book's place on the bestseller list. Such a sales system threatened the survival of many small bookstores and made it more difficult for readers to find shops willing to stock, or even order, volumes that lacked mass appeal.

Many would-be authors complained that a similar trend toward concentration in the publishing industry limited opportunities for new literary talents, especially younger novelists. As a consequence of the general consolidation of American business, most American publishers became subsidiaries of large corporations, often "communications groups" that included newspapers, electronic media, and records. The results, according to critics, were not always pleasant. First, publishing executives were anxious to show their superiors in the corporate hierarchy that books, like other products, could generate sizable profits. The easiest way to do this, of course, was to publish only those volumes likely to find a mass readership and to avoid more esoteric titles. Critics, such as Noam Chomsky, warned that the consolidation of the publishing industry raised the threat of a powerful new censorship of unorthodox styles and ideas.

A fierce critic of American foreign policy, Chomsky charged that a subsidiary of Warner Communications suppressed one of his studies because corporate executives considered the book unpatriotic. Although Warners fulfilled their commitment to print the book, the conglomerate failed to promote or even distribute it. Ultimately, it was republished and distributed by a small publishing cooperative in Boston. The Chomsky-Warners affair defied simple analysis. Some observers ridiculed the suggestion that Chomsky had been censored. His book, after all, had never been the subject of government pressure, and it *had* been published—twice—and eventually marketed. Yet the incident remained troubling. In an age of relatively inexpensive photo-duplication techniques, publication of a book was often a minor obstacle. In an age of mass-communications networks, distribution and promotion were more crucial. If authors wished to publish their own books or to work with smaller presses, they found themselves at a great disadvantage in reaching a wide audience. Was the denial of access to the channels of mass distribution a new form of corporate censorship that could impede the flow of dissenting views?

With the trend toward "McDonaldization" in publishing, authors discovered that their ability to market their works might be more important than their ability to write them. Some publishers conceded that, before making a final commitment to publish a book, they considered the author's potential charm on television talk shows. The publisher of the best-selling *Your Erroneous Zones* recalled that he had been more enthusiastic about the television personality of the author, Dr. Wayne Dyer, than about his book. The tie-in between book publishing and the electronic media grew even closer as the communications groups began to "package" expensive media products. The ultimate in commercialized "art" might span the entire communications spectrum: a TV mini-series for the domestic market; a theatrical movie for distribution overseas; a record album of the sound track; and a mass-market paperback for drugstore racks and large bookstore chains.

Many veterans of the literary establishment condemned such trends.

Publishing, they conceded, had never been a purely philanthropic enterprise, but never had it been so crassly commercial. The metamorphosis of the highly prestigious National Book Awards—prizes selected by prominent literary critics and by celebrated authors—into the American Book Awards—which were to be chosen by committees that included mass-market publishers and individuals from the bookstore chains—symbolized the new developments. A number of prominent authors, including Norman Mailer and Philip Roth, declared that they would have nothing to do with the new awards, and some of the old-line publishers denounced them as an obvious attempt to mimic the Emmy and Oscar awards of television and motion pictures.

Similar trends toward consolidation and commercialization affected American journalism. Continuing a pattern that had been evident for more than half a century, the American newspaper business became increasingly concentrated. By the 1980s only readers in the largest cities could turn to competing daily papers. Although financial pressures forced some papers to fold, including the widely acclaimed *Chicago Daily News,* many more, especially in smaller cities, became the property of large newspaper chains. For those who could afford the new computerized technology, journalism was more profitable than ever. Although not all chains imposed a single editorial policy upon their papers, there could be no doubt that fewer and fewer hands wielded the power of the press. Because of such concentration, critics of the media complained, journalists became too complacent; lacking competition, they also lacked incentive to dig out material on local affairs. Reluctance to probe into the dark corners of municipal life, it was further charged, reflected the close, interlocking relationships between newspapers and powerful corporate interests.

Critics of the media also complained that the press showed too much concern with "celebrity journalism." Recognizing that most Americans relied upon network television's evening news programs as their primary source of information, afternoon newspapers increasingly emphasized "soft" features on popular culture, living styles, and prominent personalities. Readers in New York City were treated to the most spectacular example of this change when Australian news magnate, Rupert Murdoch, purchased the staid *New York Post* and converted it into an updated version of the old tabloids of the 1920s. Celebrity journalism also spawned "personality magazines," including the very successful *People.* Devoted almost entirely to the rise and fall of celebrities and distributed only at magazine counters and on supermarket racks, *People* was Time, Incorporated's answer to the *National Enquirer* and the *Midnight Globe.* The New York Times Corporation soon responded with a clone of *People* entitled *US.* The trend toward celebrity journalism reached its logical conclusion when the media began to cover its own celebrities—in a publication appropriately entitled *Media People.*

Although the catch phrases "consolidation" and "celebrification" accurately summarized the dominant trends in publishing in the 1960s and 1970s, there were other forces at work. Despite the growth of publishing conglomer-ates, smaller houses continued to survive on the fringes of the industry. Many publishers, regardless of size, remained committed to bringing out what they considered works of quality, even if they did not seem to be candidates for the best seller lists or for TV mini-series. Meanwhile, the fragmentation of the old cold-war consensus was reflected in the magazine-publishing business. Many of the magazines that had sought a "general" readership—such as *Look,* the *Saturday Evening Post, Life,* and *Harpers*—either folded or underwent drastic overhauls. More specialized journals, such as the *National Review* on the political right and *The Nation* on the left—gained in circulation and prestige. Even in the newspaper business, diversity survived. Most of the "underground" papers of the 1960s, including the famous *Berkeley Barb,* ultimately failed, but alternative journalism survived in the form of community-based newspapers. The going was always rough for these publications, but many journalists, especially younger ones who could not find other jobs in a glutted market, were willing to make the sacrifices. Finally, the growing amount of criticism directed at the publishing industry by publications such as the *Columbia Journalism Review* offered a healthy contrast with the smug complacency that had prevailed during the cold-war era.

The Motion-Picture Industry

Significant changes affected the motion-picture industry as well as the publish-ing industry during the 1960s and 1970s. For more than four decades film making and the huge Hollywood studios had been synonymous. Using their sprawling back lots and deploying vast armies of contract players and stars, the major studios steadily nourished the dreams of millions of moviegoers. Young men dueled alongside Errol Flynn or Clark Gable, and women floated through the glamorous world of Barbara Stanwyck or Lana Turner. But dur-ing the 1960s the giant studios came upon bad days. Challenged by television and victimized by urban decay, which frightened many people away from the old downtown movie palaces, Hollywood's film moguls watched box office receipts decline steadily. During the early 1960s some producers tried to reverse the slide by making long-running, multimillion-dollar extravaganzas that dwarfed the less costly fare on television. A few of these films, such as *Spartacus,* made money and displayed some cinematic style, but most were financial and artistic disasters. Seeking to reduce production costs and to bring new realism to the screen, many film makers abandoned the Hollywood sets completely and shot entirely on location, often outside the United States. At the same time, many of the old stars either died or retired; others, such as Rock Hudson and Elizabeth Taylor, suddenly discovered that their names alone no longer guaranteed a film's financial success.

Many of the successful films of the 1960s and early 1970s appealed to younger viewers, particularly to college-educated people. Stanley Kubrick—with the aid of Peter Sellers—lampooned the insanity of nuclear diplomacy in *Dr. Strangelove.* He subsequently explored the mystical science fiction of Arthur C. Clarke in *2001: A Space Odyssey* and examined the problems of violence and behavior modification in *A Clockwork Orange.* In one of the most surprising hits, *Easy Rider,* Peter Fonda and Dennis Hopper updated the theme of the open road. The story of two hippies who used a drug sale to finance a motorcycle trip across the Southwest to New Orleans, *Easy Rider* interwove all the themes of the new American cinema: social criticism, sex, and violence. Spokespersons for more traditional Hollywood films—in which stars stayed out of bed until they were married and then stayed discreetly covered—denounced the decline of old standards. But film makers recognized that only a handful of family pictures attracted as many viewers as the racier and more violent products. Producers rushed to sign new, young directorial "talents" and tried to pack more gore and naked flesh into their movies. Although some tastelessly exploited violence and sex, serious film makers also benefited from the lifting of old taboos.

By the early 1970s most producers and directors had abandoned general-audience films in favor of making special movies for special audiences. The need for more careful "targeting" of audiences became crucial as motion pictures lost their mass popular audience of the 1930s and 1940s to old age and to television. In a survey taken in 1974, only 9 percent of the respondents ranked movies as their favorite pastime. No longer able to rely upon a steady movie-going clientele, both the big studios and the small distributors constantly tried to find unique films that could lure people back into the theaters. Struggling to summarize Hollywood trends of the early 1970s, one critic described the motion-picture industry as being in a state of "creative anarchy."

Although not all critics agreed that the creativity lasted into the 1980s, much of the anarchy certainly did. Once, major studios could hand-stamp their products—every regular moviegoer could distinguish a Warner Brothers film from a Paramount production—and rely upon the drawing power of their stars. By the 1980s individual directors, not studios or stars, seemed to have emerged as the crucial element in American films. Many of the much-heralded young directors of the early 1970s, such as Dennis Hopper of *Easy Rider,* could not sustain their initial successes. By the beginning of the 1980s the most talked-about directors were even younger "young talents": Francis Ford Coppola, whose personal travails during the making of *Apocalypse Now* nearly overshadowed the controversial film itself; Steven Spielberg, who broke all of Hollywood's old box-office records with *Jaws;* and George Lucas, whose *Star Wars* shattered *Jaws'* box-office take and ultimately surpassed $400 million in gross revenues.

The popularity of traditional film genres seemed even more volatile than the reputations of directors. During the 1970s, the western, once Hollywood's most reliable moneymaker, all but disappeared. Old age had forced John Ford to quit making westerns in the 1960s, and cancer finally halted his favorite star, John Wayne, in the 1970s. (Ironically, in his last film, *The Shootist,* Wayne played an old gunfighter stricken with cancer.) Despite some attempts to revive musicals, this genre did no better in the late 1970s than it had in the previous decade. The Disney studios found that the G-rated family picture was not a sure winner any longer. For their annual holiday release of 1979-1980 the Disney people chose their first PG-rated film, *The Black Hole.* Even that old reliable, the B picture, appeared to be dying out, a victim of the decline of the drive-in-movie culture and the disappearance of smaller theaters.

Although some critics decried the baneful effects of the emphasis on giant blockbusters, such as *Star Wars,* a trend necessitated by the rising costs of marketing a film, American film culture was in many ways stronger in the 1980s than it had ever been before. Increased popular attention to the styles and themes of individual directors, for example, reflected the popularization of more sophisticated styles of film criticism. During the 1970s most urban areas began to support "retrospective houses "—commercial theaters that specialized in previously released classics—and theaters that emphasized foreign movies and the type of thoughtful films once dismissed as noncommercial "art" movies. And even as Hollywood's revenues declined in relation to those of television (or even the record and book-publishing industries), more Americans were coming to take the motion picture itself more seriously. The study of film, both Hollywood's products and documentary works, became a part of most university and many high-school curriculums during the 1970s. Journals devoted to film criticism, film theory, and film history proliferated as more and more people came to appreciate the subtle connection between the world of the movies and the world of Americans themselves.

Sports

Sports also reflected the expansive trends in American life. There were more fans, more teams, and more television coverage. At the beginning of the 1960s big-league baseball still dominated the sports scene, and the two major leagues expanded into new cities during the 1960s and 1970s. But despite its growth, the national pastime lost ground to other spectator sports, particularly to the faster-moving, more violent games of football, basketball (a noncontact sport only in theory), and ice hockey. Pro football's much ballyhooed Super Bowl replaced baseball's World Series as sports' most talked-about annual attraction. Cities competed vigorously for almost any type of professional franchise; lucrative television contracts and generous tax write-offs made the possession of a team even more alluring.

Always seeking new forms of competition to sell, promoters aggressively marketed golf tournaments (women's as well as men's), imported soccer, tried (unsuccessfully) team competition in tennis, and even formed "major leagues" for slow-pitch softball and volleyball. Similarly, the growing popularity of women's sports produced a women's professional basketball league, a women's professional football league, and increased visibility for women's tennis and golf. Predictions that the energy shortage was ending America's love affair with the automobile did not cool sports fans' ardor for all types of racing. The Indianapolis 500 rivaled the Super Bowl as sports' biggest one-day event, and Jimmy Carter's favorite spectator sport, stock-car racing, retained its great popularity in the South.

Even professional boxing, once considered on the ropes because of the taint of fixed matches and the declining supply of "hungry" fighters, staged a vigorous comeback in the late 1960s and throughout the 1970s. The dominant figure was Muhammad Ali, the three-time heavyweight champion of the world. Ali modestly claimed that he was the best-known person on the planet, and there seemed little reason to doubt him. Certainly, he made boxing a worldwide enterprise. In 1964 he made his first title defense before a handful of people in a hockey rink in Lewiston, Maine; fifteen years later, he could boast that he had fought before millions of people from Malaysia to Zaire. Ali noted accurately that governments, and not simply promoters, bid for his services. Ali's success in the top weight classification was matched, at least pound for pound, by smaller fighters; not since the 1920s had boxers outside the heavyweight division attracted so many fans and earned so much money.

Sports figures remained society's special heroes. Some, like football's Jim Brown, retired in favor of full-time acting; while others, such as O.J. Simpson and Joe Namath, found it more profitable to hop back and forth between stadium and sound stage. Many sports celebrities discovered that business ventures could handsomely supplement their athletic contracts. During the heady 1960s, some challenged Colonel Sanders and McDonald's in the highly risky franchise food business, but most contented themselves with a safer course—product endorsements. After breaking Babe Ruth's lifetime home-run record, Hank Aaron signed a $5-million contract with Magnavox.

Inevitably, politicians tried to supplement their own fading glamor by tapping that which surrounded big-time sports celebrities. Richard Nixon assiduously cultivated his image as the nation's number-one sports fan. (He even contributed a trick play to the 1972 Super Bowl; perhaps an evil omen, the play lost thirteen yards.) During presidential campaigns candidates rushed to sign up prominent athletes for their campaign squads, and a former pro football player, Jack Kemp, became a vice-presidential aspirant himself in 1980.

Most of the professional team sports went through considerable turmoil during the 1960s and 1970s. Players achieved at least partial emancipation from the once dictatorial control of their "owners." Professional athletes had long complained that they received a disproportionately small share of the profits, but through the 1950s the laws applying to sports stood fully on the side of capital. A new generation of athletes, armed with union advisers and spurred on by the sight of burgeoning sports revenues, changed this. Hockey, basketball, and football players made some gains when rival leagues began to bid for their services in the late 1960s and early 1970s, but not until the mid-1970s were their victories, and new breakthroughs by baseball players, written into law. In 1970 baseball's owners narrowly escaped defeat when the Supreme Court, after considerable internal squabbling, finally voted five to three to reject a suit challenging the national pastime's reserve clause as the basis of a form of involuntary servitude. The owners' victory was short-lived.

By the early 1980s other legal decisions had given athletes in all major sports a new freedom, the freedom to "play out their options" to their old team and to auction off their services as "free agents" in the marketplace. The result was hefty inflation in the entire salary structure of professional sports. In 1979 Nolan Ryan, owner of baseball's fastest fast ball, became a million-dollar-a-year player when he switched his allegiance from Gene Autry (the owner of the California Angels) to the Lone Ranger (the old cowboy hero who had become the promotional symbol of the Texas Rangers). Although some fans grumbled about the new salaries—especially when high-paid players failed to deliver—most owners adjusted smoothly, especially after they found that steadily rising revenues could generally cover the salaries specified in the new contracts.

The growing commercialization of big-time sports, even at the collegiate level, provoked lively debate. Traditionalists continued to defend amateur sports as character-building enterprises, and some social observers, such as Michael Novak, celebrated the thrill of watching highly skilled professionals perform their special magic. Reflecting upon the improvisational moves of basketball players like Julius Irving ("Dr. J."), Novak compared the game to jazz. But other observers, including former players, such as Dave Meggyesy and Peter Gent, took a more critical approach. Culminating a trend toward more iconoclastic sports journalism, Robert Lypsyte of the *New York Times* condemned Americans' infatuation with "Sportsworld, an amorphous infrastructure that acts to contain our energies, divert our passions, and socialize us for work or war or depression."

Writing in a different vein, Christopher Lasch argued that the real tragedy of recent years had been the "trivialization" of once legitimate, highly conventionalized athletic contests into debased, prepackaged spectacles. The nearly criminal violence in professional hockey, Lasch suggested, resulted from the extension of the game to areas without any authentic ice-hockey tradition: unaware of the subtle aspects of the game, fans could react only to mayhem and bloodletting. A cult of violence was clearly evident in professional boxing and wrestling. Boxing's resurgence was accompanied by a rash of ring fatalities, signs of careless matchmaking, inadequate medical supervision, and complacent officiating. Though the mayhem in professional wrestling was obviously feigned, scenarios became much more violent than they had been in the "golden days" of the 1950s: wrestlers routinely promised to maim or cripple opponents, and promoters eagerly pushed spectacles featuring cages, chains, crowbars, and all manner of theoretically lethal weaponry.

Television

The key to the rejuvenation of boxing, and the *sine qua non* for almost every other sport, was television. At the beginning of the 1970s professional football, along with Howard Cosell, invaded Monday night's prime-time schedule and, to the surprise of most sports and media experts, ran away with the ratings contest. Two years later, even before a terrorist attack upon Israeli athletes gave the 1972 summer Olympic Games new political significance, the Munich Olympics confirmed the drawing power of sports, including previously obscure ones such as women's gymnastics. By 1980 the air time devoted to sports by the three major networks had more than doubled. The reason was simple. Sports brought "good numbers"—high ratings; good numbers produced another set of happy figures—increased advertising revenues; and together, the two sets of numbers translated into greater corporate profits for ABC, CBS, and NBC. Between 1970 and 1975 the percentage of NBC's advertising take that came from sports nearly doubled. And higher television revenues *from* sports inevitably meant higher payments *to* sports for the privilege of carrying events on television. In 1976 the rights to telecast the Montreal Olympics cost ABC $25 million; four years later, the same network paid more than $200 million dollars more for rights to the 1984 summer games.

This symbiotic relationship between sports and television helped to solidify TV's position as the most popular of the popular arts. First of all, this American medium remained popular in terms of its ability to attract mass audiences, not only in the United States but throughout most of the world. Various types of surveys documented Americans' fascination with the tube. By the end of the 1970s, 97 percent of the homes in the United States had at least one television set. According to a study completed in the mid-1970s, nearly half of the population ranked watching television—as opposed to watching motion pictures, reading, playing cards, talking with friends, or any other activity—as their favorite pastime. Surveys also showed that people were spending more and more time with their sets: in 1961 respondents indicated that they watched television slightly more than two hours a day; by 1974 the figure had jumped to more than three hours per day. By the time a child graduated from high school, it was estimated, he or she had spent more time with television sets than with a twelve-year supply of schoolteachers.

The content of TV shows was shaped by its broad-based audience. Throughout the 1950s a number of network executives had hoped that TV would somehow emphasize "serious" programming, such as symphony concerts, sophisticated dramas, and in-depth news analyses. At the same time, some prominent sponsors helped to develop their own high quality shows, and some corporate image-makers considered critical acclaim as important as massive audiences, if not more so. By the 1960s and 1970s, though, a new breed of executives, individuals such as James Aubrey and Fred Silverman, aimed nearly all their programming schedule at a mass audience. The fundamental measure of a good program was "good numbers." The result, critics charged, was a steadily declining level of program quality, a trend that reflected the search for maximum ratings and the fact that the amount of time people spent watching television *increased* as their educational level and occupational status *decreased*.

Despite such critiques of the ratings wars, the search for "good numbers" did not always determine programming, even in the late 1970s and early 1980s. In some cases, in fact, the "right numbers" proved important. Few sponsors, for example, wanted to buy advertising time on shows that appealed primarily to older people with small disposable incomes, and some programs with respectable ratings—westerns and "The Lawrence Welk Show," for instance—disappeared from network schedules. In a few cases the "right numbers" could preserve low-rated shows, such as "All in the Family" and "60 Minutes," until they developed a broader audience. Moreover, although the frantic pace of television tended to "use up" talent quickly, even the most jaded viewer could still discover good scripts, superb acting, and solid productions. Programs such as "The Mary Tyler Moore Show," James Garner's "The Rockford Files," and the various productions of Norman Lear bent hackneyed television formulas into new and interesting angles. With the emphasis these programs gave to character development—not just that of the stars but of featured players as well—regular viewers could find a continuity that was missing from most television shows.

There were other brights spots. CBS's "60 Minutes," an innovative "television magazine," finally caught on with viewers in the late 1970s and even ranked in the Neilson Survey's list of the ten most popular programs. In the late 1970s, as Hollywood's film archives were depleted and its current production schedule shrank, the networks began to make their own "feature-length" films and the longer "mini-series." (The most successful mini-series turned out to be TV's most spectacular effort—the much-watched and exhaustively discussed production of Alex Haley's *Roots*.) Although scripts and production values varied widely, some of the made-for-television epics easily outclassed many theater films. During the late 1970s and early 1980s, television films tackled controversial subjects such as the Vietnam war and racial conflict, subjects that had rarely intruded into regular programming in earlier years.

By the early 1980s viewers could select a highbrow alternative to network television, but few actually did so. Public television, authorized by Congress in 1967 and expanded (with the help of corporate and foundation grants) in the 1970s, attracted only about 5 percent of the viewing audience for its most popular adult shows. (Children's programs, such as "Sesame Street" and "Mr. Rogers' Neighborhood" did considerably better.) Moreover, the public-broadcasting bureaucracy produced considerable controversy. In 1972 Richard Nixon tried to block public television's appropriations because of the allegedly left-liberal bias of its public-affairs offerings. Private broadcasting interests complained bitterly about the steadily increasing federal subsidies. Public television's most popular programs, critics liked to point out, were purchased from British television rather than produced by PBS' own staff. Finally, noting the large number of programs bankrolled by oil companies, some wags claimed that PBS stood for the Petroleum Broadcasting System, not the Public Broadcasting System. When in 1979 the Carnegie Commission coupled a general endorsement of the existing system with calls for a dramatic increase in federal funding, both the White House and Congress ignored the recommendation, and in 1981 Ronald Reagan slashed the appropriation for PBS.

Most people who touted television's potential did not place their faith in either the networks or PBS; instead, they claimed that new technologies, some of which were unveiled in the 1970s, seemed the best hope for innovation and greater diversity. "Mini-cams" and new video-tape equipment greatly increased television's mobility and the speed with which it could send images back to viewers. The new communications satellites allowed live transmissions from most parts of the world. Expansion of cable-television systems gave millions of subscribers new options, including channels reserved for "public access" programming. Public-access channels, supporters claimed, would finally give citizens a real chance to explore the limits of media; even the instant arrival of X-rated television in some cities did not cool the enthusiasm for future breakthroughs. The mass marketing of video-tape machines allowed more affluent viewers to record programs for replay at their convenience, a small step toward breaking the tyranny of the network schedules. Indeed, some futurists predicted that the arrival of satellites and video tape decks marked the beginning of the end for the traditional network system. By the early 1980s viewers could already purchase equipment that would allow them to scan the hundreds of programs and motion pictures carried by satellite and bring the ones they wanted into their homes—for instant viewing or for recording and viewing at their convenience.

Popular Music

Many pop-music stars surpassed television personalities and sports figures in popularity and wealth. Performers received huge fees for concert appearances and staggering royalties from album sales. Some of the superstars of the 1960s—Janis Joplin, Jimi Hendrix, and Jim Morrison, for example—lived at a frantic pace, spending money wildly while killing their talent and ultimately themselves with drugs and alcohol. When Morrison succumbed to a heart attack at twenty-seven, physicians reported that his internal organs resembled those of a person in his fifties. Other stars displayed more concern about their health and their financial balance sheets. Bob Dylan, the Beatles, and James Brown became multimillionaires. Even the Grateful Dead, the group most closely associated with San Francisco's original hippie movement, eventually concentrated upon cash flows and tax write-offs as much as upon musical arrangements. In 1973 the business magazine *Forbes* estimated that at least fifty rock superstars earned between $2 million and $6 million a year. "The idea all along," explained Alice Cooper, "was to make $1 million. Otherwise the struggle wouldn't have been worth it." As one study put it, "Rock and Roll was here to pay."

In addition to obtaining great financial rewards, rock musicians gained serious critical attention. The success of the Beatles and Dylan helped rock music escape its be-bop-a-lula image in the 1960s, and both rock and folk-rock became widely accepted as serious forms of artistic expression. The poetic lyrics of Dylan and Paul Simon reflected the frustrated dreams of restless youth, their concern about the "sounds of silence" ("people talking without listening"), and their outrage against the persistence of social injustice. Young composers blended various types of musical styles into the rock idiom: traditional folk music, black blues, jazz, and country-and-western music all influenced trends in the progressive rock of the late 1960s.

During the 1970s, though, popular music was in a state of flux similar to that of the late 1950s and early 1960s. Although Bob Dylan could sing about being "forever young," rock-and-roll, like its founding fathers, seemed to be aging. The death of Elvis Presley in 1977 prompted admirers of his early work to lament, once again, the predictability and the posturing that had characterized the last fifteen years of his career. Publications as diverse as *Cream* and *The New York Review* reflected on the significance of Elvis's rise, fall, and death. By the late 1970s rock found itself mired in bubble-gum music, engulfed by the prepackaged pyrotechnics of Kiss, and under siege by disco.

Outwardly, the popular-music industry retained much of the casual countercultural image of the 1960s, but the business of poplar music became a larger corporate enterprise than ever before. Recording companies, which surpassed the Hollywood film industry in yearly revenues during the 1970s, naturally placed their greatest emphasis upon expanding their incomes. Competition among record executives, who were expected to anticipate not only the next new musical fad but the following one as well, encouraged corruption and discouraged real innovation. The major labels, which were generally owned by giant multinational firms, were more than eager to package the latest trend, subsidizing journalistic puffs for the rock magazines and concert tours for the latest products of their hit-making machinery, but were extremely reluctant to invest the time and money to explore significant new directions in music.

The same situation prevailed in the radio industry. The expansion of FM stations during the 1960s and early 1970s had helped to break the tyranny of the old Top-40 play list. Formats became freer; the range of music expanded; and local and regional artists could usually get their recordings on the air. By the 1980s, though, the expansion of radio-programming services had again narrowed the musical spectrum. Relying upon sophisticated survey data, the programming services carefully packaged each minute of air time, eliminated the discretion of disc jockeys, and emphasized the music that their data said would appeal to their clients' desired audience. The inevitable result was elimination of artists and musical styles that did not fit "the program." Local talents lost out to well-known national recording stars, and individuals on the smaller record labels lost out to artists being promoted heavily by the majors.

With the arrival of the 1980s, though, there were some signs of change. The recording industry finally discovered that "new-wave" rock was not synonymous with "punk," and the emerging union between some rock musicians and the antinuclear movement indicated that the old musical-political synthesis of the 1960s might be recaptured. Even so, the simple optimism of "Woodstock Nation" was clearly a thing of the past. For those who could not remember the bloodshed of Altamont there was a tragedy in Cincinnati in late 1979: several thousand concertgoers trampled hundreds of others, killing eleven, in a headlong rush for the general-admission seats at a concert by The Who.

While rock music was "running on empty," country and country-rock had energy to spare during most of the 1970s. Even before Jimmy Carter conquered the northern electorate, the music associated with the honky tonks of Dixie had swept over the northern states. During the 1950s and even much of the 1960s northerners who wanted to hear country music on the radio often had to wait until evening, when they could pick up high-beaming stations from the deep South. By the 1980s, though, every metropolitan area had several country-music stations, and a number of country artists were "crossing over" to the pop and rock stations. Singers, such as Kris Kristofferson, Dolly Parton, and Willie Nelson (the first country artist to win a platinum record, symbolic of sales of one million albums) became nationwide celebrities with television and movie careers.

The spreading appeal of country music was difficult to explain. Some people claimed that they liked its simplicity and honesty, its stories of broken hearts and faded loves—"Your Cheatin' Heart Will Tell on You." Others seemed attracted by its nostalgic overtones, its celebration of rural life and simple virtues—"My Heroes Have Always Been Cowboys." But perhaps in the uncertain 1970s, when the old liberal consensus was gone, country music's deeply rooted quality, its sense of limits and its acceptance of failure, articulated a southern idea that came home to the rest of the nation.

Give Me That Old-Time Religion/
Give Me That Big-Time Religion

During the 1950s some observers happily noticed that Americans were becoming an increasingly religious people. Church membership climbed steadily; President Eisenhower spread "piety along the Potomac"; and the Reverend Norman Vincent Peale's popular *Power of Positive Thinking* seemed to carry faith and optimism to Protestants throughout the land. In 1955 the sociologist

Will Herberg noted that the Judeo-Christian religious tradition was merging with American ideals to produce a consensus on deep-seated values among Protestants, Catholics, and Jews. A few skeptics reminded Americans that church attendance did not necessarily measure religious commitment and charged that churches emphasized form over substance, fund-raising over worship. But if the religious messages were vacuous, at least the sanctuaries were full. Most churchgoers seemed content with the way things were.

Churches, however, mirrored the society at large, and they did not escape the turmoil of the 1960s—the bureaucratization, the splits over social issues, and the disenchantment of the young. By the end of the decade established churches had been wracked by factionalism, had lost membership, and were threatened by an array of newer sects and evengelical movements.

During the 1960s the merger movement became almost as fashionable in religion as in business. Mainstream Protestant denominations seemed preoccupied with consolidation and centralization. Lutherans, Methodists, and Congregationalists each approved important mergers arranged by their national decision-making bodies and accepted by most local congregations. Greater centralization crept into other functions as well. More and more, national church boards set church policy, raised funds, budgeted money, and directed missionary and social efforts. The umbrella organization for Protestant churches, the National Council of Churches, revamped its structure in mid-decade to further the centralized direction of policy. But the interjection of national-level decisions into affairs of individual churches often created dissension within congregations.

When national church bodies, which were fairly liberal politically, began to express themselves on controversial issues, such as civil rights and the war in Vietnam, factional disputes in local congregations became severe. Many Americans wanted their church to remain detached from social issues, as it had in the 1950s; others pressed for the church to be even more active in protest against injustice and inhumanity. The split over the role of the church was basic, and it was bitter. Many pastors walked a tightrope, fearing that a lean toward either side might cost them part of their congregation. Lack of a clear identity drove many people out of the church and into agnosticism or uninstitutionalized personal religion. According to surveys conducted by the Gallup Poll, there was a marked decline in church attendance during the 1960s; this drop was most evident in the "main-line" denominations.

The Catholic Church had to contend not only with social issues—Catholics were bitterly divided between deep-seated conservatism and the "Catholic Left radicalism" of priests, such as Daniel and Philip Berrigan—but also with the even more explosive matter of church policy. The Second Vatican Council of 1962-65 ushered in a reformist period by substituting English for Latin in the liturgy. Subsequently, demands accelerated for greater changes. While religious traditionalists looked on in horror, some Catholics pressed for liberalization of rules concerning priestly celibacy, the role of women in the church, and birth control.

American Jews confronted a problem even more baffling than divisions over doctrine and social policy: how to maintain an ethnic and religious identity. Large numbers of Jewish young people failed to understand or follow their Hebrew school lessons; many married gentiles. In fact, the majority of American Jews, while still identifying themselves as part of a Jewish ethnic group, belonged to no synagogue or temple. Economic success and the decline of anti-Semitism now seemed to pose as great a threat to the Jewish faith than old-style persecutions.

Discontent within established churches and general social turmoil helped produce new movements and faiths. Evangelism swept the country, turning individuals, such as Billy Graham, Oral Roberts, and Billy James Hargis into the heads of multimillion-dollar enterprises. Although their religious organizations were huge bureaucracies relying upon mass media and the latest advertising techniques, their evangelism attracted people through its appeal to personal religion and past virtues. Evangelical fundamentalism provided an anchor for many Americans who felt buffeted by uncontrolled change.

Some popular preachers, such as Hargis and Carl McIntire, closely linked Christianity, anticommunism, and ultra-right-wing politics. Hargis charged that the Equal Rights Amendment would bring the nation to the brink of hell, and his organization carried on a well-funded campaign against women's liberation. McIntire joined Hargis in an attack on the environmentalist movement. He charged, "It has been thought that the great emphasis upon ecology was a diversionary tactic to turn people's minds away from...what the Communists are doing throughout the world to take over. But now it is seen to be even deeper than that; it involved the rejection of Christianity."

While Hargis and McIntire occupied the far right, Oral Roberts and Billy Graham became important establishment figures. Roberts financed his own university in Oklahoma and used the school's successful basketball team as a promotional device. (During one stretch the squad lost only 19 of 134 games.) He also built a huge television empire, which rivaled that of the acknowledged king of evangelists, Billy Graham. Still, Graham continued to be the most revered fundamentalist leader. He took his crusades around the world, preaching to crowds of over a hundred thousand people, and he became an important spiritual counselor to President Nixon, often leading prayer breakfasts at the White House. Year after year he stayed near the top of the list of "most admired Americans."

During the 1960s wholly new religious movements sprang up, particularly among the young. The Bahai faith built several breathtaking and expensive structures in the United States and gained numerous converts; members of the Hare Krishna sect, with their shaved heads and robes, appeared on the streets and in the airports of larger cities; "Jesus freaks" replaced political agitators on some college campuses; the Children of God and other communal cult groups attracted middle-class youth who were willing to renounce their families and adopt a new life and loyalty. Religion took on other dimensions as well. Americans became fascinated with spiritualism, mysticism, and transcendental meditation. Bookstores expanded their sections on religion and the occult, and the success of *The Exorcist* indicated that such subjects had wide appeal to moviegoers. Many people of all ages and political persuasions, it seemed, looked to religion for escape from a bureaucratic, centralized, and oversized society.

The same phenomena continued through the 1970s. Although attendance at Catholic masses leveled off after the declines of the 1960s, main-line Protestant and Jewish congregations continued to lose members. At the same time, all of the major denominations still struggled to heal internal divisions, especially those involving the role of women in the church. By the 1970s feminism had spilled over into religious affairs, and women in all three major denominations argued that they were entitled to participate fully in nearly all phases of spiritual life. The Roman Catholic Church reaffirmed its opposition to such changes—including papal bans on female priests and on artificial methods of birth control—but most Protestant denominations agreed to modify at least some patriarchical practices. The situation in Judaism was complicated by the division between the Orthodox, Conservative, and Reform movements. While Conservative and Reform congregations changed some traditional rituals and doctrines, the Orthodox movement, the only wing of Judaism to gain members in the 1970s, held firm. Finally, the evangelical revival of the 1960s gained momentum in the 1970s. Even though main-line Protestant denominations lost members, the total number of Protestants attending church remained constant because of the growth of evangelical congregations.

The growth of evangelicalism could be measured in watts, in dollars, and in political power—as well as in the number of people actually attending evangelical churches. Radio and television ministries remained central forces in the evangelical surge; Billy Graham and Oral Roberts were joined by hundreds of other media preachers. Among the most prominent were Robert Schuller, who preached an updated, California version of Norman Vincent Peale's *Power of Positive Thinking;* Rex Humbard of Ohio, a family-oriented evangelist in the Oral Roberts mold; and dynamic, gospel-singing Jimmy Lee Swaggart, a cousin of country-rockers Jerry Lee Lewis and Mickey Gilley. In an even less traditional vein, Pat Robertson, a former corporate lawyer turned evangelist, hosted the "700 Club," a born-again Christian version of "The Johnny Carson Show."

Although the major television networks refused to sell any of their prime time to religious broadcasters, the media evangelists used their burgeoning bank accounts to purchase time from local stations and even to establish their own networks. Pat Robertson's Christian Broadcasting Network (CBN) boasted of its own satellite system and of its ability to reach hundreds of stations and cable-TV systems on an around-the-clock basis. By the end of the 1970s there were more than 1400 radio stations and 30 TV outlets that specialized in religious broadcasts; every week they were joined by another radio station and every month by another television station.

Many born-again Christians also turned to a new generation of old-fashioned charismatic, evangelistic faith healers, including Jimmy Carter's sister, Ruth Carter Stapleton. While her "therapeutic ministry" kept faith healing low-key, others, such as Ernest Angley, bellowed in the old style. Angley, who relied heavily on television, ministered to the lame and the deaf and directed his healing powers at diabetes—"I command no more sugar in the blood!"—and cancer—"I command no more cancer and command you to gain weight!" More and more faith healers, though, came to emphasize the more restrained style of Oral Roberts, and "healing ministries" came to lose much of the sleazy image attached to them in films, such as *Elmer Gantry* and *Marjoe*.

By the late 1970s some of the more conservative evangelicals had become potent political forces. While many Americans were claiming to have little faith in established institutions, especially the national government and the public school systems, evangelical religious faiths were attracting new converts and gathering political strength. Evangelists like Pat Robertson and Jerry Falwell promised to lead their followers, and the nation, out of the wilderness. Joining with political figures on the far right, evangelical groups helped to unite a number of disparate interest groups in opposition to many existing federal programs and in favor of new action to protect the nuclear family and old moral values. For example, Jerry Falwell's political lobby, The Moral Majority, campaigned against rights for homosexuals, federal involvement in education, and the Equal Rights Amendment. The Moral Majority also ran workshops and seminars for budding evangelical politicos and issued its own "morality rating" for members of Congress. By the early 1980s an alliance between the right wing of the GOP and the ultra-conservative evangelicals was clearly evident: the 1980 Republican platform promised to tear down the signs of an oversized government and to put the nation back on a proper moral footing by, among other things, appointing as federal judges only those individuals who opposed abortion laws.

At the same time, the Hare Krishna and other cults condemned by the Moral Majority continued to flourish. These groups, like the evangelicals, seemed to gain support as a result of continued popular doubts about many social institutions. A powerful cult, the Unification Church, was headed by South Korea's Moon Sun-Mung, a staunch anticommunist who reportedly had ties to the South Korean CIA. Using sophisticated behavior-modification methods to gain followers and corporate-management techniques to handle the church's growing wealth, the "Moonies" converted thousands of young people who thought they had found a new sense of community. Moon's church also gained the endorsement of prominent supporters, including some conservative academics who liked Moon's political outlook. Unlike apolitical movements, such as Hare Krishna, Moon's sect pushed right-wing politics, laissez-faire capitalism, and a hard-line anticommunist foreign policy. From 1969 to 1974 Moon's group funneled a considerable amount of money—much of it coming from young Moonies selling flowers—to various groups supporting Richard Nixon. Moon's activities finally provoked several federal investigations.

The crusade against cults, which grew alongside the increasing visibility of the Hare Krishna and the Moonies, gained grisly evidence when 918 members of the People's Temple cult died in a mass-suicide ritual in Guyana in 1978. Led by a charismatic and increasingly paranoid preacher, the Reverend Jim Jones, the People's Temple appealed to the very poor, to those who could find no secure place in the oversized society. Loosely aligned with the political left, Jones offered the promise of both religious salvation and social progress. He gained thousands of followers, especially among poor black people in the San Francisco Bay area, and many of them moved with him to the jungles of South America. Though concerned about a very different set of issues, Jones and his followers ultimately reached a conclusion similar to that of the conservative evangelicals on the far right: America was a fundamentally flawed society. Lacking the financial resources and political clout of the evangelical right, the most desperate members of the People's Temple believed they could save themselves and their families only through flight—from this country and, finally, from life itself.

The Education Labyrinth

The pressure of the baby-boom generation, the demands of a rapidly expanding economy, and concern with minority groups brought enormous changes to America's educational establishment in the postwar era. Thousands of new schools had to be built and equipped, and many corporations stood ready to sell the latest in instructional devices. Under Lyndon Johnson's Great Society programs, federal funds became available for expanding and upgrading education. Almost every suburban classroom had its arsenal of audio-visual equipment. Some instructors began to use "teaching packages" containing all kinds of material to help students understand a particular topic or concept. Most of the new techniques sought to involve students as active participants rather than as passive listeners. In some schools, architects eliminated walls, creating an open and airy environment in which students would, it was hoped, become more expressive.

The educational revolution affected course content as well as teaching techniques. The "new math" and the "new English" substituted analysis and understanding for traditional categories and extensive memorization; the "new social studies" emphasized personal evaluation of documents rather than regurgitation of names and dates. Under pressure from women's organizations and minority groups, most schools replaced the stereotyped middle-class characters of Dick and Jane. At its best, the educational revolution promised to produce individuals who could think, evaluate, and make critical judgments. At its worst, it could degenerate into multimedia entertainment with little intellectual substance. Undoubtedly, changes in method outstripped changes in educational personnel, and many older teachers found themselves confused and resentful. New approaches that worked in a laboratory school did not automatically succeed in the average classroom. Brighter pupils easily adapted to the new math, but slower students graduated without the basic skills needed to balance a checkbook. After more than a decade of experimentation, critics of the new techniques contended that "Johnny still can't read, and he can't add, either."

During the 1960s one answer to the failure of traditional classrooms was to offer education outside the school system. Some parents who disliked the "authoritarianism" of traditional public schools sent their children to experimental "free schools." In response to criticism of education for minority children (such as Jonathan Kozol's *Death at an Early Age*), some reformers attempted to use the free-school concept in ghetto areas. Head Start, originally a Great Society program, attempted to provide educational experiences for poor and minority preschoolers so that they would enter kindergarten on a par with more "privileged" middle-class children. Educational television also helped preschoolers and reached dropouts, adults, and school-aged youngsters with educational material ranging from American history to language instruction to guitar playing. Public television developed the most successful venture in children's shows—*"Sesame Street."* Colorful and fast-moving, *"Sesame Street"* had its viewers reciting numbers, letters, and difficult words (some in Spanish) before they entered kindergarten. Although *"Sesame Street"* captivated both parents and children, traditionalists disliked the program's flashy style, and some innovators criticized its emphasis on repetition.

Many schools experienced rapid changes in their student bodies during the 1960s. Especially in rural areas, public officials worked to consolidate small schools into better-equipped large ones. As a result, the size of educational institutions increased dramatically. In 1950 there were over 86,000 school systems in the country, averaging about 300 students each; by 1965 there were fewer than 30,000 systems, averaging 1,400 students each. Most children no longer knew all their classmates or teachers, and many students rode buses to school. The undeniable educational gains of consolidation came at the expense of nearby facilities and a feeling of community.

As long as school buses assisted consolidation of small schools they were generally welcomed as symbols of educational progress, but when courts began to order busing to fulfill another educational function—racial integration—many white people began to view them as part of a sinister plot. In the late 1960s and particularly in the political campaigns of 1970 and 1972, busing provided the focus of discussion on civil-rights questions. Using buses to achieve racial balance raised complicated social, legal, and educational problems. Even some minority-group parents denounced forced integration, fearing that their children would lose traditional cultural values in white-dominated schools. They called for community control rather than desegregation.

The baby-boom generation also strained institutions of higher education during the 1950s and 1960s. Universities contended not only with the natural population increase but also with a rising percentage of youth who chose to go to college. In 1955 only 27 percent of college-aged people attended school; by 1965 the figure had risen to 40 percent. The flood of new students stemmed from private affluence, government-assistance programs, and the desire of many young men to avoid the draft by staying in school. Graduate schools also boomed. By the mid-1960s there were about a quarter of a million full-time graduate students, three of five receiving some form of financial support. Half of all the Ph.D. degrees granted in the United States between 1861 and 1970 were earned in the 1960s. A researcher writing in 1971 accurately observed that "we have created a graduate education and research establishment in American universities that is about 30 to 50 percent larger than we shall effectively use in the 1970s and early 1980s."

The large numbers of students gave university life the appearance of a business (or a factory, some students said). During the mid-1960s most state universities computerized registration and record keeping, an innovation that increased both the efficiency and the impersonality of college life. As universities expanded their physical plants, administrators had to devote more time to land purchases, financial arrangements, and construction problems. Even feeding and housing so many students required bureaucracies of substantial size. Sometimes, it seemed, education was purely incidental. In this business atmosphere, teachers' unions inevitably developed. Such organizations helped instructors obtain job security, fringe benefits, and retirement plans. But the growing adversary relationship between faculty and administration further fragmented the university community and sometimes distracted attention from the primary goal of education.

The debates of the 1950s and 1960s—over the size and structure of schools, over philosophies and techniques of instruction, and over the content and the rigor of the curriculum—became more bitter and complex during the 1970s. First, the declining birth rate of the 1960s finally caught up with education: for the first time in several decades students were not crowding the education labrynth. Already faced with rising costs and declining revenues, school officials responded at the primary and secondary levels by consolidating some schools and closing down others completely. Even without busing for racial balance, neighborhood schools would not be nearly as close to most people's homes as they had been during the 1950s and 1960s.

Although colleges and universities also began to face the necessity of contraction, they enjoyed greater flexibility than primary and secondary schools. They, unlike the lower-level schools, could create students. Increasingly, colleges and universities sought to attract "the nontraditional student." Foreign students and "adult scholars"—individuals (especially women) slightly or considerably older than the traditional 18-22 age group—became obvious targets. Four-year institutions also began to compete more actively with two-year colleges for students. And, of course, colleges and universities vied with one another to attract a steady number of students from an ever-shrinking pool of high-school graduates. Admissions offices became "recruiting centers," relying upon advertising consultants to provide their college with an attractive image and a new set of recruiting tools. A number of smaller colleges gave up and closed their doors during the 1970s, and even the most optimistic forecasts predicted gloomy days for institutions of higher education during the 1980s.

In contrast with the generally flush 1960s, all levels of education confronted economic problems during the 1970s. Even Harvard and Yale, well-endowed private institutions that attracted large sums of federal money, worried about their ability to maintain, let alone expand, their programs. Public schools, which had to depend upon tax dollars, faced growing popular protests against higher property taxes and new school-revenue bonds. As a result, many school districts throughout the country were forced to slash educational staff, instructional programs, and extracurricular activities. The problem was most serious in large cities, where shrinking tax bases and rapidly escalating costs added to difficulties produced by reluctant taxpayers.

But the problems of American education transcended issues of revenue and taxation. There were more subtle forces contributing to what appeared to be a growing backlash against a strong commitment to education of the young. Put simply, more and more people saw public schools, especially in urban areas, as educational and social failures. In some schools, traditional discipline problems—truancy, smoking in rest rooms, scuffles on the playground—seemed trivial when compared with the everyday reality of hard drugs and violent attacks on both teachers and students. At the same time, educational results, as measured by standardized tests, steadily dropped. (To be fair to urban schools, the decline was a nationwide phenomenon: between 1966 and 1976 the average score on the verbal portion of the SAT test plummeted from 467 to 429.) The hope that school integration would introduce children to a heterogeneous environment began to fade as more affluent families left for the suburbs or sent their children to private schools. The vast majority of urban public schools came to serve primarily children from poor and nonwhite families. In Pasadena, California, for example, more than 35 percent of white parents removed their children from public schools after court-enforced busing went into effect; nationwide, it was estimated, 40 percent of middle-class black families sent their children to private schools.

One prominent, controversial explanation for the problems of urban public schools focused on busing and on other efforts to achieve racial balance. But the broadest analyses of what the historian-social critic Christopher Lasch called "the spread of stupefaction" rightly viewed racial issues as only one part of a complex situation. Many indictments, including those of Lasch and Neil Postman, the educational critic, focused on the curriculums and on the teachers instead of simply on the students. Writing in 1970, in *Teaching as a Subversive Activity,* Postman had endorsed the individualized, open school that was popularized in the 1960s. A decade later, in *Teaching as a Conserving Activity,* he had retained his faith in individualized learning, but he also stressed the importance of creating an educational atmosphere that emphasized social order and group cooperation. Postman even advocated dress codes so that students would recognize schools as "a place of dignity and a special kind of learning"—a place different than other parts of the youth culture. Lasch also condemned misguided educational philosophies (especially those that denigrated the teaching of basic skills in favor of teaching "life adjustment") and slipshod teaching methods (particularly those that made few demands on students). But he placed the ultimate blame on the "narcissistic," consumer-oriented ethos of American society. The decay of the over-bureaucratized educational system, he argued, reflected "the waning social demand for initiative, enterprise, and the compulsion to achieve." In his view, the problems of education could not be separated from the other flaws of an oversized society.

The Fragmented Seventies

Despite numerous efforts to characterize the decade, few people could agree upon the nature of the 1970s. To some, the decade's apparent aimlessness indicated a "lack of leadership" in public and private sectors. In a much-discussed report prepared for the Tri-Lateral Commission, the political scientist Samuel Huntington argued that this "failure of leadership" was linked to "an excess of democracy"; the egalitarian demands of the late 1960s and early 1970s, the commission suggested, placed unreasonable and unattainable demands upon the political and economic system. By the end of the 1970s, fear about the "excess of democracy" had become one of the cornerstones of neo-conservative ideology. Others, observing the proliferation of "personal-growth therapies," the self-absorption, and the general retreat from social concerns among college students, stereotyped the 1970s as "the Me Decade" (Tom Wolfe) or as an age of "narcissism" (Christopher Lasch).

Yet all the concern about the "failure of leadership," the "excess of democracy," and the growth of "narcissism" could not obscure the signs of social renewal and the examples of people constructively experimenting to improve social arrangements and programs. Even the most bitter critic of the "narcissistic" 1970s, Christopher Lasch, could find another side to American life. "In small towns and crowded urban neighborhoods, even in suburbs, men and women have initiated modest experiments in cooperation, designed to defend their rights against the corporations and the state." In truth, in small ways that did not capture much footage in the media's nightly news shows, the so-called Me Decade was as much a time of social ferment as the 1960s.

Perhaps the most striking new departure of the 1970s was the growth of community and local self-help movements. Looking back to the "splendid decade" of the 1970s, William Braden of the *Chicago Sun-Times* called it a time of "grass-roots revival."

In part, this trend built upon movements of the 1960s. Whatever the limitations of the Great Society, it did stimulate increased participation by local citizens in a variety of community projects. Some of these efforts, such as attempts to gain community control of local schools, were defeated by more powerful, solidly entrenched adversaries. But other local efforts met with limited and even with striking success. Local arts programs contributed to a grass-roots artistic revival reminiscent of the 1930s. Neighborhood clinics, legal-aid offices, and recreational and counseling services became regular features of American life. Community organizing, a strategy pioneered by Saul Alinsky's school for "radicals" in Chicago, developed new, broader goals and spread to other parts of the country and the ideological spectrum. In a move thoroughly representative of the decade's attempt to retreat from the oversized society, large, centralized mental-health facilities were decentralized into small "group homes" in which family and community living could replace institutional standardization.

The failures of the 1960s also contributed to the new directions of the 1970s. Clearly, neither the political thrusts of the New Left nor the iconoclasm of the counterculture—both of which became directed almost exclusively at young people—constituted an effective basis for broad social change. More conventional political lobbying on behalf of the poor (the type of activity Dr. George Wiley's National Welfare Rights Organization—NWRO—mounted in Congress in 1971 and 1972) was even less successful. Reflecting upon the failure of the NWRO and other "poor people's movements," Richard Cloward and Frances Fox Piven, two social scientists committed to significant change, questioned the usefulness of organizational efforts. They argued that the only successful tactic for change was "mass defiance." Ruling elites, they argued, would concede nothing to egalitarian demands unless they were forced to do so in order to "buy off" discontent. Other observers of the 1960s, however, drew a different conclusion. The real failure of that decade, they argued, was the absence of effective grass-roots organizations; mass defiance and radical posturing were simply manifestations of fundamental organizational weaknesses.

If the economic slowdown of the 1970s encouraged greater corporate concentration and produced calls for centralized economic planning, it also seemed to confirm the importance of grass-roots organizations and self-help. In a dialectical process, crisis and centralization bred thriving localistic structures. Most black Americans, for example, found it difficult to maintain, let alone expand upon, the economic gains of the late 1960s and early 1970s. In 1978 there were twice as many blacks out of work as a decade earlier. The same year, the median income of blacks stood at only 55 percent of the median income of whites, the same percentage as in 1965, the year LBJ unveiled his Great Society. The concentration of poor blacks in decaying parts of central cities became even more intensive: by the early 1980s more than half of the nation's black population lived in the oldest, shabbiest portions of the inner cities. Meanwhile, the national black organizations and their white allies found it difficult to get significant new help from the federal government. Consequently, many blacks concluded that the most effective strategy involved a return to their own communities and a renewed effort to develop new institutions and a spirit of self-help. Jesse Jackson, the controversial leader of PUSH, headed one such movement in Chicago; Detroit became another city in which local organizations grew significantly; and a black-owned news service provided an alternative communication network for small black newspapers across the country.

Members of other ethnic groups adopted similar strategies. During the late 1970s increased immigration (both legal and illegal) and high birth rates swelled the Hispanic population—largely Mexican-American and Puerto Rican—to about 6 percent of the nation's total. Without significant help from Washington or from local governments, many Hispanics turned to community-based institutions. Cesar Chavez continued to be the most charismatic Mexican-American leader, especially in rural areas. But other Chicanos, such as Ernie Cortes of Los Angeles' United Neighborhood Organizations, worked to organize urban communities, often relying upon the resources and personnel of the Catholic Church. Russell Means also eased away from dramatic clashes with white authorities, placing a new emphasis on native American self-sufficiency. Other American Indian leaders hoped that the great energy resources on their lands might even lead to the creation of a native American version of OPEC—controlled by and for the Indian nations.

Efforts at local organizing were not limited to nonwhite minorities. Confronted with rampant inflation and with the continued surge of urban-development projects into their communities, the "unmeltable" white ethnics mobilized to protect their life savings, much of which was invested in their homes and in neighborhood businesses. In ethnic neighborhoods as well as in other parts of American cities and suburbs there was a significant growth of local neighborhood associations. According to one estimate, there were literally millions of such organizations. In some rural areas there were similar examples of new grass-roots organizations. In Minnesota and Wisconsin, for example, groups of farmers joined with city folk to protest the spread of nuclear-power plants and the proliferation of high-voltage power lines.

Moreover, the organizational ferment went beyond ethnicity and geography. Older Americans, one of the country's fastest-growing minorities, banded together to make "gray power" a reality. Recognizing that new technologies threatened not only their jobs but their health, some blue-collar workers organized to demand more control over their job sites. Neither the people who talked about "corporate responsibility" nor government inspectors who oversaw health and safety standards, these advocates of "work-place democracy" charged, appreciated the risks that American workers faced every day. In a few cases, groups of workers became owners, taking over plants that were being abandoned by large corporations and running them as worker-community ventures.

The numerous local self-help organizations occasionally banded together in order to exchange ideas and information and to lobby for political and economic help. During the summer of 1980, for example, Seattle, which had hosted the World's Fair of 1962, welcomed a very different kind of gathering—CityFair. In contrast with the fair of 1962, which displayed high-cost, massive-scale technology, 1980's CityFair featured inexpensive, grass-roots technology appropriate to the pressing needs of local communities. The exhibits included a solar greenhouse that had been built by senior citizens and low-income residents of Cheyenne, Wyoming; the plan of an underground office building that used 92 percent less energy than the conventional skyscraper; and various programs for recycling the nation's trash into energy and new products. If visitors to the CityFair traveled to nearby parts of the Pacific Northwest, they could see a number of new worker-owned-and-controlled plywood factories, operations that competed successfully with larger corporations. Consumer-cooperative ventures even had their own special lending agency. In response to pressure from cooperative supporters, Congress created in 1978 the National Consumer Cooperative Bank, an institution that provided loans to a variety of consumer co-ops.

Did all these self-help movements provide reason for optimism, or did such localistic efforts operate at cross purposes with one another? A suspicious Russell Means, for example, was not ready to rush the American Indian Movement into an alliance with western ranchers and farmers. Preferring that his people go their own way on energy and environmental issues, Means argued that he could recall few instances where the close proximity of "cowboys and Indians" had not meant warfare. Organizations of blacks and of white ethnics also traditionally drew a good deal of their energy from their mutual antagonism. Those who believed that traditional corporate and political institutions represented the best solution for the nation's pressing problems expressed great skepticism about the ability of disparate community and self-help groups to unite in any common causes. Such individual organizations, argued John Gardner, a former secretary of HEW and the founder of Common Cause, were often interested only in single issues, not in a larger vision of the American future. The successful effort by the gray-power lobby to extend the mandatory retirement age to 70, for instance, seemed only to place another hurdle in the paths of women and minority workers. And pressures to raise Social Security benefits for the elderly resulted in Congress assigning new tax burdens to younger wage earners.

Some political analysts feared that the nation's already shell-shocked political system could not handle the new pluralism. (Ironically, when the doctrine of pluralism justified the status quo in the late 1940s and the 1950s, mainstream social scientists rhapsodized about its virtues; when the social activists of the 1970s began to talk about a greatly expanded pluralism, many of the same social scientists worried about a decline of authority and an excess of democracy.) They feared that "single-issue" pressure groups would only further fragment the political process and increase the power of "media managers" and the appeal of charismatic candidates with low hairlines and resonant voices.

But the highly-publicized taxpayer revolts of the late 1970s suggested the superficiality of analyses that dismissed the authentically democratic aspirations that persisted throughout the decade. The tax revolt, at first glance, seemed to confirm liberal fears about the dangers of the new political trends. Gaining momentum after Californians enacted Proposition 13 (a 1978 measure that halved state property taxes) and marching behind pseudo-populist denunciations of government "giveaway" programs, tax-cut leaders sold proposals that appeared to attack the poor and needy. Yet, the deeper one probed the tax revolution, the more it appeared that the rank-and-file rebels still endorsed government programs to meet real social needs. Most supporters of the tax slashing crusade were fighting, through the democratic process, inequitably apportioned taxes and unresponsive governmental bureaucracies. They did not want low taxes as much as they wanted equitable rates; and they wanted better, not less, government.

Thus, advocates of localism and self-help could remain optimistic. The diverse groups might increasingly recognize their common interests and aspirations. Out of this new kind of pluralism could come a new consensus about the broader public interest. As more and more people realized that the institutions (both public and private) of an oversized society were the common enemy, a spirit of cooperation could emerge, especially in an era that required greater conservation and sharing of scarce resources. "In the crisis that's lying ahead," claimed Milton Kotler of the National Association of Neighborhoods coalition, "there's a new recognition that the country's not going to be saved by experts and bureaucracies." The future, as always, was what people could make of it.

SUGGESTIONS FOR FURTHER READING

Changes in the scale of America's social and economic institutions are critically analyzed in W. Lloyd Warner's *The Emergent American Society: Large-Scale Organizations* (1967); Morris Janowitz, *The Last Half-Century* (1978); and Kirkpatrick Sale, *Human Scale* (1980). For an analysis from a legal-constitutional perspective, see Arthur Selwyn Miller, *The Modern Corporate State* (1976).

On the relationship between large business organizations and the national government, see John Kenneth Galbraith, *Economics and the Public*

Purpose (1973); Seymour Melmon, *Pentagon Capitalism* (1970); and James L. Clayton, ed., *The Economic Impact of the Cold War* (1970). Students may also wish to compare the views presented in various studies done for the Center for Study of Responsive Law—such as Daniel Guttman and Barry Willner, *The Shadow Government* (1976)—with the views of the contributors to James Q. Wilson's anthology, *The Politics of Regulation* (1980).

On multinational corporations, see Raymond Vernon, *Storm Over the Multi-Nationals: The Real Issues* (1977); Richard J. Barnet and Ronald Muller, *Global Reach* (1974); C. Fred Bergsten, Thomas Horst, and Theodore H. Moran, *American Multi-Nationals and American Interests* (1978); and Dan Morgan, *Merchants of Grain* (1979).

Richard J. Barnet, *The Lean Years* (1980) offers a good synthesis of various issues relating to the "age of scarcity"; it also contains an excellent bibliography. On this same subject, the following titles are especially recommended: Robert Engler, *Brotherhood of Oil* (1977); John Blair, *The Control of Oil* (1976); Robert Stobaugh and Daniel Yergin, *Energy Future* (1979); Barry Commoner, *The Poverty of Power* (1976) and *The Politics of Energy* (1979); Amory Lovins, *Soft Energy Paths* (1977); and William Ophuls, *Ecology and the Politics of Scarcity* (1977). See also Rachel Carson, *Silent Spring* (1962); Commoner, *The Closing Circle* (1971); and Michael Brown, *Laying Waste: The Poisoning of America by Toxic Chemicals* (1980). For a critical view of environmental regulations, see Bernard J. Frieden, *The Environmental Protection Hustle* (1979). For a good introduction to land policies, see Robert G. Healy and John S. Rosenberg, *Land Use and the States* (2d. ed., 1979). *Paradise Lost* (1972) by Emma Rothschild and *The Car Culture* (1975) by James J. Flink chronicle the growing disenchantment with the automobile.

On education, compare the radically different analyses in the following works: Christopher Jencks and David Riesman, *The Academic Revolution* (1969); Jonathan Kozol, *Death at an Early Age* (1967); Joel Spring, *The Sorting Machine* (1976); Herbert Gintis and Samuel Bowles, *Schooling in Capitalist America* (1976); Christopher Jencks, *Inequality* (1973); David Nasaw, *Schooled to Order* (1979); Ray C. Rist, *The Urban School* (1973) and *The Invisible Children* (1978); Diane Ravitch, *The Revisionists Revised: A Critique of the Radical Attack on the Schools* (1978); and Christopher Lasch's essay, "Schooling and the New Illiteracy," in his *Culture of Narcissism* (1978).

James Monaco's anthology *Media Culture* (1978) provides a good introduction to all print and electronic media; it also contains a good section on media consolidation. On trends in publishing, see Ben Bagdikian, *The Information Machines* (1971); Richard Pollak, ed., *Stop the Presses, I Want to Get Off* (1975); Edward J. Epstein, *Between Fact and Fiction* (1975); Edwin Diamond, *Good News, Bad News* (1978); and Herbert Gans, *Deciding What's News* (1979). Although it is too rambling and anecdotal, David Halberstam's *The Powers That Be* (1978) contains fascinating anecdotes. On motion pictures, see Robert Sklar, *Movie-Made America* (1975) and the essays in journals, such as *The Journal of Popular Film, American Film,* and *Sight and Sound.* See also the collected reviews of leading film critics, such as Andrew Sarris, Pauline Kael, and Stanley Kaufmann. On television, see Erik Barnouw, *Tube of Plenty* (1977) and *The Sponsor* (1979); A. Frank Reel, *The Networks* (1979); Horace Newcombe, ed., *Television: The Critical View* (2nd. ed., 1979); Michael J. Arlen, *The View From Highway One* (1976); Jerry Mander, *Four Arguments for the Elimination of Television* (1978); and Edward J. Epstein, *News from Nowhere* (1973).

On sports, compare the contrasting views of Paul Hoch, *Rip Off the Big Game* (1972); Robert Lipsyte, *SportsWorld* (1975); Michael Novak, *The Joy of Sports* (1976); Allen Guttman, *From Ritual to Record* (1978); Edwin Cady, *The Big Game: College Sports and American Life* (1978); and Robert C. Yeager, *Seasons of Shame: The New Violence in Sports* (1979).

On popular music, see David Pichaske, *A Generation in Motion* (1979); Greil Marcus, *Mystery Train* (1976); Peter Guralnik, *Lost Highways* (1979); and Bill Malone, *Southern Music/American Music* (1980). For the business end of music, see Geoffrey Stokes, *Star-Making Machinery* (1976) and *Rock and Roll is Here to Pay* (1977) by Steve Chapple and Reebee Garofalo.

Religious developments to about 1970 are analyzed in the final chapters of Sydney Ahlstrom, *A Religious History of the American People* (1972). James Morris, *The Preachers* (1973) is a readable introduction to the evangelical crusade, but see also John Pollock, *Billy Graham* (1979); Marshall Frady, *Billy Graham* (1979); and David Harrell, *All Things Are Possible: The Healing and Charismatic Revivals in Modern America* (1974). Ben Armstrong's *The Electric Church* (1979) offers an introduction, but the best way to explore this subject is to turn on your radio or television set.

The bible for decentralists of the 1970s was E.F. Schumacher's *Small Is Beautiful* (1973). Sale's *Human Scale* is a good summary of the literature and a militant plea for decentralism. See also P.D. Dunn, *Appropriate Technology* (1979); Frances Moore Lappe and Joseph Collins, *Food First* (rev. ed., 1978); Scott Burns, *The Household Economy* (1977); Jaroslav Vanek, *The Labor-Managed Economy* (1977); Carole Goodwin, *The Oak Park Strategy: Community Control of Racial Change* (1979); Robert Kuttner, *Revolt of the Haves: Tax Rebellions and Hard Times* (1981); and Harry C. Boyte, *The Backyard Revolution* (1980).

Index